£60.00

D1583427

BCFTCS

Managing FDI in a Globalizing Economy

Managing FDI in a Globalizing Economy

Asian Experiences

Edited by

Douglas H. Brooks
Asian Development Bank
and

Hal Hill
Australian National University

First published 2004 by
PALGRAVE MACMILLAN
Houndmills, Basingstoke, Hampshire RG21 6XS and
175 Fifth Avenue, New York, N. Y. 10010
Companies and representatives throughout the world

PALGRAVE MACMILLAN is the global academic imprint of the Palgrave Macmillan division of St. Martin's Press, LLC and of Palgrave Macmillan Ltd. Macmillan® is a registered trademark in the United States, United Kingdom and other countries. Palgrave is a registered trademark in the European Union and other countries.

ISBN 1–4039–3655–2

This book is printed on paper suitable for recycling and made from fully managed and sustained forest sources.

A catalogue record for this book is available from the British Library.

A catalog record for this book is available from the Library of Congress.

10   9   8   7   6   5   4
13   12   11   10   09   08   07   06   05

Printed and bound in Great Britain by
Antony Rowe Ltd, Chippenham and Eastbourne

Contents

Tables

Figures

Glossary

ADB	Asian Development Bank
APEC	Asia Pacific Economic Cooperation
ASEAN	Association of South East Asian Nations
ASEM	Asia Europe Meeting
BCC	business cooperation contract
BOI	Board of Investment (Thailand)
bumiputera	indigenous Malaysians
CGE	computable general equilibrium
chaebol	business conglomerates (Korea)
CMIE	Centre for Monitoring Indian Economy (India)
doi moi	late 1980s program of economic reform (Viet Nam)
FDI	foreign direct investment
FIE	foreign-invested enterprise
FTA	free trade area/agreement
FTZ	free trade zone
GATS	General Agreement on Trade in Services
GATT	General Agreement on Tariffs and Trade
GDP	gross domestic product
GFCF	gross fixed capital formation
HMT	enterprises with direct investment from Hong Kong, China; Macao; and Taipei,China (PRC)
IMF	International Monetary Fund
ITA	Information Technology Agreement
M&A	merger and acquisition
MFN	most favored nation
MNE	multinational enterprise

MSC	Multimedia Super Corridor (Malaysia)
NAFTA	North American Free Trade Area
Nasscom	National Association of Software and Service Companies (India)
NEP	New Economic Policy (Malaysia)
NIE	newly industrializing economy
NTB	non-tariff barrier
OECD	Organisation for Economic Co-operation and Development
PPP	purchasing power parity
PRC	People's Republic of China
RIS	Research and Information System for the Non-Aligned and Other Developing Countries (India)
SAARC	South Asian Association for Regional Cooperation
SEBI	Securities and Exchange Board of India
SEZ	special economic zone
SIJORI	Singapore–Johor–Riau
SME	small and medium-sized enterprise
SMIDEC	Small and Medium Industries Corporation (Malaysia)
SOE	state-owned enterprise
STTCA	Special Tax Treatment Control Act (Korea)
TRIM	trade-related investment measure
US	United States
VAR	vector auto-regression
WTO	World Trade Organization

End of Year Exchange Rates: Local Currency per US Dollar

Country	Currency	Abbreviation	1990	1995	2000	2002
People's Republic of China	yuan	CNY	5.2	8.3	8.3	8.3
India	rupee	Rs	18.1	35.2	46.8	48.0
Republic of Korea	won	W	716.4	774.7	1,264.5	1,186.2
Malaysia	ringgit	RM	2.7	2.5	3.8	3.8
Thailand	baht	B	25.3	25.2	43.3	43.2
Viet Nam	dong	D	8,125.0	11,015.0	14,514.0	15,403.0

Source: International Monetary Fund, *International Financial Statistics*.

Preface

The countries of developing Asia have rapidly been integrating their economies, both with each other and with the rest of the world. To help policy-makers and other concerned parties better understand the changes taking place and the relative merits of alternative courses of action to facilitate or respond to those changes, in 2001 the Asian Development Bank (ADB) approved a technical assistance grant to support a study of the relevant economic issues. This volume is one outcome of that research project. It gathers together six country studies on foreign direct investment (FDI), preceded by a discussion of recent trends and the policy context for FDI and a comparative synthesis of the country studies. It is intended for policymakers and development practitioners with a view to helping them maximize the net benefits of FDI, as well as for scholars of economic development.

The country studies in this volume cover the People's Republic of China, India, the Republic of Korea, Malaysia, Thailand, and Viet Nam. These developing Asian economies were selected for the diversity of their levels of national and per capita income, openness to international trade, and experiences with, and attitudes toward, FDI. Professor Hal Hill of the Australian National University provided the primary international perspective. The country studies were authored by researchers with policy influence in their own countries. In particular, domestic analysis was carried out by Xiaolu Wang for the People's Republic of China, Nagesh Kumar for India, Seong-Bong Lee, June-Dong Kim, and Nak-Gyun Choi for the Republic of Korea, Tham Siew-Yean for Malaysia, Somkiat Tangkitvanich, Deunden Nikomborirak, and Busaba Krairiksh for Thailand, and Tuan Bui for Viet Nam. Authors, government officials, and staff of multilateral development agencies participated in a conference in Manila in August 2003 to discuss the preliminary findings of these studies. In particular, helpful comments were received from Duo Qin for the study on the People's Republic of China, Hans-Peter Brunner for India, Juzhong Zhuang for the Republic of Korea, Jesus Felipe for Malaysia, Cyn-Young Park for Thailand, and Alessandro Pio for Viet Nam. A number of other staff at the ADB offered additional constructive comments. Valuable suggestions were also given by Chea Vuthy of Cambodia, Soekarno Wirokartono of Indonesia, Kubanyshbek Kanimetov of Kyrgyz Republic, Krishna Gyawali of Nepal, and AMC Kulasekera of Sri Lanka.

Douglas Brooks of the ADB's Economics and Research Department designed, supervised, and coordinated the various activities of the project. He was ably assisted by Emma Xiaoqin Fan, Pilipinas Quising, Lea Sumulong, and Ma. Susan Torres. Jean-Pierre Verbiest gave helpful counsel throughout project implementation. Beth Thomson handled the copy editing of the book with skill, grace, and amazing patience. Angela Grant prepared the subject index. Lynette Mallery provided valuable advice on the overall production of the book. The views and opinions expressed in this volume are those of the authors and do not necessarily reflect those of the ADB or its board of directors.

Ifzal Ali

Ifzal Ali
Chief Economist, Asian Development Bank
December 2003

Foreword

Investment, whether domestic or foreign, is an essential ingredient for sustainable growth; productive investment translates into increased output. Especially where domestic resources are insufficient to steer a country toward its long-term potential growth path, the role of foreign investment becomes indispensable. Over the last two decades, we have seen the increasing globalization of foreign investment, with developing countries in Asia emerging as important recipients, and increasingly as sources, of foreign direct investment (FDI).

FDI has come to be welcomed by most developing countries as not just a source of investment funds and foreign exchange, but also as an important source of new technology. It is also a spur to competition that raises the efficiency of domestic firms, a stimulant to domestic investment, and a means of gaining market access abroad and integrating into global value chains of production. At the same time there are concerns that FDI may hinder the development of local firms in some sectors, may negatively impact income distribution or terms of trade, or may negatively influence governance and promote rent-seeking in host economies. To try to maximize the developmental benefits of FDI flows and minimize the potential negative impacts, host governments have enacted and implemented a wide range of investment incentives and regulations.

With the internationalization of the world economy, some countries have felt the need for more formal cooperation in the area of investment through international rules and commitments. Foreign investors desiring to protect their investments and receive favorable tax treatment on their global profits and host countries wishing to attract greater inflows of FDI have entered into thousands of bilateral and, increasingly, regional agreements related to FDI. Among some countries, interest continues in establishing a multilateral framework on investment. At the First Ministerial Meeting of the World Trade Organization (WTO) in Singapore in 1996, members established a working group to examine the relationship between trade and investment. Since then, there has been continuing debate as to whether or not there should be multilateral negotiations in this area in the context of the WTO. Asian countries have actively participated in the debate, elucidating arguments both for and against multilateral negotiations on investment.

The Asian Development Bank (ADB) encourages this debate, and we are analyzing country experiences in the search for policy recommendations that can effectively help our developing member countries (DMCs) to maximize the benefits from investment. In August 2001, even before the WTO's Fourth Ministerial Conference at Doha, Qatar, ADB approved a research project on 'Regional Integration and Trade: Emerging Policy Issues for Selected DMCs' in anticipation of a new round of multilateral trade negotiations under the WTO. In Doha, WTO members decided to step-up work on trade and investment, and agreed that in relation to investment, 'negotiations will take place after the Fifth Session of the Ministerial Conference on the basis of a decision to be taken, by explicit consensus, at that Session on modalities of negotiations.' While the Fifth Session in Cancun, Mexico, did not reach its goal of deciding on negotiating modalities, flows of FDI continue. Bilateral and regional investment agreements continue to proliferate.

This volume on FDI represents the first of a two-part series of economic country studies to emerge from the research project. The second volume will deal with another widely discussed issue—competition policy. These studies compare and contrast the countries' experiences in order to inform policy debate and decision making, and to help guide ADB's operations. It is hoped that by encouraging debate and analysis on such critical development issues, this project will raise developing countries' capacities for both policy analysis and trade negotiations.

Tadao Chino

Tadao Chino
President, Asian Development Bank
December 2003

Contributors

Douglas H. Brooks, Asian Development Bank, Manila

Tuan Bui, Institute of World Economy, Hanoi

Nak-Gyun Choi, Korea Institute for International Economic Policy, Seoul

Emma Xiaoqin Fan, Asian Development Bank, Manila

Hal Hill, Australian National University, Canberra

June-Dong Kim, Korea Institute for International Economic Policy, Seoul

Busaba Krairiksh, Thailand Development Research Institute, Bangkok

Nagesh Kumar, Research and Information System for the Non-Aligned and Other Developing Countries, New Delhi

Seong-Bong Lee, Korea Institute for International Economic Policy, Seoul

Deunden Nikomborirak, Thailand Development Research Institute, Bangkok

Lea R. Sumulong, Asian Development Bank, Manila

Somkiat Tangkitvanich, Thailand Development Research Institute, Bangkok

Tham Siew-Yean, Universiti Kebangsaan Malaysia, Kuala Lumpur

Xiaolu Wang, National Economic Research Institute, Beijing

1

Foreign Direct Investment: Recent Trends and the Policy Context

Douglas H. Brooks, Emma Xiaoqin Fan, and Lea R. Sumulong

Until the 1980s, most developing countries viewed foreign direct investment (FDI) with great wariness. The sheer size and magnitude of FDI by multinational enterprises (MNEs) were viewed as a threat by host countries, which were concerned about MNEs' capacity to influence economic and political affairs. These fears were driven by the colonial experience of many developing countries and by the view that FDI was a modern form of economic colonialism and exploitation. In addition, MNEs were frequently suspected of engaging in unfair business practices, such as rigged transfer pricing and price fixing through their links with their parent companies.

In recent years, however, FDI restrictions have been dramatically reduced as a result of a host of factors: accelerating technological change, the emergence of globally integrated production and marketing networks, the existence of bilateral investment treaties, prescriptions from multilateral development banks, and positive evidence from developing countries that have opened their doors to FDI. In addition, the drying up of commercial bank lending due to debt crises persuaded many developing countries to reform their investment policies to attract more stable forms of foreign capital, as FDI appeared to be an attractive alternative to bank loans as a source of capital inflows. In the process, developing countries aggressively offered incentives and subsidies, particularly to MNEs that supported their industrial policies.

Flows of FDI have seen a dramatic rise in the last 20 years due to the increasing openness of host economies, particularly in Asia. The growing internationalization of trade and investment has prompted a proliferation of bilateral investment treaties and led some countries to call for increased cooperation through the establishment of international investment rules

Figure 1.1   Growth of World Exports and FDI Outflows (average annual growth rate)

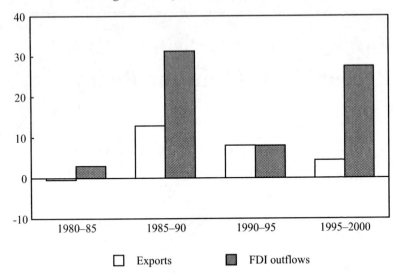

Source: Exports: IMF (2003), World Economic Outlook Database, September; FDI: UNCTAD (2003a), Foreign Direct Investment Database, September.

and commitments under the World Trade Organization (WTO). This chapter reviews recent developments in FDI flows and their effects, focusing on developing Asia, and examines the importance of the policy context in which these flows occur.[1]

1   TRENDS AND EFFECTS

From only $53.7 billion in 1980, global FDI outflows expanded rapidly, reaching $1.2 trillion in 2000.[2] Since then the weak global economy has considerably reduced outflows, which dropped by 41% in 2001 and an estimated further 9% in 2002. The upsurge in FDI over the longer period substantially changed the international economic landscape. From 1980 to 2000, the growth rate of world FDI outflows surpassed that of world exports (Figure 1.1). This swift expansion in FDI was most pronounced in 1985–90, when many host countries began to relax regulations to attract FDI, and in 1995–2000, when companies undertook scores of mergers and acquisitions in the wake of the Asian financial crisis and in response to a wave of privatization programs in Latin America.

Figure 1.2   Index of World Exports, FDI Outflows, and Output,
1990–2002 (1990 = 100)

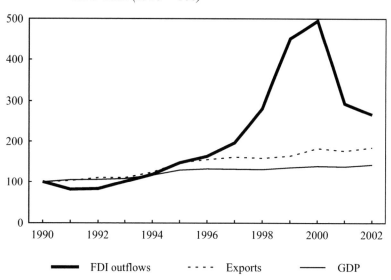

Source: Exports and GDP: IMF (2003), World Economic Outlook Database, September; FDI: UNCTAD (2003a), Foreign Direct Investment Database, September.

Relative to world output and total trade, FDI flows have risen tremendously since the early 1990s (Figure 1.2). World FDI flows increased five times from 1993 to 2000 before falling from 2001, while world trade and output grew at a more modest pace, not even doubling in value between 1990 and 2002.

The geographic pattern of FDI outflows changed slightly during the last decade. Europe and North America continued to be the world's largest sources of FDI flows, supplying at least 75 percent since 1991. In contrast, the share of Asia and the Pacific in total FDI outflows fell significantly beginning in 1998, reflecting the declining importance of Japan as an FDI supplier.

While Europe and North America continued to be major recipients of FDI, the People's Republic of China (PRC) emerged as another favored destination. Economies in Asia and the Pacific received increasingly large shares of world FDI inflows beginning in the 1990s, but the 1997 financial crisis temporarily reversed this trend. Flows soon recovered, however, particularly with the rise in the number of mergers and acquisitions after the crisis.

In terms of individual country destinations, there have been shifts in the preferences of foreign investors over the last decade. Malaysia, Singapore, and Thailand, which were among the 20 largest recipients of FDI in 1991–93, were replaced by Brazil, Finland, and Ireland in 1998–2000. In addition, Japan and the Republic of Korea (Korea) became popular locations for FDI in the post-Asian crisis era (JBICI 2002).

Among the preferred Asian destinations for FDI, there has not been as much change. Indonesia and Kazakhstan, two of the top ten FDI destinations in the early 1990s, had dropped from the list by the late 1990s, primarily due to uncertainties about their domestic economies. They were replaced by India and Viet Nam. Meanwhile, Hong Kong, China overtook Malaysia as a preferred FDI destination. While the total value of FDI inflows to the top ten Asian destinations increased substantially during the decade, the share of developing Asia in the world total dropped significantly. Average FDI inflows per capita showed remarkable increases in some Asian economies. In Hong Kong, China, for instance, they increased 7.5 times to $5,006 between the early and late 1990s, and the inflow was greater than gross fixed capital formation by the end of the decade. In other Asian economies, FDI commonly amounted to about 40 percent of gross fixed capital formation (Table 1.1).

Distinguishing characteristics of FDI are its stability and ease of servicing relative to commercial debt or portfolio investment, as well as its inclusion of non-financial assets in production and sales processes. Aside from increasing output and income, potential benefits to host countries from encouraging FDI inflows include the following.

i   *Foreign firms bring superior technology.* The extent of benefits to host countries depends on whether the technology spills over to domestic and other foreign-invested firms.

ii *Foreign investment increases competition in the host economy.* The entry of a new firm in a non-tradable sector increases industry output and reduces the domestic price, leading to a net improvement in welfare.

iii *Foreign investment typically results in increased domestic investment.* In an analysis of panel data for 58 developing countries, Bosworth and Collins (1999) found that about half of each dollar of capital inflow translates into an increase in domestic investment. However, when the capital inflows take the form of FDI, there is a near one-for-one relationship between the FDI and domestic investment.

iv *Foreign investment gives advantages in terms of export market access arising from economies of scale in foreign firms' marketing or from their ability to gain market access abroad.* Foreign firms can even act as a catalyst for unrelated domestic exporters. In an empirical analysis,

Table 1.1   Top Ten Destinations for FDI in Developing Asia, 1991–93 and 1998–2000

Rank	Host Economy	1991–93	Rank	Host Economy	1998–2000
Average annual total inflows ($ billion)					
1	PRC	14.3	1	PRC	41.6
2	Malaysia	5.0	2	Hong Kong, China	33.8
3	Hong Kong, China	3.9	3	Singapore	11.1
4	Singapore	3.9	4	Rep. of Korea	8.0
5	Thailand	2.0	5	Thailand	5.6
6	Indonesia	1.8	6	Malaysia	3.5
7	Taipei,China	1.0	7	Taipei,China	2.7
8	Philippines	0.9	8	India	2.4
9	Rep. of Korea	0.8	9	Philippines	1.6
10	Kazakhstan	0.7	10	Viet Nam	1.5
	Total Developing Asia	36.3			114.1
	(% of world total)	(19.8)			(10.8)
Average inflows per capita ($)					
1	Singapore	1,234	1	Hong Kong, China	5,006
2	Hong Kong, China	667	2	Singapore	2,826
3	Malaysia	264	3	Rep. of Korea	172
4	Vanuatu	164	4	Malaysia	154
5	Fiji Islands	104	5	Taipei,China	121
6	Solomon Islands	51	6	Vanuatu	94
7	Taipei,China	49	7	Thailand	94
8	Kazakhstan	42	8	Kazakhstan	87
9	Thailand	36	9	Azerbaijan	71
10	Maldives	29	10	Fiji Islands	63
FDI as % of gross fixed capital formation					
1	Vanuatu	53.1	1	Hong Kong, China	75.7
2	Fiji Islands	38.7	2	Armenia	47.7
3	Viet Nam	32.0	3	Cambodia	45.3
4	Solomon Islands	26.5	4	Kazakhstan	42.7
5	Singapore	23.1	5	Singapore	39.3
6	Malaysia	22.8	6	Azerbaijan	38.9
7	Cambodia	17.9	7	Papua New Guinea	36.5
8	Kyrgyz Republic	15.2	8	Georgia	36.5
9	Hong Kong, China	13.2	9	Vanuatu	28.2
10	Papua New Guinea	12.1	10	Kyrgyz Republic	24.4

Source: UNCTAD (2003a), Foreign Investment Database, September.

the probability that a domestic plant will export was found to be positively correlated with proximity to multinational firms (Aitken, Hanson, and Harrison 1997).

v   *Foreign investment can aid in bridging a host country's foreign exchange gap.* Two gaps may exist in the economy: insufficient levels of savings to support capital accumulation to achieve a given growth target, and insufficient foreign exchange to purchase imports. Often investment requires imported inputs. If domestic savings are not sufficient, or face barriers in being converted to foreign exchange to acquire imports, they may not be able to guarantee growth. Capital inflows help ensure that foreign exchange will be available to purchase imports for investment.

If both labor and capital are fully employed before and after the capital movement, the total and average returns to capital increase in the source country, while the total and average returns to labor decrease. While the source country gains as a whole, income is redistributed from labor to capital. Meanwhile, in the recipient country, income is redistributed from capital to labor, as total and average returns to capital decrease and total and average returns to labor increase. The result is potentially a win–win situation for the two countries.

However, capital inflows do not necessarily increase welfare in the host country. For example, when capital flows to an industry in which an existing firm has monopoly power in the world market, an increase in output from the new competition lowers the price of the exportable, thus reducing the terms of trade and potentially lowering welfare in the host country. Also, the benefits from foreign investment are usually evaluated under the assumption that host countries can absorb a large inflow of capital without large declines in its rate of return. But if capital grows much faster than the productivity of labor, its productivity will fall, which might reduce its rate of return.

Under full employment, a capital inflow that reduces the relative scarcity of capital and raises the productivity of labor in the host country can raise real wages across the board and reduce income disparity within the country. However, the question of distribution also arises with respect to the sharing of gains between foreign capital and host countries' factors of production. Traditionally, foreign investment was geared toward primary commodity exports. During the colonial period in Indonesia, for instance, foreign investment in Java was concentrated in tea and sugar exports and in Sumatra in rubber and oil exports. In some cases, this led to capacity expansion, productivity growth, declining prices of exportable commodities, and a deterioration in the host country's terms of trade, possibly leading to welfare losses. In addition, there were generally few spillovers to the rest of the host economy from primary commodity production. The resulting view was that the gains from capital inflows favored the source economy more than the host economy.

Many new foreign investments in developing countries are in process manufacturing because of the lower labor costs, an example being the sports shoe factories across developing Asia. The host countries often import unfinished components and export finished goods or refined components for further processing elsewhere. While wages may rise across the board in host countries, contributing to a reduction in income disparity, in practice they are likely to rise only for the small fraction of the labor force employed by the foreign investor. The result can be to improve the absolute and relative condition of workers within this favored group, in the process aggravating overall income inequality. Over time, however, and given a conducive policy environment, linkages and leakages emerge, creating a country reputation that influences other potential investors. Singapore is a case in point.

A capital inflow can lead to a rise in the prices of non-tradable goods and services relative to those of imported goods and services. If world demand for the country's exports is perfectly price-elastic, the price of non-tradables will rise relative to the price of exports as well. Consequently, the change will affect the returns to factors that are used intensively in either the tradable or non-tradable sector. Thus, a capital inflow-induced terms of trade effect may affect real income for any given level of real output, which may or may not be affected.

When the price of non-tradables rises relative to the prices of imports and exports, the 'Dutch disease' may result, in which resources are drawn from production of tradables to non-tradables, and exports fall as the macroeconomy adjusts to a new equilibrium with corresponding changes in factor demand and prices. Distributional effects will result (Cooper 2002).

When there are 'lumpy' adjustment costs for new investment and there are economies of scale in the investment technology, trade openness can trigger discrete changes in the terms of trade and thereby lead to a discrete jump in the level of investment. However, it can also lead to boom–bust cycles of investment where multiple equilibria are supported by self-fulfilling expectations (Razin, Sadka, and Coury 2002).

As foreign investors search for the location that will provide the highest return on their investment, they are often drawn to countries with abundant natural resources but low-quality institutions. Weak and inefficient institutions allow the extraction of natural resources at a faster pace than that required for sustainable development. As a result, local communities are sometimes harmed as the environment, their main source of livelihood, is damaged or destroyed. Foreign investment-led growth also promotes Western-style consumerism, with serious potential consequences for the health and food security of the host population (French 1998).

Not all investments by MNEs lead to technology transfer and positive spillovers. In their desire to protect the technology of the parent company, multinationals may limit the production carried out by affiliates in host countries to activities with low value added, thereby reducing the scope for technical change and technological learning. They may also restrict vertical integration by relying completely on foreign suppliers for their inputs. In some cases MNEs, through their sheer size, can even eliminate competition by crowding out domestic producers. As an integral part of global value chains, MNEs have a built-in advantage (in their economies of scale and scope, for example) over their local competitors.

Increasing FDI across borders has increased the impact of FDI on national economies and on the international economy as a whole, with the widely held perception in Asia that the net effect is positive. No absolute consensus on the positive effects of FDI has been reached by all governments or the general public, reflecting differences between countries in economic conditions, specific histories of utilizing FDI, cultural variation, and ideological differences. In particular, the policy framework plays an important role in determining the effects of FDI on a recipient country.

2   IMPORTANCE OF THE POLICY CONTEXT

Whether, and the ways in which, FDI is beneficial or harmful to the host country depends on the context in which the investment takes place and in which the resulting economic activity occurs. This is particularly true of the policy environment in the recipient country, and especially in the local area of the recipient country where the investment is located. It is also true of policies that may be internal to the investing firm, such as transfer pricing.

Many developing countries that have introduced policies in recent years to encourage foreign investment as part of their national reform programs, are now reaping the benefits. This strategy was implemented in the belief that economic liberalization would reduce domestic inefficiencies and stimulate growth, as illustrated by the experience of a large number of countries in Asia.

Most countries offer incentives to attract FDI. These often include tax concessions, tax holidays, tax credits, accelerated depreciation on plants and machinery, and export subsidies and import entitlements. Such incentives aim to attract FDI and channel foreign firms to desired locations, sectors, and activities. At the same time, most countries have also regulated and limited the economic activities of foreign firms operating within their borders. Such regulations have often included limitations on foreign equity ownership, local content requirements, local employment requirements, and minimum export requirements. These measures are designed to transfer benefits arising from the presence of foreign firms to the local economy. This 'carrot and stick' approach has long been a feature of the regulatory framework governing FDI in host countries (McCulloch 1991).

Tax breaks and subsidies are common, but generally influence investment location decisions only at the margin. More important to most potential investors are the size and expected growth rate of the market to be served, the long-term macroeconomic and political stability of the host country, the supply of skilled or trainable workers, and the presence of modern transportation and communications infrastructure. Once these criteria are satisfied, then financial incentives may influence the investor's choice of suitable sites.

More importantly, such incentives often create distortions and inefficiencies. Table 1.2 indicates the wide variety of both incentive-based and rule-based measures commonly used to attract FDI. By distorting the relative costs for other sectors and investment projects that are not targeted for incentives, such schemes typically discriminate against smaller and domestic investors, as well as areas of actual or potential comparative advantage that are not recognized as such by policymakers. Perhaps of greatest concern, over time these actions contribute to the development of a governance system that lacks transparency and accountability (JBICI 2002). Imperfect competition, which leads to FDI as opposed to exports, raises issues of national sovereignty and the need for a competition policy, as well as rent-seeking behavior among countries. Government action at the national level can enhance a host country's success in attracting FDI by significantly reducing the uncertainty, asymmetric information, and related search costs faced by foreign investors, as well as transaction costs—especially the amount of time and number of steps involved in acquiring approval.

Incentives and regulations are often closely linked, such as when the former are granted subject to conditions. For example, many countries allow foreign firms majority ownership on the condition that they export all or a significant proportion of their output. The length of tax holidays and the amount of tax credits granted often depend, among other things, on the market orientation of the venture and the degree of local content of its output (Ariff 1989).

Table 1.2   The Foreign Investment Regime in a Host Economy: Main Types of Regulatory and Incentive Measures

Type of Measure	Example
Screening, admission, and establishment	Closure of certain sectors, industries, or activities to FDI Minimum capital requirements Restrictions on modes of entry Eligibility for bidding on privatizations Establishment of special zones (such as export-processing zones) for FDI with legislation distinct from that governing the rest of the country
Fiscal incentives	Reductions in standard corporate income tax rate Tax holidays Reductions in social security contributions Accelerated depreciation allowances Duty exemptions and drawbacks Export tax exemptions Reduced taxes for expatriates
Financial incentives	Investment grants Subsidized credit Credit guarantees
Other incentives	Subsidized service fees (electricity, water, telecommunications, transportation, etc.) Subsidized designated infrastructure (for example, commercial buildings) Preferential access to government contracts Closure of the market to further entry or the granting of monopoly rights
Performance requirements	Protection from import competition Local content requirements (value added) Minimum export shares Trade balancing Technology transfer Local equity participation Employment targets R&D requirements

Source: JBICI (2002: 84).

Arrangements that commit host country entities to purchase fixed quantities of output on a take-or-pay basis, and especially that oblige them to pay in foreign currency, are common means of shifting risk from investors to the host government, but can be detrimental to the host government. This was evident in Southeast Asia during the financial crisis: regional currencies depreciated sharply and swiftly, but foreign investments in infrastructure (such as power plant investments in Indonesia and the Philippines) were based on continuing repayments in US dollars at rates that did not take the depreciation into account.

Too often, policies ostensibly designed to maximize the net benefits of FDI for recipient economies have resulted in subscale manufacturing plants, frequently through mandated joint ventures that are not allowed to source inputs freely and contribute little to the technological, social, or economic development of the country. Arrangements between foreign investors and host country authorities that block other new entrants to the industry or that inhibit alternative cheap sources of supply are also common but are generally not in the best interests of the host country.[3]

A host country will offer fewer incentives, and benefit less, when foreign investment is directed toward serving small and protected domestic markets.[4] The benefits to the host economy are greatest when international companies can exploit economies of scale both locally and globally, and are continually driven to update their technology and managerial practices in order to remain competitive.

An investor will invest more of the latest proprietary technology and procedures only when it feels it has the greatest control over protection of the proprietary content transferred through the investment, and greatest freedom in its use. Restrictions such as forced sharing of technology through mandatory joint ventures, local content requirements, or performance criteria reduce the incentive for the investor to apply the most modern techniques and technologies, hindering integration into the global sourcing network of the parent company.[5] Ramachandran (1993) found that subsidiaries of MNEs received greater resources than partially licensed/owned or independent firms because of the lower transaction costs involved in technology transfer. Thus, multinational investment appeared to be superior to the direct licensing of technology to independent firms. The study also found that technology transfer and the interchange of managers and technicians between parent and subsidiary firms were significantly higher for wholly owned subsidiaries than for joint venture partnerships or licensees.

Most investment measures were designed to transfer benefits arising from the operations of foreign firms to the local economy, and to promote development objectives. In essence, the primary objective of these measures is for host countries to obtain the maximum possible share of the gains from FDI. However, such regulations distort trade and investment and impose welfare losses. The various regulations used may in fact have lowered, rather than enhanced, the contribution of FDI to national development objectives. Moran (2002a) has provided much evidence to show how counterproductive and damaging domestic content requirements and joint venture requirements can be for host country development. He also demonstrates just how beneficial for host country growth and development it can be to adopt a policy of leaving wholly owned subsidiaries unfettered by local content mandates.

Thus, investment measures may be costly and inefficient. Many countries, both developed and developing, have abandoned or scaled back their use. Perhaps the most telling empirical evidence on this issue is not the number of governments that have such policies, but the number that have abandoned them. Indeed, one key feature of the use of policies such as local content schemes and export performance requirements is that they are becoming less popular. Therefore, the appropriate question to be asked is whether or not there are reasonable grounds for adopting or maintaining such policies. The most frequent response to this question is that these policies are required to 'develop' specific industries in order to allow them to compete in an open trading environment. Another reason sometimes cited for maintaining these types of policies is that the structural adjustments involved in removing them would lead to unemployment, lower levels of technology transfer, and the loss of opportunities to move into high-technology industries (Bora 2001).

The core of the debate on the use of these policies is typically referred to as the 'development dimension.' In this context, the term 'development' includes elements of self-sufficiency, national pride, and, perhaps most importantly, employment. It also has a technology transfer dimension, where FDI is supposed to induce the transfer of advanced technology to developing countries. Protection may induce an expansion of output and employment in certain sectors. But this expansion often carries a massive cost for the society implementing such a policy.

The upsurge in FDI to developing countries in the 1990s was largely caused by the unilateral liberalization of their FDI policies and regulatory regimes. Theoretical and empirical evidence provides strong support for the proposition that neutral policies designed to enhance the efficiency of investment are better suited to attracting foreign investment and enhancing its contribution to development than interventionist methods (Bora 2001). Ariff (1989) points out that some investment measures appear to be redundant. For example, export performance requirements that set minimum export–output ratios for a firm to qualify for incentives are scarcely binding in the sense that firms are required to do what they would have done anyway, even in the absence of explicit performance requirements.

A central issue is whether investment measures actually alter the allocation of resources in production and trade or merely affect the distribution of rents between firms and host countries. Both suppliers and recipients of FDI gain from the liberalization of investment measures. Foreign investors may benefit from new investment opportunities resulting from liberalized investment regulations, while the host countries may benefit from increased FDI inflows and the greater market discipline resulting from this. Since many developing countries compete with one another to offer foreign investors generous fiscal, infrastructure, and financial incentives, the scaling down of investment incentives could yield additional revenue for the governments of host countries.

Hopes have faded that import-substituting industries benefiting from infant industry protection will grow to become globally competitive. So have hopes that domestic content and joint venture requirements for foreign investors will stimulate domestic supply chains. In fact, empirical evidence accumulated in the 1990s shows that the reverse is actually more likely. FDI facilitates integration into international supply chains, allowing host economies both to increase the efficiency of existing activities and to enter into new economic activities. Allowing wholly owned affiliates of foreign firms the freedom to source from wherever they consider most advantageous is *more* likely to lead to domestic suppliers achieving economies of scale and becoming integrated into global supply chains, often under the direct supervision of the foreign buyers. Foreign buyers have increasingly helped local suppliers to export first to sister plants and later to independent purchasers in order to lower the suppliers' costs of production through economies of scale, thereby promoting contract manufacturing as a new infant industry development strategy. Externalities in the adoption of production, quality control, and managerial processes (including advice on exporting) frequently spread vertically within the invested sector and eventually to other sectors in the host economy (Moran 2002a).[6]

National-level programs to promote the development of linkages between foreign-invested and domestic firms commonly include the provision of market and business information; matchmaking by such means as trade fairs or data bases; and support for local enterprises through the provision of managerial and technical assistance, training, audits, and, occasionally, financial assistance or incentives (UNCTAD 2001: 183).

The Economic Development Board of Singapore has successfully encouraged foreign investors to serve voluntarily as scouts to identify promising local suppliers and then contribute to vendor development. This sort of *build-up* strategy is most effective in a conducive economic environment—that is, one that provides low inflation, has a realistic exchange rate, rewards saving and investment, and encourages legal and regulatory consistency (Moran 2002a). Not only does the high return to capacity building pay off in terms of income, it attracts additional FDI in higher skill areas, encouraging progression from lower to higher skilled activities with consequent improvements in worker treatment.

With strengthened interest in human resource development and skill formation in the context of FDI policy, many countries regulate the hiring of foreign workers and impose training requirements on foreign investors. Malaysia, for example, has provided incentive schemes to promote technical and vocational training (JBICI 2002). In general, attracting internationally mobile factors of production will increasingly require host countries to improve the quality of their immobile assets.

Protection of intellectual property rights also plays an important role in attracting advanced technology production processes. Weak intellectual property protection deters foreign investors in technology-intensive sectors that rely heavily on intellectual property rights, and encourages investors to undertake projects focusing on distribution rather than local production (Smarzynska 2002).

3   INTERNATIONAL INVESTMENT AGREEMENTS

In the context of international trade and investment agreements, most favored nation (MFN) treatment obliges the host country to offer equally advantageous investment conditions to potential investors from all treaty signatories. National treatment (non-discrimination) requires that both foreign and domestic investors receive the same treatment. In terms of creating a level playing field with regard to screening procedures for entry and the right of establishment as well as national treatment, Latin American countries appear to have implemented a more liberal legal framework than the larger developing Asian markets (JBICI 2002).

Over 2,100 bilateral investment treaties and 2,200 double taxation treaties were in effect by the end of 2002 (UNCTAD 2003a). Although they vary across countries, bilateral investment treaties generally contain binding commitments on the expropriation of assets, the transfer of funds, and the provision of compensation in the event of armed conflict or political instability. These commitments are provided on a national treatment or

MFN basis. Disagreements between foreign investors and the host government are usually referred to private arbitration centers of the International Chamber of Commerce or to the International Centre for Settlement of Investment Disputes (ICSID).[7]

Bilateral investment treaties are intended to protect foreign investors against unpredictable host country actions that would negatively affect the profitability of their investments. In this sense they guard against problems of dynamic inconsistency. However, their implementation may not always be effective in lower-income countries and their benefits for host countries are not clear. Empirical evidence has not found a strong link between the existence of a bilateral investment treaty and an increase in FDI flows. Furthermore, bilateral investment treaties complement, rather than substitute for, institutional quality, including the strength of property rights (Hallward-Dreimeier 2003). Tax treaties may even reduce FDI if part of the motivation for the investment is to evade taxes. At the same time, bilateral investment treaties may reduce policy options for the host country government and leave it open to being sued for substantial amounts. Decisions handed down behind closed doors by arbitration panels with no public accountability cannot be amended by the domestic legal system.

Despite the asymmetry of the benefits of bilateral investment treaties for foreign investors and host economies, such agreements have proliferated. As developing economies mature and their outward FDI flows increase, as in the case of Korea, they become more interested in protecting the rights of their investors. In the broadest international context, this has led to calls for a multilateral framework on investment.

The Agreement on Trade-related Investment Measures

In the multilateral context, the General Agreement on Tariffs and Trade (GATT)/WTO has stipulated certain rules related to trade-related investment measures (TRIMs). TRIMs are a subset of the incentives and regulations designed to influence FDI. Broadly speaking, they consist of incentives and regulations deemed to have a direct impact on international trade. The most common TRIMs are local content and export performance requirements. Local content provisions require foreign firms to purchase a specific proportion of their inputs from local rather than foreign sources. Failure to comply with this regulation may result in increased tariffs on imported inputs. Trade balancing measures are also considered to be TRIMs. In this case, governments impose restrictions on the import of inputs by a corporation, or limit the import of inputs in relation to the level of exports of the firm. Some foreign exchange balancing requirements impose a similar scheme whereby a corporation's permitted imports are tied to the value of its exports so that there is a net foreign exchange earning. Another measure used is to deny foreign corporations access to the host country's markets.

After a failed attempt to formulate a multilateral agreement on investment among mostly developed countries in the OECD, the principal multilateral agreement on FDI, the TRIMs Agreement, was formulated in the Uruguay Round of the GATT (1986–94). This agreement was designed to address certain issues related to investment policies in a multilateral framework. Formal consideration of TRIMs in a GATT forum was a long time in coming. The Uruguay Round of the GATT was the first attempt to formulate an agreement covering trade and investment.

A combination of factors led to the inclusion of foreign investment in the work program of the Uruguay Round negotiations. As mentioned above, there was a changing perception of the role of FDI in development. Foreign investment had become increasingly important and the flows far more sizeable. Perceptions had also moved from initial anxiety about FDI to a more welcoming stance. The dispute between the United States and Canada around this time over the latter's application of performance measures for foreign firms also facilitated debate on the linkages between GATT rules and foreign investment policy (Bora 2001).

The TRIMs Agreement recognizes that certain investment measures distort trade and that these distortions are not consistent with GATT principles. Export subsidies, import entitlements, minimum export requirements, and local content requirements directly affect the volumes and prices of imports and exports, and in some cases the composition of trade. For example, local content requirements mean that imports are treated less favorably than domestic inputs, violating the national treatment principle of the GATT. The trade balancing requirement that limits the quantity of inputs an MNE can import if it does not meet its export target also violates national treatment obligations. Incentives geared to attracting FDI, such as tax incentives, may influence trade flows in that they may persuade firms to favor FDI over exports as a method of foreign market penetration. As such, the inclusion of TRIMs on the agenda of the Uruguay Round of multilateral trade negotiations was favored and considered legitimate by developed countries (Balasubramanyam 1991).

Despite this, after lengthy debate, only a brief TRIMs Agreement was put into effect on 1 January 1995. It includes the following terms.

i   It covers only regulations and requirements imposed on foreign investors that directly impinge on international trade flows.

ii   Its coverage 'applies to investment measures related to trade in goods only.' This means that it excludes investment incentives and many performance requirements. Furthermore, services are covered by the WTO's General Agreement on Trade in Services (GATS), and export subsidies are covered in the Subsidies Agreement. As such, technology transfer requirements, licensing requirements, and joint venture requirements are not included in the TRIMs Agreement. One aspect of the agreement that has received much attention from academics and policymakers is export performance requirements, which are not actually included among the investment measures listed in the annex to the TRIMs Agreement. There has been ongoing debate as to whether or not the list should be extended to prohibit this policy.

iii The central provision of the TRIMs Agreement prohibits trade-distorting investment measures subject to GATT Article III (on national treatment) or Article XI (on the elimination of quantitative restrictions). Measures specifically identified as inconsistent with Articles III and XI include local content, trade balancing, import substitution, foreign exchange, and export limitation requirements.

iv The agreement sets deadlines for removing TRIMs. Member states were given 90 days from 1 January 1995 to notify the WTO Council for Trade in Goods of all measures that did not conform with the agreement. They were then given a 'transition period' to eliminate their notified TRIMs, with a member's level of development determining the length of time it would be given. Developed members were allowed two years, developing countries were given five years, and least-developed countries were given seven years.

v The agreement allows for developing and least developed countries to apply for an extension of the transition period. Ten WTO members have so far submitted requests for an extension of the transition period. The requests range from less than a year for Chile to seven years for Pakistan.

vi The agreement also makes allowance for developing country members to deviate temporarily from some of their obligations; for example, countries experiencing a balance of payments crisis would find temporary relief under the GATT 1994 provisions as they apply in the TRIMs context. The waiver of an obligation will be granted providing that three-quarters of members agree to it.

vii The TRIMs Agreement is overseen by the WTO Council for Trade in Goods, with the WTO dispute settlement mechanism to apply to its signatories. A review of the operation of the agreement took place in 2000, five years after it came into force.

The agreement does not provide an explicit definition of TRIMs, or of 'investment.' Instead, it provides an illustrative list in the annex of laws, policies, and regulations that are considered to be TRIMs and that are deemed to violate GATT Articles III and XI.

All developing countries were supposed to implement the TRIMs Agreement and eliminate their non-complying regulations by 1 January 2000. However, 26 developing country members with widely varying economic characteristics gave notice at that time that they still had a variety of problematic policies in existence. Overwhelmingly these were local content schemes, most of them involving the auto and agro-food industries. The second most frequently notified type of TRIM was foreign exchange balancing requirements (Bora 2001).

A number of countries requested extensions of the transition period. Argentina, Malaysia, Thailand, and the Philippines cited financial crises that had added to their structural adjustment problems as a major reason for their requests. Colombia and Pakistan cited specific development reasons for their extension requests. Colombia detailed difficulties in transforming its economic model, especially in terms of developing substitutes for illegal crops. It argued that it needed a local content policy to promote greater absorption of agricultural products by the domestic market and thus ensure that farmers would be able to sell their produce. Pakistan said that a rapid opening of its economy to import competition would not allow it to exploit domestic resources optimally, to promote the transfer of technology, or to promote employment and domestic linkages. Another reason cited by some countries for an extension request was inconsistency between preferential trade agreements and multilateral obligations (Bora 2001).[8]

Since 1995, the TRIMs obligations of new WTO members have depended on the terms of their accession. So far, all acceding countries have agreed to implement the TRIMs Agreement upon accession, whether or not they are developing countries.

The current TRIMs Agreement resulted from a compromise. During the Uruguay Round discussions, developed countries, including the European Union, Japan, and the United States, initially proposed establishing a comprehensive agreement on investment. Their proposed framework covered a wide range of areas, including technology transfer requirements, restrictions on the transfer of profits overseas, controls on foreign exchange flows, government reviews of foreign investment performance, and nationalization. This plan faced strong resistance from the governments of developing countries. Brazil and India maintained that investment was outside the GATT's competence, while other developing countries tended to take a defensive position with regard to TRIMs (Ariff 1989). In particular, many developing countries resisted the extent of the market access proposed for foreign firms. The result was that negotiations focused on policies that applied to the operations of foreign firms. Even then, negotiation proved difficult. Since the enactment of the agreement, the main focus has been on the effect on trade of local content and export performance requirements.

The remarkable brevity of the TRIMs Agreement in relation to the complicated issues it covers is extraordinary. Its brevity is a manifestation of the divisions that emerged between developed and developing countries during its negotiation. This lack of consensus also explains the vague nature of some of its elements. The current agreement does not contain a basic definition of investment. This requires clarification, as the definition of investment has profound implications for the scope and coverage of the agreement. The definition given in the draft OECD Multilateral Agreement on Investment, for example, went far beyond the traditional notion of FDI to include portfolio investment, debt capital, intellectual property rights, and various forms of tangible or intangible assets (Ganesan 1998).

Bora (2001) summarizes a few other areas where confusion might arise. Because the TRIMs Agreement does not introduce a new vocabulary in the context of disciplining policies, and instead refers to the GATT articles, there has been some confusion as to whether or not a policy that violates GATT articles automatically violates the TRIMs Agreement. Because it is a stand-alone agreement, the TRIMs Agreement needs to be interpreted independently of GATT rules. However, since it is independent, many developing countries question whether it goes beyond GATT rules.

The TRIMs Agreement covers measures related to foreign investment according to their impact on trade. However, since it contains nothing to suggest that the nationality of the ownership of enterprises is an element in deciding whether a measure is covered by the agreement, the TRIMs Agreement is not confined to policies targeting foreign firms. It is in fact ownership-neutral. However, some argue that the TRIMs Agreement was basically designed to govern and provide a level playing field for foreign investment, and that therefore measures relating to internal taxes or subsidies cannot be construed to be TRIMs.

There is also no well-defined phase-in period in place for members that notify under the TRIMs Agreement to bring their laws into conformity with it. This has caused some implementation difficulties. None of the notifying countries have either developed an implementation plan or identified alternative policies that could be used to achieve the objective of meeting all the requirements of the TRIMs Agreement.

TRIMs are typically used in conjunction with a number of other policies. One aspect that was not taken into account during the Uruguay Round negotiations was how the removal of certain TRIMs without addressing companion policies would affect trade. For example, local content schemes are usually combined with a subsidy. The TRIMs Agreement disciplines trade policy, but not incentives. Views are still divided on how to deal with both incentives and regulations.

Ambiguity in the wording of the TRIMs Agreement has made the interpretation of obligations difficult. The lack of capacity of some developing countries to fully understand the scope and implications of these obligations has exacerbated this problem. These problems have also created a tension between the generally accepted notion of efficiency and the broader definition of development. Some work to clarify these issues has been done recently by the WTO Council for Trade in Goods, but solving these problems will require much time and effort (Bora 2001).

The current TRIMs Agreement relies on the state-to-state mechanisms of the WTO for dispute settlement and arbitration under which, for example, a dispute settlement panel is established and makes its judgment. Some argue that it is necessary to establish investor-to-state mechanisms to ensure that investors receive a hearing (Moran 2002a).

Believing the existing TRIMs Agreement to be inadequate, developed country parties such as the European Union, Japan, and the United States largely view it as a mechanism for removing performance requirements on foreign investment (Greenfield 2001). Nevertheless, the agreement represents a step forward in ensuring that all countries are subject to the same rules respecting the use of certain investment-related performance requirements. Although most FDI has occurred between developed countries, the agreement has allowed investment issues to be discussed in the context of multilateral negotiations. These discussions have been continued through the WTO Working Group on Trade and Investment where members have further assessed the linkages between trade, FDI, and development (Bora 2001). This has also allowed disputes between member states to be settled in the WTO context, and has enforced GATT provisions.

The Ongoing Divide in Negotiating a Multilateral Framework on Investment

Investment was again put on the agenda for the WTO Doha Round of negotiations. Investment, competition policy, transparency in government procurement, and trade facilitation have been labeled the 'Singapore issues,' following the work program set out in the 1996 Singapore WTO Ministerial Declaration. The Doha Declaration continues to attach the usual operational qualifications of 'trade-related aspects only' for investment and competition policy (WTO 2001a). However, as evidenced at the Fifth WTO Ministerial Conference in Cancun, Mexico, in 2003, members still have a long way to go to reach agreement on investment issues.

In current WTO discussions, negotiations are a 'single undertaking' in which concessions in one sector can be traded off against concessions in other sectors. In Cancun, resistance from the more developed economies to making further concessions on agriculture prompted some developing countries to refuse to negotiate on the Singapore issues. In the end the discussions broke down on the issue of investment, although other factors were more likely to have been the underlying cause.

Considerable divisions continue to exist between developed and developing countries on investment-related issues in the WTO framework. Since the TRIMs Agreement came into effect in 1995, operational details have caused contention between developed and developing countries. Some developing members argue that they lack the capacity to identify measures that are inconsistent with the TRIMs Agreement and hence are unable to meet notification deadlines set out for the transition periods. In some cases, members that did notify do not appear to be willing or ready to meet the deadlines. Many members implemented strategies that seemingly addressed the implications of compliance for affected industries, but did not actually implement alternative policies.[9]

The governments of Brazil, Malaysia, Mexico, and Pakistan have argued that the process for negotiating extensions to the duration of transition periods should be undertaken through a multilateral framework. In contrast, the European Union, Japan, and the United States argued that requests for deadline extensions should only be considered on a case-by-case basis and should be negotiated bilaterally (Greenfield 2001). The bilateral nature of this process has caused concern among developing country governments that developed countries could use the threat of rejecting requests for an extension as bargaining leverage against them. Since the 1999 Seattle talks, the WTO Council for Trade in Goods has held several meetings to resolve the dispute over extension procedures. This was partly resolved in July 2000 when it was decided that the chair of the council would oversee multilateral negotiations. However, requests will still be dealt with on a case-by-case basis and are open to bilateral pressure from the European Union, Japan, and the United States.

The extremely brief preamble of the TRIMs Agreement states that it takes into account the trade, development, and financial needs of developing countries. Some applications for an extension cited the financial crises that hit East Asia and Latin America. However, some developed countries argue that structural adjustment should not be considered a defense, as this is part of any obligation to liberalize.

More fundamentally, several developing countries take the view that TRIMs and other investment measures are domestic issues that should therefore not involve GATT/WTO officials. This point was emphasized during the Fifth WTO Ministerial meeting in September 2003. Some developing countries also assert that the mandate of the GATT/WTO is confined to trade and does not extend to investment. Some fear they would be deprived of a major means of exercising control over foreign firms operating locally if their right to impose TRIMs or other investment measures were removed. India, Malaysia, and some other countries consider policies such as domestic content requirements to be essential policy tools for industrialization. At the WTO Doha Ministerial Conference, a number of countries continued to state that the use of domestic content requirements constitutes an extremely useful policy tool that effectively links FDI with domestic economic activities, and acts as an important instrument in the development process in several other ways. They also said that joint venture requirements encourage indigenization. They believe developing countries should be allowed to use TRIMs and other investment measures flexibly in pursuit of development objectives because they have unique needs and circumstances that require them to have sufficient freedom and flexibility to pursue their own policies. They are of the view that, although the TRIMs Agreement established uniform obligations for all members, it does not take account of structural inequalities and disparities in levels of development; of differences in technological capabilities; or of differing social, regional, and environmental conditions—in short that it does not incorporate a meaningful development dimension. A legally binding treaty on foreign investment would reduce the degree of flexibility available to such countries even further (Ganesan 1998).

Panagariya (2002) has identified a number of major factors behind developing countries' objections to a multilateral agreement on investment. These include asymmetries between countries in the obligations they must undertake and in the distribution of benefits, the limited capacity of some countries to negotiate adequately on their own behalf, and limited resources for implementation.

A major reason for their reluctance is that liberalization of investment is more constrained by political factors than is trade.[10] Many developing countries find that political sensitivities demand discretion in how investment liberalization proceeds. Investment is a sensitive issue in terms of national sovereignty, adding another dimension to policies aimed at controlling the extent and character of foreign production within a nation's borders (McCulloch 1991). This arises from the fact that direct investment implies long-term foreign ownership and control of assets, resources, and enterprises.

A second reason is that many developing countries wish to ensure a degree of certainty, before committing to negotiations, that the benefits of a future agreement will outweigh the risk of trade sanctions. Based on their experience with the Uruguay Round agreement, some developing countries fear that they will fail to implement the negotiated agreement in a timely fashion and then be left exposed to the risk of trade sanctions. Third, many developing countries lack the capacity to negotiate effectively on a wide-ranging agenda. The problem is not merely one of financial resources, but also involves human resources. Furthermore, since developed countries already meet the standards likely to be negotiated with respect to the Singapore issues, liberalization in these areas places a proportionately greater burden on developing countries. The use of TRIMs and other investment regulations tends to be relatively high in developing countries. Moreover, from the national standpoint, it is not clear that the implementation of an agreement as a priority represents the best use of the limited resources and political goodwill available to developing country governments.

This raft of concerns explains the ongoing reluctance of some developing countries to negotiate a multilateral framework on investment. Some countries have been concerned about the dislocations and difficult adjustments that will be forced on uncompetitive firms and workers. The tone of their comments suggests that some might even wish to renegotiate the TRIMs Agreement (Moran 2002a).

To date, it is still unclear whether the WTO will pursue investment-related issues further, and what form and scope negotiations would take if they did proceed. Furthermore, it is not clear whether any new talks would focus on extending the TRIMs Agreement or negotiating a new, comprehensive multilateral investment agreement. This reflects the continuing differences of opinion between developing and developed countries. The next subsection explores some issues that might arise in future negotiations.

Is a Multilateral Framework on Investment Necessary?

Mundell (1957) argued that free trade is a substitute for factor movements, so that in the presence of free trade there would be little or no FDI. By this logic, there would be no need for investment measures in the absence of FDI, if the latter were due to free factor movements. Ariff (1989) has also argued that investment measures arise only because of pre-existing distortions that make domestic market orientation an attractive proposition for foreign investors. Investment measures would become largely a non-issue if liberalization succeeded in dismantling tariff and non-tariff barriers to trade. For example, local content requirements tend to raise production costs and render final products uncompetitive. A local content program can only be sustained behind protectionist walls. Similarly, elimination of protection will diminish the need for export incentives. Therefore, the more successful trade liberalization is, the less need there will be to worry about investment agreements. This raises two questions: should liberalization focus on trade, and is an agreement on investment needed?

Despite different views on the relationship between trade, trade barriers, and foreign investment, it is important to acknowledge that problems of barriers or incentives for foreign investment partly result from the incomplete liberalization of trade. For example, without tariffs, quotas, and other import barriers, there would be less economic rent to extract and thus less scope for performance requirements. Thus, trade liberalization can also induce more liberal investment regimes.

The reality is that trade and FDI coexist. Impediments to trade are a factor in the growth of FDI, but other market imperfections also have an important influence on the decisions of firms to invest abroad. Real market conditions seldom approximate the free trade model. Oligopoly rather than perfect competition is a characteristic of many market structures in which foreign firms operate, and these firms have considerable discretion over the choice of market in which to operate (Balasubramanyam 1991). Even for trade barriers, it would be unrealistic to assume that all such barriers will disappear soon. In these circumstances, restrictions on foreign investment, as well as incentives to promote it, may exist for a long time.

Nevertheless, an agreement on investment might strengthen the investment climate of host countries and contribute to trade liberalization. Foreign investment and trade are not necessarily substitutes for each other; often they have a complementary relationship. The effects of restrictions on trade and on investment are empirically indistinguishable from one another. As with the multilateral trade rules introduced through the Uruguay Round, a multilateral framework of rules may or may not be necessary for investment in order to cope with the dynamics of the ongoing integration of the world economy. In recent years, TRIMs have been reduced or dismantled as the TRIMs Agreement was implemented. However, such measures have also been reduced as countries carry out economic reform and liberalization.

Is there a North–South Divide on an Investment Agreement?

Industrialized countries are still overwhelmingly the main source of FDI. Increasingly, however, capital moves not only between developed and developing countries, but also between developed countries. By the mid-1980s, the United States had emerged as the world's largest host country in terms of the total value of inward FDI. Thus, developed countries represent both major sources of, and hosts for, FDI. The increased extent of intra-industry FDI among the industrialized nations blurs the distinction, at least among industrial nations, between host and source countries. The investment issue thus is of interest to developed countries as both suppliers and recipients of FDI. Developing countries are mainly recipients of FDI. But a number of them—such as Hong Kong, China; Korea; Taipei,China; and Singapore—have undertaken investment abroad. The stake or interest of these developing countries in TRIMs and other investment issues may be similar to that of their developed counterparts.

There are different views both between and within developed and developing nations. For example, given their generally open capital markets, relatively higher income levels, and preoccupation with agricultural liberalization, countries in Latin America were not particularly opposed to the negotiation of the TRIMs Agreement. Much of the opposition to a new investment agreement derives from countries in Africa and Asia (Panagariya 2002). Notably, however, in its submission to the Working Group on the Relationship between Trade and Investment at the WTO, Korea supported the EU position on banning technology transfer requirements for foreign investment (Greenfield 2001).

Conventional wisdom holds that developing countries employ trade-distorting investment measures while developed countries do not. However, trade and investment figures clearly show that developed countries also use investment measures. Most developed countries do not use what they formally call 'screening' agencies for inward investment, but instead make available location-based incentive packages for both domestic and international investors. Ireland reports that its special incentive packages have attracted more than 1,200 foreign firms to its economy, and that these contribute 70 percent of the country's industrial output and three-quarters of its manufactured exports (O'Donovan 2000). Germany's grants to both domestic and foreign firms to settle in the economically depressed former East Germany have exceeded the already generous treatment the European Union provides to attract investment to lagging regions. The OECD found that almost 90 percent of all domestic support programs in the European Union were available to foreign investors (OECD 1996; Moran 2002a).

The divide between developed and developing countries is further bridged by the fact that MNEs invest in many countries, both developed and developing. Any multilateral effort to create a level playing field for national and international companies among home and host countries around the world would be seriously deficient if it ignored the proliferation and escalation of location-based incentives by developed countries.

Overall, it appears that with or without a multilateral framework for investment, many countries have carried out liberalization of their investment regimes. This has two possible implications: that a multilateral framework is redundant; or that a more comprehensive international agreement on investment becomes increasingly possible and necessary for facilitating the liberalization process and governing investment measures as policies converge. Which outcome emerges will depend on the bargaining positions adopted by different countries and their attitudes toward the process of negotiating a multilateral agreement on investment.

4   CONCLUSIONS

Debates on measures to regulate foreign investment need to consider the policy framework for domestic investment. Indeed, in many developing countries it is the local investors who feel that they are being discriminated against while foreign investors are being pampered. Arguably, the privileges granted to foreign investors have tended to thwart the development of local entrepreneurship. Domestic small-scale industrialists in particular often feel neglected and overlooked (Ariff 1989).

Individual countries can adopt a policy framework that is beneficial to both foreign and domestic investors, as well as to recipient economies as a whole. Transparency about investment rules and regulations, with clear identification of the agencies responsible for issuing relevant licenses, permits, and approvals, would be a basic component of such a framework.

In the long run, the establishment of a multilateral framework of rules could help to improve the investment climate; create a stable, predictable, and transparent environment for investment; enhance business confidence; and thereby promote the growth of FDI flows to developing countries. These conditions will not only foster foreign investment, but also stimulate domestic investment. Such favorable long-term outcomes may, however, be accompanied by arduous adjustment in developing countries. It is therefore important to minimize the adjustment costs faced by developing countries in the short to medium term.

There appears to be increasing acceptance that liberal policy regimes for most industries bring the highest benefits to host countries. FDI policies can be put in place at both the national and international level. At present, however, they are predominantly national rather than international. There is still much disagreement on forming and implementing a multilateral framework on investment.

The following chapters look at these and other issues in the context of a diverse group of dynamic developing economies in Asia.

NOTES

1 This chapter draws heavily on Brooks, Fan, and Sumulong (2003a, 2003b).
2 All dollar figures in this book refer to US dollars unless stated otherwise.
3 However, the host country can capture part of the rents from scale economies through a licensing fee or an increase in factor prices in the export sector as foreign firms bid up factor costs above the level sustained by the small domestic export industry.
4 Efforts to protect domestic markets offer an incentive to foreign investors to reap a secondary round of oligopoly rents from older technology.
5 *Voluntary* joint ventures to spread risk and increase market access, on the other hand, are less of a disincentive to technology transfer, at least for more established technologies.
6 However, the affiliates of foreign investors generally try to avoid horizontal technology transfers, which may create greater competition for themselves.
7 While private sector arbitration mechanisms have generally worked satisfactorily so far, this means of dispute settlement raises the potential for political disagreements in that a sovereign judicial system can be overruled by an arbitration panel that is unelected and that usually operates with little transparency.
8 Argentina's request stated specifically that it was aware of potential areas of inconsistency in the context of the proposed MERCOSUR Common Automotive Policy. Mexico did not specifically mention NAFTA in its request, but it has been noted that there is an inconsistency between its phase-out period for TRIMs under NAFTA and under the TRIMs Agreement.
9 Implementation is difficult in some cases. For example, Romania had a legally binding contract between the government and a firm that included a provision that was not in compliance with the TRIMs Agreement. Its removal would have had legal consequences for the national government.
10 Panagariya (2002) points out that trade is generally easier to liberalize than investment, which in turn is easier to liberalize than labor flows. Within trade, goods trade is easier to liberalize than services trade. Within investment, FDI is easier to liberalize than portfolio investment. And within labor, opening up to immigration of skilled labor is easier than opening up to unskilled labor.

2

Six Asian Economies:
Issues and Lessons

Hal Hill

1 INTRODUCTION

This chapter examines the role and impact of foreign direct investment (FDI) in six major Asian economies. Drawing on the general literature on foreign investment and development, we look especially at the changing FDI policy regimes in these countries and assess the developmental contribution of multinational enterprises (MNEs). Policy challenges and concerns are also addressed.

For most of the twentieth century, global capital flows grew more quickly than global trade, which in turn grew faster than world output (Crafts 2000). The six economies examined in this book—the People's Republic of China (PRC), India, the Republic of Korea, Malaysia, Thailand, and Viet Nam—differ enormously in their international commercial orientation. However, a common feature is that all of them, in varying degree, have become more open to both international trade and investment during the past decade at least, and sometimes longer. In particular, there is a general recognition that the earlier 'Japanese model' of rapid economic development with minimal FDI is costly and in many cases not feasible. Rather, the principal analytical and policy issues now focus on how to maximize the benefits of the foreign presence.

The link between trade and FDI liberalization is central to this transformation. As trade barriers have fallen, the old 'tariff factory' model of FDI has given way to a new FDI-led, export-oriented paradigm. This is sometimes characterized as a switch from 'rent-seeking' to 'efficiency-seeking' FDI. This transformation has profound links for host countries' management of FDI. The regulatory apparatus that was constructed to manage (and frequently siphon off) rents under the old regime is generally still present in most countries. Yet it has become largely irrelevant, and has usually been bypassed in the reform process, which typically has been driven by other parts of the bureaucracy. Rather, the contemporary challenge for developing countries is to develop a new approach to managing FDI. In a globalizing world, competition for FDI is no longer about rents but instead focuses on the establishment of an enabling, business-friendly commercial environment, consistent with national development objectives. In this context, a useful paradigm is the so-called 'three I's': incentives, institutions, and infrastructure. That is, as economies open up, these three factors, which are examined below, are key determinants not only of the overall rate of growth but also of the magnitude and productivity of capital inflows.

The six Asian countries examined in this book are diverse in practically every respect. There are rich and poor nations, giant and medium-sized ones, with high and moderate rates of economic growth. Some have a long history of openness while the engagement of others with the global economy is very recent. Their ownership structures range from a very large foreign presence to a quite modest one. Some have very large state-owned sectors. Some were severely affected by the recent Asian economic crisis, others minimally. There is also great variation in terms of institutional quality, infrastructure, and human capital. This diversity is an obvious strength of the study, as it permits broader generalization beyond the six.

This chapter is organized as follows. Section 2 surveys FDI policy regimes and foreign ownership patterns in the six countries, in the context of general economic reform and the institutional backdrop. Section 3 examines the effects of FDI in more detail. Some major conclusions and lessons are discussed in Section 4.

2   FDI AND THE COMMERCIAL ENVIRONMENT

This section assesses FDI inflows (and outflows), patterns, and policy regimes in the six countries, in the context of general economic trends, ownership structures, and policy reforms. One of our major arguments, as adumbrated above, is that trade reform alters the incentive of production for the domestic market relative to exports, resulting in a fundamental shift in the behavior of MNEs and in the FDI cost–benefit calculus.

Six Diverse Economies

Tables 2.1 and 2.2 present a set of comparative statistics for the six economies. These include some general economic indicators, as well as others relating to the trade regime and FDI. We also include several indicators of countries' attractiveness to FDI. Table 2.3 offers a summary of stylized facts about FDI regimes in the six economies.

The sample includes the world's two most populous nations, together with a range of intermediate-sized countries with populations of 20–100 million people. The largest economy (PRC) has GDP that is more than double that of the next largest (India) and about 35 times greater than that of the smallest (Viet Nam). Korea is a rich OECD member. Malaysia is an upper middle-income developing country. The PRC and Thailand are in the lower middle-income group, while India and Viet Nam are low-income countries. The range of per capita GDP from the richest (Korea) to the poorest (Viet Nam) is about 30:1, or 7:1 in purchasing power parity (PPP) terms.

All six have performed creditably for most of the past two decades. Their real per capita incomes in 2001 were at least double those in 1980, and more than five times higher in the case of the PRC. Since 1990, the PRC has consistently recorded spectacular economic growth, to the point where it is now the principal locomotive of East Asian growth and a major global economy. If its current growth rates are maintained, it will become the world's largest economy (in PPP terms) before 2020. Korea, Malaysia, and Thailand all grew at more than 6 percent until the crisis of 1997–98; Thailand was the world's fastest growing economy in the decade from the mid-1980s. All three experienced a sharp contraction in 1998, but recovery has been fairly rapid. Viet Nam grew strongly for most of the 1990s, with slower (but consistently positive) growth during the crisis. India has never achieved the very high growth rates of the others. However, reforms from the late 1980s have lifted its performance significantly, and it was largely unaffected by the recent Asian crisis.

All six countries have reasonably good macroeconomic management. Since 1990, all have averaged single-digit inflation. None is heavily indebted. Malaysia and Thailand have the highest debt to GDP ratios. Both were running very large current account deficits pre-crisis, albeit in the context of very high investment rates, low fiscal deficits, and (owing to their outward orientation) moderate debt-service ratios.

FDI Regimes

An Overview

In terms of their FDI regimes, it is useful to divide the six countries into three groups. The first comprises those with historically very restrictive regimes (including outright prohibition) that have opened up during the past quarter-century. The countries in this group are the PRC, India, and

Table 2.1   Summary Indicators for Six Asian Economies

Indicator	PRC	India	Rep. of Korea	Malaysia	Thailand	Viet Nam
General economic indicators						
GDP, 2002 ($ billion)	1,237	515	477	95	126	35
GDP per capita PPP, 2001 ($)	4,020	2,840	15,090	8,750	6,400	2,070
GDP per capita growth, 1990–96 (%)	9.2	3.7	6.5	6.7	7.4	5.8
GDP per capita growth, 1997–2001 (%)	6.9	3.5	3.5	0.5	–0.9	5.0
Annual average inflation, 1990–2001 (%)[a]	6.5	8.6	5.3	3.3	4.4	3.0
Total external debt/GDP, 2001 (%)	15	20	26	49	59	38
GDP per capita 2001/1980[b]	5.3	2.1	3.5	2.1	2.6	2.1
Openness						
Trade						
(Exports + imports)/GDP, 1990 (%)	31.9	17.2	59.4	147.0	75.8	81.3
(Exports + imports)/GDP, 2001(%)	49.2	29.1	83.5	214.3	126.5	111.5
Export growth, 1990–2001 (%)	17.4	12.9	13.5	11.3	9.8	22.0
Average tariff rate, 1999	18.7	30.2	7.9	8.1	5.9	20.0
Index of economic freedom, 2003[c]	3.6	3.5	2.7	3.0	2.6	3.7
Investment						
FDI as % of total capital inflows, 1990–96[d]	90	15	7	147	16	81
FDI as % of total capital inflows, 1997–2001[e]	92	22	34	32	–57	82
Total cumulative FDI inflows, 1990–2001 ($ billion)	372.2	20.9	38.3	52.5	33.1	15.8
Total FDI stock, 1990 ($ billion)	24.8	1.7	5.9	10.3	8.2	0.3
Total FDI stock, 2001 ($ billion)	395.2	22.3	47.2	53.3	28.2	15.9
Outflow/inflow FDI stock, 1990 (%)	10.1	16.8	39.2	25.9	4.9	0.0
Outflow/inflow FDI stock, 2001 (%)	7.0	9.3	86.4	35.6	9.2	0.0

a   Data for Viet Nam are for the period 1997–2001.
b   Data for Viet Nam are for the years 1984 and 2001.
c   Index of economic freedom ranges from 0 (mostly free) to 5 (highly restricted).
d   Data for India are for the period 1991–96; data for Viet Nam are for 1996.
e   Data for India are for the period 1997–2000; data for Korea and Thailand are for 1997–2002; the years 1999 and 2000 are missing for Malaysia.
f   Tertiary enrolments (regardless of age) as a percentage of the 20–22 age group. Data for the PRC and India are for 1999.
g   Data for India, Malaysia, and Thailand are for 1996, 1997, and 1998 respectively.
h   Data for India and Viet Nam are for 1999 and 1997 respectively.
i   Based on the 1–59 country ranking in the Global Competitiveness Report (1 = best).
j   The index ranges from 0 (highly corrupt) to 10 (highly clean). The world average for the 102 countries covered is 4.6, with a maximum of 9.7 and a minimum of 1.2.

Table 2.1 (continued)

Indicator	PRC	India	Rep. of Korea	Malay-sia	Thai-land	Viet Nam
Total FDI stock as % of GDP, 1990	7.0	0.5	2.3	23.4	9.6	4.0
Total FDI stock as % of GDP, 2000	32.3	4.1	13.7	58.8	20.0	46.7
FDI as % of GDP, 1990–2000						
(annual average)	4.1	0.4	0.8	6.4	2.2	6.6
Human capital						
Years of education	5.7	4.8	10.5	7.9	6.1	n.a.
Tertiary enrolment as % of age						
group, 2000[f]	7.5	10.5	77.6	28.2	35.3	9.7
R&D expenditure as % of GDP[g]	1.0	1.2	2.7	0.4	0.1	n.a.
Number of internet users as % of						
total population, 2001	3	1	51	27	6	1
Public spending on education						
as % of GDP, 2000[h]	2.9	4.1	3.8	6.2	5.4	2.8
Physical infrastructure[i]	46	54	28	18	32	57
Institutional quality and risk						
Corruption						
Corruption perception index[j]	3.5	2.7	4.5	4.9	3.2	2.4
(country ranking)	(59)	(71)	(40)	(33)	(64)	(85)
Country risk						
Composite risk rating	73.5	63.8	79	75.3	72.8	71.8
Property rights						
Index of economic freedom[k]	4	3	2	3	2	5
Bureaucratic quality						
Public institutions index, 2001[l]	4.10	4.11	4.25	4.53	4.36	3.58
(country ranking)	(50)	(49)	(44)	(39)	(42)	(63)
Fiscal/finance						
Stock market capitalization, 2002[m]	13.0	23.0	43.0	129.0	36.6	n.a.
Average corporate tax rate, 1999 (%)	33	35	28	28	30	25

k The property rights index is a composite from the index of economic freedom developed by the Heritage Foundation. The range is from 0 (very good) to 5 (very poor).
l The public institutions index is based on survey data and ranges from 2.48 to 6.59 across 75 countries. The higher the index, the higher the quality.
m The figure for India is for 2001.

Source: General economic indicators: World Bank, *World Development Indicators* (CD ROM). Index of economic freedom: Heritage Foundation, http://www.heritage.org/research/features/index/. FDI: UNCTAD, *World Investment Report*, www.http://stats.unctad.org/fdi. Total capital inflows: IMF, *International Financial Statistics* (CD ROM). Human capital and stock market capitalization: World Bank, *World Development Indicators* (CD ROM). Corruption perception index: Transparency International, http://www.transparency.org/. Country risk: UNCTAD, *World Investment Report*. All other data are from *Global Competitiveness Report 2001*.

*Table 2.2   Annual Inflows of FDI, Portfolio Investment, and Other
Capital Inflows, 1990–2002 ($ million)*

Country	1990	1991	1992	1993	1994	1995
PRC						
Total capital inflows	4,557	9,431	7,467	30,585	36,214	41,676
FDI	3,487	4,366	11,156	27,515	33,787	35,849
Portfolio	0	565	393	3,646	3,923	710
Other	1,070	4,500	−4,082	−576	−1,496	5,116
India						
Total capital inflows	n.a.	4,258	3,147	5,244	9,488	5,157
FDI	n.a.	74	277	550	973	2,144
Portfolio	n.a.	5	284	1,369	5,491	1,590
Other	n.a.	4,180	2,587	3,325	3,024	1,423
Republic of Korea						
Total capital inflows	6,506	10,519	10,606	9,686	22,591	37,101
FDI	788	1,180	728	589	810	1,776
Portfolio	662	2,906	5,875	11,088	8,713	14,619
Other	5,056	6,434	4,003	−1,990	13,068	20,706
Malaysia						
Total capital inflows	1,989	4,664	7,244	11,738	784	6,628
FDI	2,332	3,998	5,183	5,006	4,342	4,178
Portfolio	−255	170	−1,122	−709	−1,649	−436
Other	−89	496	3,183	7,441	−1,909	2,885
Thailand						
Total capital inflows	9,402	11,575	9,517	13,998	13,691	25,534
FDI	2,444	2,014	2,113	1,804	1,366	2,068
Portfolio	−38	−81	924	5,455	2,486	4,083
Other	6,996	9,642	6,479	6,739	9,839	19,383
Viet Nam						
Total capital inflows	n.a.	n.a.	n.a.	n.a.	n.a.	n.a.
FDI	n.a.	n.a.	n.a.	n.a.	n.a.	n.a.
Other	n.a.	n.a.	n.a.	n.a.	n.a.	n.a.

n.a.: not available.

Table 2.2 (continued)

1996	1997	1998	1999	2000	2001	2002
43,834	64,107	35,230	41,908	58,045	41,557	50,031
40,180	44,237	43,751	38,753	38,399	44,241	49,308
2,372	7,842	98	–699	7,317	1,249	1,752
1,282	12,028	–8,619	3,854	12,329	–3,933	–1,029
16,798	14,490	11,871	10,108	11,087	n.a.	n.a.
2,426	3,577	2,635	2,169	2,315	n.a.	n.a.
3,958	2,556	–601	2,317	1,619	n.a.	n.a.
10,413	8,357	9,837	5,623	7,152	n.a.	n.a.
48,080	6,814	–8,748	17,829	20,002	2,912	11,014
2,326	2,844	5,412	9,333	9,283	3,198	1,972
21,514	13,308	775	7,908	12,697	11,856	4,940
24,240	–9,338	–14,935	588	–1,978	–12,142	4,102
5,343	6,801	2,719	n.a.	n.a.	–942	n.a.
5,078	5,137	2,163	3,895	3,788	554	n.a.
–268	–248	283	–892	–2,145	–666	n.a.
533	1,912	272	n.a.	n.a.	–830	n.a.
17,797	–8,851	–10,591	–8,970	–8,094	–3,709	–6,500
2,336	3,895	7,315	6,213	3,366	3,820	1,075
3,585	4,598	338	77	–546	–932	–1,347
11,876	–17,344	–18,243	–15,261	–10,914	–6,597	–6,228
2,942	2,237	2,183	1,844	1,773	1,568	n.a.
2,395	2,220	1,671	1,412	1,298	1,300	n.a.
547	17	512	432	475	268	n.a.

Source: IMF, *International Financial Statistics* (CD ROM).

Table 2.3   FDI Regimes: Some Stylized Facts

	PRC	India	Republic of Korea
Ownership structures	Dominant but declining SOEs; rapidly rising private and foreign firms.	Large SOE sector; reservation schemes for small firms.	Predominantly private; *chaebol* important; high concentration; small SME presence.
FDI history	Closed until 1978; rapid increase from the 1980s, especially in the south.	Very restrictive before 1991, then gradual opening.	Restrictive until 1990s, then gradual opening; major reforms in 1998.
FDI presence	Modest but rising.	Modest, with no clear trend.	Low but rising gradually.
Trade regime	Closed until 1978, then progressive opening, especially for exports. Landmark 2001 WTO accession.	Very restrictive before 1991, then gradual opening.	From 1960s, open for exports, otherwise restrictive; major reforms in the 1990s.
International connections	Hong Kong, China important; large diaspora.	Large and active diaspora.	Large US diaspora; reverse brain drain in the 1990s.
FDI regime in practice	Continuing though declining preference for SOEs; rapid decentralization; much corruption.	Reforming, in context of dirigiste history; states are powerful; much corruption.	Business climate becoming more predictable and open; powerful nationalist sentiment.
Institutional quality	Uneven but improving.	Well developed but cumbersome.	Generally good, though legal system is still evolving.
Human capital	Pockets of excellence; uneven, rapid catch-up.	Pockets of excellence; continuing high illiteracy.	Extremely strong education and R&D base, though not very internationally oriented.

	Malaysia	Thailand	Viet Nam
Ownership structures	Always large foreign presence; active *bumiputera* promotion.	Predominantly private; Sino-Thai dominance.	Dominant SOEs, actually rising post-reform.
FDI history	Consistently open.	Consistently fairly open.	Closed until late 1980s; rapid rise from early 1990s.
FDI presence	Very high.	Substantial and rising.	Low, but rising quickly.
Trade regime	Consistently open.	Consistently fairly open.	Closed to late 1980s, then major opening, especially for exports.
International connections	Singapore ties historically strong.	No special features.	Large diaspora, still regarded with suspicion.
FDI regime in practice	Predictable commercial environment.	Reasonably predictable commercial environment.	Continuing preference for SOEs; north–south differences; private firms insecure.
Institutional quality	Generally high.	Generally quite high.	Weak; very limited investor protection.
Human capital	Generally quite good; major affirmative action program; continuing non-*bumiputera* brain drain.	Historic under-investment in post-primary education.	High literacy, but limited international commercial know-how and entrepreneurship.

Viet Nam. The second comprises those that have always been reasonably open, and become progressively more so. Malaysia and Thailand belong to this group. Finally, there is the special case of Korea, which was initially highly selective in its opening up to FDI but has become progressively more open over time. There is no instance in our sample of a country becoming less open to FDI.

The comparative FDI data reported in Table 2.1 illustrate these general characterizations. In 1990, Malaysia, the least populous of the six economies, had the largest stock of FDI after the PRC. Thailand was well ahead of the other three. The amount in Viet Nam was negligible. By 2001, the PRC had emerged as the dominant recipient, with more than seven times the stock of the next two, Malaysia and Korea. In 2002, it was the world's largest FDI recipient, overtaking the United States. India and Viet Nam still had the smallest stocks in 2001, although these had been increasing quickly, especially in the case of Viet Nam. Relative to GDP, Malaysia was the largest recipient of FDI in both 1990 and 2000, and India the smallest. The greatest absolute increase in these ratios occurred in Viet Nam, followed by Malaysia.

In some cases, it is possible to trace the opening up to FDI to a package of major general reforms. In Korea, there was gradual liberalization from the late 1980s, with major reforms in 1997–98 in the wake of the economic crisis. In the PRC the reform process commenced in 1978. It was further consolidated in the late 1980s, and again in 2001 upon the country's accession to the WTO. In India, 1991 is regarded as the key year of reform. In Viet Nam it was the *doi moi* reforms of the late 1980s, with further liberalization around the turn of the century.

By contrast, Thailand and especially Malaysia have always been quite open to FDI, and over time have become progressively more so. In neither case has there been a major swing in the policy pendulum. In the decade up to the 1997 crisis, Thailand was a huge capital importer, in some years running a current account deficit of more than 8 percent of GDP. While total capital inflows increased to record levels, an increasing proportion of this was portfolio investment and other short-term capital flows. The government's objective to promote Bangkok as a regional capital market center in competition with Singapore and Hong Kong, China was a factor here, as virtually all restrictions on capital flows were removed. Following the 1997–98 capital flight and consequent collapse of the baht, the government maintained its open posture toward FDI, despite a growing nationalist backlash, and FDI flows actually increased for a period.

In Malaysia, the principal issue has arguably been the political imperative to redistribute ownership toward the indigenous (*bumiputera*) community (Gomez and Jomo 1997), rather than the foreign presence *per se*.

Under the New Economic Policy (NEP) announced in 1970, the *bumiputera* share of the corporate sector was to rise from 2 to 30 percent. After reaching about 20 percent in 1990, albeit through sometimes controversial share allocations, the scheme was somewhat de-emphasized, especially in the wake of the mid-1980s recession and the economic crisis of 1997–98. In fact, the very high foreign presence at the outset of the NEP facilitated this transformation, as the major redistribution occurred not from non-*bumiputera* to *bumiputera* groups but rather from foreign to domestic ownership. The non-*bumiputera* share actually rose throughout the period, while the foreign share fell continuously until recently (see below).

This is not the place to analyze in any detail the dynamics of these reforms and why they took place. But it is worth pointing out that a range of internal and external factors were typically at work. At an intellectual level, these factors have included a recognition that outward-oriented economies grow more quickly, and that it is possible to achieve 'nationalist' objectives in the context of an open economy. Competitive liberalization—keeping up with one's neighbors—has been a factor. Foreign pressures, including a desire to join international agencies such as the General Agreement on Tariffs and Trade (GATT/WTO) and, for Korea, the OECD, have often coaxed countries along. Conversely, the demise of an international benefactor (the former USSR) was a major trigger in Viet Nam's reforms. Coalitions of key bureaucrats and political figures have often accelerated progress once the environment for reform was judged to be favorable.

Obviously, 'policy reform' has very different connotations across the six countries studied here. In traditionally open Malaysia and Thailand, it has implied a gradual swing of the pendulum. In other cases, reform has constituted a major change in policy emphasis, even a U-turn, in which FDI liberalization has been important. The PRC and Viet Nam are both cases of a transition from a prohibitive to a quite open FDI regime.

'Dual Policy' Regimes

Only a handful of countries in the world have completely open FDI regimes. Thus, while the FDI regimes of the six examined in this book have become more open, there remains considerable selectivity across sectors and firms. Governments have typically been slower to open up the services sector to FDI. All countries have 'national projects' where a range of non-economic considerations intrude. Among our sample, for example, even the most open economy, Malaysia, has consistently protected its uneconomic automotive industry, and restricted foreign equity participation in it.

More generally, countries typically have a mix of both rent-seeking and efficiency-seeking FDI, reflecting partial reform of their trade regimes, and the political economy of dispensing patronage. Consequently, all the country studies draw attention to what may be termed 'dual policy' regimes. For example:

- FDI policy may differ between regions. Three of the six (PRC, India, and Malaysia) feature quite high levels of decentralized economic policy-making. Thailand has been pursuing a policy of 'industrial decentralization' for some time. In all but Malaysia, economic authority is progressively being devolved away from the center in varying degree and at different speeds.
- There are large inter-industry differences in protection, and thus incentives, in all six.
- State-owned enterprises (SOEs) typically receive preferential treatment, especially in the PRC, India, and Viet Nam, and so, therefore, do their MNE joint venture partners.
- Most countries offer some sort of fiscal or financial incentives to foreign investors. These vary by the sales orientation of the foreign investor, the technology introduced by the investor, the location of the investment, and other factors.
- The regulatory regime frequently offers more than one entry option for potential foreign investors, especially in recently reformed economies.

Not surprisingly, this phenomenon of dual policy regimes is particularly pronounced in the most recently reformed economies, the PRC and Viet Nam. Governments in the 'late reformers' typically reveal the greatest ambivalence toward foreign investment. There is an awareness that, after a period of commercial isolation, special promotional measures may be required as countries attempt to enter the international commercial mainstream. Sometimes this results in more generous treatment for foreign firms at the expense of domestic firms. Such preferential treatment lacks any analytical rationale, can generally be circumvented easily (for example, the PRC 'round-tripping' phenomenon discussed below), and runs the risk of a domestic backlash.

In such cases, there is at one extreme FDI flowing into joint ventures with SOEs, often in protected, uneconomic sectors, producing negative value added at international prices. FDI also typically flows into non-tradables such as real estate and hotels where, in thin markets for international-quality assets, bubbles in asset prices may occur. Meanwhile, another group of foreign investors enters 'comparative advantage' sectors—small and medium-sized enterprises (SMEs) specializing in labor-intensive, export-oriented activities. Often the latter locate in special zones that are free of the regulatory and bureaucratic complexities found elsewhere in the economy.

Such a pattern is clearly evident in the case of the PRC. The country's initial export orientation was confined to four southern coastal zones. Most of the labor-intensive FDI in these zones originated in Hong Kong, China, and later Taipei,China. This type of FDI co-existed with foreign investment going into joint ventures with SOEs, much of it in uneconomic and protected heavy industry. Firms from OECD countries were the dominant investors in these activities. The domestic welfare implications of the different types of FDI are fundamentally important. There is no such thing as a single FDI 'model' in these economies. A major feature of the reform process is, therefore, the diminished importance of the former type of FDI, and its progressive replacement with the latter.

Even among the relatively successful late reformers, policy progress is invariably uneven and unpredictable, as is the response of investors. Viet Nam in the 1990s illustrates both these propositions. Following *doi moi*, growth accelerated and there was an initial period of euphoria among foreign investors. By the mid-1990s, however, foreign investors had become more wary as the reality of doing business in a transitional, partially reformed communist state sank in (Freeman 2003). The prolonged commercial isolation and prevailing ideology permeating much of the bureaucracy and the Communist Party meant that policy-makers frequently had very little understanding of how to manage a foreign commercial presence. For example, they typically had unrealistic expectations about FDI.[1] Moreover, many of the general problems associated with the business environment—red tape, corruption, insecure property rights, an ill-defined legal environment, poor physical infrastructure, limited financial development, and the huge, inefficient, and privileged SOE sector—had not been addressed in the first round of reforms. Finding private sector business partners was difficult, especially as much of the non-SOE business sector was either neglected or harassed.

The PRC is an excellent illustration of the political economy proposition that, in some circumstances, partial reform is desirable if it can be a precursor to successful economy-wide liberalization. Evidently, the latter was not politically feasible during the early years of reform. But as the coastal zones began to grow at a spectacular rate, they became the model for the rest of the economy to emulate, and reform was progressively extended to other regions and sectors.[2]

Reform: Rhetoric versus Reality

In any evaluation of policy regimes, it is crucial to distinguish between formal FDI and trade regimes, and their operation in practice. Nominally 'open' regimes may in fact be highly complex and corrupt. Widespread physical and technical smuggling and unrecorded capital flows are present in all six countries, especially the less reformed ones. For example, smuggling renders much of Viet Nam's formal trade regime irrelevant. The value of investment incentives in Viet Nam is significantly eroded by administrative complexities and corruption. Moreover, reform at the center does not necessarily ensure that liberalization will proceed smoothly. This is illustrated by the case of India, where power is diffused and the vested interests and philosophical predisposition toward planning and intervention built up during decades of dirigisme cannot quickly be overturned. The reforms have been a 'positive sum game,' since growth has accelerated. But there have been losers, too, among the bureaucrats who dispensed power and patronage, the SOEs sheltered from competition, and the unions in feather-bedded (especially state-owned) industries. Moreover, under India's federal structure, the states wield considerable power.[3]

In Korea, too, there seems to have been considerable ambivalence about recent reforms among sections of the bureaucracy that are reluctant to relinquish control. Considerable sectoral restrictions on FDI remain, while business surveys (for example, that conducted by AMCHAM Korea) report that foreign investors find the business environment quite difficult. To overcome these difficulties, reformers have proposed the establishment of 'free economic zones' where liberalization would be able to proceed more quickly than elsewhere. It is unlikely that Korea will achieve its current objective of becoming an 'economic hub' for Northeast Asia unless these reforms can be introduced.

One general lesson from the reform experience is that authoritarian states like the PRC and Viet Nam can reform very quickly once key leadership figures are convinced of the case for change. Democratic states such as India invariably move more slowly. Conversely, it may be that the reforms are likely to be more durable in democratic states: greater persuasion is required to get the reforms through, potential losers are more likely to be compensated, and therefore opposition is likely to be ameliorated.

Korea undertook its major liberalizations after it had become democratic, but in any case it appears that external factors were a major trigger for reform. Two in particular stand out. One was the country's desire to join international organizations (the GATT/WTO and then the OECD), membership of which required reform. The second was the 1997–98 economic crisis when, in spite of intense nationalist sentiment, the government felt it had no choice but to open up.

Frequently, the investment boards charged with regulating FDI have little general authority. 'One-stop shops' may simplify their own operations without untangling the regulatory complexities of many other, more powerful agencies. Moreover, the rationale for the existence of such boards continues to be obscure. Over a decade ago, there was concern in the literature over how Asian investment boards married their (potentially conflicting) promotion and regulatory functions.[4] Such a concern appears to be even more valid today, in the wake of the transition to outward orientation and the region's economic crisis (Buckley 2003).

Especially in larger states, subnational policy regimes matter increasingly. In countries with well-established federal structures such as India and Malaysia, states do compete for investment and the rules of the game are quite well established. But decentralization is proceeding rapidly in most of East Asia's nominally unitary states (Hill 2002). Regional authorities are now offering a range of incentives, some only quasi-legal. The general presumption is that this subnational competition for FDI (and investment in general) is desirable, since it will spur improvement in the quality of governance at the local level. However, there are dangers, especially moral hazard concerns of local governments offering excessively generous incentives secure in the knowledge that they can rely on central government bail-outs. Moreover, as international barriers to commerce are declining, paradoxically subnational barriers are sometimes rising.

Ownership Structures and the Foreign Presence

Rising FDI flows in the six economies have generally been associated with an increased foreign presence, as measured by the MNE share of output, employment, and exports. However, it needs to be emphasized that rising FDI inflows do not necessarily result in increased foreign ownership.[5] This is so for a number of reasons. First, especially in high-growth economies, increased FDI flows have been accompanied by rising domestic investment rates, and thus the share of foreign-owned firms has not necessarily risen. Second, much FDI takes the form of reinvested earnings rather than fresh capital inflows. This is especially the case in countries with long-established foreign investors. In Malaysia, for example, retained earnings have accounted for as much as half of all new FDI in recent years.

It also needs to be noted that, even in the rare instances where ownership statistics are comprehensive, the foreign presence is always recorded imperfectly.[6] There are substantial non-equity forms of foreign commercial involvement, such as licensing and franchising. In some cases, foreign firms have no choice but to enter through non-equity forms, principally licensing arrangements. It is generally—though not necessarily—the case that these commercial arrangements are less important in countries with more open FDI regimes. Thus, for example, the foreign presence is probably more accurately captured in the ownership statistics in Malaysia than in Korea or India. In addition, international labor flows are increasing, thus adding an additional element to the foreign presence.

Moreover, ownership is often an empirically slippery concept, and the distinction between foreign and domestic is likely to become blurred in the future. The existence of large diasporas abroad will hasten this trend. These are present for all six countries, particularly the PRC, India, and Viet Nam, but perhaps inevitably their commercial activities are not consistently recorded. Official attitudes also vary, from suspicion of diaspora communities to embracing them.

To place these rising FDI flows in context, and bearing in mind the serious data deficiencies, it is useful to briefly examine patterns of ownership in the six countries.

Accurate economy-wide data on ownership are not available for the PRC. The best documented sector is manufacturing, where the major ownership feature has been the rapidly diminishing importance of the once dominant SOE sector. Its share of industrial output declined from 49 percent in 1994 to just 18 percent in 2001. Over this period, the shares of the non-SOE domestic sector and foreign firms rose by approximately similar amounts: from 38 percent to 53 percent for the non-SOE sector, and from 13 percent to 28 percent for foreign firms. Among the latter, firms from Hong Kong, China; Macao; and Taipei,China account for 40–45 percent of the total. There has been some, but limited, privatization of SOEs in the PRC. The major change has been the unshackling of the non-state sector, which has been the source of the country's economic dynamism since the late 1980s.

In India, too, economy-wide ownership data are patchy, but all estimates point to minor ownership changes over time and a modest foreign presence. As would be expected, the foreign share declined prior to liberalization, from around 30 percent of industrial output in the early 1970s to about 25 percent in 1990 according to unpublished Reserve Bank of India data cited by Athreye and Kapur (2001). These figures overstate the foreign presence since they refer only to medium-sized and large public companies surveyed by the bank. As the authors note, the decline is explained by

> the restrictions placed on foreign firms by the overall regulatory framework. Greater selectivity in industrial licensing restrained the growth of many multinationals [which] were unable to compete against well-organized domestic industrial lobbies (Athreye and Kapur 2001: 409).

Post-liberalization, this trend appears to be reversing slowly. For companies listed on the Indian stock exchange—a data series that cannot be compared directly with the source above—the share of foreign firms in manufacturing output rose gradually toward the end of the century, from

9.5 percent in 1990 to 9.3 percent in 1995 and 12.8 percent in 2000. It could be that the foreign presence has risen more sharply in other sectors, especially the newly opened service industries. The foreign presence in India's manufactured exports is, as noted, minuscule, especially compared to East Asian norms.

The foreign presence has always been modest in Korea, given its historically restrictive ownership regime. Within manufacturing, at the onset of the economic crisis, foreign firms produced about 10 percent of manufacturing output and employed 5.5 percent of the industrial workforce. Liberalization and merger and acquisition (M&A) activity had raised these shares to 13.3 percent and 8 percent respectively by 1999. Over the period 1997–99, foreign firms accounted for about 15 percent of the country's manufactured exports.

The data for Malaysia confirm the historically large foreign presence in the economy. Foreign firms owned approximately one-third of the nation's share capital in 1999, down from over one-half in 1970. Within manufacturing, foreign firms generated about 44 percent of value added and 38 percent of employment in 2000. They also accounted for 73 percent of manufactured exports and 65 percent of total exports in 1995.

Ownership statistics for Thailand are the weakest among the six countries. There are no economy-wide estimates, while even for manufacturing the first reasonably comprehensive data were prepared only in 1996. They report that firms with a foreign presence (that is, a foreign share greater than zero) produced about 50 percent of the country's industrial output and employed 41 percent of its workforce. Estimates for 1999 suggest little change in the immediate aftermath of the crisis.

Ownership structures in Viet Nam are unusual. As FDI flowed in from the late 1980s, the share of the SOE sector actually increased. The explanation is that the SOEs retained their privileged access to secure land titles and the domestic banking sector for much of the reform period, and thus foreign investors were forced into joint ventures with them. Meanwhile, the policy regime suppressed the emergence of a domestic SME sector. This trend began to reverse, but very slowly, as the monopoly privileges of SOEs were eroded. One important milestone in this respect was the granting of 100 percent foreign ownership in certain circumstances (principally for firms in export zones), and the formal recognition that foreign firms were no longer part of the 'state capitalist sector.' Another was the enactment of the Law on Enterprises in 2000, which provided a more secure environment for the domestic private sector. Over the period 1995–2001, there were no major changes in economy-wide output shares by ownership, apart from a doubling in the share of foreign firms from 6 percent to

13 percent. The state sector remained virtually constant at 39–40 percent, while there was a slight decline in the share of both collectives (from 10 percent to 8 percent) and the private/household sector (from 39 percent to 36 percent). The small mixed sector remained unchanged at 4 percent. In these respects, Viet Nam has yet to experience the far-reaching ownership changes evident in the PRC. The foreign share of Viet Nam's manufactured exports has risen sharply, from around 18 percent in 1993–95 to 57 percent in 2000. This share is likely to rise still further as the country entrenches itself as an attractive destination for labor-intensive manufactured exports.

FDI Flows and Patterns

There are at least five features of the FDI flows and patterns summarized above, and explained in more detail in the country papers, that are worthy of comment.

The first concerns *inflows to the PRC* and *comparisons between the PRC and India*. Although the PRC is now the world's largest FDI recipient, the size of the inflows is a subject of debate. The principal uncertainty relates to the extent of 'round-tripping,' that is, Chinese investments being channeled through Hong Kong, China and returning as 'foreign' investment to secure the greater privileges and security that foreign investors typically receive. As the Chinese reforms progress, however, and the gap between the commercial environment in Hong Kong, China and adjoining southern regions narrows, this round-tripping FDI appears to be a diminishing proportion of total inflows.

The magnitudes of the flows to the PRC have also triggered debate about the comparative attractiveness of the PRC and India to foreign investors. On the face of it the PRC appears to dwarf India, owing to its earlier reforms, faster economic growth, and vastly greater recorded FDI inflows—some 20 times greater than India in recent years. However, a recent literature, principally emanating from India, has argued that the reported differences are greatly exaggerated.[7] At least 20 percent of the PRC's FDI is still thought to be round-tripping, while Indian statistics have until recently significantly understated the country's FDI receipts, partly owing to the way in which outflows were measured. In addition, the PRC's economy is about double the size of India's. Making these adjustments, the reported 20:1 differential in flows becomes perhaps 3:1 in terms of FDI/GDP ratios. Since the PRC's investment rate (relative to GDP) is at least one-third higher than that of India, the FDI/GDI (investment) ratio is about 2:1. Thus, in the PRC–India comparison, and more generally, the PRC emerges as less of an outlier. The magnitudes of its inflows are extremely large as much because of its size as because of its openness to FDI.

A second feature of FDI flows is their *changing sectoral composition.* Until the 1980s, most FDI in developing countries was in extractive industries and import-substituting manufacturing. The first major compositional shift was within manufacturing, from import-substituting to export-oriented manufacturing. This transition commenced in the late 1960s but really accelerated from the 1980s. A more recent shift has been toward services. By 2000, about half the total stock of FDI in developing countries was in services, more than double the figure in 1990 (UNCTAD 2002). Three factors principally account for this trend: the rising share of services in practically all countries; the increasingly tradable nature of many service outputs; and liberalized entry into many service industries previously closed to foreign businesses. However, substantial barriers to FDI in services remain.

These global changes are evident in all six economies, and have been driven in particular by the opening up of service industries to FDI. The changes are particularly pronounced in the more recently reforming economies. In the PRC, FDI began entering the banking and foreign and domestic trade sectors in the 1990s. With the country's accession to the WTO, insurance, telecommunications, and other sectors are being progressively opened. Liberalization in India has resulted in a sharp decline in the earlier dominance of manufacturing, from 85 percent to 48 percent of the economy. Most of the increase has gone into services. There is also a more even distribution of FDI across subsectors. In Korea, most service industries were closed to MNEs until the 1990s. Here too reform has led to a major reallocation of FDI flows.

Third, there are the *changing modalities of capital flows.* For a period in the 1990s, portfolio investment flows in Southeast Asia exceeded FDI (Table 2.2). During and after the 1997–98 crisis, this trend was dramatically reversed. Moreover, the nature of FDI is also changing. The old pattern of 'greenfield' FDI and durable, long-term joint ventures is increasingly being replaced by M&As and volatile, opportunistic, and short-term relationships. The extent of M&A FDI is poorly documented, but appears to be rising in most countries. Such activity certainly increased in the late 1990s in the crisis-affected countries, as exchange rates and stock markets collapsed, inducing so-called 'fire-sale FDI,' that is, foreigners purchasing distressed and much cheapened assets. In India, too, there was a sharp rise. During the restrictive era, virtually all FDI was greenfield by government dictate; now about 40 percent is M&A. However, as will be shown below, there continues to be much official ambivalence about the domestic welfare effects of this form of MNE entry.

The modalities of foreign capital entry have varied significantly among the six economies (Table 2.2). FDI has been the major source of capital flowing into the PRC, dwarfing portfolio investment owing to the semi-closed capital account, including restrictions on foreigners trading shares on the domestic stock market. Total capital flows to India have risen significantly since the 1991 reforms, with a sharp increase from 1996. FDI still remains a relatively unimportant part of these flows, though it is rising over time as MNEs adjust to the country's more open policies. Capital flows to Korea also increased sharply in the first half of the 1990s, until the crisis precipitated major capital flight. The major declines occurred in portfolio and other capital flows; as noted earlier, FDI inflows increased strongly in 1997–99.

In contrast to the other countries, and reflecting its consistently open regime, Malaysia has traditionally received most of its capital in the form of FDI. FDI declined at the onset of the crisis, though flows were still large. In the wake of the September 1998 imposition of capital controls, portfolio flows turned negative but FDI strengthened. Thailand experienced the greatest volatility in capital flows, reflecting the large swing in its capital account balance during the crisis, equivalent to about 15 percent of GDP. Capital flows were negative in 1997–2002, but FDI remained positive, increasing strongly in the immediate aftermath of the crisis. Comprehensive data on capital flows to Viet Nam are not available. It has the least internationally integrated capital market of the six. Most of its capital inflows have taken the form of FDI. Inflows declined in the wake of the crisis but remained positive.

Fourth, *the major sources of FDI vary across countries*, although there are some common patterns. The United States, Japan, and Europe are typically the major investors. In addition, in some cases much smaller, but very open, proximate and historically connected economies are major players in much larger economies. Thus, Hong Kong, China has been the largest investor in the PRC, given its traditionally important (though declining) role in connecting that country to the global economy. The round-tripping phenomenon alluded to above is also a factor. Singapore remains a significant actor in Malaysia, reflecting their historically close commercial and political ties. A major foreign investor in India is Mauritius, where, in addition to historical connections, special taxation privileges have played a key role.

The FDI debate of the 1970s about whether particular source countries matter, and whether some are more desirable than others, no longer resonates.[8] This is so for several reasons: the evidence demonstrates that well-managed FDI contributes to growth; international competition for FDI is more intense; there is a greater diversity of sources as compared to earlier periods of American and European dominance; and even quite low-income countries are now investing abroad. Much of the literature on 'FDI differences' simply reflected the particular stages of development of the home countries. These alleged 'unique' characteristics of MNEs generally faded as the source countries were transformed.

Finally, there is the issue of FDI *behavior during crises*, including the magnitude and composition of flows. Three of the six economies in the sample (Korea, Malaysia, and Thailand) were severely affected by the 1997–98 Asian economic crisis, and in another (Viet Nam) growth slowed markedly. It is therefore useful to examine briefly the behavior of FDI, and the related policy responses, during this episode. Sudden capital flight is a central feature of modern economic crises. Crisis economies typically switch quickly from current account deficits to surpluses. On the current account, expenditure switching and absorption effects reduce imports and promote exports. In addition, slower economic growth and increased economic and political uncertainty result in the rest of the world being unwilling to finance a current account deficit.

Moreover, the behavior of different forms of capital diverges. Portfolio and other forms of highly mobile capital are more likely to exit a country. By contrast, FDI flows are typically much less volatile. In fact, post-crisis FDI may well increase, along the lines postulated in Krugman's 'fire-sale FDI' thesis (Lipsey 2001). Asset prices are now cheaper, owing to depreciated exchange rates, contractions in demand, and financial collapse. Policy regimes are typically liberalized as part of the government's recovery package. Athukorala (2003) demonstrates that this is precisely what happened in most of the five East Asian crisis-affected countries during 1997–98. In aggregate there was massive capital flight, principally of portfolio investment and short-term debt. Yet FDI actually rose modestly.[9]

FDI may also play an important role in the recovery of crisis-affected economies. The analytical connection between the two starts with the collapse in aggregate demand during a crisis: consumer confidence and therefore expenditure wanes; the capacity for governments to run fiscal deficits is often constrained; domestic investment falls owing to financial fragility, weak domestic demand, and uncertainty. Exports are therefore the critical component in the immediate recovery period. Crucial to the latter are MNEs. Given their global market networks and know-how, deeper pockets, and stronger connections to global capital markets, they have the capacity to translate large increases in potential competitiveness (arising from the depreciated currency) into export growth, which in turn facilitates economic recovery.

The 1997–98 crisis also served as a reminder that restrictions on short-term capital flows may be compatible with an open FDI regime, at least in the short to medium term. This is the major conclusion from the controversial Malaysian policy experiment introduced in September 1998.[10] Nevertheless, it is important to note Malaysia's special circumstances: its very open economy, its good quality bureaucracy, and the fact that it has never had a balance of payments crisis. Moreover, the controls were introduced in the context of a sudden and dramatic political crisis—the sacking and jailing of the deputy prime minister—indicating the government's resolve to implement the controls.

FDI Outflows

Capital outflows are central to the process of globalization. Although occasionally the subject of mercantilist objections, to the effect that national savings are being employed for the benefit of others, theory and empirical evidence point clearly in the opposite direction. Outward FDI benefits the home economy, since domestic factors of production are able to maximize their returns. It is also presumed to constitute a spur to better economic policy, to the extent that the option of 'exit' for investors exerts a policy discipline on governments. Outflows present a mixed and imperfectly recorded picture, but it is clear that patterns vary across the six economies. In all but Viet Nam, these investments abroad are sizeable. In all, there has been a general relaxation of controls on outflows, although in some cases quite onerous restrictions remain in place. However, with the occasional exception of Korea, all six are net FDI recipients.

The case of Korea—which became a large investor abroad, with outflows often exceeding inflows, at a relatively low per capita income—is very unusual. This appears to have reflected a number of factors. One was Korea's traditionally restrictive approach to inflows. The second was the country's rapid loss of comparative advantage in labor-intensive activities during the 1980s and the consequent relocation on a massive scale of much of this industry to high-growth, receptive economies nearby. A third was the aggressive internationalization of the major *chaebol* (business conglomerates) from the late 1980s, with support from the government. A considerable proportion of the FDI was high-end investment in sectors where protection in the targeted markets necessitated investment rather than export from the home base (for example, the automotive and consumer electronics industries). The 'reverse engineering' type of FDI, to obtain access to host country technology, has been a factor at times. In India, too, this motive is becoming increasingly important.

The PRC is also emerging as a major investor abroad. This may seem surprising in view of its rapid growth, with the presumption that returns on capital would be higher at home than abroad. Three factors appear to be relevant in this story (Garnaut and Song 2003). One relates to macro-economic policy. The PRC is running large current account surpluses and accumulating massive international reserves, currently estimated to exceed $350 billion. Most of these reserves are held abroad, albeit largely in the form of government securities rather than FDI. The second factor is the round-tripping phenomenon referred to above. This is not of course genuine FDI, and should be discounted from the figures for outflows. The third factor is investments abroad by state-related entities in sectors deemed to be of commercial and strategic importance, such as natural resource projects.

For some countries, it is useful to distinguish between what may be termed 'state-sponsored' and 'market-driven' investments. This is evident in Malaysia, for example. The government has sponsored several major investment projects abroad, including directly through its state-related entities. Some of these have been high-profile, quasi-political investments in the 'South,' with mixed commercial results. Alongside these have been straightforward efficiency-motivated investments, principally in neighboring countries and reflecting firms' competitive advantages.

Three additional features of these outflows are worthy of mention. First, as noted elsewhere, many of the outward investment projects draw on the countries' overseas communities, as is to be expected given that this diaspora lowers the transactions costs of going abroad. Second, in countries with complex regulatory systems, outward FDI may be a means of exploiting firm-specific advantages in a less restrictive environment. This has been hypothesized in some of the Indian literature, though presumably it is now a less important motive. Third, it appears to be the case that increasing outward FDI has contributed to the liberalization of policies on inward FDI. The argument is that investing abroad does introduce an appreciation of the case for a more predictable and open regime. This has evidently been the case in Korea, particularly in the context of its accession to the OECD.

Trade Regimes

Openness to the international economy varies significantly among the six countries. All have become more open to trade since 1990, as indicated by both trade reforms and rising trade/GDP ratios. This ratio has increased by more than 50 percent in three of the countries (PRC, India, and Thailand) and substantially in the others (Table 2.1).[11] Malaysia and Thailand were among a very small group of developing economies classified by Sachs and Warner (1995) as 'always open.' Both exhibit very high trade orientation, quite low average tariffs, modest inter-industry tariff dispersion, and limited incidence of non-tariff barriers (NTBs). Qualitative indicators support this conclusion. Korea now has fairly low average tariff rates. Notwithstanding recent reforms, the PRC, India, and Viet Nam still have quite high tariffs, and a higher incidence of NTBs. Smuggling remains rampant in the more protected economies.

Among the six, Korea's trade and investment regime has arguably been the most unusual. From the early 1960s, it achieved very rapid export-led growth, but in the context of (until recently) very restrictive policies on imports (except those required by export-oriented firms) and FDI. Its adventurous industrial policy resulted in tremendous achievements, but also had high costs.[12] In addition to tariff reform and a reduction in NTBs, Korea's 1990s reforms included a reduction in the number of subsidy programs and a simplification of customs procedures. As with its FDI regime, a desire to join both the GATT/WTO and the OECD, and the imperative to reform in the wake of the 1997–98 crisis, drove much of the liberalization.

Viet Nam's re-engagement with the international economy is of very recent origin. For much of the period following the commencement of its 1986 *doi moi* reforms, it was effectively shut out of the world's largest market, the United States. The US embargo was lifted in 1993, while the two countries signed a bilateral trade agreement only in 2001. As is the case with late reformers, Viet Nam's official trade regime remains opaque and poorly documented. It is only quite recently that a formal tariff schedule was released. It still retains very high levels of protection—of several hundred percent—for its automotive, sugar, and garments industries. Much protection is firm-specific in nature, tailored to the needs of the country's inefficient SOE sector. Viet Nam aspires to WTO membership by 2005, which constitutes a powerful incentive for it to continue to broaden the reform process. ASEAN membership and the gradual introduction of ASEAN Free Trade Area commitments have constituted a useful 'training exercise' for the country's WTO application.

A central feature of trade reform in all six economies is that it was unilateral in nature. While four of the countries are members of preferential trading arrangements—ASEAN in the case of the three Southeast Asian economies and the South Asian Association for Regional Cooperation (SAARC) in the case of India—in practice these arrangements have meant practically no deviation from non-discriminatory reform.[13] Unfortunately, this may be changing. With the current US-led penchant for free trade areas (FTAs), all six have been forced to follow suit and explore FTA options. Korea and Thailand in particular have been active in this respect. If these FTAs ever become significant, MNEs will certainly respond by including preferential access to selected export markets as a factor in their decision-making processes.

The Commercial Environment

The large variations in the foreign presence among the six economies are explained fundamentally by the attractiveness of the host economies to FDI. This in turn reflects the rate of economic growth in each and the ease of entry for foreign investors. In addition to macroeconomic management and openness, a number of factors co-determine both economic growth and FDI attractiveness. Several proxies for these factors are presented in Table 2.1. Informed analytically by the 'three I's' referred to above, these variables include proxies for human capital, the quality of physical infrastructure, institutional quality and country risk, and financial conditions. The argument here is that, as economies open up, governments have to make the transition from protectionist/regulatory regimes to a new emphasis on promotion and efficiency. Thus, there needs to be more effective industrial extension, R&D, and other support schemes; better physical infrastructure; legal reform; improved education; and administrative reform and simplification. Broader still are issues of country risk and policy predictability. Hence, countries' performance according to the range of 'competitiveness' variables listed in Table 2.1 is central to economic progress.

It also needs to be emphasized that domestic investors are invariably the key players in any economy and that domestic investor sentiment weighs heavily in MNEs' international location decisions. Therefore what matters is the host economy's commercial environment in general, and not especially as it relates to foreign investment. Indeed, FDI regimes that are significantly 'pro-foreign' in their incentives or other provisions are unlikely to be fiscally or politically durable, and are therefore heavily discounted by MNEs. It is important that any study of competitiveness and the business environment recognizes this fact.[14]

The proxies and data in Table 2.1 are of course highly selective, and subject to numerous qualifications.[15] But they are illustrative, and generally accord with *a priori* notions. Moreover, they effectively draw attention to the diversity of the six countries.

The PRC's human capital base is comparatively strong, with near-universal literacy and segments of technical excellence. The PRC is also increasingly able to tap into a very large international diaspora. It has R&D strengths, some military-related, or owing to the past emphasis on heavy industry. It is rapidly opening up to foreign trade and investment, at a faster pace than either India or Russia. Its commercial institutions have historically been weak, and the country continues to score poorly in international comparisons of corruption and protection of property rights. But institutional quality is improving quickly, especially in regions most connected to the international economy. Physical infrastructure is being upgraded rapidly, although its quality is spatially very uneven.

India's human capital and R&D base has pockets of international excellence, most notably in information technology (IT) and some defense-related heavy industries. Until recently, and in contrast to much of East Asia, its educational priorities resulted in centers of international quality alongside quite high levels of illiteracy. It also differed from East Asia until recently in that its inward-looking strategy meant that it was unable to exploit its strength in human capital in the global economy. Thus, in contrast to the PRC, India's major intrusion into the international IT industry has been through services rather than manufacturing. Its commercial environment is broadly predictable, and the legal system cumbersome but independent. Economic policy-making is the most dispersed among the six countries. A large diaspora facilitates its connections to the international economy. The 1991 reforms and their aftermath have begun to transform the commercial environment, but the unfinished agenda is large and complex, and the forward momentum appears to have slowed significantly in recent years.[16]

Korea's development strategy has been underpinned by exceptional strength in some areas. It reached OECD levels of educational achievement and R&D expenditure at comparatively low levels of per capita income.[17] Its internet access and usage is one of the highest in the world. Its infrastructure and institutional quality are good though not outstanding. External factors—aspiration to membership of international organizations and the recent economic crisis—have been important in Korea's policy reforms. As with its trade and FDI regimes, the internationalization of its human capital strengths has proceeded more slowly (Dahlman and Andersson 2000; L. Kim 1997, 2000). For example, its universities remain relatively unconnected to the international mainstream.

Malaysia emerges as a country with comparatively high institutional quality, excellent physical infrastructure, and large public investment in education, much of it designed to redress past ethnic imbalances. It has had the most consistent commercial policy environment of the six. Nevertheless, there are concerns that the independence of its legal system may have been weakened over the past two decades, and there has been a persistent loss of high-level non-*bumiputera* human capital. Malaysia's very open international labor market has delayed the process of upgrading its technological capabilities. It faces particular challenges to its competitiveness from below (especially the PRC) and from above (the Asian newly industrializing economies, or NIEs).

Thailand scores well on most indicators, the principal exception being human capital. Until recently, while achieving almost universal primary enrolment, its education retention ratios were very low. In consequence, during the 1990s, as real wages began to rise quickly in the wake of rapid economic growth, it experienced difficulty managing the transition out of labor-intensive activities. It has become progressively more open in its trade and FDI policies, although nationalist sentiment became more pronounced in the wake of the 1997–98 crisis. Historically, its legal and commercial institutions have not been strong, though informal commercial rules of the game were widely understood and observed. Physical infrastructure is generally good, apart from congestion in and around Bangkok.

Having successfully completed the first round of macroeconomic and commercial policy reform, the principal challenges in Viet Nam relate to establishing the infrastructure that underpins a market-based economy; property rights, the legal system, financial intermediation, and physical infrastructure all remain poorly developed. Illiteracy levels are low, but the stock of internationally experienced entrepreneurs is also small. Many small and household enterprises operate in an insecure commercial environment. SOE reform lags. There are pronounced regional differences (especially, still, between the north and the south) in the quality of the physical and commercial infrastructure.

3   IMPACT OF FDI

An Overview

Foreign investors introduce a package of highly productive resources into the host economy, including production and process technology, managerial expertise, accounting and auditing standards, and knowledge of international markets. The challenge for the host economy is to benefit from the MNE presence, and to appropriate some of the increased income accruing from the resultant productivity growth. The large literature on the effects of FDI concludes that the benefits to host economies are uneven, both across and within countries.[18] This suggests that host country policies are an important factor in the distribution of these benefits. Of relevance here, as argued above, are the commercial environment, institutional quality, and supply-side capacities.

It should be emphasized that many of the effects of FDI are inherently difficult to measure. The academic literature typically approaches the issue in one of three ways. The first is in the context of cross-country determinants of growth. In international comparisons of economic growth, FDI, or some other measure of the foreign presence, is introduced as an explanatory variable, together with a range of interactive or 'conditional' variables (for example, trade orientation, human capital, institutional quality, or legal protection). The hypothesis is that, subject to the usual caveats, a larger foreign presence is associated with faster economic growth. The other methodologies focus on technology spillovers within countries from foreign to domestic firms, as measured either through firm-level case studies or an analysis of cross-section industry data. Both provide only a proximate and partial picture: the former is limited by the sample size and the flows are generally not quantified; the latter is presumptive and inferential rather than demonstrated. The relative importance of the various channels through which the spillovers occur—emulation, inter-firm worker mobility, subcontracting networks—is generally not conclusively demonstrated. A range of non-equity channels (international labor migration, international buying groups, licensing arrangements) could be just as important as FDI in some circumstances.

A related literature attempts to draw a distinction between the positive, 'crowding in' effects of FDI, and the negative, 'crowding out' effects. Among the former are the positive technology and trade effects alluded to above, together with various dynamic externalities such as clustering and country reputation. Among the latter are anti-competitive effects (such as the displacement of domestic firms), the luring of scarce resources (such as skilled labor and credit) away from domestic firms, and the squeezing out of domestic supply networks as new foreign entrants bring with them integrated upstream and downstream supply chains.

Against this backdrop, this section highlights the evidence presented in the six country papers. The usual indicators include international trade, employment, income distribution and poverty alleviation, technology and human capital development, and competition, concentration, and profitability. Particular attention is accorded to the trade and technology effects of FDI, given the attention they receive in the literature and from policymakers.

FDI and Trade

MNEs are playing an ever more prominent role in the global economy, with crucial implications for countries pursuing an export-oriented development strategy. Compared to a decade or more ago, FDI is now typically more export-oriented; less likely to be attracted by the old 'tariff factory' model of production for a protected domestic market; and more likely to account for an increasing share of host economy exports.[19]

Two factors have been driving these trends. The first, as noted, is the more or less simultaneous liberalization of trade and FDI regimes. The second has been technological advances in transport costs and production technologies. The rise of the 'global factory' has been made possible by much reduced international transport costs and by disaggregated, trans-border production processes, particularly in MNE-intensive industries such as electronics and automobiles. In the most successful East Asian cases of these industrial clusters, notably southern coastal PRC and to a lesser extent the Singapore-centered Singapore–Johor–Riau (SIJORI) growth triangle, production operations constitute a seamless web in which national boundaries virtually disappear.

It is now much more difficult for latecomer industrializers to achieve high rates of export growth without MNE participation (Urata 2001), the more so for transitional economies with a history of international commercial isolation. The earlier literature on this subject, in which Nayyar (1978) was the major study, argued that MNE involvement in export expansion from the NIEs was mostly low by international standards. (As a corollary, therefore, developing countries could achieve rapid economic development while maintaining relatively restrictive FDI policies.) While this generally remains the case for Korea and Taipei,China, it is important to note that in both economies the MNE share in exports did increase significantly from about the mid-1970s to the mid-1980s, as compared to the figures reported by Nayyar for the late 1960s.

In any case, however, and contrary to Nayyar's arguments, there is clear evidence that the strong export performance of developing countries since the 1970s has been closely associated with MNE involvement. Nayyar estimated the share of MNEs in total manufactured exports from developing countries to be not more than 15 percent *circa* 1974. Moreover, he found that the share had not registered any significant increase since 1966. By contrast, a similar calculation, based on unpublished estimates prepared by Prema-Chandra Athukorala of the Australian National University, suggests that MNEs accounted for 24 percent of total manufactured exports from developing countries *circa* 1980, increasing to 36 percent in 1990. When the three Asian NIEs—Korea; Taipei,China; and Hong Kong, China—are excluded, the latter estimate increases to 45 percent. Given the massive increase in manufactured exports from the PRC, and the increased share of MNEs in this export expansion (from 17 percent to 48 percent between these two years), this figure would have surpassed 50 percent by the turn of the century.

Two additional observations about the effects of MNEs on trade are relevant. One is that earlier concerns about 'immiserizing growth' are less relevant. This analytical paradigm, motivated by the experience of India and other highly distorted economies, postulated that FDI that entered highly protected industries could generate negative value added at international prices, in addition to the costs of any fiscal incentives offered to attract MNEs (Brecher and Diaz-Alejandro 1977). More open trade regimes alleviate these concerns.

Second, in any case, what matters is the efficiency of MNE investments rather than their trade orientation. As exemplified in the PRC chapter, some government officials still worry about whether MNEs generate a trade surplus or deficit. However, 'deficits' and 'surpluses' carry no normative implications; they can be either 'good' or 'bad' depending on the efficiency of firms' operations. As it happens, the trade of MNEs in the PRC is shifting from deficits to surpluses as reform progresses and the dual policy regime becomes less important. That is, the initial concentration of MNEs in joint ventures with uneconomic SOEs was a major explanation for the observed 'deficits.' The trade orientation of MNEs has changed rapidly as liberalization has proceeded.

Thus, the trade orientation of MNEs is largely shaped by the domestic policy environment. Here the differences between East and South Asia are striking. As noted, MNEs account for a trivial share (about 3 percent) of Indian exports, as compared to the 50 percent or more found in many East Asian economies. Skeptics might argue that the East Asian figures are overwhelmed by thin domestic value added in intensively traded goods such as electronics, or that East Asian governments have been more successful in imposing export performance requirements as a condition of entry. While the former does inflate both export/GDP ratios and MNE export shares, the differences fundamentally reflect the fact that the East Asian economies offer more congenial commercial environments: entry is simpler and less restrictive, and import/export procedures are less complex.

In countries where MNEs dominate host country exports, there is some concern about the potential loss of economic policy sovereignty. Malaysia, where MNEs account for about 75 percent of exports, exemplifies this issue. Decisions made in distant corporate headquarters, it is alleged, might not reflect host economy interests and priorities. By threatening large-scale exit, highly mobile MNEs might be able to extract very generous tax concessions. Intra-MNE export restrictions and franchises could inhibit export growth. The international evidence supporting these allegations is not persuasive, however. MNEs tend to put down roots in congenial environments, and FDI is not as mobile as other forms of foreign capital. MNE inter-affiliate export decisions are fundamentally driven by the same considerations as arm's-length market-based ones. Of course, regime instability and xenophobia will discourage FDI—as they do for domestic investors as well. As a country loses comparative advantage in labor-intensive activities, MNEs will shift their low-end activities to other locations. But domestic firms will do the same, and the challenge for policy-makers is to play a creative role in managing the upgrading process.

Employment and Distribution

The social and distributional effects of FDI depend principally on host country policies and institutions. For example, employment outcomes depend on the flexibility of the labor market. The growth–poverty relationship depends on the extent to which governments have pursued pro-poor policies that enable low-income groups to avail themselves of growth opportunities. Similarly, regional (subnational) impacts will be shaped by the spatial distribution of complementary production inputs such as physical and social infrastructure.

The effects on employment of FDI illustrate this proposition. The more open and less distorted Malaysian and Thai economies have experienced chronic labor shortages since the late 1980s, necessitating very large imports of mainly unskilled labor.[20] This phenomenon was interrupted only briefly by the 1997–98 economic crisis. The predominant location of MNEs in labor-intensive, export-oriented industries, combined with rapid economic growth in general, hastened the emergence of labor scarcity and, consequently, rising real wages.

By contrast, in less open and transitional economies, labor market outcomes, complicated by history and institutions, have been less satisfactory. In the PRC, there is some evidence to suggest that the effects of FDI on employment have been negative. The problems appear to be concentrated in MNE joint ventures with SOEs. The root cause lies in the hugely overstaffed SOEs; the solution is to reform this sector rather than to restrict FDI. Indeed, the entry of export-oriented, labor-intensive FDI is facilitating the process of structural adjustment. Moreover, there is the freeing up of the domestic labor market, enabling workers from poor regions in the hinterland to seek employment in the booming, FDI-connected coastal regions. While this migration has massive and sometimes disruptive social implications, and may create unemployment of the Harris–Todaro variety, it is also an important mechanism for equalizing the benefits of spatially uneven growth.

Similarly, the effects of FDI on employment in India have been mixed. With its earlier emphasis on heavy industry and the modest export performance of its labor-intensive industries, until recently India largely missed out on East Asian-style export-oriented industrialization. This was the central conclusion of the one major (albeit dated) comparative study of this issue (Little, Mazumdar, and Page 1987). Moreover, as a corollary,

India has not enjoyed the equity dividend that flows from a broader-based participation in the industrial workforce. Foreign investors are attracted to regions with good social and physical infrastructure and a business-friendly environment. In this respect they behave no differently from domestic firms. However, MNEs are likely to exhibit greater spatial concentration than their domestic counterparts, for at least three reasons. First, MNEs are generally more trade-intensive, and therefore more likely to locate in regions that are better connected to the global economy. Second, to the extent that MNEs operate in more skill- and capital-intensive activities, they are more likely to locate in regions with stronger endowments of these attributes. Third, MNEs will generally not have the operating history of local firms in the host economy, and therefore will be less 'historically attached' to a particular region.

The evidence from the six countries supports these propositions. In the case of the PRC, as power devolves rapidly from the center, the subnational effects are predictably uneven. Regional inequality in the PRC is increasing rapidly.[21] This arises primarily from the 'retreat from equality' at the center, but also from the differential effects of integration with the global economy. FDI is certainly part of this process of rising spatial inequality: 92 percent of FDI was located in the eastern/coastal regions through to 1985, declining only slightly to 87 percent by 2001. In addition, some regions, notably the southern coastal areas, are more adept than others at managing the foreign presence, that is, in attracting FDI and in maximizing the local benefits from it.[22] However, it is locational advantages and an array of policy and institutional factors (early fiscal incentives for the coastal zones, and local government capabilities), not FDI *per se*, that are the fundamental determinants of this trend. Moreover, as long as there remain powerful impediments to domestic economic integration, particularly owing to physical infrastructure constraints, regionally based fiscal incentives alone will have a limited impact on firms' locational decisions.[23]

Although its circumstances are very different, Thailand's experience again illustrates the nexus between rapid globalization and increased regional inequality. Although all regions prospered, Bangkok, one of the world's major primate cities, was at the center of the country's extremely rapid economic growth from the mid-1980s, and remains its principal gateway to the global economy. In the presence of such a powerful locational advantage, fiscal incentives alone will not persuade firms to move to the regions. The more generous incentives for remote (so-called zone 3) regions have had limited impact. At the margin, foreign (and domestic) investors have located on the boundary of the intermediate zone 2, in proximity to the better infrastructure, larger markets, and international access offered by Bangkok in zone 1.

Spatial inequalities in India have been rising, although not as quickly as in the PRC or Thailand. It is alleged that foreign firms locating mainly in richer regions with better infrastructure, better human capital, and better connections to the global economy exacerbate this trend. Yet comparable Indian firms appear to behave in a similar fashion. Moreover, FDI is presumably a minor factor in this process since it has been so small. In any case, the trend of rising regional inequality pre-dates the process of opening up.

Viet Nam illustrates the proposition that, in transitional economies, the speed of local-level reform can be a key factor in FDI location in addition to locational advantages. This is especially so because the FDI approval process commences at the local level and is completed in Hanoi. Some regions have sought aggressively to attract FDI, by simplifying regulatory procedures, developing complementary infrastructure, and facilitating land access.[24] As in the PRC, the presence of export zones has been a major factor in locational decisions: over half of FDI has located in these zones, mostly in the south. Ho Chi Minh City and the surrounding regions have a significantly more business-friendly environment, and a larger stock of entrepreneurs. Not surprisingly, they have attracted much more FDI than the SOE-dominated northern economy.

The importance of regional industrial history and entrepreneurial capacity as factors influencing MNEs' locational decisions (and the extent to which these multinationals develop local linkages) is of course not confined to transitional economies. Although central governments may have contrary spatial priorities, MNEs everywhere thrive where local governments are welcoming and industrial/commercial capabilities are better established. The experience of Penang in Malaysia, referred to below, illustrates this proposition.

Technology and Human Capital Development

Technology and productivity spillovers are central to the study of FDI impacts. They constitute the core of MNEs' competitive advantages, and they feature prominently in host governments' expectations of FDI. The major general conclusion from the country studies is that these spillovers are positive, both for the economy as a whole and for specific industries. However, there are concerns about the magnitude of the spillovers, the speed of technology transfer, and the capacity of governments to develop an enabling policy framework. We consider each of these in turn.

With regard to the magnitude of spillovers, both the aggregate and case study approaches usually, though not always, point in the same direction. In the case of Thailand, Archanun (2003a) found spillovers from foreign to domestically owned firms in the manufacturing industry to be significant. He concluded that they were more likely to occur in less protected sectors, both because these sectors were more attractive to MNEs and because of the presumed competitive impetus of lower protection.

As in most countries, MNEs have played a key role in the Thai automotive industry. The country is now the Southeast Asian leader in the industry, with major clustering effects evident among both assemblers and suppliers. Two factors appear to explain this success. Thailand possesses the largest domestic market in the region. This initially attracted MNEs during the earlier import substitution phase (which in the Thai case was relatively mild). In addition, it reaped an 'early mover advantage' in being the first country in the region to enact major trade reform in the auto industry, thus quickly building up a strong export-oriented supplier base. By contrast, although Thailand has attracted much export-oriented FDI in electronics, it has not emerged as a major player in this industry. This was because it was slower to provide the major prerequisites required in this MNE-dominated, internationally integrated industry: export zones with high-quality infrastructure, linked in a seamless manner to international markets, and allowing 100 percent foreign ownership. It is important to note also that MNEs have not been central to all of Thailand's export successes. The country's agro-based exports, including seafood, have performed very well. Several large domestic firms, most notably the CP group, have been the major players in this industry. This illustrates a more general proposition, that MNEs are particularly important in industries that are characterized by high levels of cross-border vertical integration, and where knowledge of international market chains may be firm-specific.

The literature on FDI in the PRC generally concludes that it has been beneficial for growth.[25] This has occurred through the usual channels: by augmenting investment, by connecting firms in the PRC to global markets (very important for a country that had experienced several decades of international commercial isolation), and by facilitating a rapid transition from uneconomic investments in SOE-dominated heavy industries. While its reforms are much more recent, Viet Nam's experience with FDI appears to be broadly similar. Much of the early FDI went into uneconomic joint ventures with SOEs and non-tradable sectors such as hotels and construction.[26] More recently, following policy reform and disappointment with some of the early investments, MNEs have shifted to labor-intensive, export-oriented investments. In both countries, FDI impacts are limited by institutional weaknesses and constraints on the growth of domestic SMEs, the latter because of the preferential treatment accorded SOEs and foreign firms.

A puzzling feature of the literature on FDI in Korea is that the econometric analysis suggests that spillovers have been minimal, and possibly even negative, while case studies of the electronics, retail trade, and banking sectors point to largely positive outcomes. How can these results be reconciled? Part of the explanation may be to do with timing. The econometric analysis was conducted for earlier periods when the FDI regime was significantly more restrictive, and hence the benefits presumably smaller, whereas the case studies focus on the liberalizations of the late 1990s. The case studies deal with just three industries, and therefore provide a less complete picture than the broader manufacturing analyses. On balance, however, their conclusions have greater intuitive appeal, since they illuminate the channels through which the spillovers occur. By contrast, studies of spillovers in distorted and restrictive environments leave much that is unexplained. For similar reasons, the literature on the pre-reform effects of FDI in India have to be interpreted with great caution.

A common feature of the six countries' FDI experiences is impatience with the alleged slow pace of local linkage formation. Among the six, Malaysia was the first to attract the MNE-dominated, export-oriented electronics industry. The literature on FDI in that country generally concludes that the effects have been positive. However, it is alleged that MNEs have been slow to develop a local supplier base, have undertaken little R&D, and have remained largely confined to the export zone enclaves. It is also argued that much of the local content of MNEs is in reality intra-MNE.[27]

The Malaysian experience nicely illustrates the challenges associated with maximizing technology transfers in the context of an MNE and export-led development strategy that is initially based on export zone enclaves. Linkage development and spillovers proceeded slowly, as one would expect. Malaysia's industrial history was very recent; its human capital base was quite limited, especially so for technical skills; firms had great difficulty in complying with government requirements to hire *bumiputera* employees, or source from *bumiputera* companies; and in any case the incentive regime discouraged firms in the zones from sourcing outside the enclave. But the evidence suggests that, over time, MNEs began to put down local roots, particularly as supply-side capacities improved. By the 1990s the country was quickly losing its comparative advantage in labor-intensive activities, although the government sought to prolong this advantage by opening up the labor market. From a low base, expenditure on R&D has begun to increase rapidly, and is now approximately 0.5 percent of GDP. MNEs are shedding low-skill activities and shifting to higher-value segments. Although the government will arguably have to be more activist in developing supply-side capacities,[28] Malaysia's experience with FDI and electronics has clearly been more successful than its experience with the auto industry, where a highly protected and politicized quasi-monopoly has achieved few of the original technology and export objectives set for it.

Enclave-based FDI will inevitably remain important as long as the dual policy regimes referred to above persist. For example, the Viet Nam government may lament the absence of strong linkages extending beyond the export zones, but there are in fact powerful incentives for firms within the zones *not* to cultivate commercial linkages beyond them. Customs and other administrative procedures are complex and corrupt. Infrastructure is poor. The choice of local partner may simply be either a bureaucratic and inefficient SOE or a legally insecure and occasionally harassed private firm.

As would be expected, MNEs' local linkages are quite selective, and are much more developed in conducive environments. In the PRC, for example, the spillovers have been more pronounced in the non-SOE sector. Typically, there is considerable regional diversity in these linkages. In Malaysia, the state of Penang has been the stand-out performer. It was the home of the earliest export-oriented investments, and is where the strongest SME subcontracting base has developed. Its commercial and business history, together with its effective political leadership and public institutions, is generally regarded as the key to its success.[29]

There is in fact nothing inherently desirable about local linkages. For example, there is concern in India about the apparently limited linkages between MNEs and local firms, and the fact that these may even be declining in a statistical sense. Such a trend could, rather, be interpreted positively, as indicative of Indian firms connecting to the global economy as the economy opens up. Indeed, it would be surprising if this did not occur as liberalization progressed. In other words, the interpretation of linkages is no simple matter. The former USSR had perhaps the most 'developed' domestic linkages in the world whereas Singapore has the least. But Singapore has the most important linkage—international trade—and, in consequence, international standards of efficiency.

There is also a debate about the most effective policy options to promote efficient linkages. The case studies reported in the Indian paper generally endorse past interventionist strategies, including restrictive MNE entry, conditionality, and export obligations. There can be no doubt that some technological advances have resulted from these policies. But they have come at a cost, for example, a technologically sluggish auto industry and the deterrence of potential MNE entrants. The most striking Indian success has been in IT software rather than manufacturing. Here it appears that the keys to success have been a base of domestic competence and strong human capital connections to international centers of excellence, but limited FDI. A major puzzle in the Indian story is why this success has not translated into a broad-based manufacturing industry as well. Presumably the explanation is that the East Asian exporters enjoy the agglomeration and international reputation benefits of reforming earlier, and still offer more conducive environments for export-oriented manufacturing.

It is clear that, in assessing FDI impacts, countries' stages of development and commercial histories do matter. For countries with prolonged commercial isolation, attracting MNEs is an indication that they are being recognized in the global economy. This especially applies to one-time communist states such as the PRC and Viet Nam, but it is a broader phenomenon.[30] It also explains why these late reformers frequently 'overdo' their FDI liberalizations and offer excessively generous fiscal incentives, at the expense of domestic private firms.

Moreover, the expectations of host countries toward FDI differ over the course of economic development. For low-income countries, the principal attraction is employment generation. As noted, when governments adopt export-oriented strategies, MNEs may play a very important role in exploiting a country's (hitherto latent) comparative advantage in labor-intensive activities. For countries shifting out of this phase of development, or with a stronger domestic R&D base, interest focuses on the potential contribution of FDI to enhancing the process of structural adjustment toward higher value-added activities. These shifts are amply illustrated among our sample of countries. In Malaysia, for example, the focus on MNE impacts principally concerns issues of technological upgrading. For Viet Nam it is employment and exports, together with managing the foreign presence in the context of limited bureaucratic expertise. India seeks to build on, and modernize, its domestic R&D strengths.

There have been allegations that MNEs are reluctant to undertake local R&D. In Thailand, for example, foreign firms appear to undertake less R&D than local firms.[31] Similar concerns are voiced in India. The explanation presumably is that much of MNEs' R&D is embodied in their investments and staffing, and thus is not formally recorded in local (host country) R&D statistics. The general evidence is that the R&D activities of MNEs are being internationalized, but quite slowly; typically, most is still carried out at company headquarters (Dunning 1998). Where R&D does go abroad, it is likely to be to countries whose R&D human capital is internationally cost-competitive (for example, Russia or India), or whose governments offer generous fiscal incentives for such activities (for example, Singapore).

An additional concern in India is whether MNE entrants may be motivated by a desire to appropriate domestic R&D strengths. India's research base, like the PRC's, is unusually strong for a low-income economy, owing to scale and concerted (if at times misguided) public policy interventions. Yet, the international experience suggests that interactions between domestic and foreign R&D can be mutually beneficial, as the Singaporean experience demonstrates (see below). Much depends on how it is managed.

It also needs to be noted that spillovers are not just about production technology or commercial expertise. There may also be broader implications for institutional development and the quality of corporate governance. MNEs are presumed to employ higher standards of accounting, auditing, and reporting. In a liberalized FDI regime, international providers of these business services may also establish local operations. The entry of foreign banks in several of the six economies, for example, appears to have raised standards in the industry, in addition to increasing competitive pressures and providing access to a broader range of risk-sharing portfolio instruments. There are, of course, caveats that need to be attached to this argument. The causality between MNE entry and institutional quality is arguably bi-directional, that is, better quality institutions are both a cause and a consequence of an increased MNE presence. Moreover, there is considerable evidence to suggest that MNEs adapt, often quite quickly, to local corporate cultures: if the prevailing rules of the game are characterized by extensive corruption and poor corporate transparency, MNEs do tend to adjust their behavior accordingly.

There is, finally, the question of the extent to which host economies may 'leverage' the MNE presence. In an open economy context, two main factors appear to be significant here. One is the propensity of MNEs to establish deep local roots, which in turn will be determined by the nature of the host economy's commercial and policy environment.[32] The second is whether, and how, an activist approach to tapping the MNE presence— through emulation, local R&D programs, and advanced training facilities—would work.

Although not included in this study, Singapore is a leader in the Asia-Pacific region in both these respects, and its strategy is therefore worthy of brief mention.[33] The government has displayed an ability to adjust the policy settings as the economy has shifted quickly from its labor-intensive industrialization phase to one that is increasingly technology-intensive. In addition to its excellent infrastructure, critical for highly traded industries, the government introduced a local industry upgrading program as a means of tapping into MNEs' expertise. Technical skills were upgraded continually through good-quality technical, vocational, and tertiary education. As the country began to lose comparative advantage in labor-intensive sectors, the government worked with MNEs to induce them to stay and upgrade, while shedding uncompetitive segments. On-the-job training was facilitated by the Skills Development Fund, funded in part by a levy on foreign workers. The Economic Development Board introduced schemes to fund MNEs' local R&D activities. The board was highly attentive to these firms' requirements, and was also willing to target specific MNEs considered useful for future industrial growth.

There is a view that, as a tiny, heavily managed city state, Singapore's experience is not internationally replicable. However, while Singapore's geography, history, and political economy are unique, there is no reason why other countries cannot learn from its success. To do so, at least five features would appear to deserve emphasis.

First, Singapore's economy is completely open, and so firms are immediately subjected to some sort of market discipline and test. Second, as part of the package to attract MNEs, Singapore offers the world's best physical infrastructure and an entirely predictable and business-friendly investment climate. Third, the government has demonstrated an unrivalled capacity to walk away from mistakes. A highly open economy reveals these mistakes quickly, and Singapore's meritocratic government is not hostage to the usual set of vested interests that constrain governments from adopting first-best solutions. Fourth, the government has revealed a willingness to open its labor market to an extent practically unparalleled among modern nation states. At least 25 percent of Singapore's workforce is foreign, and a much higher percentage is born overseas. With its high salary structure, it is able to recruit in the most cost-efficient labor markets, regionally and internationally. Finally, Singapore has a seemingly completely incorruptible civil service. Its public sector remuneration is one of the highest in the world, and it is insulated from political pressures. Thus, a selective industrial policy is more likely to be successful there than in practically any other country in the world.

The more follower countries depart from these features, of course, the less likely this model is likely to be replicable.

Competition and Concentration

The evidence on the effects of FDI on competition, concentration, and profitability in the six economies is mixed, as it is in the general literature. *A priori*, FDI entry might be expected to lessen concentration simply because a new entrant means more producers. Of course, in the longer term concentration could rise if the foreign firms were able to drive out local competitors, or if they entered oligopolistic industries (as they often do, to exploit firm-specific advantages). In addition, here too the host country's trade policy matters: in outward-oriented regimes, MNEs are more likely to be attracted to the country as part of their vertically integrated international production activities. Thus, if their primary motivation is export orientation, as it invariably is, competition issues are largely irrelevant.

Moreover, in open economies, high concentration levels *per se* are not necessarily a problem, certainly for tradable activities, as the industry is exposed to foreign competition. Of course, even in the most open of economies, there are public policy concerns in activities that may be characterized as natural monopolies, or that are essentially non-traded. However, it remains the case that there is much less discussion or concern about monopolies in, for example, the open Malaysian economy, as compared to countries with more interventionist regimes.

In reality, much of the analysis of concentration, including FDI impacts, focuses on a commercial environment featuring state-sanctioned monopolies combined with restrictive trade barriers. In other words, the 'competition problem' has at least as much to do with 'government failure' as with 'market failure.' In the PRC and Viet Nam, SOEs continue to receive much special assistance, some of it in the form of restrictions on competition. Where these SOEs form joint ventures with foreign firms, MNE entry may thus appear to cause increased concentration, whereas in fact the fundamental problem lies with the regulatory regime.

Although their SOE sectors have been historically smaller, similar general comments apply to Korea and India. The promotion of *chaebol* in Korea resulted in high levels of concentration and an underdeveloped SME sector. India's highly interventionist industrial planning regime stifled competition. For this reason also, studies of the effects of FDI in the pre-reform period provide little indication of likely contemporary effects.

It also needs to be emphasized that the extent of competition is best measured by some notion of 'contestability' rather than the standard indicators of concentration (such as four-firm ratios or the Herfindahl index). This proposition is illustrated by the case of Thailand. Following its recent FDI liberalization, concentration fell significantly in the banking industry, but may have risen in the retail sector as large international companies pushed out local petty traders. In the latter case, although there may have been some adverse social consequences, competitive pressure through the possibility of further new entrants appears to have lowered retail margins.

4 CONCLUSIONS AND POLICY IMPLICATIONS

Conclusions

Several key points emerge from this survey of six countries' approaches to and experiences with FDI. Notwithstanding their diversity, all six have adopted progressively more open policies toward FDI during the past decade, and this trend appears likely to continue. This more open posture has been accompanied by the adoption of more liberal trade regimes, a process that has had profound implications for the motives for, and impact of, foreign investment. These changes have been so rapid in some cases that the policy framework has not been able to keep pace.

Apart from this major generalization, it is increasingly difficult to characterize and typify foreign investment. In most economies, it enters practically all sectors. It originates from developed and developing economies. It may take the form of long-term greenfield investment or short-term, opportunistic M&As. The investors range from the world's largest MNEs to small, family-connected cross-border investments. The distinction between foreign and domestic investment is also increasingly blurred, especially when a country's diaspora is actively involved. A world of increasingly seamless national boundaries also connotes highly fluid capital whose national characteristics are often difficult to discern.

The general conclusion in the empirical literature is that FDI confers net benefits on the host economy. The capital stock is augmented, productivity rises, and at least some of the increase is appropriated by domestic factors of production. These benefits appear to be especially important in connecting to the global economy, and in the area of technology transfer. Nevertheless, there is much debate about the magnitudes, channels, and lags associated with these transfers. As noted, different methodologies may generate different results.

In assessing the impact of FDI, a key issue is one of 'attribution,' in the sense of discerning causality. That is, the entry of FDI may be associated with rising inter-personal or inter-regional inequality, the demise of petty traders, increased concentration of ownership, higher levels of pollution, and more corruption. The challenge in each case is to determine whether there is any causality in the alleged relationship. In most cases, the causality is either weak or nonexistent. For example, pollution invariably rises as countries pass through a transitional phase of industrialization characterized by greater pollution intensity. Petty traders and cottage industries experience difficulty competing with large retail outlets and factory-scale production regardless of who owns the latter. Regional inequality often rises during the process of globalization, as those regions in the domestic economy that are better connected to the global economy have the capacity to grow faster. One cannot help but note in passing that some of the strongest criticisms of MNEs emanate from countries with the smallest FDI presence.

It is also important to emphasize that MNEs generally adapt to the local commercial environment. Any assessment of their impact needs to make due allowance for this. For example, if corruption is deeply embedded in the host country environment, MNEs are presumably likely to adjust to this requirement (subject of course to home country restrictions). If tax evasion via transfer pricing occurs, it could be because tax rates are significantly above comparable benchmarks and such evasion is a general feature of local corporate behavior. If the incentive regime is strongly biased against exports, employment, or balanced regional development, MNEs cannot reasonably be expected to behave any differently from local firms in these respects. Limited technology spillovers are likely to be present when the domestic human capital base is weak. It is unlikely that MNEs will maintain high environmental standards if enforcement is lax. In other words, it is important to diagnose the root cause of a particular problem rather than engage in an exercise of guilt by association.

Policy Implications

The international benefits of FDI appear to be highly uneven. Some countries clearly benefit from the MNE presence, while for others the impacts are ambiguous or possibly negative. Since all countries face the same international commercial environment, the presumption is that host country policy regimes and institutional capacities are the key arbiter of these differences. We therefore conclude this chapter with a discussion of some salient policy issues. At least seven are worthy of mention.

A flexible and adaptable regulatory environment. A major challenge for policy-makers is keeping up with a rapidly changing international commercial environment. As noted, the calculus for mobile, export-oriented foreign investors differs from that in the import substitution era. The quality of institutions, infrastructure, and incentives matters more than before. In transitional economies, the first round of reform typically focuses on macroeconomic stabilization and partial trade liberalization, while some other, microeconomic, components of the 'three I's' often lag.

The question arises as to whether the FDI regulatory framework is able to adapt to this fast-changing environment. One worries that inert and bureaucratic investment agencies, accustomed to distributing and exacting rents, may not be able to change quickly enough. Over a decade ago, Wells and Wint (1991) observed that, with the exception of Singapore, these agencies struggled with their dual, and potentially conflicting, roles as promoters as well as regulators of FDI. These agencies have rarely been at the forefront of major economic policy reform. There often remains a mindset that views FDI primarily as greenfield, rather than recognizing the rapidly increasing post-crisis volume of M&As. The rise of the 'new economy' in various guises is transforming international business patterns. Even in relatively successful and long-lived cases of regional economic cooperation, such as ASEAN, the notion of a seamless market and business environment is far from being realized.

An unfinished reform agenda. There are still significant obstacles to FDI in all six economies, and these are typically more substantial than trade barriers. Many of them are concentrated in service industries, notwithstanding the significant liberalizations of the past decade.[34] In fact, countries with a tradition of openness toward merchandise trade have often been quite restrictive on trade in services, and FDI in this sector. Malaysia, Thailand, and even Singapore may be included in this characterization. Of course, there may be good grounds for rejecting certain FDI applicants, when their presence would harm national interests.[35] Moreover, governments everywhere have to bend to nationalist sentiment, particularly in the wake of economic crises when there is a perception that deep-pocketed foreigners are picking up distressed assets at fire-sale prices. Nevertheless, it needs to be recognized that, for all the rhetoric of 'open borders,' major commercial barriers do still exist.

Different countries, different FDI challenges. The diversity of our country sample draws attention to the fact that host countries have diverse expectations of FDI. For late liberalizers, a major objective is simply to enter the international commercial mainstream. Thus 'bagging the first contract' is a prime objective. For resource-rich economies, taxation and environmental arrangements, and the rate of resource depletion, feature prominently. For low-wage, densely populated economies, export-oriented, labor-intensive FDI is considered crucial. By contrast, as host economies lose their comparative advantage, attention shifts to how FDI may play a role in the process of upgrading to more technology-intensive activities. Where a strong domestic R&D base already exists, policy-makers often seek to build on this strength through joint ventures with MNEs.

The key point, therefore, is that while the notion of 'one size fits all' may apply at the general level to the adoption of open trade and investment regimes, there is in addition much scope for specific micro interventions to maximize the benefits of the foreign presence.

Toward a unified investment environment. A major challenge for policy-makers is the introduction of a unified investment regime that confers 'national treatment' on foreign investors, except for carefully articulated areas of national interest where domestic ownership is deemed essential.[36] Foreign and domestic investors are generally concerned with the same set of policy issues—the tax regime, labor relations, the quality of human capital and infrastructure, adequate legal protection, and so on. There is therefore little point in attempting to devise different policy regimes for foreign firms. Invariably, MNEs will be attracted to a commercial environment that domestic firms also find conducive.

The question of national treatment for FDI is particularly important for transitional economies. As part of the opening up process, their policy-makers recognize the importance of attracting MNEs into a hitherto hostile commercial environment. It is therefore not uncommon for them to 'overdo' the FDI incentive regime by offering excessively generous arrangements for foreign investors. This results in the familiar dual policy regime, and often in the round-tripping phenomenon referred to in the PRC chapter. Moreover, since these transitional economies also typically have a large, unreformed, and subsidized SOE sector, a lop-sided ownership structure frequently emerges in which domestic private firms are under-represented. In such circumstances, if domestic opposition to these privi-leged arrangements intensifies, there is a danger that the reform process itself could be jeopardized.

FDI and trade issues, again. As argued above, trade liberalization is a key driver of the reorientation of foreign investors from rent-seeking to efficiency-seeking FDI. Underpinning this transformation has been trade liberalization that has been primarily unilateral in nature, supported by a conducive multilateral environment. These twin pillars are under challenge as never before. The momentum for multilateral trade reform appears to have slowed, most recently with the disappointing results at the Cancun summit. Bilateral and regional preferential arrangements, inherently dis-criminatory in nature, are proliferating. There is a danger that a world of 'hubs and spokes' may emerge, under which trade barriers between the spokes could conceivably increase. Such a trend would constitute a rever-sal of the post-war trend toward a more liberal global environment. It would also frustrate the emergence of the global factory phenomenon, and the capacity of MNEs to source globally at the lowest cost. It is therefore possible that, if the current predilection for FTAs intensifies, MNEs will be forced to incorporate discriminatory trade barriers in their locational cal-culus. For host economies, being a predictable and efficient production site would thus be necessary but not sufficient condition for attracting FDI.

FDI in decentralized policy environments. Over time, the power of central governments in all six countries is likely to diminish, as authority devolves to the regions. In transitional economies such as the PRC and Viet Nam, this process is an inevitable outcome of the shift from plan to market. In Thailand it is by design, as a major decentralization program is being introduced. India and Malaysia are already federal entities. As this process takes root, it is possible that energetic local governments will begin to compete among themselves to seize business opportunities, in the process bypassing cumbersome national agencies. The challenge for national governments will be to encourage this competitive potential, while ensuring that it operates in a manner consistent with national development objectives.[37] The structure of center–regional fiscal relations is also a key to the success of these reforms: severe vertical fiscal imbalances may starve subnational governments of the resources they need to facilitate growth, typically resulting in chronic 'buck-passing' between tiers of government.

Fiscal incentives. Fiscal incentives are a risky and generally costly means of attracting MNEs. They are invariably second best, when a first-best approach would be to address at source the unattractive features of the host economy environment. If granted on a large scale, there is a risk that they will undermine the government's fiscal base. Foreign firms are attracted to commercially profitable and politically stable environments. Surveys of MNEs invariably record these features as the major determinants of their locational decisions when investing abroad. The empirical evidence also supports such a finding. Hong Kong, China, for example, has traditionally eschewed fiscal incentives in favor of a uniformly low tax regime. The report by the Foreign Investment Advisory Service cited in the chapter on Thailand suggests that the pay-off from incentives is very low. Moreover, in the absence of regime credibility, foreign investors implicitly discount the value of incentives because they doubt their fiscal sustainability.[38]

Fiscal incentives are also corruption-prone. Not a few governments treat these 'rents' as bargaining tools for corruption. In addition, they may be employed as a de facto instrument of industry policy by agencies without the analytical capacity to devise and implement such programs. Performance criteria often lack any clear rationale, and in any case are often not enforced. Even in the well-managed Malaysian economy, the rationale for the granting of incentives is ambiguous, and their opportunity cost has not been thoroughly assessed for a decade or more, at least in public.[39]

There may be a case for distortions of these kinds in special circumstances. For example, investment incentives may be a useful signaling device in cases where governments are seeking to press their reform credentials abroad. In such a second-best world, and to prevent vested interests proliferating around them, the key is to ensure that these incentives are time-bound and transparently costed. In all six countries, governments have struggled to introduce major reforms in their incentive regime, despite the clear case for doing so.

NOTES

I am grateful to staff at the Asian Development Bank (ADB), and the paper writers for helpful comments and much useful information, to Archanun Kohpaiboon for assistance in compiling the data, and to Prema-Chandra Athukorala for many insights on FDI issues.

1   For example, official documents state that FDI should go to 'mountainous and remote regions with difficult economic and social conditions.' MNEs are criticized for not developing greater local sourcing, and yet the policy regime inhibits the development of a vibrant SME sector.

2   See Lardy (1996) for a detailed analysis of the PRC's trade and FDI liberalization.

3   To quote Joshi (2003): 'In practice, however, the system [that is, the FDI regime] is more restrictive than it sounds, because there still remain numerous hurdles to jump, erected by State governments if not the Centre.' Athreye and Kapur (2001: 422) note the irony that 'even in sectors where foreign investment is readily allowed, firms must secure "automatic approval"!' On the Indian reforms, see also Joshi and Little (1997) and Krueger (2002).

4   See Wells and Wint (1991). In the sample of countries they studied, only Singapore appeared to have an effective separation of responsibilities.

5   See Ramstetter (1999) for a detailed empirical study of this issue.

6   Any analysis of foreign investment has to be heavily qualified by data constraints. The country chapters provide extensive discussion of data issues. Commonly found weaknesses include the following.

First, FDI flows are poorly recorded. Investment agencies typically report approved investments, which often differ significantly from actual flows. This is because realization rates fluctuate, with realizations sometimes lagging approvals by several years, and because some agencies include domestic borrowings and even equity in their 'foreign' totals.

Second, realized FDI estimates produced by central banks from balance of payments data are generally very approximate. Moreover, they do not include FDI in the form of reinvested earnings.

Third, disaggregated data on FDI flows, by sector and by source, are mostly incomplete. Often, the administrative responsibility of investment agencies does not extend to key sectors of the economy. Attempts to match home and host country FDI estimates typically reveal large discrepancies.

Fourth, accurate estimates of the FDI stock are rarely available. As noted, the data on flows are inadequate. In addition, census estimates of foreign ownership are irregular and mostly patchy.

Fifth, data on other dimensions of the foreign presence, which may include foreign equity, are even weaker. In some countries there is substantial foreign ownership via the stock market, which (except during periods of crisis) may be 'FDI-like' in its behavior. The six countries have large diaspora communities, but there is no consistent treatment of their investment activities. Associated flows of human capital and technology, which often entail some implicit or explicit FDI, are also poorly recorded.

7 For a summary of the debate, see the PRC and India chapters. A recent summary appears in *The Economist* (21 June 2003).

8 This debate included the assertion that FDI from Japan was superior to FDI from America, and that FDI from the Third World was superior to FDI from developed countries. Kojima was commonly associated with the former argument (see, for example, Kojima 1996), while Wells (1983) produced a major early study on the latter proposition.

9 Indonesia has of course been the principal outlier among the crisis-affected economies, owing to regime change and a prolonged period of political uncertainty.

10 See Athukorala (2001) for a detailed examination.

11 The usual caveats have to be attached to the data in Table 2.1. Trade/GDP ratios need to allow for country size. Average tariffs need to take account of tariff dispersion and the presence of NTBs. To varying degrees, all six countries maintain dual trade regimes that differentiate between export sectors and the domestic economy. Nonetheless, the picture presented here is a reasonably plausible characterization of the countries' differences.

12 For contending perspectives on the impact of these interventions, see, for example, Amsden (1989, 2001) and Smith (2000).

13 That is, the ASEAN Free Trade Area liberalizations have almost always been multilateralized, while the SAARC concessions have been trivial.

14 Of course, there will always be a need for some special provisions in any investment law tailored specifically for foreign investors, for example, to provide a guarantee against expropriation and to permit profit remittance.

15 Numerous data sources could have been selected. One recent and very useful series, with heavy emphasis on technological capacity and learning, is presented in UNIDO (2002). Its major drawback for this chapter is that it does not include Viet Nam. Part 3 ('Competitiveness in Developing Asia') of ADB (2003) provides a comprehensive review of various competitiveness estimates.

16 For a detailed review of these issues, see the contributors to Krueger (2002). Some of the major areas on the reform list are fiscal imbalances, public sector enterprises, trade policy (especially in consumer goods industries), labor market rigidities, SMEs and reservation schemes, the regulatory and licensing system, and center–state relations. Many of these of course intersect.

17   For example, R&D expenditure rose from 0.3 percent of GDP in 1971 to 2.8 percent in the mid-1990s.

18   See Athukorala and Hill (2002), Blomstrom and Kokko (1998), Fan (2003), Lall and Urata (2003), Lim (2001), and Moran (2002b) for recent literature surveys.

19   See Yusuf and Evenett (2003: Ch. 7) for a recent analysis of this phenomenon in an East Asian context.

20   Migrant labor flows to Malaysia have been particularly large. At the time of the economic crisis, migrant workers, many of them illegal, comprised 20–25 percent of the workforce (Athukorala and Manning 1999).

21   See Fan (2003) and Hill (2002) for references to the large literature on spatial inequality in the PRC, including the effects of FDI.

22   There are concerns, however, that some local authorities are excessively generous in their fiscal and financial incentives (for example, providing land at no cost).

23   Logistics networks—transport and telecommunications—are particularly relevant here. For example, in the PRC it is sometimes cheaper to freight goods from coastal regions to the United States than it is to transport them from the hinterland to the coast.

24   There appear to be very marked differences among Viet Nam's regions in this respect, with some completing local-level regulatory formalities in a matter of weeks whereas others may take up to two years. Of course, the nature of the proposed investment is a factor, with resource-based or pollution-intensive projects inevitably proving more complex.

25   See Fan (2003) for a summary of this large literature.

26   An extreme example is the auto industry, whose high levels of protection were referred to earlier. In 2002, 11 foreign manufacturers competed for a local annual market of less than 27,000 cars and commercial vehicles.

27   For a comprehensive analysis of these issues, see the papers in Jomo and Felker (1999), and Jomo, Felker, and Rasiah (1999).

28   It is worth remembering that Malaysia was a world leader among tropical countries in pioneering high-quality agricultural research and extension programs, partly to address problems of rural Malay poverty. However, industrial extension programs have never been developed to the same extent, the government preferring to adopt a more passive, MNE-led approach.

29   See Rasiah (2001) and Toh (2002) for interesting accounts of Penang's export-oriented industrialization, including both successes and challenges.

30   The key architect of Indonesia's dramatic FDI regime liberalization in 1967, Moh. Sadli, later expressed the context in his country as follows:

> When we started out attracting foreign investment in 1967 everything and everybody was welcome. We did not dare to refuse; we did not even dare to ask for bonafidity of credentials. We needed a list of names and dollar figures of intended investments, to give credence to our drive. The first mining company virtually wrote its own ticket. Since we had no conception about a mining contract we accepted the draft written by the company as a basis for negotiation and only common sense and a desire to bag the first contract were our guidelines (quoted in Hill 1988: 28).

31 This may be changing. For example, Toyota has recently transferred some major R&D activities to Thailand.

32 An important consideration here is whether fully owned foreign operations are permitted. The empirical evidence suggests that MNEs are more likely to develop strong local supply and content networks in a secure environment that permits 100 percent, or at least majority, foreign ownership (Moran 2002b).

33 See McKendrick, Doner, and Haggard (2000) and Wong (2003) for detailed analyses of Singapore's upgrading strategies.

34 See Hardin and Holmes (2002) for the development of a methodology to estimate FDI barriers, and some empirical estimates.

35 For example, as Stiglitz (2001: 521) notes, Singapore earned high marks 'when it excluded the Bank of Credit and Commerce International, which [later] succeeded in duping the United States' regulatory authorities.'

36 Of course, much revolves around the definition of 'essential.' It typically includes defense-related industries, and sometimes the media and major natural resources. Divestment requirements may also be stipulated, although these are contrary to the spirit of national treatment.

37 For example, in some cases of rapid decentralization, regional governments, in their desire to expand the local revenue base quickly, resort to the imposition of local trade taxes or sanction environmentally unsound practices such as deforestation.

38 See Berezin, Salehizadeh, and Santana (2002) for a recent study of Caribbean nations' proliferating fiscal incentives to attract FDI, especially in IT sectors, and which underlines this point. See also Morisett and Pirnia (2002).

39 For example, as in most countries, proposed investment per employee is one of the criteria. Yet Malaysia is also actively courting advanced IT projects, which typically have relatively low (physical) capital/labor ratios.

3

People's Republic of China

Xiaolu Wang

1   INTRODUCTION

The People's Republic of China (PRC) is the world's largest developing country and most populous nation. From 1978 to 2002, it experienced rapid economic growth of 9.3 percent on average. Even during the Asian financial crisis, the PRC managed to maintain a growth rate of over 7 percent, the fastest in the world (World Bank 2002). The government continues to target growth of 7 percent for the first decade of this century.[1]

Although the PRC ranks very low in terms of per capita GDP, its total GDP exceeded CNY10,000 billion ($1,200 billion) in 2002, making it the sixth largest economy in the world. It is the major regional economic dynamo in East Asia, in many ways assuming the role that Japan and the newly industrializing economies (NIEs) held in previous decades. At current growth rates, the economy will double in the coming decade and the PRC will become the world's third or fourth largest economy. Measured in purchasing power parity (PPP) terms, its GNP is already the second largest in the world. If the present growth rate of 7 percent is maintained, the PRC will catch up with the United States in the next 15 years.[2]

The dramatic growth of the economy can be attributed mainly to the market-oriented economic reforms of the past two and half decades. In the 1980s, the impetus for growth arose from the reallocation of resources, induced by marketization of the domestic economy, development of the non-state enterprise sector, rural industrialization, and increased export orientation. Substantial reform and structural adjustment followed in the early 1990s. Since then, growth of both exports and foreign direct investment (FDI) has accelerated. In 2002, inflows exceeded $50 billion, making the

PRC the largest recipient of FDI in the world. The sharp increases in FDI have been driven by policy changes directed at achieving greater openness and liberalization of the economy, further fueled by the PRC's accession to the World Trade Organization (WTO) in 2001.

FDI is playing a very important role in the Chinese economy and has made a significant contribution to economic development. However, there have also been policy failures, unsuccessful experiences, and unsolved problems. This chapter briefly summarizes the past and current situation of FDI in the PRC, and changes in relevant policies. It examines the effects of FDI on the Chinese economy and discusses the lessons and experiences of the previous and current policies.

The following section provides a brief review of trends in FDI. The third section assesses the effects of FDI on the Chinese economy. The fourth sketches policy changes relating to FDI, and describes how these have affected the size, quality, and regional allocation of FDI and its distribution across different industries. The fifth section reviews the implementation of international agreements on FDI and trade-related investment measures (TRIMs), and the final section provides a summary and some policy recommendations.

2   AN OVERVIEW OF FDI

The Chinese economy was centrally planned until 1978. In that year, the Central Committee of the Communist Party and the central government decided to reform the economy by allowing the market mechanism to play a 'subsidiary' role in the economy, and by opening the economy to the world. In 1981, four special economic zones (SEZs) were established in the provinces of Guangdong and Fujian to attract FDI, and in particular investment from nearby Hong Kong, China; Macao; and Taipei,China. Firms locating in the zones received low tax rates, tax holidays, and duty-free imports and exports.

Following the initial success of the SEZs, in 1984 14 cities in the eastern coastal area were allowed to establish economic and technological development zones offering preferential FDI policies similar to those that applied in the SEZs. In 1988, the government broadened the policy regime further with the listing of large parts of the nine coastal provinces and three eastern municipalities as coastal economic open zones.[3] With the decentralization of government controls on the domestic enterprise sector, market-oriented non-state enterprises mushroomed everywhere.

After a short period of stagnation in the process of reform between 1989 and 1991, Deng Xiaoping, the former leader of the Communist Party, pushed ahead with a new campaign in 1992 to convert the whole economy into a 'socialist market economy.' The market mechanism was officially elevated from a 'subsidiary' to a 'primary' position. FDI has increased dramatically since then. A large literature has examined the general profile of FDI in the PRC. Kamath (1990, 1994) and Pomfret (1991, 1994) reviewed and drew lessons from the early experience of an open door policy. Several authors have looked at the size, growth rates, location, and main features of FDI, and addressed the question of whether the large inflows would continue. Eng and Lin (1996) investigated economic penetration by foreign investors and their efforts to build a competitive edge for operations in local and international markets. Fukasaku, Wall, and Wu (1994) provided a chronological catalog and evaluation of FDI policy. Chi and Kao (1994) analyzed the general location and industrial distribution, sources, and types of FDI, by examining data from a sample of foreign enterprises registered in 1991. Freeman (1994) described the FDI profile of the PRC and Viet Nam by sector and region.

The Magnitude of FDI

FDI played a minor role in the economy until 1992, a crucial year of policy change toward marketization. Inflows exceeded $40 billion in 1996 and $45 billion in 1997, around ten times the level in 1991 and 25 times that in 1985 (Table 3.1). In 2002, following the PRC's accession to the WTO and the relaxation of service sector restrictions, FDI reached a new high of $52.7 billion. Three key sets of factors explain this dramatic growth.

First, because of its abundant supply of cheap and relatively well-trained labor, the PRC has a comparative advantage in labor-intensive manufacturing, and therefore is attractive to FDI seeking this resource.

Second, the business environment in the PRC has improved. Regulations on FDI, and on economic policy more generally, were not very transparent in earlier periods. In addition, the domestic market was heavily protected by tariff and non-tariff trade barriers that had a negative impact on FDI (although, of course, protection also generated some rent-seeking, domestic-market-oriented FDI). In the 1990s there was a gradual but significant liberalization of restrictions on FDI. The PRC's trade policies also became more open.

Third, changes in preferential policies have increased the PRC's attractiveness as a destination for FDI. The differential treatment of joint ventures and wholly foreign-owned enterprises has gradually been unified, and additional tax reductions and other privileges have been accorded to FDI in a greater number of regions.

Table 3.1   PRC: FDI Inflows, 1979–2002 ($ billion)

Year	FDI
1979–84 (cumulative stock)	3.1
1985	1.7
1990	3.5
1991	4.4
1992	11.0
1993	27.5
1994	33.8
1995	37.5
1996	41.7
1997	45.2
1998	45.5
1999	40.3
2000	40.7
2001	46.9
2002	52.7
1979–2002 (cumulative stock)	446.2

Source: National Bureau of Statistics (2002), *China Statistical Yearbook*; Ministry of Commerce (2003), <www.moftec.gov.cn>.

In 2001, FDI was estimated to account for 10.5 percent of total investment in fixed assets in the whole economy, and 24.1 percent in the industrial sector. However, these and other data on FDI in the PRC need to be treated cautiously because some FDI is 'round-tripping' capital, that is, capital that flows out of the PRC and returns disguised as foreign investment in order to receive the preferential treatment available only to FDI. Another possible source of this round-tripping capital is illegal funds from the PRC being 'money laundered' as FDI.

A considerable part of FDI from Hong Kong, China and tax havens such as the British Virgin Islands and Cayman Islands is likely to be round-tripping capital. Hong Kong, China itself accounted for 36 percent of total FDI in the PRC in 2001 (see Table 3.4 below). However, it is not possible, as some authors have suggested, that all or even most of this is round-tripping, because Hong Kong, China does have large investments in the PRC. In addition, it is reported that investors from Taipei,China and other Asian economies often route money through Hong Kong, China to avoid rousing domestic hostility by investing directly in the PRC. An estimate by an International Finance Corporation economist has suggested that as much as 30–50 percent of FDI in the PRC may be round-tripping capital (Pfeffermann 2002, cited in Gordon 2002), although the more commonly accepted figure is 10–20 percent (see, for example, Dai 2003). Whatever the magnitude, it is clear that the unequal treatment of foreign and domestic investors has induced this rent-seeking behavior.

Along with continued rapid growth in FDI, there has been increased foreign merger and acquisition (M&A) activity, converting domestic enterprises into joint ventures and foreign enterprises. In 2002, FDI increased by 12.5 percent over 2001. In the first quarter of 2003, it reached $13.1 billion, a 56.7 percent increase on the first quarter of 2002. The epidemic of severe acute respiratory syndrome (SARS) in 2003 had a negative impact on inflows, but the long-term effects are not likely to be serious since the immediate crisis has been overcome. To date, the central and western regions of the PRC have received only a small proportion of total FDI. However, a program set up in 1998 to improve the investment environment in these regions should result in faster growth of FDI in inland areas in coming years.

Small-scale investors in labor-intensive sectors were the major sources of FDI in the earlier period, when large MNEs tended to adopt a cautious attitude toward investing in the PRC. However, the role of the large MNEs is now becoming more important. Associated with this change, the technological content of FDI is increasing.

Sectoral Distribution of FDI

Owing to the PRC's comparative advantages and the policy regime, the majority of FDI has gone into the manufacturing sector, mainly electronic products, machinery, chemicals, and textiles and garments. In 2001, manufacturing received 66 percent of total FDI and services received 24 percent, much of the latter in real estate (Table 3.2).

Table 3.3 estimates cumulative FDI by sector. Column (1) shows total cumulative investment by foreign-invested enterprises, including investment by their Chinese partners. Column (2) shows the foreign share of registered capital (data on actual investment are unavailable). Based on these shares, cumulative FDI in each sector, and its proportion of the total, is estimated in columns (3) and (4). Cumulative FDI in the manufacturing sector accounted for 55 percent of the total in 2001, and 36 percent in serv-

Table 3.2   PRC: Realized FDI by Sector, 1993–2001[a]

Sector	1993[b]		1997		2001	
	($ billion)	(%)	($ billion)	(%)	($ billion)	(%)
Total	27.5	100.0	45.3	100.0	46.9	100.0
Agriculture[c]	0.3	1.1	0.6	1.4	0.9	1.9
Industry	12.6	45.8	31.2	68.8	34.0	72.4
Manufacturing	n.a.	n.a.	28.1	62.1	30.9	65.9
Construction	1.0	3.5	1.4	3.2	0.8	1.7
Services	13.6	49.6	12.1	26.6	11.2	24.0
Real estate	10.8[d]	39.3[d]	5.2	11.4	5.1	11.0
Transport & telecommunications	0.4	1.3	1.7	3.7	0.9	1.9
Wholesale, retail, & catering	1.1	4.0	1.4	3.1	1.2	2.5
Social services	0.0	0.0	2.0	4.4	2.6	5.5
Banking & insurance	0.0	0.0	0.0	0.0	0.0	0.1

n.a.: not available.
a   For simplicity, some small subsectors are not listed in the table.
b   Information on the sectoral composition of realized FDI in 1993 is not available. The data shown for this year are based on approvals by sector.
c   Agriculture includes farming, forestry, animal husbandry, and fisheries.
d   Includes social services.
Source: National Bureau of Statistics (1995, 1998, 2002), *China Statistical Yearbook*.

ices. Both Table 3.2 and Table 3.3 indicate an increasing proportion of FDI in the manufacturing sector between 1993 and 2001, probably as a result of increased investment activity by MNEs. Following the WTO accession in 2001, there are likely to be significant increases in FDI in service sectors such as banking, insurance, and telecommunications.

Sources of FDI

FDI in the PRC is officially defined as follows:

Foreign Direct Investment refers to the investments inside China by foreign enterprises and economic organizations or individuals (including overseas Chinese, compatriots from Hong Kong, Macao and Taiwan, and Chinese enter-

Table 3.3   PRC: Cumulative FDI by Sector, 2001[a]

Sector	Total Investment by FIEs ($ billion) (1)	Foreign Share in Registered Capital[b] (%) (2)	Estimated FDI in FIEs ($ billion) (3)	Distribution of FDI by Sector[c] (%) (4)
Total	875.0	71	621.3	100.0
Agriculture	9.1	77	7.0	1.1
Industry	544.1	69	375.4	60.4
Manufacturing	491.3	70	343.9	55.4
Construction	21.5	65	14.0	2.3
Services	300.3	75	224.8	36.2
Real estate	149.1	77	114.8	18.5
Transport & telecommunications	41.4	75	31.1	5.0
Wholesale, retail, & catering	24.6	72	17.7	2.8
Social services	56.3	68	38.3	6.2
Banking & insurance	2.1	70	1.5	0.2

FIE: foreign-invested enterprise.

a   For simplicity, some small subsectors are not listed in the table.

b   Where total registered capital of foreign-invested enterprises in each sector is 100 percent.

c   Where total accumulated FDI in the PRC is 100 percent.

Source: National Bureau of Statistics (2002), *China Statistical Yearbook*.

prises registered abroad), following the relevant policies and laws of China, for the establishment of ventures exclusively with foreign-owned investment, Sino–foreign joint ventures, and cooperative enterprises, or for the cooperative exploration of resources with enterprises and economic organizations in China. It includes the reinvestment of foreign entrepreneurs with the profits gained from the investments and the funds that enterprises borrow from abroad in the total investment of projects which are approved by the relevant department of the government (NBS 2003: 686).

According to this definition, FDI includes investment from Hong Kong, China; Macao; and Taipei,China. Hong Kong, China has in fact

Table 3.4   PRC: Sources of FDI Inflows, 1987–2001[a]

Country/ Region	1987 ($ billion)	1994 ($ billion)	2001	
			($ billion)	(%)
Total	2.3	33.8	46.9	100.0
Asia	1.9	28.6	29.6	63.2
Hong Kong, China	1.6	19.8	16.7	35.7
Japan	0.2	2.1	4.4	9.3
Taipei,China	–	3.4	3.0	6.4
Republic of Korea	–	0.7	2.2	4.6
Singapore	–	1.2	2.1	4.6
Other	–	1.4	1.3	2.7
North America	0.3	2.8	5.1	10.9
United States	0.3	2.5	4.4	9.4
Other	–	0.3	0.7	1.4
Europe	0.1	1.7	4.5	9.6
Germany	–	0.3	1.2	2.6
United Kingdom	–	0.7	1.1	2.2
Other	–	0.7	2.2	4.7
Latin America	–	0.2	6.3	13.5
Virgin Islands	–	0.1	5.0	10.8
Cayman Islands	–	–	1.1	2.3
Other	–	–	0.2	0.4
Oceania & the Pacific islands	–	0.2	1.0	2.2
Africa	–	–	0.3	0.7
Other	0.1	0.6		

a   A dash indicates a value of zero or close to zero. The table is based on annual
    data.
Source: National Bureau of Statistics (2002), *China Statistical Yearbook.*

been the largest source of FDI, with estimated inflows of $19.8 billion in 1994 and $16.7 billion in 2001, accounting for 59 percent and 36 percent of total FDI inflows in these two years (Table 3.4). Other major investors, apart from the tax havens mentioned earlier, include the United States, Japan, Taipei,China, the Republic of Korea, and Singapore. Although still relatively small in amount, FDI from the United States, Japan, and Europe has been increasing quickly in recent years.

Capital Outflows and Round Tripping

The PRC experienced trade deficits in the 1980s and surpluses in the 1990s (with the exception of 1993). The capital account has been in surplus since the 1980s. Gross capital inflows (that is, FDI, other foreign investment, and foreign loans) stood at around $50 billion in the mid-1990s (Table 3.5). The PRC's foreign exchange reserves increased rapidly to reach $300 billion in the first quarter of 2003. A large part of this was used to buy US government bonds, a move that has been criticized as an inefficient use of the reserves. Outgoing direct investment is now increasing. Both the capital account and the foreign exchange regime are still controlled by the state.

Table 3.5   PRC: Trade Balance and Gross Capital Inflows, 1990–2002 ($ billion)

Year	Trade Balance	Capital Inflows
1990	8.7	10.3
1991	8.1	11.6
1992	4.4	19.2
1993	−12.2	39.0
1994	5.4	43.2
1995	16.7	48.1
1996	12.2	54.8
1997	40.4	64.4
1998	43.5	58.6
1999	29.2	52.7
2000	24.1	59.4
2001	22.5	49.7
2002	30.4	55.0

Source: National Bureau of Statistics (2002, 2003), *China Statistical Yearbook*.

Table 3.6   PRC: Capital Outflow and Capital Flight, 1990–98 ($ billion)

Year	Capital Outflow		Capital Flight			
	Han (World Bank)	Song (World Bank)	Han (Morgan Guaranty)	Song (Song)	Han (Cline)	Han (Cuddington)
1990	13.9	9.6	10.2	4.8	5.4	3.6
1991	10.2	9.1	7.3	12.9	1.3	7.0
1992	24.4	20.3	21.3	12.0	12.1	11.7
1993	24.0	21.8	18.0	21.0	9.0	13.7
1994	17.5	18.0	11.4	14.4	−1.7	12.8
1995	26.8	20.1	18.9	25.7	6.0	17.3
1996	23.6	21.8	15.1	18.6	2.0	13.9
1997	51.2	47.4	41.0	40.8	33.3	16.1
1998	77.0		74.5		50.6	14.3

Source: Han (1999); Song (1999); Yang and Chen (2000); Han (1999).

Unregistered capital outflows, or capital flight, are also large. Two approaches have been developed to measure the extent of these outflows. The first, developed by Cuddington (1986), was to measure capital flight directly using the errors and omissions term in the balance of payments in addition to short-term capital outflows from the private non-banking sector. Because the errors and omissions term reflects not only capital flight, but also statistical errors, this approach is not very accurate. The second approach, developed by the World Bank (1985), derives capital outflow indirectly from capital account residuals. That is:

capital outflow = current account earnings + net FDI inflow
+ foreign loans − foreign reserve increases.

Note that capital flight is only part of the outflow. To derive unregistered capital flight, the Morgan Guaranty Trust Company (1986) deducted short-term financial assets held by the banking system and the monetary authorities from the World Bank formula. Cline (1987) further deducted tourism and border trade earnings from the Morgan Guaranty Trust Company formula.

Table 3.6 shows estimates of the PRC's capital outflows and capital flight by Han (1999) and Song (1999). Both used the World Bank approach

Figure 3.1   PRC: Capital Inflows and Capital Flight, 1990–2001
($ billion)

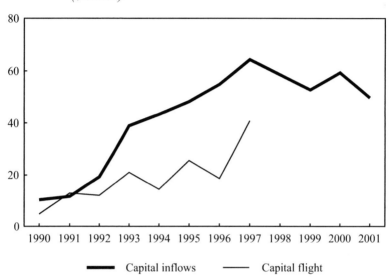

Source: Capital inflows: National Bureau of Statistics (2002, 2003), *China Statistical Yearbook*; capital flight: Song (1999).

to calculate outflows. To calculate unregistered capital flight, Han used the Cuddington, Morgan Guaranty Trust Company, and Cline approaches, whereas Song subtracted from capital outflows the banks' net assets held overseas, approved Chinese investment and loans overseas, and export earnings. He also undertook price conversions and error adjustments.

According to these estimations, capital outflows amounted to $10–20 billion in the early to mid-1990s and then increased rapidly to $47–77 billion in 1997–98. Estimates of capital flight diverge. In general, the indirect approaches lead to large estimates of around $30–40 billion in 1997, whereas the direct approach produces smaller estimates of about $16 billion. According to Song's estimates, capital flight has accounted for such a high proportion of capital inflow that it has largely neutralized FDI inflows (Figure 3.1).

Several reasons have been advanced to explain the extent of capital flight (see, for example, Song 1999). The first is the round tripping of capital that sees domestic capital reinvested in the PRC as FDI, because of a discriminatory taxation policy that favors FDI over domestic investment. Assuming 20 percent of total FDI is round-tripping capital, in 1997–98 the amount could have been in the order of $9 billion. This would account for 20–50 percent of the PRC's total capital flight according to Song's and Han's estimates. The second explanation lies in the money laundering of illegal funds leaked from state-owned enterprises (SOEs) and state banks. This particularly relates to corruption among civil servants and SOE managers, and there are no reliable estimates of the amounts involved. Other explanations given for capital flight include deficiencies in the legal system and differences in interest rates between Chinese and international sources.

3   THE EFFECTS OF FDI

It is now commonly agreed that FDI has been beneficial to capital formation, output, income, and export growth in the PRC (Kueh 1992; Lardy 1996). In a discussion of the effects of FDI on economic development, regional growth, and trade, Hiemenz (1989) argued that a more efficient use of resources had been more important than increases in investment in achieving the positive economic performance of the PRC in the 1980s. Chen, Chang, and Zhang (1995), who assessed the effects of FDI on GDP, domestic savings, fixed asset investment, and foreign trade during the transition to a market economy, concluded that FDI had contributed to economic growth by augmenting the resources available for capital formation, and by increasing export earnings. Shan, Tian, and Sun (1997) constructed a vector auto-regression (VAR) model on the basis of quarterly time-series data for 1985–96, concluding that there was two-way causality between FDI and growth.

Assessments differ as to FDI's contribution to technology transfer. Huang (1995) found that FDI had led to the introduction of advanced technology. Lan and Yong (1996) reached a similar conclusion based on interviews with 36 firms in the northeastern city of Dalian. However, many others have argued that relatively little advanced technology has been transferred. Kamath (1990), for instance, found that, given the preponderance of FDI in real estate, commerce, tourism, and labor-intensive manufacturing, the majority of transfers have involved low-level technology, much of it in areas classified by the government as 'non-productive.'

Despite the large number of studies, the relationship between FDI and spillovers is far from clear. There is limited in-depth, quantitative analysis, owing to the difficulty of obtaining data and the complexity of defining the relationships. Most studies are based on intuitive reasoning and are descriptive in nature. There are also few comparative studies of firms in different ownership categories and industries. One exception is Pan and

Parker (1997), who compared management attitudes in three kinds of firms. However, their study was based on a sample of only 16 enterprises, and their conclusions may therefore be limited by the small sample size. We now look at the effects of FDI in more detail, with reference to output and employment, international trade, income distribution, competition, and linkages and technology transfer.

Output and Employment

Value-added data on foreign-invested enterprises are available only for the industrial sector, and even then are incomplete. It is therefore not possible to undertake a growth accounting analysis for foreign-invested enterprises. Nevertheless, it is clear from their contribution to gross industrial output that they are playing an increasingly important role.

Statistically, foreign-invested firms comprise enterprises with direct investment from foreign countries and those with direct investment from Hong Kong, China; Macao; and Taipei,China. To distinguish between them, we refer to the former as foreign-funded enterprises and to the latter as HMT enterprises. Together, these two types of enterprises contributed 28 percent of gross industrial output by value in 2001, compared with only 13 percent in 1994 (Table 3.7).[4] This rapid increase in the foreign share between 1994 and 2001 was accompanied by an equally rapid rise in the share of the domestic non-state sector (from 38 to 53 percent), but a sharp drop in the SOE sector (from 49 to 18 percent). This indicates a dramatic restructuring of ownership during this period.

Employment in foreign enterprises and joint ventures is small, and has grown far more slowly than their output (Table 3.8). It seems likely that the employment of foreign firms is under-reported. However, it is still the case that foreign enterprises are more capital-intensive than domestic enterprises and therefore employ relatively fewer people.

Tables 3.7 and 3.8 show only the direct contribution of FDI to output and employment. Although not reflected in the figures, there may also be a 'crowding out' effect of FDI on domestic enterprises. In an environment of intense competition in the domestic market, the rapid output growth of foreign-invested enterprises may imply slower or declining growth among domestic enterprises, or even closures. This trend has been evident in motor vehicles, food, beverages, chemicals, and pharmaceuticals. However, it is also clear that foreign-invested enterprises are generally more productive, thereby making a positive contribution to economic growth. In such cases, crowding out may mean an improvement in factor allocation, even though this may cause dislocation in some domestic sectors.

Set against this are the taxation and other policies that have favored

Table 3.7   PRC: Gross Industrial Output of Foreign and Domestic Enterprises, 1994–2001[a]

Type of Enterprise	1994 (CNY billion)	(%)	1997 (CNY billion)	(%)	2001 (CNY billion)	(%)
Total	5,337	100	7,075	100	9,545	100
State-owned	2,620	49	2,903	41	1,723	18
Non-state domestic	2,053	38	2,732	39	5,100	53
Foreign-funded	349	7	827	12	1,537	16
HMT	315	6	613	9	1,185	12
Contribution of FDI to output[b]	417	8	949	13	1,936	20

HMT: enterprises with direct investment from Hong Kong, China; Macao; and Taipei,China.

a The data for 1994 and 1997 exclude 'individual enterprises' with up to eight employees and some small rural enterprises; the data for 2001 exclude enterprises with annual sales of less than CNY5 million. Foreign-funded and HMT enterprises include Sino–foreign joint ventures.

b The contribution of FDI to output is based on the the foreign share in registered capital of the two types of enterprises with FDI (foreign-funded and HMT).

Source: National Bureau of Statistics (1995, 1998, 2002), *China Statistical Yearbook.*

foreign-invested enterprises, generating unfair competition against domestic enterprises and distorting factor allocation. Some analysts have indicated that the favorable policy treatment accorded FDI has stymied the development of an indigenous private sector (see, for example, Huang and Khanna 2003). Economists have called for equal treatment (national treatment) of domestic and foreign-invested enterprises, but this has not yet been achieved.

The real employment effect of FDI is less clear. Because of the lower labor intensity of foreign-invested enterprises, the crowding out effect is likely to imply a negative effect on total employment in the short run. Currently the PRC is facing serious unemployment problems. Although the official rate of urban unemployment is low, surveys suggest that actual

Table 3.8   PRC: Employment in the Foreign and Domestic Sectors,
             1995–2001

Sector	1995		2001	
	(million persons)	(%)	(million persons)	(%)
Urban employment	190.4	100.0	239.4	100.0
State sector	112.6	59.1	76.4	31.9
Non-state sector[a]	72.7	38.2	156.3	65.3
Foreign-funded sector	2.4	1.3	3.5	1.4
HMT sector	2.7	1.4	3.3	1.4
Rural employment	490.3		490.8	

HMT: enterprises with direct investment from Hong Kong, China; Macao; and Taipei,China.

a   Urban non-state sector employment is calculated as the residual of total urban employment minus urban employment in the state, foreign-funded, and HMT sectors.

Source: National Bureau of Statistics (1996, 2002), *China Statistical Yearbook.*

unemployment is significantly greater than is implied by the registered number of job seekers. Millions of urban workers have been laid off from SOEs, many of which have been privatized or closed in recent years. Some of these workers, including those still registered as SOE workers but in fact underemployed, are not included in the unemployment statistics. In 2001, according to official statistics, there were 24.4 million job seekers registered with employment agencies, equal to about 10 percent of the urban workforce. In the east coast provinces, urban workers who have been laid off are likely to find alternative employment in the non-state sector quite quickly, but this is not the case in the central and western provinces where the non-state sector is less developed.

The rural employment situation is even more serious. In 2001, the PRC had 491 million rural workers out of a total workforce of 730 million. Most work in the labor-abundant agricultural sector in which there is limited arable land. The rural industrial sector created about 130 million jobs in the two decades from the late 1970s to the late 1990s. But growth in this sector then began to stagnate and employment to shrink, due to sharp compe-

Table 3.9   *PRC: Exports and Imports of Foreign-invested Enterprises,*
1992–2002 ($ billion)

Year	Total		Foreign-invested Enterprises			
	Exports	Imports	Exports	Imports	Net Exports	Export Share (%)
1992	84.9	80.6	17.4	26.4	−9.0	20.5
1993	91.7	103.9	25.2	41.8	−16.6	27.5
1994	121.0	115.7	34.7	52.9	−18.2	28.7
1995	148.8	132.1	46.9	62.9	−16.0	31.5
1996	151.0	138.8	61.5	75.6	−14.1	40.7
1997	182.7	142.4	74.9	77.7	−2.8	41.0
1998	183.8	149.2	80.9	76.7	4.2	44.0
1999	194.9	165.7	88.6	85.9	2.7	45.5
2000	249.2	225.1	119.4	117.3	2.1	47.9
2001	266.1	243.6	133.2	125.9	7.3	50.1
2002	325.6	295.2	169.9	160.3	9.6	52.2

Source: National Bureau of Statistics (various years), *China Statistical Yearbook.*

tition from the urban sector, including foreign-invested enterprises (NBS, various years).

Exports, Imports, and the Balance of Payments

Foreign-invested enterprises incurred a trade deficit until the late 1990s, demonstrating the ineffectiveness of the earlier policy of imposing export–import balancing conditions and export performance requirements on foreign firms. The national trade surplus was generated entirely by domestic enterprises until 1998, when the exports of foreign-invested enterprises finally exceeded their imports, and thus made a positive contribution to the PRC's balance of payments (Table 3.9). Since then, the share of foreign-invested enterprises in exports and imports has increased dramatically; in 2002, their exports accounted for over half the national total.

Meanwhile, FDI has contributed greatly to the upgrading of the PRC's export structure. Manufactures now make up 90 percent of total exports. In 2001, foreign-invested enterprises accounted for 64.4 percent of the PRC's

*Figure 3.2   PRC: Inflows of FDI and Exports of Foreign-invested
            Enterprises, 1992–2001 ($ billion)*

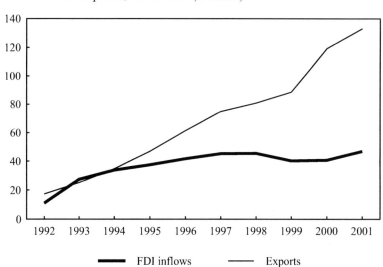

Source: National Bureau of Statistics (various years), *China Statistical Yearbook.*

exports of mechanical and electrical products and 81.5 percent of its high-tech exports (Jiang 2002).

The significant contribution of foreign-invested enterprises to exports is mainly attributable to the higher quality of foreign firms' products and their market access abroad. However, the earlier trade deficits of these enterprises suggest that FDI does not automatically bring about a trade surplus in host countries. Even after 1998, the trade surplus of foreign-invested enterprises was small in relation to their total exports and imports, although it has increased significantly since 2001.

Figure 3.2 also shows no direct relationship between FDI growth and export growth since 1992. This is for several reasons. First, FDI itself induces large imports of capital goods, albeit in the short run. Second, because imported components usually account for a large proportion of the output of foreign enterprises, and local value added is relatively small, the domestic sale of even a small proportion of foreign firms' output may lead to a trade deficit. Third, when sales to the domestic market are more profitable than exports, foreign-invested enterprises will naturally focus on the former. This was certainly the case before 1998, when protection resulted in price differentials between the domestic and international markets. One

Table 3.10   *PRC: Average Annual Wage Rates of Foreign and Domestic Enterprises, 1999–2001 (CNY)*

Year	Foreign-invested Firms		Domestic Firms		National Average[a]
	Foreign-funded	HMT	State-owned	Ltd	
1999	12,951	10,991	8,543	8,632	8,346
2000	14,372	11,914	9,552	9,766	9,371
2001	16,101	12,544	11,178	10,993	10,870

HMT: enterprises with direct investment from Hong Kong, China; Macao; and Taipei,China.

Exchange rate: CNY8.28 = $1.

a   The national average is lower than the totals for domestic firms because some low-wage, non-state enterprises for which data are not available have been excluded.

Source: National Bureau of Statistics (2002), *China Statistical Yearbook.*

clear lesson from the PRC and elsewhere is that high protection retards exports and encourages firms to concentrate on the domestic market.

Income Distribution

In general, average wage rates are higher in foreign enterprises, although HMT firms pay less than other foreign firms (Table 3.10). Foreign firms pay higher wages because they employ more skilled workers and are not bound by the SOEs' egalitarian salary structures. Their higher wages may also reflect the harder work and greater efficiency demanded of employees in foreign firms. In the process, FDI has increased income disparity. Field surveys show that whereas highly qualified workers in foreign firms can command significantly higher wages than those in domestic enterprises, unskilled workers in both types of firms receive broadly similar wages. Thus an income gap arises not only within foreign-invested enterprises, but also between foreign and domestic enterprises. The positive effect is that higher returns to human capital increase the incentive for education and technical innovation, at the social cost of increased income disparity.

Competition and Competition Policy

FDI has created increased competition in the domestic market. For instance, in the automobile industry, the few large domestic manufacturers have all set up joint ventures with major auto makers such as Volkswagen, General Motors (GM), Daimler-Chrysler, Citroen, and Toyota, while many of the small, less efficient domestic manufacturers are closing down (Box 1). In mobile phone production, domestically produced Motorola, Nokia, and Siemens phones have taken the major share of the market. P&G and Unilever are the largest producers of shampoo, detergent, and soap. In beverages, domestically produced Coca-cola and some international fruit juice brands dominate the market, forcing some domestic producers out of business or into mergers.

In general, in industries that have a relatively high technology intensity or a strong brand name, foreign-invested enterprises either dominate the market or can be counted among a few major competitors. The exception is home electrical appliances, where Chinese brands of television sets, washing machines, refrigerators, and air conditioners have a dominant position in the domestic market. They have achieved this without government protection, although many such products are produced by joint ventures (Box 2).

Table 3.11 shows the output and share of foreign-invested enterprises by sector. In eight of the 37 sectors shown—food; garments; leather, fur, and down; furniture manufacturing; cultural, educational and sporting goods; plastic products; electronic and telecommunications equipment; and instruments, meters, and office machinery—foreign enterprises and joint ventures account for 40 percent or more of gross industrial output by value. Most of these sectors are growing rapidly.

Foreign-invested enterprises have certainly contributed to technological progress and increased efficiency. In Table 3.12, several efficiency indicators are calculated for the various ownership groups. Foreign enterprises and joint ventures have higher rates of return and better labor productivity than domestic enterprises. Their capital productivity is higher than that of SOEs but lower than that of non-state enterprises (because their capital intensity is higher than that of the latter). Their liability/assets ratio is lower than that of domestic enterprises, indicating a relatively low financial risk.

The possibility that the entry of MNEs has been accompanied by an increase in monopolistic or oligopolistic market structures has not been examined carefully. Such situations arise when a market is dominated by one or a few suppliers, and may be harmful to consumers. In the case of PC software, for instance, Microsoft has a monopoly in the legal software market (although an illegal market also exists), including Chinese-language software, and some Chinese software companies have exited.

The PRC has not yet introduced an anti-trust law against monopolies,

BOX 1   A CASE STUDY OF FDI
IN THE MOTOR VEHICLE INDUSTRY

The government has long had a policy of high tariffs (of 100 percent on completely built-up vehicles) and quantitative restrictions on motor vehicle imports, in order to promote the industry. With FDI from the world's major auto producers, the output of the PRC's motor vehicle industry has grown rapidly, as the following table shows.

PRC: Output of Motor Vehicles, 1983–2002 (million units)

Year	All Motor Vehicles	Cars
1983	0.24	n.a.
1985	0.44	n.a.
1990	0.51	0.04
1995	1.43	0.36
2000	2.07	0.60
2001	2.34	0.70
2002	3.25	1.09
Annual growth, 1988–2002 (%)	13.70	30.20

Source Teng (2003).

However, in terms of efficiency and competitiveness, the industry's achievements have been less impressive. Many small manufacturers were set up under the shelter of local government protection, in spite of the central government's policy of limiting the entry of new manufacturers operating on an inefficient scale. Currently the PRC has 123 motor vehicle producers, excluding component manufacturers. Most are very small in size and economically inefficient: 95 have an annual output of less than 10,000 units, and 70 an annual output of less than 1,000 units. Only a few producers are relatively large, and only two truck manufacturers have achieved efficient scale economies. Of the PRC's 31 mainland provinces, 26 have motor vehicle plants, but the output of 13 of these was below 50,000 units in 2002.

Some of the world's largest car makers from Germany, the United States, Japan, and Korea have entered the PRC and established joint ventures with a few large Chinese manufacturers. These joint ventures include First Motor (Changchun)–Volkswagen, Shanghai–Volkswagen, Shanghai–GM, Dongfeng–Citroen, Beijing–Daimler–Chrysler, Guangzhou–Honda, and Tianjin–Toyota. Most produce superseded models at well above world market prices. Their production costs are typically 20–30 percent higher than international levels.

Several factors explain the industry's lack of competitiveness. First, high tariffs and import restrictions have induced investment in small and inefficient plants. Second, local governments at the provincial, municipal, and county levels have taken advantage of economic decentralization to avoid or disregard central government stipulations on the minimum scale of plants. Indeed, some local governments have protected local auto markets against competition from better quality vehicles produced in other provinces. Third, while central government regulations have failed to prevent the proliferation of small and inefficient producers, they have restricted the activities of the larger manufacturers. Investment in new production lines, new car models, and changes in factory gate prices all have to be approved by the State Planning Committee. The fortunes of existing manufacturers have depended more on their ability to extract special deals from the government than on their competitiveness. This has restricted technical innovation and efficiency. Fourth, the PRC's TRIMs, in particular the 40 percent local content requirement for components, resulted in high input costs, because some local manufacturers were too small and inefficient to supply parts at a competitive price. And finally, because of its limited technological capacity, the PRC has had to rely on MNEs for vehicle design and key production techniques, yet trade barriers have protected the oligopolistic status of a few large joint ventures.

To meet its WTO commitments, the PRC has reduced its tariffs on motor vehicles from 100 percent to around 70 percent. These will fall further to 25 percent by 2006, while tariffs on auto parts will fall to 10 percent. Quota restrictions on vehicle imports, from a base of $6 billion, will increase by 15 percent annually, and will be eliminated in 2005. The 40 percent local content requirement for components has been eliminated, and the 50 percent ceiling on foreign ownership in auto joint ventures has been relaxed. For example, the government recently approved the establishment of the Guangzhou–Honda joint venture with a 65 percent foreign ownership share.

These reforms have resulted in significant declines in car prices and an increase in the number of new models. Sales and output are both increasing rapidly. Total sales increased by 34 percent to CNY671 billion ($81 billion) in 2002, and total profit increased by 73 percent to CNY46 billion ($5.5 billion). In 2002, output rose by 39 percent over 2001. The number of vehicles produced reached 3.25 million units, making the PRC the world's fifth largest manufacturer after the United States, Japan, Germany, and France. Three large groups, First Motor (Changchun), Dongfeng, and Shanghai, were responsible for 51 percent of the total vehicle output.

Source: National Bureau of Statistics (2002, 2003), *China Statistical Yearbook*; Teng (2003); NWMI (2002); author's interview with Tianjin Motor and the Chinese Auto Industry Institute, August 2003.

BOX 2 A CASE STUDY OF FDI IN THE HOME ELECTRICAL APPLIANCES INDUSTRY

The home electrical appliances industry has been less regulated and protected than autos, and was opened up earlier. The industry was initially dominated by imports. In the 1980s, foreign firms set up production facilities in the PRC, often in the form of joint ventures. Spurred by intense competition in the domestic market among local producers and importers, both the quantity and quality of domestic production increased rapidly. As a result, a few large producers emerged, and many small ones either merged or closed down.

Tariffs were not a major obstacle to imports. Although the nominal tariff rate was high, actual rates were far lower. For example, in 1995 the average nominal tariff rate on electronic products was 40 percent, but the actual rate (that is, tariffs actually collected as a share of the value of imports) was only 11.8 percent.

As the competitiveness and quality of domestic products has improved to rival that of international producers, production and exports have expanded rapidly. This has turned the PRC into one of the world's major exporters of household electrical appliances. As the table shows, the PRC produced 51.5 million color television sets, 16 million household fridges, 16 million washing machines, and 31 million air conditioners in 2002, accounting for 23 percent, 19 percent, 26 percent, and 32 percent of world output respectively. The PRC exported 19.2 million color television sets in 2002, with exports of all household electrical appliances valued at $9 billion. Chinese exports of household electrical appliances rose from 6.6 percent of the global total in 1994 to 11.4 percent in 2000, and have certainly risen further since then.

---

although it has enacted an Anti-iniquity Competition Law (1993). The latter mainly deals with the protection of intellectual property rights and has little to say about anti-monopoly issues.

Linkages and Technology Transfer

There have been few studies of the effect of FDI on input–output linkages. However, the available evidence suggests that, to date, the linkage effect of FDI on domestic industry has been relatively weak, because foreign-invested enterprises rely heavily on international markets for both inputs and output. In the 1980s and most of the 1990s, the imports of foreign-invested enterprises exceeded their exports, as noted earlier (Table 3.9). In 2001, the exports and imports of foreign-invested enterprises were $133.2

PRC: Output of Main Household Electrical Appliances,
1980–2002 (million units)

Year	Refrigerators	Washing Machines	Color Television Sets	Air Conditioners
1980	0.05	0.24	0.03	0.01
1985	1.45	8.87	4.35	0.12
1990	4.63	6.63	10.33	0.24
1995	9.19	9.48	20.58	6.83
2000	12.79	14.43	39.36	18.27
2002	15.99	15.87	51.55	31.35

Source: Shanghai Electronics Information Website.

While FDI continues to play an important role in the industry, some local manufacturers have also become major suppliers to the world market. For instance, Haier Fridge, a major Chinese fridge producer located in Qingdao, has a 40 percent share of the mini-fridge market in America. In 2002, foreign brands, mainly produced by joint ventures in PRC, held a 45 percent share of the domestic household electrical appliance market, with local producers accounting for the remainder. A few of these local producers have invested abroad in Asia, Europe, and America.

Source: National Bureau of Statistics (2002, 2003), *China Statistical Yearbook*; CEAF (2003); Shanghai Electronics Information Website, <www. 265.com>, accessed July 2003.

and $125.9 billion respectively, or 42 percent and 40 percent of their gross industrial output (when non-tradable outputs, namely power, gas, and water, are deducted from the gross output value).

Jiang (2002) has suggested that about 40 percent of foreign-funded projects utilize high technology or advanced equipment, although what constitutes 'high technology' and 'advanced equipment' is not clearly defined. It is commonly recognized that most FDI in the PRC has gone into labor-intensive industries using a low level of technology,[5] with high-tech investment lagging far behind (see, for example, OECD 2003). However, recent evidence indicates that foreign-invested enterprises are shifting their focus to more capital-intensive industries with a relatively higher technology content, for example, electronic products, automobiles, communica-

Table 3.11   PRC: Gross Industrial Output and Share of Foreign-invested Enterprises by Sector, 2001

Sector	Total (CNY100 million)	Foreign-invested (CNY100 million)	(%)
1 Coal mining & dressing	1,531.3	14.6	1.0
2 Petroleum & natural gas extraction	2,780.1	209.7	7.5
3 Ferrous metals mining & dressing	191.0	1.7	0.9
4 Non-ferrous metals mining & dressing	419.2	4.8	1.1
5 Non-metal minerals mining & dressing	373.5	15.9	4.3
6 Logging and transport of timber & bamboo	112.1	....	....
7 Food processing	4,097.9	976.7	23.8
8 Food manufacturing	1,627.7	655.7	40.3
9 Beverage manufacturing	1,824.3	545.8	29.9
10 Tobacco processing	1,694.7	11.7	0.7
11 Textile industry	5,621.6	1,230.8	21.9
12 Garments & other fiber products	2,596.3	1,194.5	46.0
13 Leather, fur, down, & related products	1,572.6	856.9	54.5
14 Timber processing, bamboo, cane, palm fiber, & straw products	741.2	213.2	28.8
15 Furniture manufacturing	434.9	198.8	45.7
16 Paper making & paper products	1,804.3	569.4	31.6
17 Printing & recorded media	726.0	243.2	33.5
18 Cultural, educational, & sporting goods	680.7	408.2	60.0
19 Petroleum processing and coking	4,587.8	418.5	9.1
20 Raw chemical materials & chemical products	6,303.7	1,372.5	21.8
21 Medical & pharmaceutical products	2,040.9	453.3	22.2
22 Chemical fiber	1,022.5	226.3	22.1
23 Rubber products	893.8	310.9	34.8
24 Plastic products	2,136.6	934.6	43.7
25 Non-metal mineral products	4,026.0	768.1	19.1
26 Smelting & pressing of ferrous metals	5,707.3	464.2	8.1
27 Smelting & pressing of non-ferrous metals	2,369.2	286.1	12.1
28 Metal products	2,852.3	1,017.5	35.7
29 Ordinary machinery	3,505.3	771.9	22.0
30 Special purpose equipment	2,352.3	417.0	17.7
31 Transport equipment	6,475.0	2,001.8	30.9
32 Electric equipment & machinery	5,481.1	1,830.6	33.4
33 Electronic & telecommunications equipment	8,990.3	6,631.3	73.8
34 Instruments, meters, cultural & office machinery	937.7	546.5	58.3
35 Production & supply of electric power, steam, & hot water	5,087.7	900.1	17.7
36 Production & supply of gas	184.9	43.5	23.5
37 Production & supply of tap water	344.5	7.3	2.1
Total	95,449.0	27,220.9	28.5

Source: National Bureau of Statistics (2002), *China Statistical Yearbook.*

*Table 3.12 PRC: Economic Efficiency of Foreign and Domestic
Enterprises in the Industrial Sector, 2001*

Type of Enterprise	Return Rate (total profit/ total assets) (%)	Capital/ Output Ratio (total assets/ value added)	Labor Productivity (value added/ employment)	Liability/ Assets Ratio
Total	3.5	4.8	5.3	58.3
State-owned	2.7	6.0	5.5	58.6
Non-state	4.7	2.9	n.a.	63.1
Foreign-funded	5.7	4.0	7.6[a]	53.6
HMT	4.3	4.0		55.2

HMT: enterprises with direct investment from Hong Kong, China; Macao; and Taipei,China.

a   Includes HMT enterprises.

Source: National Bureau of Statistics (2002), *China Statistical Yearbook.*

tions equipment, instruments and apparatus, medicines, and chemicals. This is already strengthening the PRC's industrial structure. As of the end of 2001, large MNEs had set up more than 110 independent R&D organizations in the PRC (Jiang 2002).

Some technology transfer and diffusion from foreign-invested enterprises to domestic industries has certainly taken place. In the home electrical appliances industry, for example, technology has spilled over to domestic producers even though some core technologies are still held by foreign producers. More commonly, technology is transferred through imported equipment. Studies have not found strong evidence indicating any technology spillover effect of FDI on economic growth (Wang 2000).

Domestic Sentiment toward FDI

In general, domestic sentiment is in favor of FDI, believing it has contributed to growth, export expansion, higher productivity, increased tax revenue, and an improved business environment. However, surveys have found that in the less developed central and western regions, where domestic enterprises (often SOEs) are less efficient and therefore more affected by competition from foreign-invested enterprises, public opinion is less supportive of FDI. Millions of workers have been laid off from SOEs in recent years. Most remain unemployed, especially in the center and west. Economists have raised the following concerns about the negative impact of FDI (see, for example, Zuo 2000).

Market monopoly. MNEs are much more advanced than domestic companies owing to their large size and financial power. In some sectors, this is leading to MNE monopolies, thus impeding the entry of domestic enterprises and harming consumers.

Crowding out and unemployment effects. Because foreign-invested enterprises are less labor-intensive, their entry has arguably resulted in higher unemployment and increased the potential for social instability.

Technology dependence. MNEs may employ their technological and financial advantages to the point that domestic companies become highly reliant on them for technology.

Profit outflow. Foreign investors import their inputs and use the PRC as a processing base, with little in the way of value-added earnings. A large proportion of their profits may be repatriated.

Corruption. Large foreign investors may bribe government officials and distort market outcomes.

National security. With MNEs holding a dominant position in sensitive industries such as telecommunications and the supply of core equipment and software for the information technology (IT) industry, there is a danger that the strategic interests of host and home countries may not coincide.

Of course, some of these arguments may not be persuasive. For example, foreign investors are not the only ones to bribe government officials; corruption owes much to the effectiveness of the domestic legal system and the transparency of government administration. Again, many MNEs have set up regional headquarters in the PRC, and this seems likely to result in reduced profit outflow. And monopoly concerns could be addressed by anti-trust legislation.

4   PAST AND PRESENT FDI POLICIES

The PRC opened the door to FDI in the early 1980s. Since then the country's FDI policies have changed substantially, including when the PRC entered the WTO in 2001 (OECD 2003). We now provide a summary picture of the changing FDI regime.

Entry and Restrictions

In the 1980s, in effect only the industrial and agricultural sectors were open to FDI. Preference was given to high-technology and export-oriented investment. The possibility that FDI in non-tradable service sectors might cause balance of payments deficits was an important consideration. Moreover, some service sectors, such as banking and telecommunications, were regarded as key activities that should not be under the control of foreign investors.

No upper limit was placed on the share of foreign ownership in foreign-invested enterprises; that is, 100 percent foreign ownership was allowed from the beginning, except in certain industrial branches. However, in the 1980s some incentives favored joint ventures over wholly foreign-owned enterprises. In addition, some industrial sectors were open only to joint ventures.

Until the early 1990s, the industrial sector was the major recipient of FDI. FDI was prohibited or restricted in mass media, domestic and foreign trade, insurance, posts and telecommunications, public utilities, transportation, and real estate. A negative effect of these policy restrictions was that, whereas the manufacturing sector experienced significant increases in efficiency, some major service sectors (such as banking and insurance) remained as state monopolies and continued to suffer from poor financial performance.

There were exceptions to the PRC's restrictive FDI regime. As indicated by Table 3.2, real estate absorbed 39 percent of total FDI in 1993, while wholesale and retail trade absorbed 4 percent. These were mainly investments in the SEZs (including Hainan Island) and in the economic and technological development zones.

Most of the restrictions on FDI were later recognized to be unnecessary. In particular, it was decided that the PRC's national security and foreign exchange concerns were generally not justified. Thus, the regime became a good deal more open from the mid-1990s. From 1994, foreign banks, foreign financial companies, and jointly owned banks were allowed to register in the PRC subject to certain conditions, for business related to foreign currency transactions only. In 1995, some foreign companies were allowed to list on the stock market. In the same year, a new regulation classified FDI into four categories: 'encouraged,' 'restricted,' 'prohibited,' and 'allowed.' All areas not specified in the first three categories fell into the last category.

The 172 encouraged areas included agriculture, infrastructure, energy, high technology, environmental protection, exports (including products with a high export potential), and business activities in the less developed central and western regions. The 114 restricted areas included products in 'oversupply' on the domestic market, out-of-date technologies and equipment, rare and precious resources, salt and cigarettes, and sensitive areas such as drugs, nuclear power generators, satellite components, air and water transport, domestic and foreign trade, finance, and the media. The 32 prohibited areas included certain biological and mineral resources, national security sectors (such as military weapons, radioactive mining, posts and telecommunications, broadcasting, and television stations), and activities considered harmful to human health.

In 1996, Sino–foreign joint ventures in foreign trade were permitted, with the foreign share to range from 25 to 49 percent. The list of FDI categories was further revised in 1997, expanding the number of encouraged industrial areas from 172 to 186 and reducing the number of restricted areas from 114 to 112.

In 1999, certain foreign companies were permitted to invest in wholesale and retail trade in joint ventures, with the maximum foreign share set at 49 percent. An obvious positive outcome of this has been the appearance in cities of foreign-managed supermarkets that are more efficient and better managed than the domestic ones. These have been welcomed by consumers, and have provided positive demonstrative effects for domestic retailers. In 2000, the government adopted a new policy that broadened the categories of encouraged and allowed FDI in the central and western regions.

Following the PRC's accession to the WTO in 2001, several restrictions on foreign investment were removed or relaxed. Foreign investment is now allowed in telecommunications, in which the maximum foreign share in joint ventures has been set at 49 or 50 percent depending on the business. Restrictions on the ability of foreign banks to negotiate yuan transactions will soon be removed. The insurance sector has also been opened to FDI.

Until 2001, the relaxation of restrictions on FDI in services had a limited impact on the sectoral structure of FDI. Table 3.2 indicates only small increases in the proportion of FDI in social services, banking, and insurance. However, this situation is expected to change in the near future as additional FDI flows into the banking, insurance, and telecommunications sectors. Many foreign banks have already set up offices in the PRC and are preparing to compete with domestic banks.

Preferential Taxation Policies for FDI

Tax policies have been the most important measure used to attract FDI. In the 1980s, income tax rates generally favored foreign-invested enterprises over domestic enterprises. The tax rate for Sino–foreign joint ventures was 30 percent of total profits plus 3 percent local income tax.[6] For wholly foreign-owned enterprises, there were five progressive levels of income tax ranging from 20 to 40 percent, plus the 3 percent local income tax. During this period, the tax rate for the then dominant SOE sector was 55 percent. Income tax rates for other domestic enterprises varied according to their ownership.

In addition, joint ventures and 100 percent foreign-owned enterprises received various other concessions. First, joint ventures scheduled to operate for at least ten years were exempted from income tax in the first and second years of operation and given a 50 percent deduction in the following three years—the so-called two-year exemption and three-year deduction policy. In contrast, tax concessions were given only to those wholly foreign-owned enterprises operating in 'low-profit' industries such as agriculture and forestry, and the periods during which exemptions and deductions applied were shorter. The difference in treatment between wholly and partially foreign-owned enterprises was eliminated in the 1990s.

Second, joint ventures engaged in low-profit sectors or located in underdeveloped or remote areas enjoyed a further deduction of 10–30 percent on income tax for an additional ten years following the close of the 50 percent tax deduction period.

Third, to encourage reinvestment, 40 percent of the income tax paid by foreign investors could be refunded if profits were reinvested.

Fourth, to encourage exports and technology progress, from 1987 all income tax paid by foreign investors that exported all their products or used advanced technology could be refunded if profits were reinvested.

The many different kinds of preferential policies based on ownership, industry, location, and sales orientation resulted in an unclear policy framework, a complex and non-transparent policy regime, and unequal competition among firms. Moreover, the evidence suggests that these policies were in many cases ineffective.

In 1991, the income tax rate for both joint ventures and foreign enterprises was set at 30 percent of total profit plus 3 percent local income tax (thus 33 percent in total). The two-year exemption and three-year deduction policy was extended to all enterprises with foreign investment, including wholly foreign-owned firms. The difference in the tax rate between joint ventures and wholly foreign-owned enterprises was eliminated because it was found to have had a limited effect in attracting FDI to invest in the former as opposed to the latter. One disincentive to investment in joint ventures was the difficulties often experienced by the partners due to their different business customs and cultural backgrounds. The local partner was often an SOE with a business culture that had developed under the old centrally planned system, whereas the foreign investor was accustomed to operating in a market environment. Moreover, MNEs were more at ease in transferring technology to their own affiliates than to joint ventures.

In 1994, the tax rate for domestic enterprises was changed to the unified rate of 33 percent, although the two-year exemption and three-year deduction policy was still not extended to these enterprises. Indirect taxes, which also generally favored foreign-invested over domestic enterprises, were addressed through the introduction of a unified value-added tax and business tax to apply to both domestic and foreign enterprises. The value-added tax rate is 17 percent for most industrial sectors.

Regional Differentials in the Policy Regime

The four SEZs set up in the early 1980s were located in Shenzhen, Zhuhai, and Shantou in Guangdong province and Xiamen in Fujian province. Hainan Island was declared an SEZ in 1988. The policies that apply in SEZs are similar to those of export-processing zones in other countries. Imported inputs for producing exports, and for consumption within the SEZs, are exempt from customs duty. Many of the policy restrictions on investment and trade that applied in the 1980s were relaxed in the SEZs.

In addition, for foreign-invested enterprises located in an SEZ, the income tax rate is 15 percent of total profit, or half the rate in other areas. The two-year exemption and three-year deduction policy applies equally to enterprises in and outside the SEZs, but foreign-invested enterprises in the zones also receive a five-year holiday on business tax.

The government had three main reasons for offering special privileges in the SEZs during the initial stage of economic reform. First, it was far easier for it to start by creating a better business climate for FDI in small areas than in the country as a whole when the economy had been isolated from the world for such a long period. Second, the government wanted to open the door gradually, without imposing a violent shock on the economy. And third, it wanted to learn from these pilot areas before introducing nationwide reforms. In general this strategy was successful. FDI increased gradually throughout the 1980s, although the magnitudes were small compared with later inflows (Table 3.1), and the economy grew by close to 10 percent annually during the decade. Nevertheless, there were some undesirable side effects. One was the large-scale smuggling that occurred via the SEZs. Also, regional differences in the policy regime led to delays in opening up inland areas, leading to increased regional disparities.

In 1984, because of the initial success of the SEZs, the government decided to extend the preferential arrangements to 14 cities in the coastal region. They were allowed to establish their own economic and technological development zones offering policies similar to those of the SEZs. In

Table 3.13   PRC: Allocation of FDI among Key Provinces, 1985–2001
(%)

Region	1985	1990	1995	2001
Total FDI ($ billion)	0.9	3.2	37.3	46.4
Eastern provinces	92.2	93.3	86.6	87.0
Guangdong	58.3	45.2	27.3	25.7
Fujian	13.3	9.0	10.8	8.5
Jiangsu	1.3	4.4	12.8	14.9
Shanghai	7.1	5.5	8.7	9.3
Total	80.1	64.0	59.7	58.4
Central provinces	4.0	3.5	8.8	8.8
Hubei	0.0	0.9	1.7	2.6
Hunan	2.0	0.3	1.3	1.7
Henan	0.6	0.3	1.3	1.0
Total	2.6	1.6	4.3	5.3
Western provinces	3.9	3.2	4.6	4.1
Sichuan	0.0	0.3	0.8	1.3
Shaanxi	1.6	1.3	0.9	0.8
Guangxi	1.4	0.9	1.8	0.8
Total	3.0	2.6	3.4	2.8

Source: National Bureau of Statistics (1999), *Comprehensive Statistical Data and Materials on 50 Years of New China*, (2002), *China Statistical Yearbook*.

1988, the preferential policy regime was broadened further with the listing of 144 cities and counties as coastal economic open zones.

These and other reforms resulted in dramatic growth in FDI in the early 1990s (Table 3.1). Arguably, improvements in the general business environment rather than specific policy inducements were the key to this rapid growth. As indicated by Table 3.13, the allocation of FDI across the coastal provinces has been uneven. In 2001, 87 percent of FDI in the PRC went to the 11 east coast provinces, but 58 percent was concentrated in only four provinces: Guangdong, Jiangsu, Shanghai and Fujian. The allocation of

FDI across the central and western provinces has also been uneven. In 2001, the eight central provinces received 8.8 percent of total FDI, nearly half of which was in Hubei and Hunan provinces. In the same year, the 12 western provinces received 4.1 percent of total FDI, 2.8 percent of which was concentrated in the provinces of Sichuan, Shaanxi, and Gaungxi.

This provides clear evidence that the uneven allocation of FDI is a result not only of regional preferential policies, but also of the business environment, including infrastructure, supply of public utilities, geographic location, and, possibly more importantly, the institutional climate. These continue to favor the east coast and undermine the capability of inland regions to attract FDI, despite the government campaign to promote the west by providing preferential treatment for FDI in underdeveloped areas. A common problem for all investors is that the approval of an investment project may require tens or even hundreds of stamps from various government departments at different tiers of government. This process may take months, especially in some central and western regions. To make matters worse, rent-seeking behavior and corruption among government officials are commonplace.

Industry-specific Tax Deductions

Since the early 1980s, tax incentives have been offered to FDI that is accompanied by the introduction of advanced technology, although the definition of what constitutes 'new' and 'advanced' technology has been unclear and arbitrary. In 1988, income tax on foreign-invested enterprises located in the coastal economic open zones was lowered from 30 percent to 24 percent for a wide range of industrial sectors, including machinery, electronics, metallurgy, chemicals, building materials, light industry, textiles, medical apparatus, medicines, agriculture, forestry, animal husbandry, and architecture. Other sectors were subsequently added to this list. And, as noted earlier, some foreign firms have enjoyed tax rates as low as 15 percent as well as other tax concessions since the 1980s.

But how effective were these preferential policies? Various surveys point to their limited success in introducing advanced technology in the 1980s and early 1990s, when most FDI entered labor-intensive, low-technology industries. Moreover, concessions were often awarded in a non-transparent manner, and were insufficient to compensate firms for the major costs associated with the introduction and employment of advanced technology. The technology content of FDI has increased since the mid-1990s, partly because of more clearly specified preferential policies, but mainly as a result of improvements in the overall business environment.

Land Use

Preferential land access has been an important measure by which local governments have attracted FDI. Legally, urban land is owned by the state. Before 1990, foreign-invested enterprises could obtain access to land through the Chinese partner of a joint venture, through a free land transfer, or by renting land. In the latter case, a schedule of fees applied. Foreign-invested enterprises are exempt from land tax and, since 1990, have been able to obtain long-term, renewable leases over land of up to 70 years.

In recent years there has been intense competition among local governments to attract FDI, with the amount received being treated as a performance indicator for local government officials. Because tax policy is regulated by the central government, and local governments therefore have limited resources to offer tax concessions, they commonly compete by offering cheap or even free land (Zhou 2001).[7] The cost of such subsidies is borne by the government. While some regions have succeeded in attracting FDI by this means, the result can be inefficient land use and unfair competition between domestic and foreign enterprises.

Regulations and Government Administration

In the lead-up to and following its accession to the WTO, the PRC tried hard to improve the business environment. Many restrictive regulations at the central, provincial, and lower levels of government that were inconsistent with WTO principles were either abolished or revised, and others are under review. Administrative procedures for FDI approval and firm registration have been simplified. Many local governments have established 'one-stop' shops to enable investors to complete the required paperwork in a shorter period of time. And government policies have become more transparent.

Yet there are still many problems in the 'software' component of the investment climate (OECD 2003). When foreign investors face regulatory obstacles, they may be able to resolve their problems by complaining directly to the county head or mayor. Domestic investors, especially small private ones, are generally not so fortunate. Not only are there preferential policies for FDI, but policy transparency and simplified administrative procedures are not equally available to domestic investors. Firm surveys have found that domestic private enterprises, especially the smaller ones, still suffer from excessive regulation, government intervention, and rent-seeking behavior by public servants (see, for example, IFC 2000; Huang 2001). A recent survey by the author of small and medium-sized enterprises in the southwestern provinces found only limited improvement in these areas.

5   INTERNATIONAL AGREEMENTS

WTO Accession and the Government Position

In the wake of the PRC's accession to the WTO, there have been several important changes in the government position on FDI.[8]

TRIMs. The government has complied with the requirement of the TRIMs Agreement that the PRC abolish its foreign exchange balancing and export–import balancing requirements, domestic content rules, and export performance obligations for foreign-invested enterprises (see below). Laws and regulations in violation of the agreement have been amended or repealed, or are no longer enforced.

Non-discrimination. The Chinese government has agreed to accord equal treatment to all foreign-invested enterprises operating in the PRC. This includes equality in all aspects of production, purchasing, and marketing, and in the supply and pricing of goods and services provided by the government. All dual pricing arrangements are being removed, and differences in the treatment of goods sold domestically and exported will be eliminated.

Foreign exchange and payments. The PRC has accepted the principle that no restrictions should be placed on payments and fund transfers related to international trade. The PRC does not now employ foreign exchange earnings as a basis for restricting access to foreign exchange for international trade.

SOEs. The PRC has confirmed that the purchasing and marketing decisions of SOEs will be based only on commercial considerations of price, quality, tradability, and usability. It guarantees non-discriminatory treatment in the purchase and sale of foreign products and services.

Pricing. The PRC does not practice price control on goods and services other than those listed in Appendix IV of the WTO agreement (including salt, grain, water, education, and transport), and will make every effort to reduce and eliminate such controls.

Transparency. To create a more transparent environment for FDI, the PRC is committed to the principle of consistency and public openness of central and regional laws and regulations. The government intends to proceed cautiously with approvals in the financial services sector, but will not impose any quantitative restrictions.

The government has also implemented new policies at the sectoral level. These include opening several important service industries to FDI and further removing restrictions in the manufacturing sector. The most important policy changes relating to FDI are as follows (WTO 2001b; He 2002).

Banking. The PRC has agreed to remove a number of restrictions on foreign banks. Several foreign banks are already allowed to conduct foreign exchange transactions with local individuals. With the removal of some of the geographic restrictions on foreign banks in 2001, they may also now conduct local currency transactions in a number of cities. All geographic restrictions on foreign banks are to be removed by 2006.

Insurance. FDI is allowed in life and non-life insurance companies up to a limit of 50 percent following the WTO accession, and 100 percent within five years.

Telecommunications. Joint ventures are permitted in the telecommunications sector. Within two years of accession, geographic restrictions on FDI were to be removed and the limit on the foreign share of joint ventures was to be increased to 50 percent.

Professional services. FDI in professional services such as accountancy, construction project management, urban design, medical services, and real estate is allowed in the form of joint ventures. Foreign investors may hold a controlling share.

Cultural services. Cultural services such as films, cinemas, and television are open to joint ventures with FDI for the first time. The foreign partner may hold up to a 49 percent share.

Wholesale and retail trade. With the exception of grain and petroleum products, wholesale and retail trade is open to FDI, and foreign control is allowed.

Education, tourism, and the environment. Foreign control is allowed in education, tourism, and environmental protection.

Transport. Sino–foreign joint ventures are allowed in sea, river, road, and rail transport, and in oil extraction and associated services.

Bilateral International Agreements

The PRC has signed agreements with 98 countries on the protection of investments. These bilateral investment protection agreements commonly cover tangible and intangible property, a company's shares or other interests, claims for payment, intellectual and industrial property rights, and any rights conferred by law or under a contract permitted by law. The Chinese government has promised to ensure fair and equitable treatment for investments on a basis no less favorable than that accorded to investments by the nationals of any third country. It has also promised not to expropriate or nationalize any investments, unless the measures taken are in the public interest, non-discriminatory, and in accordance with the law of the contracting party. In such circumstances, reasonable compensation must be paid based on the market value of the investment, with the funds freely transferable internationally. The government has agreed to permit foreign investors to transfer all the earnings related to their investments abroad without undue delay. In the event of a dispute, either party may initiate proceedings before a competent judicial or administrative body in the PRC. To protect foreign investors, disputes may also be referred to an international center for dispute settlement.

In addition to its bilateral investment protection agreements, the PRC has concluded bilateral agreements with 70 countries on the avoidance of double taxation and the prevention of tax evasion. These adopt the format provided by the United Nations and the OECD.

TRIMs

As noted, the PRC has long used TRIMs to restrict the imports and increase the exports of foreign-invested enterprises. These restrictions were eliminated in 2000–01 at the time of the PRC's accession to the WTO. There are no remaining compulsory foreign exchange balancing, local content, or export performance requirements. In any case, the PRC's experience indicates that these TRIMs were not particularly helpful in 'balancing' national exports and imports, or in strengthening linkages between foreign and domestic enterprises. Despite the requirements, foreign-invested firms recorded a trade deficit until 1997, mainly owing to the higher profits they could earn in the domestic market under import protection. The recent opening of the trade regime played a more important role than the removal of TRIMs in shifting the trade balance of foreign-invested enterprises into surplus.

It is not clear whether local content requirements helped domestic industry, but they probably lowered product quality. For example, despite the high tariffs on imported cars and the 40 percent local content requirement on auto manufacturing, the domestic auto industry, which mainly consisted of Sino–foreign joint ventures, remained inefficient and lacking in competitiveness until the late 1990s. The production costs of domestic auto makers were higher than those of the major international producers, and the quality of their products poorer. The recent reduction of protection and elimination of TRIMs may revitalize the auto industry.

The PRC's experience also indicates that a gradual approach to reform is a better strategy for developing and transition countries than a 'big bang' approach. It is hard to imagine that the Chinese government could have removed TRIMs in the 1980s without first reforming the country's high trade barriers, because this would have led to rent-seeking behavior and an increased trade deficit.

There may be a case for local content requirements in some developing countries, in certain periods and in some industrial sectors. Even if they do result in lower quality or higher production costs, they may also provide opportunities for local component producers to learn technical, quality control, and even management skills from their foreign partners. After a transitional period, the 'infants' are likely to grow up and become more competitive.

The PRC still uses preferential policies to encourage exports and promote import substitution. Exporters, whether foreign or domestic, can continue to claim refunds of tariffs and value-added tax on imported materials, components, and equipment used in the production of exports. And, as already mentioned, income tax incentives continue to be given to foreign-invested enterprises that export most or all of their products.

6 SUMMARY AND POLICY RECOMMENDATIONS

Summary

The PRC experienced rapid growth of FDI in the 1980s and 1990s, with annual inflows exceeding $50 billion in 2002. This trend is likely to continue. FDI is playing an important role in the PRC's economic development in terms of capital formation, output growth, technological progress, and exports. Foreign-invested enterprises provide an example for domestic enterprises to emulate, resulting in improved management, quality control, and marketing. Nevertheless, concerns remain about the possible negative effects of FDI, including problems of monopoly creation, unemployment, technology dependence, profit outflow, and national security.

A very important attraction for foreign investors is the PRC's abundant, cheap, well-trained, and disciplined workforce. The openness pursued over the past two decades is another key factor in attracting inflows of FDI, as are policy incentives such as tax holidays, cheap land, and tariff exemptions. But in particular it is the institutional environment—including policy transparency, legal protection, non-discriminatory competition policies, and clean and efficient public administration—that is crucial in attracting FDI. The better performance of the PRC's eastern regions compared with the central and western regions is explained by institutional factors as well as by the locational, infrastructural, and policy advantages enjoyed by the east.

The various preferential policies based on ownership, location, industry, and activity have generated incentives, but have also resulted in unclear or non-transparent policies and unequal competition among firms. Although the tax regime has been equalized, many preferential policies for FDI still exist.

With the PRC's accession to the WTO, the services sector is finally being opened up. This, together with the elimination of TRIMs and the removal of trade barriers, is likely to underpin rapid growth in FDI for the foreseeable future.

Policy Recommendations

The PRC has already removed many policy restrictions on FDI. At the same time, foreign-invested enterprises continue to enjoy preferential treatment in several areas. This has led to significant differences in profitability between domestic and foreign firms, some unfair competition, outflows of local capital, and rent-seeking behavior. It has also weakened the development of the domestic private sector. Therefore, the tax differential between domestic and foreign investors should gradually be eliminated. Any temporary preference (for example, to encourage technology transfer or to reduce regional disparities) should be granted according to the location, activity, and sector specified by the policy target, rather than the ownership of the business.

While the business environment is improving, further reform is important and urgent. This means improving the legal framework and practice, simplifying government administration, and promoting market competition and policy transparency. These reforms will be especially important for less developed regions, and would arguably be more effective than preferential FDI policies.

For example, in Guizhou province, a new system has been put in place to monitor and evaluate the investment environment in different localities. Information is collected from investors on the efficiency and transparency of different levels of local government and collated for the various government departments. This information is being used to create an index to evaluate both the investment environment in different cities and counties and the performance of government departments. This is generating pressure on, and competition among, these local governments and departments. Such a system could be a useful and effective means of improving the regional investment environment if it were adopted nationally.

The increasing regional disparity between the rapidly developing eastern provinces and the less developed central and western provinces is a continuing problem to which rapid growth in FDI has indirectly contributed. There is a strong case for the gradual unification of taxation across regions, while retaining some special treatment to encourage development in the less developed areas.

NOTES

I am indebted to Emma Xiaoqin Fan for permission to draw heavily on her recent working paper (Fan 2003) in the preparation of some sections of this chapter.

1 Speech by Zeng Peiyan, director of the State Development Planning Commission, as quoted in *China Economic Times*, 31 March 2000.

2 This estimate is approximate since it has been argued that the PPP measure of GNP may be overstated.

3 These municipalities are Beijing, Tianjin, and Shanghai. In this chapter, all municipalities and autonomous regions that are administratively at the provincial level are called provinces.

4 The data on gross industrial output for 1994 and 1997 employ a slightly different definition from that used for 2001 (see Table 3.7, note a). As the difference is small, the results are still comparable.

5 Even though the labor intensity of foreign-invested enterprises is initially lower than that of domestic enterprises.

6 In addition, there were specific rates in several regions and zones, as noted later.

7 For example, whereas developed land in south Jiangsu typically sold for CNY90,000 per mu (1/15 hectare)—CNY135 per square meter—in 2001, foreign investors paid only CNY20,000–50,000 per mu.

8 This section draws on Economic Research Centre, State Committee of Economics and Trade (2002).

4

India

Nagesh Kumar

1 INTRODUCTION

The attempt of developed countries to extend the international trade rules to investment using multilateral trade negotiations has attracted much debate in recent times. Developing countries believe that investment is more a development than a trade issue, and hence that the World Trade Organization (WTO) is not an appropriate forum for negotiating investment-related matters. Developing countries need the policy space and flexibility to formulate rules and regulations on foreign direct investment (FDI) that are in tune with their development policy objectives. They feel that this would be undermined by a multilateral framework on investment. The decision as to whether or not to launch negotiations on an investment framework was to be made at the failed Fifth Ministerial Conference of the WTO held in Cancun in September 2003.

Against this backdrop, this chapter discusses the experience of India in mobilizing and employing FDI inflows (and outflows) in the development process. It also briefly summarizes India's approach to international investment agreements in general, and to the attempt of developed countries to establish an investment framework modeled on the General Agreement on Tariffs and Trade (GATT) in particular. The structure of the chapter is as follows. Section 2 summarizes the evolution of India's policy on FDI in the context of the economic reforms dating from 1991. It also describes the country's approach to international investment agreements, including bilateral investment treaties, the Trade Related Investment Measures (TRIMs) Agreement, and the proposed multilateral framework on investment. Section 3 outlines broad trends and patterns in FDI inflows and outflows for India, especially since the policy reforms of the 1990s. Section 4 examines the impact of FDI in terms of various development parameters, highlighting in particular the role of government policy. Section 5 summarizes some policy lessons with regard to FDI, and details some considerations to guide discussions on the proposed multilateral framework on investment.

2 GOVERNMENT POLICY ON FDI, INTERNATIONAL TRADE, AND INVESTMENT AGREEMENTS

A Brief Review of FDI Policy, 1948–2003

The policy of the Indian government on FDI has evolved over time, in line with the requirements of the development process during different phases.[1] Soon after independence, India embarked on a strategy of import-substituting industrialization to improve the local capability in heavy industry, especially the machinery manufacturing sector. As the domestic base of 'created' assets (technology, skills, entrepreneurship) was limited, the government became increasingly receptive to FDI as a means of bridging this gap. FDI was sought on mutually advantageous terms, though majority local ownership was preferred.

The government adopted a more restrictive attitude to FDI in the late 1960s as the local machinery manufacturing base strengthened, local entrepreneurship developed, and outflows of remittances (such as dividends, profits, royalties, and technical fees to service FDI and technology imports) grew sharply. Restrictions were placed on proposals that would not be accompanied by any transfer of technology, and on projects seeking more than 40 percent foreign ownership. From 1973 onward the activities of foreign companies (along with those of large local industrial houses) were further restricted to a select group of core or high-priority industries. The Foreign Exchange Regulation Act of 1973 required all foreign companies to register as Indian companies with up to 40 percent foreign equity. Exceptions to this general limit were made for companies operating in high-priority or high-technology sectors, tea plantations, and firms producing predominantly for export.

In the 1980s the government's attitude to FDI began to soften slightly. As part of a strategy to modernize industry, it liberalized imports of capital goods and technology, thereby exposing domestic industry to foreign competition and assigning a larger role to MNEs in the promotion of manufactured exports. The policy changes adopted during this decade included the liberalization of industrial licensing (approval) rules, the creation of a host of incentives, and exemptions from foreign equity restrictions under the Foreign Exchange Regulation Act for firms that exported all of their output. A degree of flexibility was introduced into the foreign ownership provisions, with exceptions to the general ceiling of 40 percent being given in some cases.

After four decades of restrictive FDI policies, in the 1990s India embarked on a broader process of reform designed to increase its integration with the global economy. The liberalization of trade policy, capital flows, and the financial sector was announced on 24 July 1991 as part of a package of reforms known as the New Industrial Policy.[2] The liberalization of inward and outward FDI flows in the 1990s was part of a broader process of reform that included a major overhaul of trade policy. The import-licensing system was dismantled. All non-tariff barriers in the tradables sector were phased out by April 2001, two years ahead of schedule. By 1999, peak tariff rates had been reduced to a maximum of 35 percent (from a previous level of up to 355 percent), and the average tariff rate had fallen from 87 percent to 20 percent. India has bound over 3,298 (70 percent) of its 4,701 tariff lines (at the six-digit level of the Harmonized System classification), 99 percent of these at rates of 40 percent or less. The applied rates are much lower than the bound rates for most products.[3]

The partial convertibility of the rupee on the trade account was announced in the 1992/93 budget. This was broadened to full convertibility on the current account in August 1994. India is cautiously moving toward full capital account convertibility, with the accumulation of foreign exchange reserves of $80 billion in 2003. The Capital Issues Control Act was repealed and the Securities and Exchange Board of India (SEBI) set up as a watchdog for regulating the functioning of the capital market in 1992. SEBI has focused on regulatory reform of the capital market as well as market modernization. Online trading has been introduced. Companies are now allowed to buy back their own shares subject to SEBI regulations.

In September 1992, the government announced guidelines for investments by foreign institutions in the Indian capital market. They were now allowed to invest in all types of securities traded on the primary and secondary markets, with full repatriation of benefits, no restrictions on the volume of trading, and no lock-in period for capital. In January 1993 the government introduced a package of financial sector reforms that permitted the establishment of new private sector banks, including foreign joint ventures. The government has also established a policy regime to rate the creditworthiness of private non-banking finance companies and agencies.

The New Industrial Policy of 1991 and subsequent policy amendments have changed the industrial policy regime beyond recognition, especially as it applies to FDI. The industrial approvals system has been abolished for all industries, except where required on strategic or environmental grounds. In order to bring greater transparency to the FDI approval process and expedite clearance, an automatic clearance system was put in place for proposals that fulfilled certain conditions, such as a foreign ownership level ranging from 50 to 100 percent depending on the sector. Other proposals would still be subject to the usual approval procedures. A new package for enterprises in export-processing zones and for 100 percent export-oriented units was announced, including automatic clearance for proposals that met the specified parameters for capital goods imports, location, and value added. The Foreign Exchange Regulation Act of 1973 was amended in 1993 to lift the restrictions it had placed on foreign companies.

New sectors—mining; banking; insurance; telecommunications; the construction and management of ports, harbors, roads, and highways; airlines; and defense equipment—have been thrown open to privately owned, including foreign-owned, companies. However, the extent of foreign ownership is limited in some service sectors.[4] Foreign ownership of up to 100 percent is permitted in most manufacturing subsectors—even on an automatic basis in some cases—except defense equipment, where it is limited to 26 percent, and items reserved for production by small-scale industries, where it is limited to 24 percent. However, FDI above 24 percent is permitted in the latter case subject to a mandatory export obligation of 50 percent of annual production. Large domestic enterprises making products reserved for manufacture by small-scale industries are subject to the same export obligation. The dividend balancing condition and related export obligation placed on foreign investors, which had applied to 22 consumer goods industries, was withdrawn in 2000.

Policy governing outward FDI was also liberalized during the 1990s. The Guidelines for Indian Joint Ventures and Wholly Owned Subsidiaries Abroad, as amended in October 1992, May 1999, and July 2002, provided for the automatic approval of outward FDI proposals up to a limit that has been expanded progressively from $2 million in 1992 to $100 million in July 2002.

To sum up, the liberalization of FDI policy has included pruning the negative list of industries requiring approval to the minimum required for security or environmental reasons; expanding the list of industries open to FDI; gradually expanding the list of industries subject to automatic FDI approval subject to certain conditions being fulfilled; removing the general restriction of 40 percent on foreign ownership and increasing the level of permissible foreign equity to up to 100 percent for most industries; providing national treatment for companies with more than 40 percent foreign ownership; and gradually dismantling performance requirements. The lat-

ter have included phased manufacturing programs (local content requirements), dividend balancing requirements (where companies manufacturing
consumer goods were required to balance the dividends repatriated abroad
against export earnings so that there was no adverse impact on the balance
of payments), and foreign exchange neutrality requirements (where enterprises were required to earn sufficient foreign exchange to cover their
imports and dividend remittances). Export obligations are now limited to
companies entering industries reserved for small-scale units, those entering the export-processing zones, and those availing themselves of incentives offered to export-oriented units (Kumar and Singh 2002).

India's Approach to International Trade and Investment Agreements

India has been a member of the GATT/WTO since its inception and has a
deep faith in multilateralism. As observed earlier, India's trade policy has
been influenced considerably by its WTO commitments: quantitative
restrictions on imports were removed two years ahead of schedule and
most tariff lines have been bound. Trade policy has also been influenced
by the regional and bilateral trade agreements established over the past
decades. As a founding member of the Bangkok Agreement, India has
exchanged trade preferences with several member countries. Signed in
1975, it is one of the oldest preferential trade agreements in Asia. India is
also a member of the South Asian Association for Regional Cooperation
(SAARC) Preferential Trade Agreement signed in 1995, of which four
rounds of tariff negotiations have so far been concluded. Since 1991, India
has consciously tried to strengthen its economic links with Southeast and
East Asian countries as part of the Look East Policy. As a dialogue partner
of ASEAN, India took part in a summit-level meeting in 2003 at which it
signed a framework regional trade and investment agreement, to be implemented over ten years. India is also party to several bilateral free trade
agreements, either already signed or under negotiation.

India has increasingly resorted to bilateral investment promotion and
protection agreements over the past decade in order to promote investment
inflows. As of January 2002, it had signed such agreements with as many
as 45 countries. Agreements of this type aim to promote inflows by providing protection for foreign investment. Since the objective is protection, a
broad definition of investment is adopted. Foreign investment that has
been admitted in accordance with the host country's policies, laws, and
regulations is guaranteed fair and equitable treatment, legal security, and
access to a framework for dispute resolution.

Under the TRIMs Agreement, India was required to phase out trade-
distorting performance requirements such as local content and foreign

exchange neutrality regulations by 1 January 2000. As observed above, India has already phased out its manufacturing programs in the auto industry, which were in effect local content requirements. Dividend balancing and foreign exchange neutrality requirements have also been phased out. Therefore, India's FDI policy regime is now fully consistent with the provisions of the agreement.

The TRIMs Agreement provided for a review of its implementation within five years. In October 2002, in a joint submission to the WTO Committee on TRIMs, India and Brazil argued that the agreement should be amended to incorporate specific provisions that would give developing countries greater policy flexibility. In particular, they proposed that developing countries should be allowed to use investment measures or performance requirements to promote domestic manufacturing capabilities in high value-added sectors, to stimulate transfer and the indigenous development of technology, to promote domestic competition, and to correct restrictive business practices.

Like other developing countries, India resisted a negotiating mandate on investment at the Singapore Ministerial Conference of the WTO in 1996. It also resisted the attempt of some developed countries to obtain a negotiating mandate on trade and investment at the Doha Ministerial Conference in 2001, arguing that the study process initiated after the Singapore conference should be concluded before a decision on a multilateral framework on investment was taken. As a compromise, the decision was postponed to the Fifth Ministerial Conference at Cancun to be held in 2003, subject to an explicit consensus.

In the meantime, in its submissions to the WTO Working Group on Trade and Investment, India took the position that the WTO should focus solely on trade issues. It argued that, as the free movement of capital carries the risk of economic crisis, developing countries should not subscribe to any policy that would limit their policy flexibility to deal with such a crisis. Bilateral treaties are a better instrument than multilateral treaties in this respect, because they give developing countries the policy flexibility to channel foreign investment in accordance with their domestic interests and priorities. India continued to argue that performance requirements should remain available to ensure that foreign investment contributes to the achievement of development goals, and that balance of payments exceptions are important. In a submission to the working group in October 2002, the government said that

> if disciplines aimed at freer movement of capital are being considered then in the interests of development needs of developing countries, the need to simultaneously build in disciplines facilitating movement of labor, particularly professionals and skilled personnel, could be a compelling argument.

India has sought to balance the interests of home and host countries by incorporating legally binding obligations on investors and home country governments along with those proposed for host country governments. These obligations would cover such areas as restrictive business practices, technology transfer, balance of payments, ownership and control, consumer protection, environmental protection, disclosure, and accounting. Because of its deep concern about the impact of a multilateral investment framework on developing countries, India—as a member of a group representing about 70 developing countries—firmly opposed a negotiating mandate on investment at the failed Cancun Ministerial Conference held in September 2003.

3   LIBERALIZATION AND TRENDS IN FDI INFLOWS AND OUTFLOWS

Inflows

The reforms of the 1990s have affected the magnitude and pattern of FDI inflows (Figure 4.1). Inflows increased markedly during the decade to peak at $3.6 billion in 1997. A period of stagnation followed, with flows of around $2.5 billion annually. In 2001 FDI inflows rose again to $3.4 billion.

In an analysis of flows through to 1997, Kumar (1998a) found that liberalization explained only part of the increase in FDI inflows; the sharp expansion in the global scale of FDI outflows during the decade was another factor. The decline in inflows since 1997, despite continued liberalization, also suggests that policy liberalization alone does not provide an adequate explanation for FDI inflows. In inter-country analysis of FDI inflows, the macroeconomic fundamentals of the host economy emerge as the most powerful explanatory variable. This becomes clear from Figure 4.2, which plots FDI inflows against fluctuations in annual rates of growth of industrial output for the 1990s. There is a good correspondence between industrial growth in one year and FDI inflows in the following year. That is, industrial growth appears to serve as a signal to foreign investors about economic prospects. Thus policy liberalization may be a necessary but not sufficient condition for FDI inflows.

The sectoral composition of FDI in India has undergone significant change (Table 4.1). Three trends are evident. First, the share of plantations, mining, and petroleum has fallen markedly, from around 9 percent in 1980 to only 2 percent in 1997 (the latest year for which data are available). Second, the share of the manufacturing sector, which declined only marginally between 1980 and 1990 (from 87 to 85 percent), fell significantly following liberalization to 48 percent in 1997. During the 1990s services clearly

Figure 4.1   India: Inward Flows of FDI, 1991–2001 ($ billion)

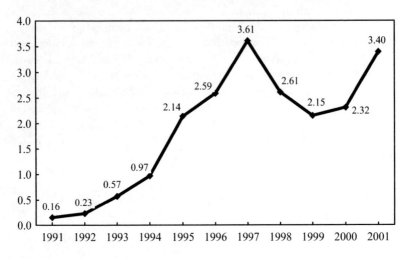

Source: UNCTAD (various years), *World Investment Report*.

Figure 4.2   India: Industrial Growth Rates and FDI Inflows, 1991–2001

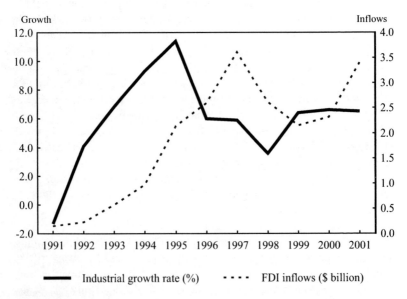

Source: Kumar (2003b).

Table 4.1 *India: Industrial Distribution of Inward FDI Stock, 1980–97*[a]

Industry Group	1980		1990		1997	
	(Rs million)	(%)	(Rs million)	(%)	(Rs million)	(%)
Plantations	385	4.1	2,560	9.5	4,310	1.2
Mining	78	0.8	80	0.3	410	0.1
Petroleum	368	3.9	30	0.1	3,330	0.9
Manufacturing	8,116	87.0	22,980	85.0	175,230	48.0
Food & beverages	391	4.2	1,620	6.0	24,310	6.7
Textile products	320	3.4	920	3.4	10,390	2.9
Transport equipment	515	5.5	2,820	10.4	24,570	6.7
Machinery & machine tools	710	7.6	3,540	13.1	19,310	5.3
Metal & metal products	1,187	12.7	1,410	5.2	7,600	2.1
Electrical goods & machinery	975	10.5	2,950	10.9	29,400	8.1
Chemicals & chemical products	3,018	32.3	7,690	28.4	32,530	8.9
Other manufacturing	1,000	10.7	2,030	7.5	27,120	7.4
Services	320	3.4	890	3.3	54,650	15.0
Other	65	0.7	510	1.9	127,170	34.8
Total	9,332	100.0	27,050	100.0	365,100	100.0

a Figures are for the end of March.
Source: Reserve Bank of India (April 1985, August 1993, October 2000), *RBI Bulletin*.

emerged as a significant FDI recipient. Power generation among other infrastructure sectors (included in the 'other' category) also attracted substantial FDI during the decade.

The FDI stock was more evenly distributed across manufacturing subsectors in 1997, in contrast to the very heavy concentration in relatively technology-intensive sectors such as machinery, chemicals, electrical goods, and transport equipment up to 1990. Infrastructure, which commanded nearly half of total approved investment in 1997, had not previously been open to FDI inflows; hence the sharp increase in FDI in this sector could be attributed to liberalization.

*Table 4.2   India: Structure of Approved FDI in the Services Sector,
Cumulative, 1991–2000*

Sector	Approvals		
	(no.)	(Rs billion)	(%)
Telecommunications	698	458.8	61.0
Air & sea transport	169	27.8	3.7
Ports	16	12.5	1.7
Consultancy services	591	20.7	2.8
Financial & banking services	382	106.2	14.1
Hospitals & diagnostic centers	88	6.5	0.9
Hotels & tourism	449	46.5	6.2
Trading	470	21.5	2.9
Other services	377	31.3	4.2
Total	3,240	731.8	100.0

Source: Ministry of Industry (2000), *SIA Newsletter*.

A more detailed picture of services is provided in Table 4.2.[5] About 61 percent of approved FDI in this sector during 1991–2000 went to the telecommunications subsector. Financial services gained about 14 percent of approvals. Other important branches were hotels and tourism (6 percent) and air and sea transport (4 percent).

Europe was the major source of FDI flows to India until 1990. However, its relative importance has declined steadily in the post-liberalization period: the share of FDI stock of the major European source countries (the United Kingdom, Germany, France, Switzerland, Sweden, Italy, and the Netherlands) fell from 69 percent in 1980 to 66 percent in 1990, then to just 31 percent in 1997. The decline in the relative importance of Europe as a source of FDI was made more prominent by the diversification of sources of FDI during the decade.

The United States emerged as the most important source of FDI during this period. Its share of the FDI stock stood at nearly 19 percent in 1992, then appears to decline to 13.8 percent in 1997 (Table 4.3). However, this latter figure is deceptive, as a large proportion of US FDI has been routed through Mauritius since the signing of a double taxation avoidance agree-

Table 4.3   India: Sources of FDI Stock, 1992–97

Country	1992		1997	
	(Rs billion)	(%)	(Rs billion)	(%)
Mauritius	–	–	65.5	17.9
United States	7.1	18.6	50.2	13.8
United Kingdom	15.5	40.2	43.8	12.0
Germany	4.8	12.4	20.8	5.7
Japan	2.1	5.6	19.6	5.4
Netherlands	1.6	4.3	11.8	3.2
Switzerland	1.9	4.8	7.9	2.2
Singapore	–	–	4.5	1.2
Canada	1.1	2.8	3.7	1.0
Other	4.4	11.4	137.5	37.7
Total	38.4	100.0	365.1	100.0

Source: Reserve Bank of India (October 2002), *RBI Bulletin*.

ment that enables investors to take advantage of the latter's status as a tax haven. Mauritius thus appears as the largest source of investment in India, with Rs 65.5 billion (18 percent) of the total in 1997.

An important feature of FDI flows to India during the 1990s has been the emergence of mergers and acquisitions (M&As) as a major source of FDI. In 1997–99, for instance, 39 percent of inflows took the form of M&As by foreign companies of existing Indian enterprises, whereas in the pre-reform period FDI entry was invariably greenfield in nature (Table 4.4). This trend may have implications for the impact of FDI if, as is sometimes argued, greenfield FDI adds to the stock of productive capital and generates more favorable spillovers of knowledge and competitive effects.

For instance, Kumar (2000b) has pointed out that, because the majority of M&As have been acquisitions by the Indian affiliates of MNEs, with their internal fund accruals and resources raised from domestic banks and long-term financial institutions, such FDI is unlikely to have added much to India's stock of domestic capital. Moreover, he argues that the per unit inflow of knowledge (such as new production, marketing, and organizational know-how) is much higher for greenfield than for M&A-led FDI.

Table 4.4   India: Share of M&As by Foreign Firms in FDI Inflows, 1997–99

Year	FDI Inflows ($ million)	M&As	
		($ million)	(%)
1997	3,200	1,300	40.6
1998	2,900	1,000	34.5
1999 (Jan–March)	1,400	500	35.7
Total	7,500	2,800	39.4

Source: Kumar (2000b).

Greenfield FDI also promotes competition, by increasing the number of market players, whereas M&As often lead to increased concentration by reducing the number of enterprises that are active in the market. Mergers among MNE affiliates in India following mergers among their parents are also likely to increase concentration. Finally, Kumar points to the possible adverse effect of M&A-led FDI on employment if an MNE introduces labor-saving managerial techniques following the merger or acquisition.

Although its FDI inflows increased considerably during the 1990s, India's share of global flows to developing countries would appear to be very small, especially compared with those received by the People's Republic of China (PRC). The reported inflows of about $3.4 billion in 2001 represented a mere 1.7 percent of total inflows attracted by developing countries. In contrast, the PRC received an estimated $46.8 billion, representing nearly 23 percent of total developing country FDI inflows.

However, as first noted by Pfeffermann (2002), the FDI data for India and the PRC are not directly comparable, for several reasons. First, the Indian data do not conform with the definition for FDI given in the widely used IMF *Balance of Payments Manual*. The principal difference is that the Indian figures count only fresh inflows of equity as FDI, and do not include reinvested earnings by foreign affiliates or inter-corporate debt flows. Second, the statistics on inflows to the PRC are believed to overestimate actual FDI inflows, in view of the round-tripping of Chinese capital to take advantage of the more favorable tax treatment of FDI routed through Hong Kong, China; Macao; and Taipei,China.

Table 4.5 compares FDI inflows to India and the PRC in 2000. The pro-

Table 4.5 Comparison of FDI Inflows to the PRC and India, 2000

	FDI to India		FDI to PRC	
	Reported	Adjusted	Reported	Adjusted
Net inflows (balance of payments basis, current $ billion)	2.3	8.0	39.0	20.0
Net inflows (% of GDP)	0.5	1.7	3.6	2.0

Source: Reported FDI: Srivastava (2003), based on World Bank (2002), *World Development Indicators*; adjusted FDI: Pfeffermann (2002), based on International Finance Corporation (2002), *World Business Environment Survey: Economic Prospects for Developing Countries*, Washington DC, March.

portion of net inflows as a share of GDP reported for the PRC is 3.6 percent, compared with 0.5 percent for India. However, when the Indian figures are revised upward to take reinvested earnings and inter-corporate debt into account, and the Chinese figures are moderated to take round-tripping into account, the gap in the FDI/GDP ratios narrows to 1.7 for India and 2.0 for the PRC.

The Indian government has taken steps to revise its definition of inward as well as outward FDI. In June 2003, it announced that the adoption of international norms would lead to a near doubling of the figures for inflows, from $2,342 million to $4,029 million in 2000/01 and from $3,906 million to $6,131 million in 2001/02.

Even after taking measurement problems into account, India's inflows of FDI are low compared with those of other economies in the region. Studies of the determinants of inflows have found that a country's attractiveness to FDI is affected by structural factors such as market size (income levels and population), the extent of urbanization, the quality of infrastructure, geographical and cultural proximity to major sources of capital, and policy factors such as tax rates, investment incentives, and performance requirements (Kumar 2000a, 2002). While India's large population base is an advantage, the country's low income levels, low levels of urbanization, and relatively poor-quality infrastructure are disadvantages. Moreover, India is at an obvious disadvantage compared to the PRC in terms of geographical and cultural proximity to major sources of capital such as Japan and the Republic of Korea.

Outflows

Although a few Indian enterprises were investing abroad in the mid-1960s, outward investment activity became significant only in the 1990s. The cumulative value of outward FDI flows from India has been estimated at $4,263 million for the ten years to March 2001, compared with a figure of $223 million at the end of March 1990.

The nature of outward investment has undergone considerable change in the post-liberalization period, in terms not only of the magnitude but also the geographical focus and sectoral composition of flows. As is clear from Table 4.6, the focus of outward investment has shifted away from developing countries in the pre-liberalization period to developed countries during the 1990s. The sectoral composition of FDI has shifted from manufacturing to services, as is evident from Table 4.7.

It has been argued that much of the outward investment activity before 1991 was of the 'market-seeking' type where Indian enterprises established a presence in developing countries on the basis of their intermediate technologies in relatively low-technology industries such as light engineering. In the 1990s, however, most outward investment has been undertaken to support the exporting activities of Indian firms through a local presence (Kumar 1998b). It is clearly concentrated in the countries that are key export destinations (the European Union and North America), and in sectors in which India has particular strengths (such as IT software services).

4   IMPACT OF FDI INFLOWS ON THE ECONOMY

Given their intangible assets, MNE affiliates can contribute to a host country's development by generating output, employment, exports, balanced regional development, and technological capability. A lack of data on the economic activities of enterprises operating in India classified by nationality of ownership constrains a fuller appreciation of the role played by FDI in the country's economic development. Nevertheless, in this section the findings of existing studies as well as observations based on comparisons of samples of enterprises are used to gain some idea of the economic effects of FDI.

Several attempts have been made to estimate the share of output or sales of foreign affiliates in the industrial sector. Kumar (1990a) estimated that in 1980–81, foreign-controlled firms accounted for nearly 25 percent of sales by large private sector enterprises in industry as a whole, and 31 percent in manufacturing. Athreye and Kapur (1999), following the same methodology, found that foreign firms accounted for about 26 percent of sales in manufacturing in 1990–91. The declining trend in the share of

Table 4.6 *India: Geographical Distribution of Outward FDI Flows,*
1975–2001

Region	1975–90				1991 – March 2001			
	(no.)	(%)	($ million)	(%)	(no.)	(%)	($ million)	(%)
Southeast & East Asia	67	29.3	80.8	36.3	379	14.8	399.4	9.4
South Asia	30	13.1	20.9	9.4	197	7.7	157.4	3.7
Africa	29	12.7	37.8	17.0	254	9.9	513.9	12.1
West Asia	19	8.3	21.5	9.7	185	7.2	376.5	8.8
Central Asia	4	1.8	23.2	10.4	49	1.9	51.0	1.2
Latin America & the Caribbean	2	0.9	0.6	0.3	36	1.4	180.6	4.2
All developing countries	165	72.1	191.5	86.1	1,176	45.9	1,719.8	40.4
Western Europe	40	17.5	17.3	7.8	565	22.1	1450.2	34.0
North America	23	10.0	13.5	6.1	749	29.2	1,029.5	24.2
All developed countries	64	28.0	30.9	13.9	1,386	54.1	2,542.6	59.7
Total	229	100.0	222.5	100.0	2,562	100.0	4,262.5	100.0

Source: RIS database.

foreign-controlled enterprises between 1980 and 1990 can be explained by
the restrictive FDI policies of the period. Similar estimates for the post-
liberalization period are not available.

To examine post-liberalization trends in the share of foreign enterprises
in manufacturing, we have computed the shares of foreign firms in total
value added and total sales for a sample of large private sector companies
quoted on the Indian stock exchange and included in the database of the
Research and Information System for the Non-Aligned and Other Developing Countries (RIS) (Figure 4.3). The data were compiled by extracting
information about relevant companies from the (online) Prowess Database
of the Centre for Monitoring Indian Economy (CMIE); they are useful
only for observing trends, as the sample may not be representative. The
shares of foreign enterprises in both value added and sales reveal a gradu-

Table 4.7   India: Composition of Outward FDI Flows by Sector,
1975–2001

Sector	1975–90			
	(no.)	(% of total)	($ million)	(% of total)
Extractive industries	3	1.3	4.0	1.8
Manufacturing				
Oilseeds, food products, & processing	10	4.4	9.1	4.1
Textiles & garments	12	5.2	9.0	4.1
Wood, pulp, & paper	3	1.3	11.5	5.2
Leather, shoes, & carpets	4	1.7	20.6	9.2
Chemicals, petrochemicals, & paints	18	7.8	7.8	3.5
Drugs & pharmaceuticals	8	3.5	4.7	2.1
Rubber, plastic, & tires	6	2.6	2.3	1.0
Cement, glass, & building materials	2	0.9	4.2	1.9
Iron & steel	10	4.4	16.2	7.3
Electrical & electronic equipment	6	2.6	2.1	1.0
Automobiles & auto parts	6	2.6	3.2	1.4
Gems & jewelry	1	0.4	0.0	0.0
Electronic goods & consumer durables	2	0.9	0.3	0.1
Beverages & tobacco	7	3.0	3.2	1.5
Engineering goods & metallurgical items	18	7.8	8.5	3.8
Fertilizer, pesticides, & seeds	5	2.2	39.9	18.0
Miscellaneous	10	4.4	2.6	1.2
All manufacturing	128	55.7	145.2	65.3
Services				
IT, communications & software	6	2.6	5.6	2.5
Hotels, restaurants, tourism	24	10.4	25.0	11.2
Civil contracting & engineering services	6	2.6	1.8	0.8
Consultancy	7	3.0	0.4	0.2
Trading & marketing	27	11.7	12.5	5.6
Media, broadcasting, & publishing	2	0.9	0.0	0.0
Financial services & leasing	17	7.4	26.3	11.8
Transport services	3	1.3	0.6	0.3
Other professional services	7	3.0	1.1	0.5
All services	99	43.0	73.2	32.9
Total	230	100.0	222.5	100.0

Table 4.7 (continued)

Sector	(no.)	(% of total)	($ million)	(% of total)
		1991–March 2001		
Extractive industries	7	0.3	61.1	1.4
Manufacturing				
Oilseeds, food products, & processing	91	3.6	69.3	1.6
Textiles & garments	158	6.2	112.6	2.6
Wood, pulp, & paper	11	0.4	17.7	0.4
Leather, shoes, & carpets	63	2.5	28.4	0.7
Chemicals, petrochemicals, & paints	94	3.7	92.1	2.2
Drugs & pharmaceuticals	163	6.4	270.2	6.3
Rubber, plastic, & tires	45	1.8	85.8	2.0
Cement, glass, & building materials	58	2.3	79.8	1.9
Iron & steel	47	1.8	50.7	1.2
Electrical & electronic equipment	63	2.5	90.9	2.1
Automobiles & auto parts	26	1.0	24.0	0.6
Gems & jewelry	56	2.2	17.9	0.4
Electronic goods & consumer durables	29	1.1	20.8	0.5
Beverages & tobacco	37	1.4	142.1	3.3
Engineering goods & metallurgical items	84	3.3	66.2	1.6
Fertilizer, pesticides, & seeds	27	1.1	327.0	7.7
Miscellaneous	184	7.2	183.6	4.3
All manufacturing	1,236	48.3	1,678.9	39.4
Services				
IT, communications & software	761	29.7	1,354.5	31.8
Hotels, restaurants, tourism	53	2.1	112.5	2.6
Civil contracting & engineering services	44	1.7	16.6	0.4
Consultancy	31	1.2	8.1	0.2
Trading & marketing	146	5.7	96.5	2.3
Media, broadcasting, & publishing	61	2.4	739.6	17.4
Financial services & leasing	96	3.8	95.5	2.2
Transport services	44	1.7	48.3	1.1
Other professional services	82	3.2	50.7	1.2
All services	1,318	51.5	2,522.2	59.2
Total	2,561	100.0	4,262.2	100.0

Source: Author's computation based on RIS database.

*Figure 4.3   India: Share of Foreign Firms in Total Sales and Value
Added of the Manufacturing Sector, 1990–2001 (%)*

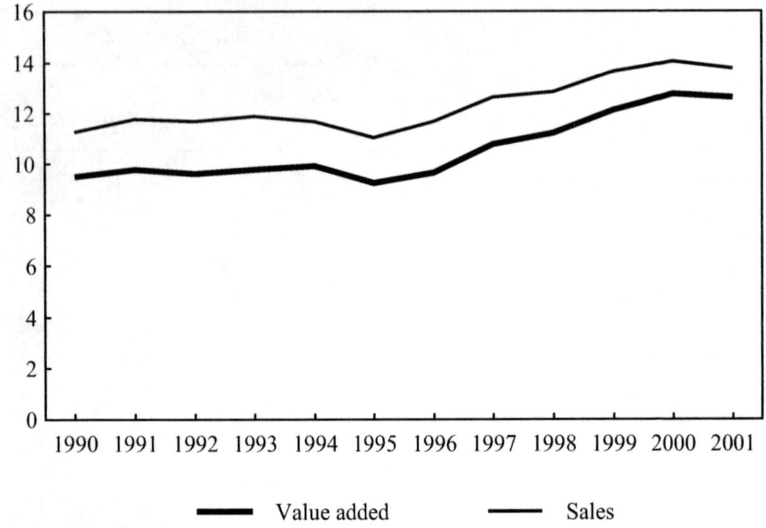

Source: RIS database; Centre for Monitoring Indian Economy.

ally increasing trend during the 1990s, particularly toward the end of the decade, suggesting that liberalization led to a rise in the foreign presence in Indian industry.

The literature has debated the relationship between FDI and growth given the two-way causality that is possible between these two variables. Elsewhere, we have made an empirical examination of the direction of causation between FDI and growth for a sample of 107 countries between 1980 and 1999 (Kumar and Pradhan 2002). This study found a Granger-neutral relationship for India, as the direction of causation was not pronounced.

It has also been shown that some FDI projects may actually 'crowd out' domestic investments from product or capital markets through the market power of their brand names and other resources, and may thus be immiserizing (Fry 1992; Agosin and Mayer 2000). Therefore, it is important to examine the effects of FDI on domestic investment in order to evaluate its impact on growth and welfare. Our study did not find a statistically significant effect of FDI on domestic investment in the case of India (Kumar and Pradhan 2002). It appears that some FDI has crowded in domestic investment and some has crowded it out, with no predominant pattern emerging.

Empirical studies on the nature of the relationship between FDI and domestic investment suggest that the effects of FDI depend on host government policies. Governments have employed selective policies and imposed performance requirements to deepen the commitment of MNEs to the host economy. The Indian government has imposed phased manufacturing programs in the auto industry to promote vertical inter-firm linkages and encourage the development of a domestic auto components industry (and thus crowd in domestic investment). A case study of the auto industry in India shows that these policies (in combination with other performance requirements such as foreign exchange neutrality) were successful in building an internationally competitive, vertically integrated auto sector (Box 1). In this regard, the Indian experience in this industry is similar to that of Thailand, Brazil, and Mexico as documented by Moran (1998).

A number of developing countries have used FDI to exploit MNE resources such as globally recognized brand names, best practice technology, and access to global production networks as a means of expanding their manufactured exports. Early studies analyzing the export performance of Indian enterprises in the pre-liberalization phase reported no statistically significant difference between foreign and local firms (Kumar 1990a; Kumar and Siddharthan 1994). Sharma (2000), using a simultaneous equation model, examined the factors explaining export growth in India over the period 1970–98. He found FDI to have had no significant effect on export performance, although its coefficient had a positive sign. Obviously, in a highly protected setting, both local and foreign firms found it more profitable to concentrate on the domestic market.

For the post-reform period, Agarwal (2001) found weak support for the hypothesis that foreign firms had performed better than local firms, although the estimates were not robust across the various technology groupings, and the foreign ownership dummy turned out to be significant at the 10 percent level in the case of medium to high-technology industries only. Controlling for several firm-specific factors, fiscal incentives, and industry characteristics, Kumar and Pradhan (2003) recently analyzed the export orientation of over 4,000 Indian manufacturing enterprises during 1988–2001. They found the Indian affiliates of MNEs to be performing better overall than their local counterparts in terms of export orientation, although with some variation across industries. It would therefore seem that reforms have prompted foreign MNEs to begin to explore the potential of India as an export platform for production, on a modest scale at least.

A study analyzing the determinants of export orientation among MNE affiliates across 74 countries in seven industry branches at three points in time has shown trade liberalization to be an important factor in explaining

---

BOX 1 PERFORMANCE REQUIREMENTS AND THE
DEVELOPMENT OF A COMPETITIVE MANUFACTURING
CAPABILITY IN THE AUTO INDUSTRY

In the early 1980s, the Indian government entered into a joint venture agreement with Suzuki Motor Corporation of Japan to set up a manufacturing facility in Gurgaon near Delhi to produce small passenger cars. The Maruti–Suzuki joint venture, in which both the government of India and Suzuki were equal partners, involved a phased manufacturing program that required local content to increase to 75 percent within five years.

In order to comply with this requirement, Suzuki initiated a vendor development program under which Indian manufacturers of auto components would be assisted to produce components to its design and specifications. It also set up joint ventures that involved technology transfer to a number of these suppliers. In addition, a number of Suzuki's original equipment manufacturer (OEM) suppliers in Japan were prompted to license technology to, or set up joint ventures with, Indian component manufacturers in order to be able to supply to the Maruti venture.

Over time a cluster of auto component manufacturers sprang up around the Maruti plant in Gurgaon. The proportion of local value added increased steadily, even though exports of cars and components remained relatively insignificant. In the 1990s, as part of the measures taken to deal with the foreign exchange crisis of 1991, the government imposed foreign exchange neutrality conditions and dividend balancing requirements on consumer goods industries, including passenger car manufacturers. These obligations pushed Maruti to obtain a product mandate from its Japanese partner to export compact cars to Europe.

The extensive network of auto component manufacturers created by the phased manufacturing programs imposed on Maruti laid the foundations for an internationally competitive auto components industry. Subsequent entrants to the industry in the 1990s not only found a good base for their indigenization efforts, but were easily able to meet their export obligations. This is evident from case studies of Ford, General Motors (GM), and Daimler-Chrysler (Kumar and Singh 2002). Export obligations prompted these

---

the export orientation of foreign affiliates. Furthermore, in host countries with large domestic markets, export obligations have been found to be an effective way of promoting export orientation among foreign affiliates (Kumar 1998c).

India has imposed export obligations only on MNE affiliates entering sectors reserved for small-scale industries. However, as discussed earlier,

companies to consider buying some components from India for export to their operations in other countries.

Ford was initially hesitant to import components from India, fearing poor quality. But following a visit in 2000 to suppliers in India, it launched a joint program with the Automotive Component Manufacturers Association to source components in the country. Ford has set up two dedicated ventures in India to handle the sourcing of components, and is exporting increasing numbers of completely knocked down (CKD) kits of the Ford Ikon to Mexico and South Africa. Thus, while export obligations prompted Ford to discover an important source of quality components, from the host country point of view they have helped local auto component manufacturers develop linkages with one of the world's largest automobile manufacturers.

General Motors India Ltd (GMI) also claims to have helped its parent company source components from India, including a major order from GM Europe that helped the Indian company meet its export obligation. GMI is pursuing partnerships with domestic suppliers as part of a strategy to supply components to GM overseas units worldwide. To fulfill its export obligation, Daimler-Chrysler India has established over 20 joint ventures for the manufacture and export of auto components to Daimler-Chrysler plants in Germany.

The performance requirements imposed until recently on the auto industry in the form of export obligations and phased manufacturing programs were successful in meeting the government's policy objective of developing a local manufacturing base and increasing exports. Most manufacturers have achieved high levels of local content. For instance, as of March 2002, Ford had achieved a level of 74 percent; GM had achieved levels of 70 and 64 percent for the Astra and Corsa models respectively; Mercedes and Toyota had close to 70 percent; and Honda had reached a level of around 78 percent. Export obligations helped overcome the information asymmetry with respect to India's capabilities as a supplier of high-quality components, and led to a fuller realization of the export potential of the local industry through the establishment of vendor–OEM linkages between Indian component producers and global auto majors.

Source: Kumar (2003a).

until 2000 indirect export obligations in the form of a dividend balancing requirement were imposed on enterprises primarily producing consumer goods. Sometimes a condition of foreign exchange neutrality was also imposed. The evidence suggests that such regulations have prompted foreign enterprises to expand their exports. In the case of Pepsi Foods, for example, indirect export obligations prompted the company to develop a

---

BOX 2 EXPORT OBLIGATIONS AND TECHNOLOGY DIFFUSION: PEPSI FOODS AND CONTRACT FARMING IN PUNJAB

Pepsi Foods Ltd was established in the late 1980s as a joint venture between PepsiCo Inc. of the United States, Voltas (a member of India's Tata Group), and Punjab Agro Industries Corporation (PAIC). It subsequently became a wholly owned subsidiary of PepsiCo. Pepsi Foods manufactures soft drinks and snack foods and runs several fast food chains. It has an annual turnover of Rs 40 billion and exports of around Rs 4 billion.

Apart from the joint venture requirement, the company had a dividend balancing requirement placed on it as a producer of consumer goods. Pepsi was also required to make an export commitment of Rs 2 billion over ten years and meet other export obligations attached to capital goods imports. Because its main business was the bottling of soft drinks for the domestic market from imported concentrate, meeting the export obligations was a formidable challenge. However, the company turned this into an opportunity through a pioneering approach to contract farming.

Pepsi proposed to meet the export obligation by exporting tomato puree and other processed foods. In 1989, when Pepsi set up its tomato and food-processing plants in Punjab, it faced problems of raw material supply. At the time local farmers grew only table varieties of tomatoes available in small quantities over a 25–28-day period. Pepsi needed large quantities of processing tomatoes for its huge plant, over a minimum 55-day time frame. To resolve these problems, Pepsi turned to contract farming of improved varieties that would fit its quality requirements. The company assembled an

---

model of contract farming that led not only to increased export earnings for the country as a whole, but also to the transfer of new technology to the farmers of Punjab (Box 2).

Foreign firms in the manufacturing sector appear to be spending more than their local counterparts on R&D, although the gap between their R&D intensities has tended to narrow (Table 4.8). A recent study found that, after controlling for extraneous factors, MNE affiliates had a lower R&D intensity than local firms, presumably because of their access to parent company laboratories. The study also observed differences in the nature or motivation of the R&D activities of foreign and local firms. Local firms seem to be directing their efforts toward the absorption of imported knowledge and providing a backup for their outward expansion. MNE affiliates, on the other hand, have tended to focus more on customizing parent company technology for the local market (Kumar and Agarwal 2000).

R&D team consisting of scientists from Pepsi headquarters and Punjab Agricultural University to develop the technology to improve productivity and decrease production costs. Under the direction of PAIC, a Pepsi team educated farmers about the benefits of contract farming, gave them seed or seedlings along with written instructions in the local language, and loaned them equipment. The team inspected crops regularly and offered an advisory service on crop management. Pepsi agreed to procure a certain quantum of the farmers' output at a pre-arranged price.

This led to an increase in the tomato yield from 16 to 52 tons per hectare between 1989 and 1999, helping the company to obtain an assured supply of raw materials. Contract farming by Pepsi Foods—starting with R&D inputs and followed by regular fine-tuning through experimental trials—has now been extended to other crops (potatoes, basmati rice, chili peppers, peanuts, garlic, groundnut) and has spread to several other states. The technology is also being used by non-Pepsi growers, who buy from the company's nursery and use its other extension services without any buy-back arrangement. This implies benefits to a broad-based spectrum of users.

Thus the export commitment imposed on Pepsi has forged a mutually rewarding partnership among farmers, Punjab Agricultural University, PAIC, and Pepsi. It has also fueled a horticultural revolution in Punjab, with significant improvements in yields and technology. Although the export obligation was phased out in 1996, the company's exports are booming and Pepsi has become engaged in exporting other agricultural commodities such as rice.

Source: Kumar and Singh (2002).

The evidence on the contribution of FDI to local technological capability and diffusion is mixed. A study of 305 Indian private sector firms by Fikkert (1994) found that firms having foreign equity participation had an insignificant direct effect on R&D and tended to depend significantly more on purchases of foreign technology. In view of these findings, he concluded that 'India's closed technology policies with respect to foreign direct investment and technology licensing had the desired effect of promoting indigenous R&D, the usual measure of technological self-reliance.'

The evidence suggests that knowledge spillovers from foreign to domestic enterprises are positive when the technology gap between foreign and local enterprises is not wide. When it is wide, the entry of foreign enterprises may adversely affect the productivity of domestic enterprises, that is, there could be negative spillovers.

Some governments have imposed technology transfer requirements on

Table 4.8   India: R&D Intensity of Manufacturing Firms by Ownership, 1990–2001 (%)

Year	All Firms	Foreign Firms	Domestic Firms
1990	0.053	0.114	0.046
1991	0.082	0.086	0.082
1992	0.148	0.213	0.139
1993	0.201	0.365	0.178
1994	0.217	0.378	0.196
1995	0.272	0.377	0.259
1996	0.312	0.376	0.303
1997	0.413	0.447	0.409
1998	0.341	0.559	0.309
1999	0.352	0.477	0.332
2000	0.311	0.386	0.298
2001	0.343	0.320	0.346

Source: RIS database.

foreign enterprises, but these do not appear to have been very successful (UNCTAD 2003b). Other types of performance requirements, such as local content or domestic equity requirements, may be more effective, as illustrated by the case studies presented in Boxes 1 and 2. Similarly, the case studies presented in Box 3 suggest that domestic equity requirements may facilitate the quick absorption of knowledge brought in by foreign enterprises. Some have expressed the view that domestic equity requirements may adversely affect the extent or quality of technology transfer (Moran 2001). However, it has been shown that MNEs do not necessarily transfer key technologies even to their wholly owned subsidiaries abroad, because of the risk of dissipation or diffusion through mobility of employees. The content and quality of technology transfer may be superior in the case of a sole venture, but from the host country point of view, joint ventures offer more desirable externalities in terms of local learning and diffusion of the knowledge transferred (UNCTAD 2003b: Ch. 3).

A recent trend in FDI is for the globalization of R&D, including knowledge-based activities such as the development of customized software and business process outsourcing. With India's reputation as a competitive

BOX 3 LOCAL LEARNING IN JOINT VENTURES:
A CASE STUDY OF THE TWO-WHEELER INDUSTRY

Joint ventures between MNEs and local enterprises in developing countries can be instrumental in the learning and technology absorption of
local partners, and hence can contribute significantly to the building of a
local technological capability. In both of the following two cases, the
local partner was able to design and manufacture independently developed new products soon after the joint venture had ended, suggesting
that considerable learning and absorption of knowledge had taken place.

TVS Motor Company Ltd (formerly Ind-Suzuki Motorcycles Ltd)
started in 1982 as a joint venture between the Sundaram Clayton Group
and Suzuki Motor Corporation to produce motorcycles. Over two
decades, the local partner in the joint venture absorbed technology and
knowledge brought in by Suzuki and built a capability to design and
develop new models of two-wheelers. In 2000/01 the company produced
139,000 scooters, 358,000 motorcycles, and 369,645 mopeds. In 2001
Sundaram Clayton and Suzuki disengaged in an amicable manner and
the company was renamed TVS Motor Company, run entirely by the
Sundaram Group. Within 24 months TVS had launched its own indige-
nously developed 110cc four-stroke motorcycle, the TVS-Victor, developed entirely in-house by the company's R&D team of 300 people, with
an investment of Rs 250 million. The new product has been described as
a 'stunning success' by the business press and has captured a 16 percent
share of the market. Building on this success, the company decided to
double its R&D spending to 3.6 percent of sales in 2002. It plans to
launch several new products and expand its presence in several Asian
markets.

Kinetic Motor Co. Ltd. (formerly Kinetic Honda Ltd) started in 1984
as a joint venture between the Kinetic Group and Honda Motor of Japan
to manufacture scooters in India. In 1998 the partnership was down-
graded to a technical collaboration, with Honda pulling out from the
joint venture to launch its own wholly owned subsidiary. On the basis of
the learning and knowledge it had absorbed from Honda, Kinetic has
launched several new products, including the Kinetic Nova and the
Kinetic Zing. The Nova is a 115cc four-stroke scooter with a ground-
breaking design and best-in-class performance. It competes directly with
the erstwhile joint venture partners' Honda Activa, a 102cc auto-geared
scooter. The Zing is a 65cc 'scooterette' custom-designed for college
goers. Like TVS, Kinetic is planning a major export push.

Source: Kumar and Singh (2002).

BOX 4 FDI AND THE SOFTWARE INDUSTRY

The remarkable expansion of India's IT software and services industry over the 1990s represents a spectacular achievement for the Indian economy. The industry has grown at an incredible rate of 50 percent per annum over the past few years, is highly export-oriented, and has established India as an exporter of knowledge-intensive services to the world. It has brought a number of spillover benefits such as employment creation and the development of a new pool of entrepreneurship. India's software exports rose from $100 million in 1989/90 to nearly $10 billion in 2002.

This export success has been driven primarily by local enterprise, resources, and talent. The role played by MNEs in software development has been quite limited. Although all the major software companies have established development bases in India, their overall share in total software exports is just 19 percent. MNEs do not figure among the top seven software companies in India, whether ranked on the basis of overall sales or exports. Of the 572 member companies of India's National Association of Software and Service Companies (Nasscom), 79 are reported as being foreign subsidiaries. Some of these—Mastech, CBSI, IMR, Syntel—are actually the subsidiaries of companies owned by Indians resident in the United States, not American MNEs *per se*. Others were Indian, but have subsequently been taken over by foreign companies; Hinditron, for example, was taken over by TAIB Bank E.C., Bahrain, and IIS Infotech was taken over by FI Group of the United Kingdom. The foreign subsidiaries include software development centers set up by mainstream developers and subsidiaries set up specifically to develop software applications for use by parent MNEs. The latter include the subsidiaries of financial services companies (Citicorp, Deutsche Bank, Churchill Insurance, Phoenix Life Mutual) and telecommunications companies (Hughes, Motorola). In addition to the 79 foreign subsidiaries identifed by Nasscom, MNEs have set up 16 joint ventures with local enterprises (British Aerospace with Hindustan Aeronautics, Bell South with Telecommunication Corporation of India, British Telecom with the Mahindra Group). Thus in all, 95 companies have controlling foreign participation. The bulk of MNE entries has taken place since 1994, by which time India's potential as a base for software development was already well established.

Source: Kumar (2001a).

---

location for software development established by the mid-1990s, MNEs began setting up dedicated software development centers in the country. These multinationals included world-class software and IT manufacturers such as Oracle, Microsoft, and Hewlett-Packard, telecommunications

Table 4.9 *India: Average Sales of Manufacturing Firms by Ownership,*
1990–2001 (Rs 10 million)

Year	All Firms	Foreign Firms	Domestic Firms
1990	97.3	119.8	95.1
1991	90.3	125.1	87.0
1992	95.9	141.3	92.0
1993	92.8	153.4	88.1
1994	88.2	172.7	82.8
1995	94.3	191.6	88.7
1996	113.3	247.3	105.7
1997	119.8	269.0	110.9
1998	130.0	285.8	120.3
1999	134.9	304.3	124.0
2000	149.3	348.9	136.5
2001	187.5	395.6	172.9

Source: RIS database.

giants such as British Telecom, and major banks and financial companies such as GE Capital and Citicorp (Box 4).

With the establishment of these centers, India began to emerge as an R&D hub for MNEs. In addition to the longstanding use of R&D to adapt products for the local market, a recent trend has been for MNEs to locate their global or regional R&D laboratories in India in order to benefit from the country's abundant, talented, but cheap human resources, and from R&D spillovers from its publicly funded centers of excellence (Kumar 2001b). Over 100 MNEs have reportedly set up R&D laboratories in India over the past five years. The economic impact of this trend has yet to be analyzed, however.

Foreign affiliates are generally larger than their local counterparts, as measured by their average sales (Table 4.9). This is to do with their strategy of employing non-price rivalry such as product differentiation, which entails substantial economies of scale (Kumar 1991). Early studies of profitability in Indian industry suggested that foreign affiliates enjoyed higher profit margins on sales than their local counterparts in most branches of Indian manufacturing (Kumar 1990a). Further analysis of the determinants of profit margins indicated that the higher profitability of foreign firms was due to their preference for the less price-elastic upper end of the market with its scope for product differentiation, leaving the more price-competitive lower end of the market to local firms. Kumar (1990b) did not find any evidence that they were more profitable because they were more efficient. The trend for foreign firms to continue to have higher profit margins in the post-liberalization period is corroborated by the data for a sample of larger firms presented in Table 4.10. It appears that foreign affiliates have enjoyed not only consistently higher profit margins, but also more stable profit margins, than local firms.

In the pre-reform period, the industrial licensing system was used to ensure balanced regional development, with some industrial approvals subject to firms locating in industrially backward or poorer states. With the liberalization of the approvals system, spatial distribution is now essentially left to enterprises. Thus the bulk of FDI inflows continues to be concentrated in the relatively well-developed states (Table 4.11). Six relatively well-developed states have accounted for 55 percent of cumulative approvals of FDI since 1991, while the eight least developed states have received negligible inflows. The inter-state distribution of FDI therefore mimics the pattern observed in the inter-country context. Inter-country studies of patterns of FDI find per capita income levels, levels of urbanization, and quality of infrastructure to have a very strong influence on the location of FDI. That pattern holds good for the Indian states as well. Another factor that has probably affected the inter-state pattern of FDI location is the attitude of state governments: some have been much more aggressive than others in promoting their states as investment locations.

FDI cannot be expected to foster balanced regional development. Government policy, especially to promote infrastructure development, is required to develop poorer regions, by crowding in both domestic and foreign investment.

5 POLICY LESSONS

Increasing the Quantity of FDI Inflows

Market size is a key determinant of both the quantity and quality of FDI inflows. Regional economic integration can be used as a strategy to overcome the market size constraints faced by developing countries, especially smaller ones. The importance of geographical and cultural proximity as a determinant of FDI inflows provides an additional rationale for regional cooperation. The formation of blocs such as the European Union and the North American Free Trade Area (NAFTA) has facilitated inflows of FDI

Table 4.10 *India: Ratio of Profits to Sales of Manufacturing Firms by Ownership, 1990–2001 (%)*

Year	All Firms	Foreign Firms	Domestic Firms
1990	3.8	6.2	3.5
1991	3.7	7.0	3.3
1992	3.6	6.5	3.2
1993	3.4	6.0	3.1
1994	5.1	7.4	4.8
1995	6.7	9.0	6.4
1996	6.3	8.0	6.0
1997	4.6	7.8	4.1
1998	3.2	8.0	2.5
1999	1.6	7.6	0.7
2000	1.6	8.0	0.6
2001	1.4	7.9	0.3

Source: RIS database.

Table 4.11 *India: Cumulative FDI Approvals by State, 1991–2000 (%)*

State	Share of Cumulative FDI Approvals	
	No.	Value
Six richest states[a]	50.5	55.0
Eight least developed states[b]	0.8	0.9
Remaining 15 states	19.6	17.0
State not indicated	30.1	27.9

a Maharasthra, Delhi, Karnataka, Tamil Nadu, Andhra Pradesh, and Gujarat.
b Arunachal Pradesh, Assam, Jammu and Kashmir, Lakhsadweep, Manipur, Mizoram, Nagaland, and Tripura.

Source: *Economic Times*, 28 May 2001.

to member states, as is evident from their rising share of global inflows. Asian countries should also consider forming a broader Asian Economic Community to consolidate the various subregional groupings that already exist: ASEAN, ASEAN+3 (PRC, Japan, Korea), ASEAN+1 (India), and SAARC.

Harnessing the Benefits of FDI for Development

Although quality is at least as crucial as magnitude, the quality of FDI inflows varies widely. One way to maximize the contribution of FDI to host country development is to improve the chances of FDI crowding in domestic investment, and minimize the chance of FDI crowding it out. Empirical studies of FDI and domestic investment across countries suggest that the relationship has been dominated by crowding in among Asian developing countries and by crowding out among Latin American countries. This difference can be attributed to the policies pursued by Asian developing countries, such as selective policies to target the more desirable types of FDI, and the imposition of performance requirements. A number of countries in the region, such as Malaysia, Korea, the PRC, and Thailand, have tried to channel FDI into export-oriented manufacturing through selective policies and export performance requirements imposed at the time of entry. Export-oriented FDI minimizes crowding out and generates favorable spillovers for domestic investment by creating demand for intermediate goods.

Another policy that could help to maximize the contribution of inflows is to direct FDI toward newer areas where a local capability does not exist and there is thus minimal chance of conflict with domestic investment. Some governments have employed pioneer industry programs to attract FDI in industries that have the potential to generate more favorable externalities for domestic investment. Similarly, because MNE entry through the acquisition of domestic enterprises is likely to generate less favorable externalities for domestic investment than greenfield investment, some governments have discouraged acquisitions by foreign enterprises (Agosin and Mayer 2000).

Another sphere where governmental intervention may be required to maximize the gains from globalization is in the diffusion of knowledge brought in by foreign enterprises. Vertical inter-firm linkages with domestic enterprises are an important channel of knowledge diffusion. Many governments have imposed local content requirements on MNEs to intensify the generation of local linkages and technology transfer. Host governments could also consider proactive measures to encourage both foreign and local firms to deepen their local content, a tool employed successfully by a number of countries (Battat, Frank, and Shen 1996). Another way to accomplish greater diffusion of knowledge would be to create subnational or subregional clusters of inter-related activities in which informal and social contacts among employees, in addition to the traditional buyer–seller links, could be expected to facilitate spillovers. UNCTAD (2001) also highlights the policy measures employed by different governments to promote linkages.

Finally, it is of critical importance that host governments preserve the policy flexibility to pursue selective policies and impose performance requirements on FDI if necessary. Some performance requirements are already outlawed under the TRIMs Agreement. Developed countries are attempting to expand the scope of the present international trade rules and further limit the policy flexibility of developing countries by creating a multilateral framework on investment. Developing countries therefore need to coordinate their approach to the ongoing WTO discussions to ensure that their policy flexibility is not curtailed.

Trade and Investment Policy in the WTO Framework

A basic question before entering into any negotiations on a multilateral framework on investment is to determine the necessity, costs, and benefits of such a framework for developing country members. Against this back-drop, we now summarize the main issues from a developing country perspective.[6]

- There is a conceptual basis for trade liberalization on the principle of comparative advantage and gains from trade. On the other hand, FDI flows emerge because of differences in countries' levels of development and in the bundles of created assets of national enterprises. From the start, therefore, MNE entrants enjoy an edge over local enterprises.

- FDI, like domestic investment, is a development and industrialization issue rather than a trade issue. That the WTO lacks competence to deal with the investment and development issue is clear from the fact that the Working Group on Trade and Investment set up at the Singapore Meeting in 1996 has not been able to complete its work.

- Countries at different levels of development receive different types of FDI. For instance, an underdeveloped country will attract resource-seeking or labor-seeking FDI and investments in capital and intermediate goods industries in subsequent stages. The one-size-fits-all approach to FDI offered by a multilateral framework on investment cannot serve the best interests of all countries at different levels of development.

- As argued above, host government policies play an important role in extracting the benefits of FDI. A multilateral regime would take away the ability of host governments to direct FDI in accordance with their development policy objectives, and thus would affect the overall 'quality' of FDI inflows.

• Proponents of a GATT-type multilateral framework on investment argue that it would help developing countries to increase their attractiveness to foreign investors. However, as numerous empirical studies have shown, FDI inflows are largely driven by 'gravity' factors such as market size, income level, extent of urbanization, geographical and cultural proximity to major source countries of FDI, and quality of infrastructure. Policy factors and investment treaties play a relatively minor role.

• A general impression created by the protagonists of an investment framework is that an adequate framework for investment protection and dispute settlement does not at present exist. However, there is already an extensive network of about 2,100 bilateral investment promotion and protection agreements or treaties for the protection and guarantee of international investments, as well as a number of multilateral instruments. The latter include the Multilateral Investment Guarantee Agency, the International Centre for Settlement of Investment Disputes, the UN Committee on International Trade Law, and the International Chamber of Commerce.

• Bilateral investment treaties provide more flexibility for partners and are much easier to conclude than multilateral agreements; consider, for example, the failed OECD negotiations for a multilateral agreement on investment. Contrary to the general impression, bilateral investment treaties would still be necessary even if a multilateral agreement on investment were concluded, just as the presence of GATT in trade is not a substitute for bilateral trade agreements.

• Proponents of a multilateral framework on investment seek to protect only the rights of investors; nothing is said about investors' obligations or the protection of host country interests. MNEs command enormous resources and power by virtue of the global scale of their operations, and these can be misused to pursue restrictive business practices. While the ability of host governments to impose performance obligations would be curbed under an investment arrangement, that of corporations to impose restrictive clauses on their subsidiaries would not be regulated. An ideal accord would provide symmetry between the rights and obligations of host and home country governments and investors.

• The proposed framework on investment proposes to liberalize capital movement without providing for labor mobility, hence creating an asymmetry. However, the economic arguments for the free movement of labor are no weaker than those for the free movement of capital.

To sum up, a GATT-type multilateral framework on investment is not justified on either conceptual or policy grounds. It could lead to considerable loss of welfare in developing countries by reducing their policy space, and it does not offer any reciprocity with regard to either FDI or labor mobility.

Developing countries therefore resisted a negotiating mandate on investment at the Doha Ministerial Conference in November 2001. The Doha Declaration recognized a 'case' but not a 'need' for a multilateral framework. Although the language of the declaration suggested the need for a consensus on negotiation modalities, the chairman's clarification (which enabled the adoption of the declaration) indicated that the negotiating mandate would itself be subject to an explicit consensus. This gave developing countries the scope to continue to resist a negotiating mandate on investment. As a coalition, developing countries have continued to draw attention to the practical problems involved in arriving at a consensus on the subject of investment, especially in light of the OECD's failed negotiations on a multilateral investment agreement. The wide variation in levels of development among WTO members further limits the chances of arriving at a consensus.

At the 2003 Cancun Ministerial Conference of the WTO, which could not be concluded, nearly 70 developing countries spoke against the proposal to launch negotiations on an investment framework. In view of this popular resistance, the main proponent of negotiations—the European Union—appeared willing to give up its demand. Developing countries should continue to coordinate their position on this issue at the next ministerial conference, when a decision on this issue will finally be taken.

NOTES

This paper has benefited from the insightful comments on earlier versions of Ifzal Ali, Hans-Peter Brunner, J.P. Verbiest, anonymous reviewers within the Asian Development Bank (ADB), and participants of seminars organized by the ADB in Bangkok and Manila. Jayaprakash Pradhan assisted in the preparation of a number of tables based on the RIS database. The usual disclaimer applies.

1 See Kumar (1998a) for more details.
2 There has been extensive debate within and outside India concerning the scope, coverage, sequencing, and economic and social impact of the reforms. Although the average rate of economic growth achieved in the post-reform period is no higher than the 6 percent achieved during the 1980s, growth is

more sustainable in the sense of maintaining manageable fiscal and current account balances. A detailed discussion of the economic reforms is beyond the scope of this chapter, but interested readers may consult Ahluwalia and Little (1998), Kumar (2000a), and Ahluwalia, Reddy, and Tarapore (2002), among others.

3 See Mehta (2003) for details of India's trade policy.

4 Foreign ownership is limited to 49 percent in banking, 26 percent in insurance, 51 percent in non-banking finance companies, 49 percent in telecommunications, 74 percent in internet service provision, 40 percent in airlines, 74 percent in shipping, 51 percent in export-oriented trading, 49 percent in broadcasting, 74 percent in advertising, and 51 percent in health and education. Foreign equity of up to 51 percent was permitted on an automatic basis in the automobile sector in 1991. This was increased to up to 100 percent on a case-by-case basis in early 2000, and under the automatic route as per the March 2002 policy. For full details, see the Ministry of Industry website: <http://indmin.nic.in/policy/default.htm>.

5 Disaggregated stock data for services are not available.

6 For a detailed treatment of this issue, see Correa and Kumar (2003) and Kumar (2003c).

5

Republic of Korea

Seong-Bong Lee, June-Dong Kim,
and Nak-Gyun Choi

1 INTRODUCTION

The Republic of Korea (Korea) has consistently worked to liberalize its foreign direct investment (FDI) policy regime since receiving its first inflows of foreign capital in 1962. The clear premise has been that liberalization is the best way to utilize FDI inflows as a force for economic development. FDI is recognized as having been an important factor in enhancing the competitiveness of Korean companies. In the wake of the Asian financial crisis, it played a crucial role in helping the Korean economy get back on its feet. Korea's experience with FDI provides insights into the relationship between foreign investment and economic development that should prove useful for discussions on a multilateral framework on investment as proposed by the World Trade Organization (WTO). This chapter examines trends in FDI in Korea and assesses its economic effects, before discussing the country's position on investment issues at the WTO.

2 RECENT TRENDS AND DEVELOPMENTS IN FDI

Overview of the FDI Regime

FDI has been permitted in Korea since 1962, when Chemtax made an initial investment of $579,000.[1] However, for the next two decades, the Korean government pursued a development strategy that depended more on foreign borrowings than on FDI. There were two main reasons for this: first, the government was concerned that foreign firms might obtain a dominant position in the economy; and second, among the various forms of foreign resources, foreign borrowings were the easiest for the government to control.

In the early 1980s, the government adopted a new economic development strategy aimed at upgrading the existing industrial structure. With the focus now on increasing the level of technology and skills, FDI was gradually liberalized. In 1984, the government replaced its 'positive list' of industries that were permitted to receive FDI with a 'negative list' of barred industries; henceforth, all industries that were not on the negative list would become eligible for FDI approval. The upper limit on foreign equity participation, which had been set at 50 percent for all industries without exception, was also revised to allow the ceiling to vary by industry. In 1991, a notification system was introduced under which cases of FDI would be approved automatically upon notification, with a few exceptions. On becoming a member of the OECD in December 1996, Korea relaxed its FDI regulations further to permit mergers and acquisitions (M&As) and some other forms of investment. As these reforms took effect, the country's inflows of FDI steadily increased. However, until the Asian crisis hit in 1997, Korea's commitment to FDI liberalization did not extend beyond the minimum obligations set out in the Uruguay Round and OECD agreements, and many restrictions were still in place.

In late 1997, at the height of the crisis, the Korean government adopted an aggressive policy to attract FDI and began an export drive to increase foreign exchange reserves. It pared back the number of industries on the negative investment list, lifted the ban on hostile M&As, and relaxed the rules barring foreign investors from acquiring land. In 1998 the government enacted the Foreign Investment Promotion Act, which greatly expanded the range of incentives available to foreign investors, while also establishing a 'one-stop' administrative service for investors. The principal objective of the act was to create a more transparent, stable, and predictable investment climate by bringing Korea's policy regime in line with international norms and standards. Two factors in particular prompted the government's actions. First, at a time of great volatility, it regarded FDI as a stable source of capital for increasing the country's foreign exchange reserves and boosting the economy. And second, it recognized that FDI could facilitate the corporate and financial restructuring process—a top priority at the time.

Recent Trends in Inward and Outward FDI

In response to the government's newly introduced policy measures, FDI rose sharply from $3.1 billion in 1997 to a record $10.6 billion in 1999 (Table 5.1). Inflows were slightly more subdued in 2000 and then fell sharply in 2001 to $4.9 billion, less than half the previous year's total. FDI plummeted again in 2002 to $2 billion on a balance of payments basis. The

Table 5.1   Korea: Inward Flows of FDI, 1962–2002 ($ million)[a]

Year	FDI Inflows			With- drawn
	Notified	Actual (arrived)	Balance of Payments	
1962–81[b]	93.3	73.9	67.8[c]	10.2
1982–86[b]	353.5	231.6	188.2	38.3
1987–88[b]	1,173.5	759.8	815.2	34.3
1989	1,090.3	812.3	1,117.8	75.1
1990	802.6	895.4	788.5	136.2
1991	1,396.0	1,177.2	1,179.8	47.3
1992	894.5	803.3	728.3	240.2
1993	1,044.3	728.1	588.1	193.1
1994	1,316.5	991.5	809.0	205.0
1995	1,947.2	1,361.9	1,775.8	114.2
1996	3,202.6	2,310.0	2,325.4	308.5
1997	6,970.9	3,088.4	2,844.2	449.9
1998	8,852.5	5,221.2	5,412.3	250.3
1999	15,541.5	10,597.9	9,333.4	1,370.6
2000	15,696.7	10,134.5	9,283.4	1,615.9
2001	11,291.8	4,859.4	3,527.7	1,203.5
2002	9,101.0	1,133.6[d]	1,971.7	116.8[e]
Cumulative, 1962–2002	84,650.0	43,562.2[d]	45,612.0	6,793.0[e]

a   The notified amount of FDI and the amount of actual capital inflows (comprising purchased equity and long-term intra-company loans) do not necessarily coincide, resulting in a large difference in some years between the two measures. The balance of payments measure combines three elements (purchased equity, retained earnings, and net lending from parent companies to subsidiaries) and is close to the arrival-based measure for most years. Withdrawn FDI is the amount of capital withdrawn from foreign-invested enterprises by foreign investors.

b   Annual averages for the period shown.

c   Annual average for 1976–81, calculated from IMF (1999).

d   Includes investment up to April 2002.

e   Includes investment up to January 2002.

Source: Notified and actual FDI: Ministry of Commerce, Industry, and Energy (various years), *Trends in Foreign Direct Investment*; balance of payments: Bank of Korea, *Balance of Payment Statistics*, <http://www.bok.or.kr>; IMF (1999), *Balance of Payments Statistics Yearbook*.

Table 5.2   Korea: Inward Flows of FDI to Selected Industries in the Manufacturing Sector, 1991–2001 ($ million)[a]

	1991–95[b]	1996	1997	1998	1999	2000	2001
All manufacturing	596.1	1,298.1	1,835.0	2,878.7	6,246.3	5,767.9	2,569.9
(% of total FDI)	(58.8)	(56.2)	(59.4)	(54.9)	(57.8)	(56.7)	(52.9)
Food	31.6	42.2	463.9	629.9	327.1	78.5	550.3
(% of total FDI)	(3.1)	(1.8)	(15.0)	(12.0)	(3.0)	(0.8)	(11.3)
Chemicals	179.9	233.9	255.8	438.2	760.7	199.9	296.2
(% of total FDI)	(17.8)	(10.1)	(8.3)	(8.4)	(7.0)	(2.0)	(6.1)
Medicine	33.1	25.6	38.6	119.8	42.0	74.3	28.5
(% of total FDI)	(3.3)	(1.1)	(1.2)	(2.3)	(0.4)	(0.7)	(0.6)
Petroleum	93.3	214.6	3.0	0.9	542.3	0.1	11.6
(% of total FDI)	(9.2)	(9.3)	(0.1)	(0.0)	(5.0)	(0.0)	(0.2)
Machinery	68.0	136.3	95.9	531.3	588.5	1,490.0	225.2
(% of total FDI)	(6.7)	(5.9)	(3.1)	(10.1)	(5.4)	(14.6)	(4.6)
Electrical & electronic equipment	73.1	281.5	219.3	255.8	2,528.8	1,921.6	946.3
(% of total FDI)	(7.2)	(12.2)	(7.1)	(4.9)	(23.4)	(18.9)	(19.5)
Transport equipment	44.4	251.1	358.4	170.4	425.1	911.8	83.0
(% of total FDI)	(4.4)	(10.9)	(11.6)	(3.3)	(3.9)	(9.0)	(1.7)
Other	72.7	112.9	400.1	732.4	1,031.8	1,091.6	428.7
(% of total FDI)	(7.2)	(4.9)	(13.0)	(14.0)	(9.6)	(10.7)	(8.8)

a   Based on actual investment.

b   Annual average.

Source: Ministry of Commerce, Industry, and Energy (various years), *Trends in Foreign Direct Investment.*

recent decreases in flows were mainly the result of a global recession. Another factor was the slowdown in sales of domestic firms to overseas investors following a spate of sell-offs in the wake of the financial crisis.

The data on FDI notifications highlight a similar trend: inflows rose from $7.0 billion in 1997 to $15.5 billion in 1999, remained steady in 2000, then decreased by 28.0 percent to $11.3 billion in 2001, and again by 19.3 percent to $9.1 billion in 2002. It is apparent that the gap between notified and actual inflows has widened considerably since 1997.

The manufacturing sector has been the recipient of more than 55 percent of total FDI inflows since 1991, with nearly all of the remainder going to the services sector (Tables 5.2 and 5.3). FDI in agriculture, mining, and

Table 5.3 *Korea: Inward Flows of FDI to Selected Industries in the*
Services Sector, 1991–2001 ($ million)[a]

	1991–95[b]	1996	1997	1998	1999	2000	2001
All services	416.1	1,011.1	1,203.8	2,176.6	4,499.3	4,400.7	2,280.7
(% of total FDI)	(41.1)	(43.8)	(39.0)	(41.5)	(41.7)	(43.3)	(47.0)
Wholesale & retail trade	20.7	330.5	255.6	536.3	511.8	452.4	341.1
(% of total FDI)	(2.0)	(14.3)	(8.3)	(10.2)	(4.7)	(4.4)	(7.0)
International trading	79.3	111.9	196.5	249.3	202.5	239.6	103.0
(% of total FDI)	(7.8)	(4.8)	(6.4)	(4.8)	(1.9)	(2.4)	(2.1)
Hotels	72.5	115.8	95.6	0.0	64.5	4.7	4.8
(% of total FDI)	(7.2)	(5.0)	(3.1)	(0.0)	(0.6)	(0.0)	(0.1)
Restaurants	12.0	2.6	4.5	6.3	3.3	21.3	11.7
(% of total FDI)	(1.2)	(0.1)	(0.1)	(0.1)	(0.0)	(0.2)	(0.2)
Transport and storage	2.0	120.0	30.2	5.7	7.5	18.4	9.8
(% of total FDI)	(0.2)	(5.2)	(1.0)	(0.1)	(0.1)	(0.2)	(0.2)
Finance	142.1	178.3	302.5	473.2	1,830.4	1,421.2	886.8
(% of total FDI)	(14.0)	(7.7)	(9.8)	(9.0)	(16.9)	(14.0)	(18.3)
Insurance	31.6	16.1	7.2	73.1	331.6	440.8	156.7
(% of total FDI)	(3.1)	(0.7)	(0.2)	(1.4)	(3.1)	(4.3)	(3.2)
Construction	4.3	31.7	48.1	5.6	4.2	9.5	1.9
(% of total FDI)	(0.4)	(1.4)	(1.6)	(0.1)	(0.0)	(0.1)	(0.0)
Other	51.7	104.3	263.7	827.1	1,543.6	1,792.9	764.9
(% of total FDI)	(5.1)	(4.5)	(8.5)	(15.8)	(14.3)	(17.6)	(15.8)

a Based on actual investment.
b Annual average.
Source: Ministry of Commerce, Industry, and Energy (various years), *Trends in Foreign Direct Investment*.

fisheries has been marginal. Within the manufacturing sector, investment in the most important subsectors—chemicals, electrical and electronic equipment, and transport equipment—increased sharply in 1997–99, mainly as a result of the FDI liberalization and promotion policies put in place by the government in response to the financial crisis (Table 5.2). However, by 2001 flows had decreased significantly, both in absolute amounts and as a share of total FDI, falling from 57.8 percent in 1999 to 52.9 percent in 2001. Inflows to the machinery and transport equipment sectors fell particularly steeply in 2001 compared with the previous year. The electrical and electronic equipment industry also suffered a decline of more than 50 percent in absolute amount, despite a marginal increase in its relative share of total FDI. The only subsectors to attract more FDI in 2001 than in 2000 were food, chemicals, and petroleum.

Within the services sector, finance has attracted the largest amount of cumulated FDI since 1991, a trend that accelerated after the financial crisis (Table 5.3). Wholesale and retail trade has also received steady inflows since 1996, when the industry was almost completely opened to foreign investment. The share of 'other services' has risen significantly since the financial crisis, reflecting increased investment in telecommunications, consulting, market research, and advertising.

Nevertheless, like manufacturing, services experienced a sharp decrease in the amount of FDI inflows in 2001 compared with the previous year, although its share of total FDI continued to increase marginally (a trend that began in 1997). FDI in finance, insurance, and 'other services' was especially hard hit, while flows to wholesale and retail trade as well as to international trading also decreased noticeably.

The United States, the European Union, and Japan are the major sources of FDI in Korea, together accounting for 75 percent of total flows. As of June 2002, the United States had contributed the largest share—$24.5 billion based on notified investment—followed by the European Union ($23.8 billion) and Japan ($11.7 billion). However, Figure 5.1, which tracks FDI flows from these three regions since 1993, reveals that FDI from the European Union surpassed that from the United States by a large margin in 1999 and 2000. In part, this is a reflection of the large number of European companies already operating in Korea that were active in acquiring the shares of their domestic partners following the financial crisis.

M&As have become an increasingly popular means for foreign firms to invest in Korea since first being permitted in 1996. The number of cross-border mergers increased significantly following the onset of the Asian crisis, in response not only to the deregulation of laws restricting hostile M&As, but also to lower asset prices and the depreciation of the won. In many cases, rescue funds flowed in from existing foreign partners to ease liquidity constraints. Common forms of M&As have included foreign partners buying out their domestic joint venture partners; acquisitions of existing investments by foreign-invested firms; and the creation of new business entities in collaboration with Korean partners to acquire existing business units.

Foreign acquisitions of major shareholdings in Korean firms increased from just $0.7 billion (10 percent of total FDI) in 1997 to $2.3 billion (15 percent of total FDI) in 1999 (Figure 5.2). These figures are based on notifications for acquisitions of more than 10 percent of a company's total out-

Figure 5.1 Korea: Inward Flows of FDI by Major Source Country ($ billion)[a]

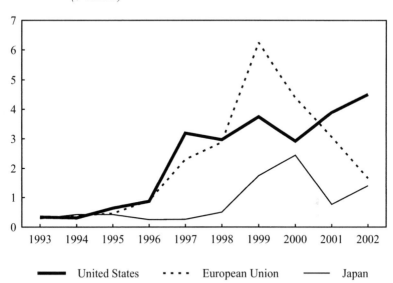

a   Based on notifications.
Source: Ministry of Commerce, Industry, and Energy (various years), *Trends in Foreign Direct Investment*.

standing shares; if acquisitions of assets were also included in the statistics, the value of cross-border M&As would be even greater.[2] Although the number of cross-border M&As decreased from 314 in 2000 to 292 in 2001, in terms of their value, they had almost recovered in 2001 to the peak level of 1999.

The initial surge of cross-border M&As mainly involved buyouts by foreign investors of their Korean joint venture partners. This and the next wave of cross-border M&As were the result of restructuring and downsizing efforts on the part of Korean partners, domestic firms, and financial institutions as they sought to cope with the effects of the financial crisis. Some of these early deals have been criticized as being fire sales in which company assets were undervalued and sold for less than fair prices. The sale of Korea First Bank to New Bridge Capital, for example, was not only made at a favorable price, but also included put-back options that made the government liable to pay compensation for any future financial difficulties incurred by the new owner involving, for instance, non-performing loans.

Figure 5.2   Korea: Trends in Cross-border M&As, 1997–2001[a]

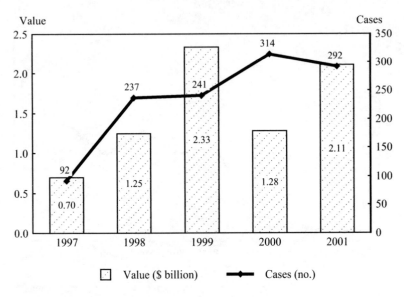

Value   Cases

☐ Value ($ billion)   ◆ Cases (no.)

a   Based on notifications for acquisitions of existing shares only.

Source: Ministry of Commerce, Industry, and Energy (various years), *Trends in Foreign Direct Investment.*

As the Korean economy recovered in 1999, partly due to a global information technology (IT) boom, the number of firms put up for sale decreased. Korean firms and the government became less desperate to sell ailing subsidiaries and financial institutions at bargain prices.[3] Creditors—largely comprising the domestic banks—also became more reluctant to expedite the sale of bankrupt firms, preferring instead to raise their value in the hope of achieving a better price. This change of attitude on the part of the government, conglomerates, and banks may have been a factor in the decline in the number and value of cross-border M&As since the peak year of 1999 (Figure 5.2).

As well as being a recipient of FDI, Korea has increasingly invested overseas (Figure 5.3). Overseas direct investment began to increase from the late 1980s, aided by balance of payments surpluses and an environment of low oil prices, favorable exchange rates, and low interest rates. It continued to rise in the 1990s, peaking at $4.25 billion in 1996, one year before the financial crisis. During this period, many of the Korean business

Figure 5.3   Korea: Outward and Inward Flows of FDI ($ billion)

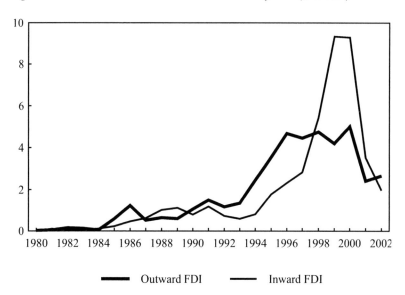

Source: Balance of payments data provided by the Bank of Korea.

conglomerates (*chaebol*) that had experienced rapid growth in the 1980s were looking to expand globally in order to gain access to overseas markets and advanced technology.

With the eruption of the financial crisis, however, domestic firms were forced to reassess their overseas investment strategies. Outward FDI had been heavily dependent on local borrowings, resulting in high debt ratios and low profitability (Lee 2000). A large number of Korean companies canceled their overseas investment plans in order to deal with the domestic liquidity problems caused by the crisis, thereby reducing the scale of outward FDI.

Figure 5.3 tracks the level of outward and inward FDI over the past two decades. For most of the 1990s Korea was a capital-exporting country, with outward flows of FDI surpassing inward flows, but in the four years following the financial crisis, the situation was reversed. In 2002, outward FDI once again surpassed inward FDI. This trend is expected to continue in 2003 for two main reasons: inward FDI is decreasing sharply; and many Korean companies that have lost cost competitiveness domestically are once again investing abroad, mainly in developing countries.

An Evaluation of FDI Trends

FDI trends in Korea provide a good example of how a developing country's FDI flows can be highly related to its economic development policy. In its initial stage of economic development—from the 1960s through 1970s—Korea received insignificant flows of FDI because the government pursued an economic development strategy based on foreign borrowings rather than foreign investment. All FDI proposals had to undergo a strict screening process before being approved.

In the early 1980s, the government began to recognize that a new input, technological innovation, was essential for achieving sustainable economic growth. FDI was gradually liberalized because it was regarded as an important means of achieving the necessary technological upgrading. Moreover, many foreign companies were attracted by the good business opportunities available in Korea throughout the 1980s and early 1990s, a time of high economic growth. FDI began to increase steadily, with most of it being used to take advantage of Korea's skilled workforce and low labor costs.

As the Korean government adopted globalization strategies aimed at deepening economic development, it accelerated the pace of FDI liberalization, especially in the lead-up to joining the OECD in 1996. The result was a remarkable increase in FDI in comparison with past decades. Much of the FDI in this period sought not only production efficiency but also access to domestic markets.

The financial crisis affected FDI flows and policies in a very different way. Recognizing the importance of FDI in stabilizing the level of foreign exchange reserves and facilitating financial and corporate restructuring, the government reviewed all restrictions on FDI and revised its regulations aggressively to promote investment. Flows increased sharply, to the extent that FDI in the four years following the financial crisis exceeded total FDI before the crisis.

3   THE POLICY REGIME FOR FDI AND RELATED TRADE ISSUES

Overview of Trade Liberalization Measures

The trade liberalization measures implemented by Korea since the financial crisis include a reduction of tariff barriers, the elimination of quantitative restrictions and prohibited trade-related subsidies, and enhancements to the transparency of import certification procedures.

The simple average bound tariff rate fell from 24.4 percent in 1997 to

18.5 percent in 2001, and the applied tariff rate from 13.4 percent to 8.8 percent,[4] thereby substantially narrowing the gap between the bound and applied rates. Korea instituted these changes in tariff rates mainly to meet its commitments under the Uruguay Round and the Information Technology Agreement (ITA).[5] At present, 6.4 percent of Korea's tariff lines are duty free, almost four times as many as in 1997.

To fulfill the conditions attached to an emergency loan package provided by the IMF following the crisis, and to meet its Uruguay Round commitments, the Korean government has removed quantitative restrictions on the eight remaining items subject to balance of payments protection as of 1 January 2001 (USTR 2001). These items consist mainly of live cattle (dairy and beef) and beef products. Korea has also abolished its import diversification system, implemented in 1978 to restrict imports from Japan. Following complaints from major trading partners such as the United States and the European Union—not to mention Japan—that these quantitative restrictions constituted an unfair trade practice, the system was abolished in June 1999.

The number of subsidy programs in Korea has fallen from 26 in 1997 to 19 in 2001. Under an economic stabilization package agreed with the IMF, the government eliminated four prohibited export subsidies in March 1998, several months ahead of the original December deadline. As part of an overall rationalization of its subsidy regime, it has notified the WTO of its remaining 19 programs, as required by reporting obligations, and will eliminate or reduce benefits available under 68 other programs that are not required to be reported to the WTO (such as government support for R&D, regional development, and environmental protection) (USTR 2001: 285).

Under the IMF program, the Korean government agreed to gradual steps to streamline its import-licensing and certification procedures. The customs service will shortly introduce an advanced, IT-based clearance system to speed up the clearance of import and export cargo. It will also introduce a new audit system to reduce delays in determining final duty amounts.

Korean government policy emphasizes a multilateral trade system under international bodies such as the General Agreement on Tariffs and Trade (GATT) and the WTO. However, as regionalism emerges as a new axis of the global trade system, the government has increasingly recognized the need to engage actively in establishing free trade agreements (FTAs). FTAs are not only able to circumvent trade barriers, but may also act as a catalyst for the restructuring of trade and industrial structures. They can therefore be used as a pre-emptive policy to avert an economic slowdown, by promoting the reform of domestic economic structures and regulations and thereby increasing efficiency. FTAs also have an important part to play in improving the trade and investment regime, because, in general, they stipulate an open investment regime among member countries. The level of investment protection and liberalization required by an FTA is normally higher than that required by a bilateral investment treaty.

It is not surprising, then, that FTAs are increasingly becoming an important plank of Korean trade policy. The government has already completed negotiations for an FTA with Chile, and is considering similar agreements with Japan, ASEAN, and the United States. Korea's plan to negotiate FTAs with its main economic partners can be expected to result in a more favorable investment environment both for foreign investors in Korea and for Korean investors abroad.

The Policy Regime for FDI

Investment Liberalization and Promotion

Following the crisis of 1997, the government liberalized FDI extensively. Ten business categories, including real estate rentals and sales, securities dealings, and insurance-related businesses, were fully opened to FDI in April 1998. Twelve more business categories, including gas stations, land development, commodity exchanges, investment companies, and investment trusts, were opened in August 1998.

The business categories in which FDI remains restricted are presented in Table 5.4. Most of the remaining restrictions are in the services sector, including the government sector, for instance, electric power generation. In addition, some professional areas requiring a Korean practitioner's license, such as legal, medical, and educational services, are effectively closed to foreign investment.

Most notable among the government's efforts was its full liberalization of the real estate sector in April 1998, regardless of property size or the intended use. Foreign investors rightly regard this as one of the most far-reaching changes initiated by the Korean government in response to the onset of the economic crisis (AMCHAM Korea 1998). Considering the symbolic significance of land to the Korean people, this change demonstrated the sincerity of the government in its pledge to open the country's markets to foreign investment.

A second ambitious measure undertaken in the same year was to permit hostile M&As of Korean firms by foreign companies. The government also simplified the FDI approval process: foreign investors were no longer required to obtain government approval when acquiring shares in a Korean company with assets of more than W2 trillion; and the investment procedure was changed from a report and approval process to one requiring noti-

Table 5.4   Korea: Business Categories Restricted to FDI as of March 2001

Wholly Restricted	Partially Restricted
Radio broadcasting	Inshore and coastal fishing
Television broadcasting	Cereal grains production
	Animal husbandry
	Meat wholesaling
	Publishing (newspapers, periodicals)
	International media agencies
	Coastal water transport
	Air transport
	Telecommunications
	Specialized banking
	Trusts and trust companies
	Cable and satellite broadcasting
	Electric power generation

Source: Ministry of Commerce, Industry, and Energy (2002), *Consolidated Announcement of Foreign Investment*, March.

fication only. The Foreign Investment Promotion Act enacted in 1998 was designed to strengthen Korea's investment incentive regime and increase the country's competitiveness *vis-à-vis* other Southeast Asian countries. The act substantially expanded the range of incentives available to foreign investors, giving them access to tax exemptions and reductions, reduced rental on government-owned factory sites, and a range of subsidies (Table 5.5). It signified a change in government policy from passive liberalization to the active promotion of FDI.

To reduce the cumbersome administrative procedures involved in establishing a foreign-invested company, in 1998 the government set up a one-stop agency for foreign investors, the Korea Investment Service Center (KISC). KISC provides a wide range of services, including investment planning, procedural assistance in requesting tax incentives, help in selecting factory sites, advocacy on behalf of investors in obtaining government approvals, and even counseling services to help foreign investors settle in Korea. The government has also established an Office of the Investment Ombudsman to address grievances filed by foreign companies. Local gov-

Table 5.5   Korea: Tax Incentives for FDI

Tax	Foreign-invested Enterprises	Foreign Investors
Income and corporate tax	Applicable to business income. Initial seven years of full exemption, 50% reduction thereafter for three years. Source: Article 121-2, Paragraph 2, STTCA.	Applicable to dividend income. Initial seven years of full exemption; 50% reduction thereafter for three years. Source: Article 121-2, Paragraph 3, STTCA.
Local taxes: acquisition tax, registration tax, property tax, aggregate land tax	Applicable to properties acquired by foreign-invested enterprises. Applies for eight years (five years of full exemption, three years of 50% reduction), with up to another seven years of reduction (decided by each local government). Source: Article 121-2, Paragraph 4, STTCA.	Not applicable.
Customs duties, special excise tax, value-added tax	Applicable to imported capital goods required by foreign-invested enterprises. Full exemption on imported capital goods for three years from the date of notification of FDI. Source: Article 121-3, Paragraph 1, STTCA.	Applicable to imported capital goods used for investment. Source: Article 121-3, Paragraph 1, STTCA.

STTCA: Special Tax Treatment Control Act.
Source: Lee (2001: 497).

ernments have instituted their own programs to support foreign investment—providing grants for employee training programs, for instance.

Remaining Internal Barriers

The efforts of the Korean government to liberalize and promote FDI, coinciding with favorable external conditions, were conducive to a rapid increase in FDI in 1999 and 2000. Nevertheless, a number of internal barriers to investment remain.

Table 5.6   Korea: Grievances Filed by Foreign Investors (no. of cases)

Area	Jan–Jun 2001	Jan–Jun 2002
Labor	27	51
Tax	20	36
Legal issues	19	27
Investment procedures	7	22
Tariffs/customs	38	21
Finance/foreign exchange	15	19
Construction	10	16
Other	77	51
Total	213	243

Source: Office of the Investment Ombudsman (2002), '2002 Report on Foreign Investor Grievances and Resolutions on Korea,' Seoul, July (draft).

In December 2001, the American Chamber of Commerce in Korea (AMCHAM Korea) surveyed about 2,000 executives working for 120 multinational enterprises (MNEs) with business interests in Asia to discover how they rated the overall investment environment of five major Asian cities (AMCHAM Korea 2002).[6] The survey found that Seoul ranked last among the cities surveyed, behind Hong Kong, China; Singapore; Shanghai; and Tokyo. It identified five major areas in which there was a need for improvement: tax, foreign exchange controls, labor flexibility, English language capability, and living and working conditions. Korea's lack of competitiveness in the areas of taxation and labor is confirmed by the number of grievances filed on these subjects with the Office of the Investment Ombudsman; these rose markedly in the first half of 2002 compared with the same period in 2001 (Table 5.6).

Respondents to the survey ranked Seoul third after Hong Kong, China and Singapore with respect to its tax regime (AMCHAM Korea 2002: 23–4). As of January 2002, Korea's maximum tax rate was 29.7 percent for corporations and 39.6 percent for individuals. Respondents identified the ambiguity of the country's tax laws as one of the most serious impediments to foreign investment in Korea. A common difficulty faced by foreign businesses is that regulations, especially those related to tax laws, are subject to various interpretations by different regulatory authorities.

Respondents also claimed that Korea's foreign exchange controls were too complex, making it difficult for MNEs to move funds freely in and out of the country (AMCHAM Korea 2002: 23–4). Many of the executives doing business in Korea pointed out that the current regulations prohibiting off-setting were making it unnecessarily complicated to conduct intra-company transactions. In addition, the burdensome reporting and approval requirements for inward and outward remittances, accompanied by the possibility of sanctions for failure to comply, were a serious impediment to attracting multinationals to Korea, let alone persuading them to make Seoul their regional headquarters in Asia.

Labor flexibility was another category in which Seoul ranked last compared to other Asian cities. The overwhelming majority of respondents (92 percent) felt that the ability to make adjustments to the workforce in response to changes in demand was vital. However, Korean labor law places restrictions on 'dismissal for managerial reasons.' This means that companies are not permitted to downsize unless they are facing a financial crisis, by which time it would usually be too late to respond effectively.

Respondents felt there was a need to upgrade the country's level of English language communication skills (AMCHAM Korea 2002: 25–6). Many of them commented that although over 90 percent of those who take the Test of English for International Communication (TOEIC) obtain an above average score, their verbal and written English language communication skills were surprisingly ineffective.

The regional executives perceived Korea to be the least attractive place to live and work, according to the survey. However, whereas most expatriates living in other Asian cities rated Seoul negatively, business executives living in Seoul viewed Korea more favorably (AMCHAM Korea 2002: 26).

Internal barriers of the type identified by the AMCHAM Korea survey may have aggravated the decrease in FDI in 2001 and 2002. There needs to be a sustained improvement in the overall investment environment, particularly in those areas attracting the most frequent complaints, to halt the recent decline in FDI.

Future Challenges for FDI Policy

FDI was undoubtedly an important factor in reviving the fortunes of the Korean economy after the financial crisis. However, it is doubtful whether the high level of recent inflows—averaging approximately $13 billion per year for the four years from 1998 to 2001—will continue, for several reasons. First, now that the People's Republic of China (PRC) has become a member of the WTO, foreign investors are turning to it as the country of primary concern in northeast Asia. And second, the opportunities for foreign investors to acquire Korean firms as part of domestic corporate restructuring efforts are gradually decreasing. With Korean corporations now less likely to sell off their assets or subsidiaries to foreign investors, the government will need to look at other ways of maintaining a continuous inflow of FDI. It has set itself the objective of raising FDI by as much as 20 percent over the 1999 level of 6.9 percent of GDP by 2010. At the current rate of inflows, this target is unlikely to be met.

The challenges for FDI policy can be crystallized by asking the following two questions: what needs to be improved within the existing system to persuade more foreign corporations to invest in Korea; and what new concepts can be incorporated into FDI policy to enhance the future competitiveness of the Korean economy?

The former question is primarily a matter of improving the overall business environment for foreign investors. At an institutional level, Korea's FDI regime is already similar to that provided by developed countries. However, as the survey results mentioned above indicate, the business environment that foreign investors actually experience in Korea is quite different from the one defined by the institutional regime. The government needs to close this gap and create a more business-friendly environment. One positive move would be to provide training for local and central government officers at the policy implementation level. In addition, the prompt conclusion of negotiations for a bilateral investment treaty between Korea and Japan, and between Korea and the United States, would increase investor confidence in the environment for FDI in Korea.

Foreign investors want the Korean government to create an environment of fair competition in which foreign-invested and domestic corporations can compete on equal terms. Most foreign investors do not want to receive special treatment, whether positive or negative; rather, they want the certainty of knowing that they can carry out their business activities in a liberal and fair environment.

The key to answering the second question may lie in a proposal to make Korea the business hub of northeast Asia, a strategy in which FDI would play a central role. This proposal assumes that northeast Asia will develop into a dynamic economic region centered on Korea, the PRC, and Japan. The economic relations between these three countries are expected to intensify as physical barriers continue to fall to developments in IT, and as the effects on free trade of the PRC's entry into the WTO continue to widen. The rise of a new business region in northeast Asia is both a threat and an opportunity for Korea. But if the country were to succeed in becoming the hub of business in northeast Asia, the implications for the long-term development of the Korean economy would be enormous.

The government proposes establishing a number of free economic zones in selected areas—Incheon Airport, Busan, and Kwangyang—as an important policy instrument for achieving this vision. The zones would offer foreign investors tax and other financial incentives, unparalleled support, and far freer business and living conditions than in other parts of Korea. Laws and regulations relating to labor and foreign exchange would be relaxed within the zones, as would restrictions on foreign investment in some service sectors (broadcasting, law, medicine, education). English would be the official language, concurrently with Korean. The Korean government expects to enact or revise the necessary laws by the end of 2003.

4   IMPACT OF FDI IN KOREA

There have been only a few studies of the impact of FDI in Korea. They include empirical studies of the spillover effects of FDI (J.-D. Kim 1997; Yun 2000; Kim 2003; Kim and Kim 2003); several case studies (Kim and Hwang 2000; Lee 2002); and a study of the economic effects of FDI following the financial crisis (KIET 2001).

Empirical Studies of Spillover Effects

Using industry-level (two-digit) data, Kim and Hwang (2000) did not find any statistically significant spillover effects of FDI on changes in productivity. However, a later study using panel data on Korean manufacturing firms did find such an effect. Lee (2002) found, first, a positive and statistically significant effect at the industry level for foreign-invested firms. Second, he found a positive and statistically significant effect for firms with a high level of foreign equity participation, with the improvement in productivity greater in firms in which foreign investors were the majority shareholders—implying that spillover effects are positively correlated with foreign management control. And finally, he found a positive and statistically significant effect for US FDI (but a negative effect for Japanese FDI).

Case Studies

Evidence for the spillover effects of FDI on productivity is also found in several case studies. Here we look at the experiences of three sectors: semiconductors, distribution, and banking.[7]

Semiconductors

The semiconductor industry has played a pivotal role in the rapid development of the Korean economy (Box 1).[8] In the latter half of the 1980s, the industry emerged as a leading sector in the country's hugely successful electronics industry. By 1992, Korea had become the world's third largest producer of semiconductors, with Korean firms, led by Samsung, dominating the market for memory chips.

In the early years, it was foreign firms—especially US and Japanese firms—that constructed the foundation for the industry. In 1965, as part of a strategy to promote export-led growth, the Korean government encouraged MNEs to invest in semiconductor assembly and testing operations in Korea.[9] The American MNE, Komy, invested in transistor production facilities in 1965; Signetics and KMI followed in the same year, Motorola in 1967, and Fairchild in 1969. By 1974, there were nine US-owned facilities in Korea, compared with eight in Hong Kong, China, three in Taipei,China, nine in Singapore, eleven in Malaysia, and six throughout the rest of Asia.

Following the normalization of relations between Korea and Japan in the mid-1960s, Japanese multinationals also set up assembly and testing facilities in Korea, led by Toshiba and Sanyo in 1969. By 1973, there were

---

BOX 1 THE CASE OF MOTOROLA KOREA

Founded by the US firm, Motorola Semiconductor, in 1967, Motorola Korea has been carrying out production on an original equipment manufacturing (OEM) basis through its two subsidiaries, ANAM and Korea Electronics. Motorola has continually improved the quality of the products made by these two companies, through on-the-job training, technical training, and the transfer of production technology. Both have become world-class semiconductor manufacturers, with many of their technicians going on to found an indigenous semiconductor capacity at other companies such as Samsung and LG Semiconductors.

Motorola Korea also helped to establish a domestic industry to supply the chip industry. It not only set up suppliers itself, but also encouraged promising former employees to establish start-up firms to supply it with components. The nitrogen factory founded by Motorola Korea in 1968 provided the impetus for the transfer of know-how to the domestic gas industry, assisting local companies such as Daesung Sanso to develop high-purity nitrogen for industrial use. Because the Korean electronics industry was heavily dependent on imported moldings, Motorola Korea set up a molding production division operated by employees trained at its US headquarters. Some of these technicians went on to establish their own supply firms, with support from Motorola Korea in the form of reduced prices for production facilities and a commitment to purchase their products.

Source: Kim (1999: 42–3).

at least seven such Japanese facilities, operated by firms such as Toko, Rohm, and Sanken.

In the 1970s, Korean firms took the initial steps toward indigenous semiconductor manufacture through joint ventures with foreign firms. One of the first was a tie-up between Goldstar and National Semiconductor, the US multinational, in 1972 to produce transistors.

In the 1990s, Korean firms moved into the supply industry, again through joint ventures. Samsung led the way, forming a joint venture with Japan's Dai Nippon Screen to produce spinners and wet stations at Chunan. Samsung also instigated a joint venture with POSCO Steel and MEMC (USA) to supply them with silicon wafers.

Technology transfer agreements—not only between Korean firms and MNEs but also between domestic and foreign research institutes—were another important driver of the Korean semiconductor industry. In the early stage, the Korean government played a critical role in the transfer of technology. In 1974, it formulated a six-year plan to promote the production of electronic components, including semiconductors. This was to be achieved through the establishment of research institutes, the tertiary training of electronics engineers, technology acquisition through licensing from overseas firms, and the use of consultants. The first experimental semiconductor fabrication facility was established in 1976 by the Korea Institute of Electronics Technology using technology transferred from the US firm, VLSI Technology. The institute opened a liaison office in Silicon Valley in 1978 to enable it to build contacts with high-tech firms and keep abreast of the latest advances in semiconductor technology.

The leadership role played by the government in promoting the semiconductor industry was relatively short-lived, lasting only until the late 1980s. With Korean conglomerates rapidly developing expertise in the production of semiconductors and carrying out their own R&D, the government no longer needed to play a direct role through its research institutes. The Korea Institute of Electronics Technology abandoned its R&D capacity in semiconductors and sold its fabrication facilities to Goldstar.

Distribution

Along with financial services, distribution was one of the least developed sectors in Korea up until the mid-1990s.[10] However, a remarkable transformation has taken place in the industry since 1996, when the government lifted some of the restrictions that had been keeping foreign service suppliers out of the country (Table 5.7).[11] Notable among the reforms was the elimination of restrictions on the number and size of stores that could be operated by both domestic and foreign retailers. The number of large dis-

Table 5.7   Korea: Timetable of Liberalization in Distribution Services

Year	Liberalization Measure
1989	FDI in the wholesaling of medicines allowed. Range of permissible imports by branches of foreign companies expanded.
1991	FDI in retailing liberalized, with each foreign-invested company allowed to establish up to ten stores, each with a floor area of up to 1,000 square meters.
1993	Store and space-related limits expanded to 20 stores of up to 3,000 square meters for each foreign-invested company.
1996	Store and space-related limits eliminated (allowing the establishment of hypermarkets). Five business categories liberalized, including commodity chains and meat retailing.
1997	Ten business categories liberalized, including general trading and grain retailing.
1998	Economic needs tests on department stores and shopping centers abolished. Operation of gas stations liberalized.
2000	FDI in meat wholesaling allowed.

Source: Unpublished internal report of the Department of Distribution, Ministry of Commerce, Industry, and Energy.

count stores or hypermarkets had increased to 207 by June 2002, more than a quarter of them established by foreign firms (Table 5.8).

The rise of the hypermarkets has changed the structure of Korean retail industry. Their huge buying power put price setting in the hands of the retailers rather than the manufacturers, leading to increased price competition. The entry of foreign retail firms was accompanied by the transfer of advanced merchandising and inventory management techniques such as point-of-sale (POS) systems, leading to rapid increases in productivity.[12] The role of liberalization in enhancing competition is apparent in the lower price margins of supermarkets and department stores, which fell from 17.8 percent and 24.2 percent respectively in 1995 to 13.6 percent and 21.7 percent in 1998 (Table 5.9). These figures reflect the extent to which supermarkets and department stores faced a direct challenge from foreign competitors.

Table 5.8   Korea: Trends in the Establishment of Hypermarkets,
1997 – June 2002 (no. of stores)[a]

Name	1997	1998	1999	2000	2001	Jan–Jun 2002
Foreign companies						
Carrefour (1996)	3	6	11	20	22	22
Wal Mart (1996)	4	4	5	6	9	12
Costco (1998) (1994)[b]	2	3	3	4	5	5
Tesco (1999) (1997)[b]	1	1	2	7	14	16
No.	10	14	21	37	50	55
(% of all hypermarkets)	(17.2)	(17.3)	(19.6)	(24.5)	(26.2)	(26.6)
Korean companies						
No.	48	67	86	114	141	152
(% of all hypermarkets)	(82.8)	(82.7)	(80.4)	(75.5)	(73.8)	(73.4)
Total (all hypermarkets)	58	81	107	151	191	207

a   Year of entry is given in brackets after the company name.
b   Year of entry of the acquired local company.
Source: Korea Chainstore Association (2002), *Discount Merchandiser*, Seoul, July.

It seems fair to say that the liberalization measures of the 1990s resulted in increased competition and improved productivity in the distribution sector, although we cannot provide firm evidence of this due to limited data. The opening of hypermarkets by foreign firms challenged domestic retail stores to match their competitors' superior management techniques. The changes in shopping patterns that accompanied the introduction of discount stores may well have forced many small stores to specialize, and existing domestic retail firms to expand their operations in order to take advantage of scale effects.

Banking

Foreign investment in financial services increased sharply after the financial crisis to record the largest share of FDI inflows in the services sector in 1999.[13] This is not surprising given the extensive liberalization measures undertaken in this sector in 1998 (Table 5.10). Within the space of a

Table 5.9   Korea: Price Margins of Supermarkets and Department Stores, 1995–98 (%)

	1995	1996	1997	1998	Change, 1995–98
Supermarkets	17.8	16.1	15.0	13.6	–4.2
Department stores	24.2	24.8	22.6	21.7	–2.5

Source: Bank of Korea (2000), *Impact of Changes in Distribution Structure on Price Levels* [in Korean], 26 January.

Table 5.10   Korea: Timetable of Liberalization in Financial Services

Date	Liberalization Measure
April 1998	Foreign banks allowed to establish subsidiaries. FDI allowed in insurance, and in insurance-related services such as brokerage and risk assessment.
May 1998	FDI allowed in the securities industry through the establishment of subsidiaries. Hostile takeovers of domestic financial services companies allowed. Portfolio investment in bonds, investment trusts, money market instruments and financial derivatives completely liberalized. Equity market completely opened, with the exception of some public enterprises.
July 1998	FDI allowed in investment companies and investment trusts, and in credit granting and credit rating agencies.
December 1998	FDI allowed in investment advisory service companies and securities trust companies.

Source: Ministry of Finance and Economy (2000), Korea's Liberalization of Financial Services: Experiences and Lessons, Paper presented at the APEC Group on Services Meeting, 18 February.

few months, foreign banks and securities firms were permitted to establish subsidiaries in Korea; the country's bond and money markets were opened; and FDI in investment companies and investment trusts, credit rating services, and other activities auxiliary to financial intermediation were completely liberalized.

Foreign investors were quick to take advantage of these reforms, acquiring significant holdings in some domestic banks by the end of 1999 (Table 5.11). Most notable was the acquisition by New Bridge Capital Consortium (an American firm) of a majority shareholding in Korea First Bank in September 1999. This was the first case in which management control of a Korean bank was handed over to a foreign investor.

Only a few studies have looked at the spillover effects of foreign penetration of the Korean banking sector. This may be because it is still too early to conduct any meaningful investigation of the impact of liberalization, and because of the lack of available data. A study by Hwang, Kim, and Shin (2001) examined whether the penetration of foreign banks had increased competition in the banking sector, thereby decreasing the profitability of the domestic banks, during the period 1994–99. They found that an increase in the share of foreign banks in total banking sector assets had had a negative impact on return on assets, as had an increase in foreign banks' share of total number of branches and an increase in their share of total deposits. The authors concluded that the penetration of foreign banks had reduced the profitability of local banks by increasing competition in the banking sector.

However, the participation of foreign investors has clearly strengthened company boards, helping to resolve some of the corporate governance issues facing the sector.[14] An important illustration of this was Korea First Bank's refusal to provide additional loans to save Hynix from bankruptcy in January 2001, despite a government request. This incident demonstrated the determination of boards under improved governance standards to resist government control or 'guidance' of the sector, which had been widespread before the financial crisis.

The Role of FDI in the Recovery Process

A study by the Korea Institute for Industrial Economics and Trade identified five areas in which foreign investment flows had assisted the country's recovery from the financial crisis (KIET 2001). First, at a time of severe shortages, FDI had helped to secure Korea's foreign exchange reserves. Because FDI is a long-term and stable source of capital compared with foreign borrowings or short-term portfolio investment, an increase in flows ensures the accumulation of foreign exchange reserves. In 1998, when the

*Table 5.11   Korea: Share of Major Korean Banks Held by Foreign
Investors as of the End of 1999 (%)*

Domestic Bank	Share of Government	Foreign Investor	Share of Foreign Investor
Korea First	49.0	New Bridge Capital	51.0
Korea Exchange	35.9	Commerz Bank	23.6
Kookmin	6.5	Goldman Sachs	18.0
Korea Housing & Commercial	14.5	ING Group	10.0
Shinhan	–	Japanese (Overseas Korean)	49.4
KorAm	–	Bank of America	16.8
Hana	–	International Finance Corporation	3.3

Source: Financial Supervisory Committee, cited in Hwang and Shin (2000: 24).

shortage of reserves was at its most serious, FDI flows to Korea increased by $5.4 billion, equivalent to 17 percent of that year's total increase in foreign exchange reserves of $31.6 billion. The following year FDI reached $9.3 billion, as much as 42 percent of that year's total increase in foreign exchange reserves of $22 billion.

Second, FDI had helped to increase domestic production and employment. According to KIET (2001), foreign-invested enterprises in the manufacturing sector increased their production by W20 trillion between 1997 and 1999, as well as providing jobs for an additional 51,300 people (Tables 5.12 and 5.13). This was 44 percent of the overall increase in production of the domestic manufacturing sector during that period, helping to stave off a large-scale drop in employment in the domestic manufacturing sector.

Third, FDI had helped to ameliorate Korea's balance of payments problem by boosting exports (Table 5.14). With exports of $21.3 billion and imports of $16.5 billion in 1999, foreign-invested enterprises generated a $4.8 billion trade surplus for Korea. At 20 percent of the total trade surplus, this was a sizable contribution toward the country's economic revival. If industries with high relative importance in oil importing, such as the oil refinery sector, are excluded, foreign-invested enterprises can be considered to have made an even greater contribution of approximately $5.95 billion.

Table 5.12   Korea: Relative Importance of Foreign-invested Enterprises in Manufacturing Sector Production, 1997–99

Year	Manufacturing Sector (W trillion)	Foreign-invested Enterprises (W trillion)	Relative Importance (%)
1997	434.9	44.0	10.1
1998	425.0	48.2	11.3
1999	480.2	64.0	13.3
Increase, 1997–99	45.3	20.0	–

Source: KIET (2001: 32).

Fourth, FDI had improved the technological capability of Korean industry, had stimulated R&D, and had intensified technological consultation between foreign-invested enterprises and their Korean subcontractors. The flow of advanced technology and managerial know-how from abroad helped to raise levels of productivity, encouraging Korean manufacturers to add value to their operations.

And finally, FDI had triggered rapid progress in corporate and industry restructuring. As affiliates of MNEs operating under a global management

Table 5.13   Korea: Relative Importance of Foreign-invested Enterprises in Manufacturing Sector Employment, 1997–99

Year	Manufacturing Sector (thousand persons)	Foreign-invested Enterprises (thousand persons)	Relative Importance (%)
1997	2,697.6	149.0	5.5
1998	2,323.9	136.2	5.9
1999	2,507.7	200.3	8.0
Increase, 1997–99	−189.8	51.3	–

Source: KIET (2001: 33).

*Table 5.14   Korea: Effect on the Balance of Payments of Foreign
Participation in the Manufacturing Sector, 1999 ($ million)*

	Exports	Imports	Trade Surplus
Manufacturing sector	143,685	119,752	23,933
Contribution of foreign-invested enterprises (estimate)	21,364	16,517	4,848
Contribution of foreign-invested enterprises excluding oil refinery sector	19,575	13,623	5,953
Relative importance of foreign-invested enterprises (%)	14.9	13.8	20.3

Source: KIET (2001: 35).

strategy, foreign-invested enterprises insisted that their Korean business partners adopt more transparent management practices; this led to a general improvement in the management standards of domestic corporations. The corporate restructuring process was accelerated in particular by the wave of sell-offs of subsidiaries of the *chaebol*, in which foreign investors were active participants. The increase in FDI that accompanied the crisis intensified competition within industries, forcing firms to restructure in order to survive.

Concerns about the Impact of Post-crisis Increases in FDI

Two main criticisms have been made concerning the effects of the recent surge in FDI. These are, first, that the entry of multinationals has had an anti-competitive impact, and second, that national wealth has been dissipated by the fire sale of valuable national assets.

Anti-competitive Effects

Media reports about the loss of Korean industry icons as a result of the rapid penetration of FDI are commonplace (Lee and Yun 2002). The *Korea Economic Daily* (10 July 2000) reported that multinationals had acquired 80 percent of the domestic aluminium market, 75 percent of the newsprint paper market, and more than 50 percent of the petroleum market. Elevators, automotive components, food and advertising are other industries said to be dominated by MNEs.

There is, however, a fallacy to the argument that such acquisitions are 'anti-competitive,' in that the aspect of competition among foreign firms themselves is generally ignored. The 'multinational companies' dominating the market are not usually single entities, but several foreign-invested firms, some of which are not wholly foreign-owned (even though foreign investors may have managerial rights). In addition, it should be noted that the divestments of parts of the *chaebol* have been made to not one but a number of different foreign entrants, the outcome generally being an increase in the number of players in the economy. Thus, discussion in the popular press is more about ownership (national versus foreign) than about market power and the lessening of competition *per se*.

Generally, the impact of FDI seems to be pro-competitive at entry, especially because of the high level of concentration in the Korean market. The open FDI regime that Korea now maintains should therefore not be reversed. This conclusion presupposes, however, that foreign-invested firms will be fully subject to competition policy scrutiny, and assumes increased effectiveness in applying competition law to MNEs.

Dissipation of National Wealth

The sweeping investment measures taken to liberalize FDI undoubtedly made it easier for foreign investors to acquire Korean corporations, with many being sold for less than the book value of their assets. Critics point to this difference between book value and the price paid for a firm's assets to support their claim that corporations have been sold to foreign investors at giveaway prices, leading to an outflow of national wealth.

It would be hard to justify some of the sell-offs that took place during the crisis on grounds of liquidity, but the sale of non-viable corporations should not be regarded as a national loss. Non-viable corporations are defined as those firms that would be unable to meet their liabilities even through the sale of all their assets, and whose liquidation could have a catastrophic effect on, or even bankrupt, third and fourth party victims such as financial institutions and other interest groups of the corporations. Even more problematic are the huge but non-viable conglomerates whose bankruptcy could severely harm not just other firms but the national economy. The most common strategy of such a corporation when faced with a loss of competitiveness is to dump products on overseas markets. This can cause the failure of more competent domestic corporations, as well as artificially enlarging the non-viable corporation itself. It is this sort of drain on national wealth that overseas sales, even at giveaway prices, are designed to halt. The alternative would be a continual drain on national resources through public subsidies.

5 AN INTERNATIONAL FRAMEWORK FOR TRADE AND INVESTMENT LIBERALIZATION

The WTO and Trade-related Investment Measures

Korea has been participating in multilateral trade negotiations since joining the WTO on 1 January 1995. Since then, it has modified many of its economic policies to comply with WTO rules on the implementation and enforcement of international free trade (Sohn, Yang, and Yim 1998). As well as abolishing direct export subsidies, reducing concessional tariff rates, and amending domestic laws on copyright, patents, and food hygiene, the government has altered its industrial subsidy and tax regime for domestic companies to satisfy WTO requirements.

The Agreement on Trade-related Investment Measures (TRIMs), negotiated during the Uruguay Round, states that in general WTO member countries will not apply any TRIM that is prohibited under the provisions of Article III (on national treatment) or Article XI (on quantitative restrictions). Korea has notified the Council for Trade in Goods that it does not maintain any TRIMs that are inconsistent with these requirements.

Korea's Preliminary Position on a Multilateral Framework on Investment

The WTO has been considering the establishment of a multilateral framework of rules to govern international investment, with the objective of securing a stable and predictable climate for FDI worldwide. Korea favors the establishment of such a framework, on the grounds that it would enhance the predictability and transparency of the international investment environment and promote and accelerate free flows of investment at the global level. With regard to the level of investment protection and liberalization that the framework would afford, Korea supports a realistic approach that would be flexible enough to accommodate the diverse development needs of participant countries. The following paragraphs outline Korea's preliminary position on the core elements of a multilateral framework on investment.

Scope and definition of investment. Korea supports the position that there should be substantive discussions on the scope and definition of investment after a consensus is reached among WTO member countries on the main direction of a multilateral framework on investment. Assuming that the aim of the framework would be to facilitate liberalization and protect international investment, Korea feels that the best way forward may be to adopt an enterprise-based definition for investment liberalization and an asset-based definition for investment protection. An enterprise-based definition in the area of liberalization would provide developing countries with the policy flexibility to reflect their development needs; specifically, it would help them avoid the negative effects of volatile short-term portfolio investment flows. The application of an asset-based definition in the area of protection would enhance the usefulness of the multilateral investment framework by clarifying the protection that would be afforded to the assets of foreign firms located in host countries.

Transparency. The transparency provisions in the proposed multilateral framework on investment could impose a heavy administrative burden on developing countries. To help them comply with transparency rules, Korea suggests providing a package of technical assistance as an integral part of the transparency provisions.

Non-discrimination. Korea supports the principle of non-discrimination as the linchpin of an open and efficient investment regime, while recognizing the need to reconcile the development needs of developing countries with the need to create a more favorable environment for international investment. A realistic approach would be to implement the multilateral framework on investment in two stages. During the first stage, countries would maintain a positive list of industries open to FDI; in the second, they would maintain a negative list of the industries that would remain closed to FDI.

Specifically, Korea supports the application of the most favored nation (MFN) principle of non-discrimination among a member's trading partners as a general obligation on parties to a multilateral framework on investment, in both stages of implementation. At the same time, Korea agrees with the view of the WTO Working Group on the Relationship between Trade and Investment that 'applying MFN treatment does not interfere with a developing country's ability to impose measures that give any competitive advantage to national producers over their foreign competitors.'

Korea also supports the principle of national treatment—that foreign and domestic companies should be treated equally—and believes that a two-stage approach may be appropriate in this area as well. During the first stage of 'conditional national treatment,' member countries would provide specific commitments in the form of a positive list of industries in which free market access would be provided to all firms, whether domestic or foreign. These commitments could initially be set at a low level to take account of the development needs of the host country, but would gradually be broadened.

During the second stage of 'unconditional national treatment,' Korea believes that national treatment should be accepted as a general obligation on parties to the multilateral framework on investment, as is the case with most existing international investment agreements. There are two reasons for this position. First, there is little ground for discriminating against foreign-invested enterprises if they are established in accordance with a host country's laws. Second, FDI creates 'sunk costs,' making it unlikely that a firm will move out of a host country in reaction to a policy change. It should therefore be a minimum requirement of the multilateral investment framework that the host country provide a stable environment for foreign investors. Nevertheless, Korea recognizes the need to allow certain exceptions to the principle of unconditional national treatment, for economic, political, or administrative reasons. Such exceptions should be transparent, however, and might be designated in the form of a negative list of industries closed to foreign investment.

The GATS approach as a model for a multilateral framework on investment. Under the General Agreement on Trade in Services (GATS), which provides a set of multilateral rules governing international trade in services, members are not obliged to make commitments on the whole universe of service sectors, but to designate a positive list of sectors in which commitments would apply. Such an approach takes account of the different requirements of countries at different stages of development, and allows members to balance the need to liberalize FDI and encourage inflows against the need to maintain national sovereignty over domestic policy. In this sense, Korea believes that the GATS approach could serve as a good starting point for the development of a multilateral framework on investment. It is therefore encouraging the Working Group on the Relationship between Trade and Investment to launch a background study on areas of compatibility between GATS and the proposed multilateral framework on investment.

Exceptions and balance of payments safeguards. Korea recognizes the need to allow exceptions to the general principle of non-discrimination in a multilateral framework on investment. Basically, these would be of two kinds: general exceptions and other exceptions. It seems likely that general exceptions for the purpose of protecting national security and maintaining public morals would be accepted without any great debate, since existing WTO rules already allow such exceptions. More problematic are other exceptions, in the context of national treatment and MFN treatment. Korea believes that member countries should first reach a consensus on the type of multilateral framework on investment that would be appropriate for WTO members before tackling the issue of other exceptions.

Balance of payments safeguards will also be necessary to enhance the flexibility of the multilateral framework on investment, but Korea believes that such provisions should apply only in exceptional circumstances and be subject to strict conditions. Notably, they should be limited to the duration of the balance of payments problem and should be phased out as the situation improves. Korea holds this position for two reasons.

First, it is unclear whether capital controls are an effective way of dealing with a balance of payments crisis: they may provide a temporary breathing space for a host country to implement policy measures to deal with the crisis, but on the other hand, it is widely accepted that they damage international confidence in the host country's economy. Thus, in the long run, capital controls have a negative effect on FDI inflows. In practice, it may be difficult for a country to protect its domestic economy from the international financial market quickly and effectively using capital controls.

Second, balance of payments safeguards are inconsistent with the principle of investor protection, which is the main purpose of an international investment agreement. Most of the world's existing bilateral investment treaties do not contain safeguard provisions restricting the free transfer of funds during a balance of payments crisis; those that do contain such provisions place strict conditions on the types of payments that can be repatriated by foreign-invested firms and on methods of payment. International investment agreements provide stronger protection for current transactions, including FDI-related payments, than they do for capital transactions. Notably, the Articles of Agreement of the IMF stipulate that restrictions can be imposed on payments and transfers for international capital transaction accounts, but not on those for current transaction accounts. The GATT and GATS both stipulate that their balance of payments safeguard provisions should be consistent with the IMF Articles of Agreement.

Dispute settlement procedures. The existing WTO rules cover only disputes between states. In line with this practice, Korea's preliminary position is that the multilateral framework on investment should not cover disputes between investors and states even if an investor's right to an arbitral tribunal has been denied; rather, investors should have access to an indirect method of appeal through a state-to-state dispute settlement mechanism. Another important question concerns the kind of dispute settlement mechanism that would be appropriate. Korea supports the view that the current procedures set out in the WTO's Dispute Settlement Understanding work well, and should be extended to the multilateral framework on investment.

6 CONCLUSIONS AND RECOMMENDATIONS

Korea's rapid economic development over the last decade has been spurred by three important events. The first was the establishment of the WTO in January 1995. Since then, open and fair competition has been the principal guideline for Korea in formulating its domestic and international economic policies. Under this guideline, the government dramatically liberalized both inward and outward FDI and industrial restructuring accelerated. Domestic companies operating in labor-intensive industries have continued to move abroad, and the *chaebol* have invested competitively overseas to serve international markets and benefit from the latest developments in high technology. Inward FDI was another avenue for the introduction of advanced technology.

The second important event was Korea's accession to the OECD in 1996. This event further accelerated liberalization, not only in trade but also in international capital flows. During negotiations for membership, Korea drew up a liberalization schedule for investment and foreign exchange transactions that served to increase the transparency of investment-related laws, regulations, and procedures, and make them more investor-friendly.

The third important event was the 1997 Asian financial crisis. The liberalization schedule established when Korea joined the OECD was accelerated under a stand-by arrangement agreed between the government and the IMF. FDI was totally liberalized so that Korea's regulations are now on a par with those in developed countries; even foreign exchange transactions were almost entirely liberalized. While some of the impetus for Korea's rapid economic transition came from outside, without the domestic policy priority placed on liberalization, it would not have been possible for the country to experience such rapid development.

Inward and outward FDI stands at the core of Korea's economic transition. Despite the huge increase in FDI after the financial crisis, more inflows are needed to allow Korea to further develop its high-tech industries and its high-value-added service industries. Korean companies also need to invest abroad to enhance their competitiveness. In view of the need for increased flows of both inward and outward FDI, the government believes that this is an appropriate time to create a more favorable environment for global investment. If the discussions at the WTO on a multilateral framework on investment bear fruit, this could contribute to the creation of a more transparent and stable international investment environment.

The Korean government therefore fully supports the launch of negotiations on a multilateral framework on investment. Without the voluntary participation of developing countries, these talks will not be effective. That is why it is essential for Korea and other countries that support a multilateral investment framework to design flexible approaches that will accommodate the needs of developing countries and encourage them to participate. Korea believes that a good way to help developing countries achieve the level of capability that is required to understand and implement the framework is to provide various types of technical assistance as an integral part of the agreement. More resources should be directed toward achieving this goal.

NOTES

1   The Foreign Investment Promotion Act of 1998 defines FDI as an investment in a domestic firm of more than 10 percent of equity capital by a single foreign person or firm. This is similar to the definition given in the IMF's *Balance of Payments Manual*, which regards FDI as the acquisition by a foreign company of 10 percent or more of the ordinary shares or voting power or equivalent of a domestic firm.

2   In the statistics, FDI is considered to fall into one of three categories: acquisitions of new shares, acquisitions of outstanding or existing shares, and long-term loans. At present, the acquisition of business units and assets is included in the first category. There are thus no official data on cross-border M&As involving the acquisition of both a company's outstanding shares and its assets or business units. The Ministry of Commerce, Industry, and Energy (1999) estimates that in 1998, 53 percent of all FDI projects involved the acquisition of both the shares and the assets of a company.

3   This trend toward being more mindful of selling conditions became evident around the time of the 2000 general elections, when the opposition party accused the government of conducting fire sales of national assets leading to an 'outflow of national wealth.'

4   Average tariff rates for 1997–2001 are calculated from data provided by the Ministry of Finance and Economy.

5   Negotiated by the WTO, the ITA provided for participants to eliminate duties on IT-related products covered by the agreement by 1 January 2000. Developing country participants were granted extensions for some products.

6   The response rate was 85 percent.

7   Kim (1999) provides anecdotal evidence of spillover effects in some other manufacturing industries.

8   This section draws on J.-D. Kim (1997, 1999).

9   In this respect, Korea was following the example of Taipei,China, which had already adopted a similar strategy (Mathews 1995: 121).

10 This section draws on Kim and Kim (2003).

11 In most of the service subsectors, the Korean government implemented domestic deregulation and external liberalization almost simultaneously. It used the

external commitment to liberalization to reduce any opposition or resistance to domestic deregulation, and implemented domestic deregulation to help domestic firms establish their market position before foreign penetration. Hence, it is difficult to differentiate the impact of domestic deregulation from that of external liberalization.

12 POS systems record a comprehensive range of information about a sale at the time and place at which the transaction is made, using specialized equipment such as optical scanners and magnetic card readers. This information is used to track sales, update inventory, check credit, and so on, all at the point of sale.

13 This section draws on Kim (2003).

14 Through its influence on the board of Hansol PCS, Bell Canada played a similar role in resolving some of the corporate governance issues facing the telecommunications sector. See Yun (2000) for a more detailed discussion of this episode.

6

Malaysia

Tham Siew-Yean

1 INTRODUCTION

Historically, foreign direct investment (FDI) has played an important role in Malaysia's economic development. Its roots can be traced back to the colonial government, which brought foreign capital into the country to develop the plantation and mining sectors. Following independence in 1957, FDI was tapped first for the development of import substitution industries and then, from the late 1960s, for the development of export-oriented industries. Despite calls in the early 1990s and again in 2003 for Malaysia to reduce its dependence on FDI and promote domestic investment, FDI has continued to play an integral part in the development process.

The next section of this chapter examines the development of, and broad policy framework for, FDI in Malaysia. The specific policies that have been implemented to attract and govern foreign investment are examined in Section 3. Section 4 analyzes the impact of these policies, while Section 5 focuses on Malaysia's international obligations under the World Trade Organization (WTO). A concluding section summarizes the main findings and provides some policy recommendations.

2 AN OVERVIEW OF FDI IN MALAYSIA

Pattern of Inflows

To create the enabling environment for multinational enterprises (MNEs) to operate in Malaysia, the government invested heavily in basic infrastructure and education while also nurturing overall macroeconomic stability. Malaysia's relatively well-developed legal infrastructure, based on the British system, also helped to make the country an attractive destination for FDI. With the exception of selected heavy industries (the national car projects, steel, petrochemicals, and cement), which were protected between 1980 and 1985 during a second round of import substitution, Malaysia has pursued an export promotion strategy since 1970. Hence, the overall trade regime in Malaysia can be said generally to have been outward-oriented.

Tariffs have been the main instrument of protection used in Malaysian trade policy; quantitative restrictions and import licensing are relatively less important. According to Menon (2000: 238), the average import-weighted tariff rate in the primary and manufacturing sectors rose from 9.7 percent in 1980–83 to 14.7 percent in 1984–87. It subsequently fell to 11.5 percent in 1988–90 and further to 11.2 percent in 1991–93. Tariff rates continued to fall progressively as Malaysia sought to meet its commitments to the WTO. The simple average applied most favored nation (MFN) tariff rate fell to 8.1 percent in 1997, before rising slightly to 9.2 percent in 2001 following an increase in tariffs on some products in 1998 during the Asian financial crisis.

The effective rate of protection fell from 50 percent in 1966 to 24 percent in 1979, then increased slightly to 28 percent in 1987 during the second round of import substitution (Rokiah 1996: 174). There was a wide range in the effective rate of protection, with some subsectors, such as wood products, furniture, non-metallic mineral products, basic metals, and transport and equipment, receiving relatively high levels of protection.

Malaysia has maintained a relatively open stance toward FDI, providing specific incentives to attract MNEs into the domestic manufacturing sector. The pro-trade environment, coupled with Malaysia's policy focus on FDI since the late 1960s, has yielded a steady inflow of foreign capital. A program of FDI liberalization, especially after 1985, coincided with fortuitous external circumstances in the region to garner large inflows in the late 1980s and early 1990s. By 1993, Malaysia had become one of the ten largest host countries for FDI inflows and stock among developing economies. In that year FDI accounted for as much as 8.6 percent of GDP and 23.4 percent of gross fixed capital formation (Table 6.1).

Following the advent of the Asian financial crisis, which slashed corporate profits and retained earnings and triggered a loss of investor confidence, inflows dropped sharply to 3.8 percent of GDP and 14 percent of gross fixed capital formation in 1998. Although Malaysia imposed selective capital controls in September 1998, there is no evidence to suggest that these contributed to the contraction in FDI. The rapid recovery of the econ-

Table 6.1   Malaysia: Trends in FDI, 1991–2002

Year	Net FDI[a] (RM billion)	Nominal GDP (RM billion)	FDI as % of GDP	GFCF (RM billion in current prices)	FDI as % of GFCF
1991	11.1	135.1	8.2	30.6	36.3
1992	13.1	150.7	8.7	53.5	24.5
1993	14.8	172.2	8.6	63.4	23.4
1994	12.0	195.5	6.1	76.4	15.7
1995	14.6	222.5	6.6	107.8	13.5
1996	18.4	253.7	7.2	121.4	15.1
1997	17.8	281.8	6.3	121.5	14.6
1998	10.6	283.2	3.8	76.0	14.0
1999	14.8	300.8	4.9	65.8	22.5
2000	14.4	342.2	4.2	87.7	16.4
2001	2.1	334.6	0.6	83.3	2.5
2002	12.2	361.6	3.4	86.0	14.2

GFCF: gross fixed capital formation.

a   Net FDI is inflows of FDI after taking account of outflows arising from the liquidation of FDI in Malaysia and loan repayments to related companies.

Source: Net FDI and GDP: Central Bank of Malaysia; GFCF: Ministry of Finance, Malaysia (various years), *Economic Report*, Kuala Lumpur.

omy in 1999 helped to restore inflows to 4.9 percent of GDP and 22.5 percent of gross fixed capital formation. However, a global slowdown in manufacturing, stock market declines across the world (Brooks, Fan, and Sumulong 2003b: 2), and the terrorist attack on New York on 11 September 2001 exacerbated competitive pressures for FDI, resulting in an all-time low in inflows of foreign capital in 2001. In that year, FDI accounted for a mere 0.6 percent of GDP and 2.5 percent of gross fixed capital formation, improving subsequently to 3.4 percent of GDP and 14.2 percent of gross fixed capital formation in 2002.

There are no published data on the components of Malaysia's total FDI flows. However, the Central Bank of Malaysia (2001: 55) estimates that retained earnings have accounted for approximately 50 percent of inflows since the early 1990s, with the remainder made up of new equity (36 percent) and loans (14 percent). Since Malaysia's policy response to the financial crisis did not include the widespread sale of assets to foreigners, inflows since the crisis have mainly been in the form of new production facilities and an expansion in production capacity rather than mergers and acquisitions. Data from the Malaysian Industrial Development Authority (MIDA) on the composition of capital investment in approved manufacturing projects reveal that the foreign equity component fell from 35.6 percent in 1991 to 9.3 percent in 2001. From this, it appears that the non-equity components of FDI (loans and retained earnings) have been increasing in importance.

There has been a discernable shift in the distribution of FDI across the main sectors of the economy. The share of the manufacturing sector—the main recipient of FDI before the financial crisis—fell from 65 percent of total FDI in 1990–97 to about 43 percent in 1998–2000 (Central Bank of Malaysia 2001: 55). The decline in the relative attractiveness of the manufacturing sector may be attributed to the loss of Malaysia's low-wage locational advantage in this sector, combined with a shortage of skilled and professional workers that is constraining the drive to attract technology-oriented FDI in manufacturing.

In contrast, the share of services jumped from 10 percent of total FDI in 1990–97 to 35 percent in 1998–2000. Within services, financial services, trading, marketing, communications, and information-related services such as computer software have been the most favored subsectors, in response to increasing liberalization in these areas. Inflows of FDI in the oil and gas sector have remained more or less stable at 18 percent of total inflows in 1990–97 and 19 percent in 1998–2000. The level of foreign ownership in the sector has, however, declined, from over 80 percent before the crisis to about 70 percent afterwards (Central Bank of Malaysia 2001: 57).

Within manufacturing, foreign companies accounted for about 60 percent of total manufacturing investment before the Asian financial crisis, but only 40 percent afterwards (Central Bank of Malaysia 2001: 56). The electrical and electronics subsector became the largest recipient of FDI in 1989, overtaking food manufacturing (Table 6.2). The relative importance of FDI in textiles and textile products declined from 1985 through to 1994. The subsector has subsequently rebounded, and was the third largest recipient of FDI in 1998 after electronics and petroeum and coal. Data based on companies in production are not available after 1998. However, subsequent data based on approved projects show that the electrical and electronics subsector has continued to dominate inflows of FDI, followed by the chemical and petrochemical industries. In 2001, the top three recipients

Table 6.2   Malaysia: FDI by Manufacturing Subsector, 1986–98 (%)[a]

Industry	1986	1987	1988	1989	1990	1991	1992	1993	1994	1995	1996	1997	1998
Food manufacturing	14.3	14.9	16.6	15.3	11.3	8.8	8.4	8.0	8.5	7.5	6.5	5.7	5.1
Beverages & tobacco	8.9	8.4	7.7	7.2	4.2	2.3	2.4	2.1	2.8	2.6	2.6	2.8	2.6
Textiles & textile products	10.4	10.2	9.5	9.5	8.7	7.1	6.5	5.5	6.4	10.4	9.4	9.3	8.1
Leather & leather products	0.4	0.4	0.4	0.3	0.2	0.3	0.2	0.2	0.2	0.2	0.2	0.1	0.2
Wood & wood products	1.7	1.7	1.8	1.6	2.3	2.5	3.5	3.8	3.3	3.5	3.5	3.4	3.3
Furniture & fixtures	0.3	0.3	0.3	0.4	0.4	0.5	0.8	0.7	0.7	0.6	0.6	0.5	0.5
Paper, printing & publishing	1.4	1.5	1.4	1.4	2.3	1.9	1.3	1.1	0.9	0.9	0.9	1.0	1.0
Chemicals & chemical products	11.1	7.9	7.6	7.2	6.8	5.9	5.6	6.8	9.6	8.1	9.8	5.8	6.1
Petroleum & coal	8.4	10.4	9.2	8.1	11.2	9.3	5.2	8.3	5.6	4.8	4.9	9.1	8.9
Rubber products	3.6	4.0	4.2	3.9	3.8	4.1	3.7	3.1	3.2	2.8	2.8	2.7	2.6
Plastic products	0.7	0.7	0.9	1.2	1.4	2.5	2.7	3.0	3.1	3.2	2.9	2.7	2.4
Non-metallic mineral products	8.9	9.7	8.9	8.1	8.3	6.1	7.4	6.4	6.2	5.7	4.9	4.7	4.8
Basic metal products	6.9	6.6	5.9	4.4	3.8	4.2	5.5	5.0	4.8	5.0	4.8	5.8	5.4
Fabricated metal products	4.5	4.5	4.6	4.2	3.8	4.5	4.8	5.1	4.1	4.0	3.9	3.8	3.8
Machinery manufacturing	1.9	2.0	2.0	2.0	2.2	2.0	1.6	2.5	3.2	4.0	4.3	4.3	5.0
Electrical & electronic products	10.8	10.8	12.8	19.1	23.2	30.9	32.3	30.2	30.3	30.4	31.9	32.4	33.7
Transport equipment	4.2	4.3	4.0	3.7	4.0	3.1	3.8	4.5	4.2	3.8	3.5	3.3	3.0
Scientific & measuring equipment	0.9	0.9	1.3	1.1	1.0	2.8	3.1	2.6	1.8	1.7	1.5	1.7	3.0
Miscellaneous	0.8	0.9	0.9	1.1	1.0	1.0	1.1	1.1	1.0	0.9	0.9	0.8	0.6
Total	100.0	100.0	100.0	100.0	100.0	100.0	100.0	100.0	100.0	100.0	100.0	100.0	100.0

a   Based on companies in production. Data are available only until 1998.
Source: Malaysian Industrial Development Authority (various years), *Statistics on the Manufacturing Sector*, Kuala Lumpur.

BOX 1 THE AUTOMOBILE INDUSTRY IN MALAYSIA

The first national car project, Proton—Perusahaan Otomobil Nasional, or the National Automobile Enterprise—was established in 1983 as a joint venture between Mitsubishi Motor Corporation and Mitsubishi Corporation (each with equity of 15 percent) and the Malaysian firm HICOM (with equity of 70 percent). The objective of the project was to rationalize the local motor vehicle industry and foster growth in the rest of the industrial sector through technical spin-offs and linkage effects. Another goal was to accelerate indigenous (*bumiputera*) participation in the automotive industry.

The first car produced by Proton was the Saga—essentially a modified version of the Mitsubishi Lancer. The domestic plant was responsible for body stamping, assembly, painting and trim, and final assembly (Machado 1994: 301). The cars were assembled from imported kits, so it is not surprising to find that the Saga had a local content of less than 20 percent (Jomo 1994: 280). Under the government's vendor development program, local content was progressively increased over time. In 2000, when Proton launched its first domestically designed car, the Waja, local content in value terms was reported to be 80 percent, with only the engine and transmission still being imported from Mitsubishi. The Waja was made possible by Proton's strategic shift into design in 1996. In acquiring 80 percent of Lotus Group International, it acquired 80 percent of the design skills needed to design an indigenous car.

Proton is the best known but not the sole national car project in Malaysia. Over the past two decades two other such projects have been launched, each with a different technology partner. These were Perodua, launched in 1993 to produce mini passenger cars with Daihatsu (a subsidiary of Toyota Corporation), and a national truck project set up in 1997 with the assistance of Isuzu Motors.

The introduction of the national car projects radically altered the struc-

---

of approved foreign investment in manufacturing were electrical and electronic products; paper, printing and publishing; and non-metallic mineral products (MITI 2001: 114).

Malaysia's national car projects have contributed to the decline in the attractiveness of the automotive subsector for FDI (Table 6.2, Box 1). Foreign assemblers that had previously formed minority joint ventures with local distributors to produce cars behind high protective tariff walls have been unable to compete against the national cars, which until very recently have continued to attract favorable treatment from the government (OECD 1999: 139).

ture of the domestic automotive industry. Previously, automotive assembly had been fragmented and inefficient, with 13 assembly plants producing a large number of makes and models for the domestic market. With the arrival of the national car projects, these assemblers became increasingly marginalized in terms of production and sales, leaving them to either focus on the upper segment of the market or shift into component manufacturing. Supported by both protection and subsidies, the domestic market share of the national cars increased steadily from 64 percent in 1991 to 93 percent in 2000. However, this has failed to translate into success abroad: exports of the national cars are quite small.

The impending liberalization of the automobile sector in 2005 under the ASEAN Free Trade Area agreement has forced Proton to accelerate its development in a bid to retain its post-liberalization market share. It has reportedly spent about RM4.2 billion over the past five years on R&D and the construction of a new manufacturing facility at Tanjung Malim, Perak (*New Straits Times*, 23 April 2003: B2). The new plant will make increased use of automation and will have five times the capacity of the existing Shah Alam plant, which itself has a maximum capacity of 230,000 units. The envisioned production efficiencies and scale economies generated by the new plant should substantially lower the costs of production.

In the meantime, global players are increasing their presence in Malaysia. For example, a joint venture formed between DRB-HICOM Bhd. (holding equity of 36 percent), Honda Motor Co. Ltd. (49 percent), and Oriental Holdings (15 percent) was formed in July 2000 to manufacture and distribute Honda cars in Malaysia from early 2003 (*Star*, 13 June 2001: 3). As Honda already has plants in three other ASEAN countries—Thailand, Indonesia, and the Philippines—it is clear that it is positioning itself to establish a stake in the ASEAN Free Trade Area market. The acceleration of competition in this sector is indeed good news for the consumers of Malaysia.

In contrast to the open courtship of foreign investment in the manufacturing sector, the government has practiced a more selective approach to FDI in services. The foreign equity ownership limit that prevails in services has, however, been liberalized for high-technology companies operating in the Multimedia Super Corridor (MSC), a new type of zone set up in 1996 to attract businesses specializing in multimedia and information and communications technology (ICT). As of 2001 there were 40 such companies, with another ten expected to be accorded the right to operate in the corridor by 2003. Approvals for foreign investment in the MSC increased from RM2 billion in 1997–99 to RM4.2 billion in 2001 (Central Bank of Malaysia 2001: 57). There are currently 14 wholly foreign-owned banks in Malaysia. Foreigners account for 20 percent of total shareholder funds in the banking sector and 40 percent in the insurance industry. Limits on foreign equity ownership have been lifted in key non-financial service sectors such as telecommunications, forwarding agencies, and shipping agencies, while foreign participation is also allowed at the management level in the energy, ports, and airline sectors (Central Bank of Malaysia 2001: 58). This has led to several acquisitions and strategic alliances in recent years. For example, British Telecom acquired a stake in the telecommunications company Binariang in 1998, Maersk-Sealand in the port of Tanjung Pelepas in 2000, and Hutchison Port Holdings in the port of Westport in 2000.

As liberalization has proceeded in services, foreign investment as a share of total investment in the sector has increased substantially—from about 5 percent before the crisis to 50 percent in recent years. It is likely that this trend will continue in view of the impending liberalization of the services sector to meet General Agreement on Trade in Services (GATS) commitments.

The regional distribution of FDI within Malaysia shows a consistent bias toward the three relatively rich states on the west coast of Peninsular Malaysia: Selangor, Penang, and Johor. Osman-Rani (1992: 132) found that these three states together attracted about 62 percent of total investment approved for the manufacturing sector between 1980 and 1989. Because of their good infrastructure and amenities, they continued to be the main recipients of foreign investment for projects approved between 1991 and 2002 (Table 6.3). Trengganu on the east coast, which received only 3.6 percent of foreign investment in 1980–89 (Osman-Rani 1992: 132), saw an increase in its share to 11.8 percent in 1991–2002 as a result of an influx of petrochemical industries to exploit the availability of petroleum and gas there. Overall, the distribution of FDI across Peninsular Malaysia has become more even over the past decade, with the share of the other 12 states (that is, all except Selangor, Penang, and Johor) increasing to 54.6 percent in the 1990s compared with 38 percent in the previous decade.

Table 6.4 shows inflows of FDI to Malaysia by source country. The appreciation of East Asian currencies following the Plaza Accord of 1985, the rising costs of domestic production in East Asia, and the withdrawal of preferential duty-free entry for products under the US Generalized System of Preferences prompted an outflow of investment from East Asia in the second half of the 1980s, particularly from Japan, which was experiencing

Table 6.3   Malaysia: Approved Manufacturing Projects by Location, 1991–2002

State	Establish-ments (no.)	Employ-ment (thousand)	Total (RM million)	Amount Invested			
				By Local Firms (RM million)	(%)	By Foreign Firms (RM million)	(%)
Kuala Lumpur	288	20.6	2,848.4	2,149.8	1.5	698.6	0.4
Labuan	15	1.1	556.2	343.4	0.2	212.8	0.1
Selangor	2,988	293.3	59,574.3	30,053.8	21.2	29,520.5	16.1
Penang	1,400	192.1	30,358.9	8,165.9	5.8	22,193.0	12.1
Perak	712	92.7	19,373.9	9,452.6	6.7	9,921.3	5.4
Johor	2,431	266.8	40,080.4	12,142.9	8.6	27,937.4	15.2
Negeri Sembilan	472	59.8	18,156.4	5,023.4	3.5	13,133.0	7.2
Malacca	406	62.8	20,286.7	5,700.8	4.0	14,586.0	8.0
Kedah	695	110.6	26,324.0	8,248.6	5.8	18,075.4	9.9
Pahang	243	37.5	15,010.0	6,255.2	4.4	8,754.8	4.8
Kelantan	89	13.5	1,845.8	1,526.5	1.1	319.3	0.2
Trengganu	181	48.6	45,150.2	23,421.1	16.5	21,729.2	11.8
Perlis	61	7.6	3,847.2	2,866.4	2.0	980.8	0.5
Sabah	418	72.8	13,304.1	8,184.5	5.8	5,119.6	2.8
Sarawak	443	81.0	28,331.8	18,086.5	12.8	10,245.3	5.6
Total	10,842	1,360.7	325,048.3	141,621.5	100.0	183,426.8	100.0

Source: Unpublished data from the Malaysian Industrial Development Authority, Kuala Lumpur.

Table 6.4   Malaysia: Sources of Inward FDI, 1986–98 (%)[a]

	1986	1987	1988	1989	1990	1991	1992
Asia-Pacific							
Australia	3.0	2.8	2.7	2.7	2.8	2.2	2.2
Canada	1.2	1.2	1.1	1.2	1.2	1.0	0.1
Hong Kong, China	5.9	5.2	4.7	4.5	4.8	4.0	3.8
Indonesia	0.7	0.8	0.8	0.7	0.7	0.6	0.5
Japan	20.1	19.7	21.1	25.7	25.9	32.3	35.5
Rep. of Korea	0.1	1.3	1.2	1.0	1.0	0.9	0.8
New Zealand	0.2	0.1	0.1	0.1	0.1	0.1	0.1
Philippines	0.6	0.5	0.5	0.6	0.4	0.4	0.3
Singapore	29.2	28.9	30.5	30.3	28.7	24.1	22.0
Taipei,China	0.5	0.5	1.1	1.3	2.0	6.9	8.5
Thailand	0.7	0.8	0.8	0.7	0.6	0.5	0.4
United States	6.4	5.8	5.5	5.4	7.1	4.4	4.4
Europe							
Denmark	1.8	1.8	1.9	1.5	1.8	1.5	1.4
France	0.3	0.3	1.0	0.2	0.2	0.4	0.1
Germany	2.7	2.5	2.6	3.0	3.5	2.7	2.4
Luxembourg	1.6	1.5	0.1	0.8	1.3	0.2	0.1
Netherlands	2.6	3.1	3.3	3.4	2.5	3.2	2.8
Norway	0.2	0.2	0.2	0.1	0.2	0.1	0.1
Sweden	0.8	0.1	0.2	0.2	0.1	0.1	0.1
Switzerland	2.3	2.5	2.2	2.0	2.2	1.6	1.4
United Kingdom	15.5	16.2	13.3	11.6	10.0	9.3	8.9
Other	3.6	4.2	5.1	3.0	3.1	3.5	4.1

n.a.: not available.

a   Based on companies in production. Data are available only to 1998.

Table 6.4 (continued)

	1993	1994	1995	1996	1997	1998
Asia-Pacific						
Australia	1.8	2.0	1.6	1.6	2.0	1.8
Canada	0.1	0.1	0.1	0.1	0.5	0.4
Hong Kong, China	2.5	4.2	3.4	3.1	2.2	2.2
Indonesia	0.5	0.4	0.4	0.4	1.4	1.3
Japan	33.7	34.6	32.0	32.7	33.9	33.2
Rep. of Korea	1.1	1.1	1.4	1.6	1.3	1.2
New Zealand	0.1	0.0	0.0	0.0	0.0	0.0
Philippines	0.2	0.2	0.2	0.2	0.1	0.1
Singapore	21.2	21.0	19.1	17.7	15.7	14.8
Taipei,China	9.3	9.5	15.0	15.2	14.7	12.3
Thailand	0.4	0.4	0.3	0.3	0.3	0.3
United States	6.1	6.4	6.2	7.5	7.6	9.5
Europe						
Denmark	0.8	1.1	0.6	0.8	0.4	0.5
France	0.1	0.3	0.2	0.2	0.4	0.2
Germany	2.8	2.6	2.4	2.8	2.9	3.1
Luxembourg	0.1	0.1	0.1	0.1	0.1	n.a.
Netherlands	4.5	3.6	3.4	3.9	3.6	6.7
Norway	0.1	0.1	0.1	0.0	0.1	0.1
Sweden	0.1	0.1	1.2	0.1	0.1	0.1
Switzerland	1.3	1.1	1.0	0.9	0.9	0.8
United Kingdom	7.0	6.1	5.7	4.6	4.0	2.9
Other	6.2	8.1	5.6	6.2	7.8	8.5

Source: 1986–89: Ariff (1991); 1990–98: Malaysian Industrial Development Authority (various years), *Statistics on the Manufacturing Sector*, Kuala Lumpur.

a shortage of blue-collar workers. Malaysia's proactive FDI policies allowed it to benefit from these outflows, as reflected in the rising share of investment from Japan and Taipei,China during the early 1990s (Table 6.4). In 1991 Japan became the single largest investor in the country, overtaking Singapore, whose historical ties with, and geographical proximity to, Malaysia had given it a longstanding position as the country's most important investor.

Although Japan remains important, the United States overtook it as the largest source of FDI in 1999–2000. In 2001, the United States and Japan ranked as the top two investor countries, followed by the People's Republic of China (PRC), Germany, and Singapore (MITI 2002: 117). Investment from other East Asian countries, such as Taipei,China and the Republic of Korea, has also continued to flow into the country.

Determinants of Inflows

It is clear from the discussion so far that Malaysia has been relatively successful in attracting FDI, especially before the onset of the Asian financial crisis. Both push and pull factors have contributed to this success. Malaysia's advantages as a location for FDI have included its macroeconomic and political stability, good basic infrastructure, and established, relatively transparent legal framework. Foreign investors have also been attracted by the country's relatively liberal trade regime and low cost of labor, although the emergence of excess demand for labor in the 1990s has eroded this latter advantage.

Malaysia's rapid recovery from the economic crisis of 1998 restored stability, laying the foundations for a restoration of FDI inflows. In response to the crisis and subsequent fall in FDI as a proportion of GDP, the government further liberalized its policies while also implementing capital controls to regulate portfolio flows. Malaysia's WTO commitments complemented the moves to liberalize FDI, with foreign investors viewing the removal of local content requirements positively. Consequently, both the investment and the trade regime became more open.

Outflows

As with inflows, an interplay of internal and external factors led to a rise in investment outflows, or reverse investment, in the 1990s. Domestically, Malaysia's robust economic performance from the second half of the 1980s through to the onset of the financial crisis in 1997 increased the income and profits of Malaysian firms, spurring them to venture abroad in search of strategic alliances (Tham 1998: 104). Based on a case study of seven Malaysian firms with overseas investments (or planning to invest overseas), Ragayah (1999: 485) concluded that the need to find new markets was the main motivation for firms to invest abroad. Rising labor costs and labor shortages in the domestic market had prompted some Malaysian firms to relocate to labor surplus economies such as Viet Nam and the PRC. Another impetus for investment abroad was the desire to acquire foreign technology. Among the external factors for investment outflows were the increasingly open door policies of some labor surplus economies, which had enhanced their attractiveness as host economies.

The government has actively encouraged reverse investment through the provision of incentives, such as a 50 percent reduction of tax on remitted income earned from overseas investments. Incentives have been directed especially toward areas in which Malaysian firms have special expertise, such as resource-based manufacturing and the processing of agricultural products. As with inflows, investment guarantee and double taxation agreements concluded with other countries provide the legal framework for the security and protection of Malaysian investors overseas. Since the financial crisis, Malaysian companies investing abroad have been required to repatriate all interest, dividends, profits, and proceeds from the sale of investments as soon as such funds are received.

Jomo (2002: 4) argues that the government has in some cases taken a leading and proactive role in the promotion of investment abroad, in line with the South Commission's promotion of South–South investment.[1] Padayachee and Valodia (2002: 32) found that Malaysia was the second largest investor in South Africa between 1994 and 1999. Some of the companies that had invested there were closely linked to the Malaysian governing party, thereby lending credence to the authors' contention that some Malaysian investment in South Africa is politically motivated.

Unlike information on investment inflows, data on outflows are quite sparse. However, the Central Bank of Malaysia, which monitors the flow of investments through payment and receipt forms submitted to its balance of payments department, does publish some rudimentary data on Malaysian investment abroad (Table 6.5). Total investment outflows increased from a mere RM318 million in 1980 to RM554 million in 1990, then rose sharply to RM1,310.2 million in 1992 (Tham 1998: 114). More significantly, direct investment in business activities jumped from 22.6 percent of total Malaysian investment abroad in 1980 to 77 percent in the first three-quarters of 1994, showing the shift away from the dominance of real estate acquisition in Malaysian investment abroad between 1980 and 1985 (Tham 1998: 112).

Despite the Asian crisis, Malaysian investment abroad continued to increase from RM10,715 million in 1996 to RM13,391 million in 1999

Table 6.5   *Malaysia: Gross Investment Overseas in Selected Countries, 1992–2001 (RM million)*[a]

Country	1992	1993	1994	1995	1996
United States	93.9 (7.2)	627.6 (18.4)	445.3 (8.0)	478.0 (7.2)	1,005.1 (9.4)
United Kingdom	63.0 (4.8)	372.2 (10.9)	436.9 (7.9)	439.8 (6.6)	595.1 (5.6)
PRC	20.1 (1.5)	112.2 (3.3)	216.3 (3.9)	326.8 (4.9)	451.3 (4.2)
Australia	99.9 (7.6)	137.4 (4.0)	461.0 (8.3)	542.2 (8.2)	425.2 (4.0)
New Zealand	51.0 (3.9)	9.4 (0.3)	98.6 (1.8)	41.2 (0.6)	30.1 (0.3)
Indonesia	10.0 (0.8)	10.6 (0.3)	87.9 (1.6)	309.5 (4.7)	394.3 (3.7)
Philippines	5.9 (0.5)	54.0 (1.6)	223.2 (4.0)	643.9 (9.7)	252.0 (2.4)
Singapore	258.6 (19.7)	686.1 (20.1)	987.4 (17.8)	2,063.8 (31.1)	1,689.2 (15.8)
Thailand	24.0 (1.8)	32.7 (1.0)	43.4 (0.8)	78.0 (1.2)	126.0 (1.2)
Viet Nam	13.3 (1.0)	7.6 (0.2)	69.2 (1.2)	94.5 (1.4)	106.6 (1.0)
Cambodia	6.5 (0.5)	7.4 (0.2)	4.3 (0.1)	16.2 (0.2)	57.2 (0.5)
Myanmar	0.9 (0.1)	3.2 (0.1)	3.7 (0.1)	0.4 (0.0)	17.7 (0.2)
Other	663.1 (50.6)	1,352.0 (39.6)	2,459.4 (44.4)	1,609.4 (24.2)	5,565.2 (51.9)
Total	1,310.2 (100.0)	3,412.4 (100.0)	5,536.6 (100.0)	6,643.7 (100.0)	10,715.0 (100.0)

a   Gross investment overseas refers to direct equity investment, real estate purchases, and loans to non-residents abroad, and includes capital invested or loans extended by foreign-owned companies to parent companies abroad. For the purpose of compiling balance of payments statistics, capital invested in parent companies abroad must be offset against the capital invested in Malaysia by these

Table 6.5 (continued)

Country	1997	1998	1999	2000	2001
United States	1,334.8	1,653.8	513.4	3,924.0	4,013.7
	(12.9)	(14.2)	(3.8)	(28.4)	(30.6)
United Kingdom	1,715.3	822.4	553.3	532.5	269.9
	(16.5)	(7.1)	(4.1)	(3.9)	(2.1)
PRC	331.1	79.4	201.5	152.7	313.2
	(3.2)	(0.7)	(1.5)	(1.1)	(2.4)
Australia	504.3	2,747.8	103.5	72.6	303.8
	(4.9)	(23.6)	(0.8)	(0.5)	(2.3)
New Zealand	48.6	18.0	9.3	11.9	15.9
	(0.5)	(0.2)	(0.1)	(0.1)	(0.1)
Indonesia	648.5	229.4	397.8	535.6	1,682.9
	(6.2)	(2.0)	(3.0)	(3.9)	(12.8)
Philippines	299.6	105.9	99.9	109.5	53.8
	(2.9)	(0.9)	(0.7)	(0.8)	(0.4)
Singapore	1,783.6	2,095.5	1,634.9	2,920.4	2,081.7
	(17.2)	(18.0)	(12.2)	(21.1)	(15.9)
Thailand	132.5	540.1	151.2	292.4	134.4
	(1.3)	(4.6)	(1.1)	(2.1)	(1.0)
Viet Nam	142.7	71.0	141.8	49.8	87.6
	(1.4)	(0.6)	(1.1)	(0.4)	(0.7)
Cambodia	40.1	88.0	7.4	39.4	4.9
	(0.4)	(0.8)	(0.1)	(0.3)	(0.0)
Myanmar	8.5	83.8	78.6	2.5	2.9
	(0.1)	(0.7)	(0.6)	(0.0)	(0.0)
Other	3,395.1	3,085.3	9,498.5	5,165.5	4,142.4
	(32.7)	(26.6)	(70.9)	(37.4)	(31.6)
Total	10,384.7	11,620.4	13,391.1	13,808.8	13,107.1
	(100.0)	(100.0)	(100.0)	(100.0)	(100.0)

parent companies. At present, the central bank's Cash Balance of Payments System is not able to segregate this type of transaction. In the table, figures shown in parentheses are the proportion of total overseas investment.

Source: 1992–95: Ragayah (1999); 1996–2001: <http://www.bnm.gov.my/files/publication/msb/2003/10/xls/viii_13.xls>, accessed 16 December 2003.

(Table 6.5). Unfortunately it is not possible to apportion this increase between direct equity investment, purchases of real estate, and loans to non-residents since no published data are available on the categories of investment abroad for the post-crisis period. There is, however, some anecdotal evidence to indicate that the crisis may have affected the sustainability of some Malaysian investment abroad, as documented by Padayachee and Valodia (2002: 40) for the case of the South African investments of Renong and SMG Holdings.

Singapore was the largest recipient of Malaysian investment abroad in 1992–96; the United States emerged as the largest host economy in 2000–01. The share of other ASEAN economies has tended to increase over time. For instance, Indonesia's share of outward investment increased until 1996, fell during the economic crisis, and has since recovered substantially, comprising 12.8 percent of the total in 2001.

3   PAST AND CURRENT POLICIES ON FDI

Fiscal and Non-fiscal Incentives

Malaysia has utilized fiscal incentives to attract FDI since its first formal effort to promote modern manufacturing: the enactment of the Pioneer Industries Ordinance (1958), which provided fiscal incentives for all pioneering firms. Fiscal and related incentives that provided either partial or full relief from income tax payments were also instituted in the Investment Incentives Act of 1968, which heralded the shift in government policy from import substitution to export promotion in 1970. It provided significant tax savings: the corporate tax rate generally prevailing in 1977–93 was as high as 40 percent, although it has since been progressively reduced to the current rate of 28 percent. The tax rate alone may not be a major factor in influencing the decisions of MNEs in their locational choice, however.

In 1986, the Investment Incentives Act was replaced by the Promotion of Investment Act, enacted to expand the scope and coverage of incentives and cater for the changing needs of industrial development. It extended the range of incentives available to the agricultural and tourism sectors, exempted industries awarded pioneer status from tax for extended periods, and removed the employment incentive, which had encouraged investors to use labor-intensive production techniques.

More importantly, it marked a shift in the granting of incentives from an investment basis to a product/activity basis (Ariff, Mahani, and Tan 1997: 13), in order to channel investment into the 12 subsectors targeted for industrial development under the country's First Industrial Master Plan

(1986–95). Since then selective intervention has continued, with the targeted industries and activities changing over time in accordance with changes in the priorities for industrial development. Initially, for example, some incentives were reserved for industries with export potential. Subsequent revisions to the incentives given under the Promotion of Investment Act have increasingly focused on the promotion of high-technology industries, strategic projects, R&D, small and medium-sized enterprises (SMEs), industrial linkages, machinery and equipment manufacturing, and training (Table 6.6). The act also provides specific incentives for the acquisition of proprietary rights and the use of information technology (IT). To keep potential investors informed of the latest changes, MIDA posts updates on the incentives provided under the act on the internet (see <www.mida.gov.my>).

Other incentives that allow manufacturers to offset some taxes, thereby enabling them to operate at a world price level, include exemptions from import duty on 'direct' raw materials and components; exemptions from import duty and sales tax on machinery and equipment as well as on spare parts and consumables; drawbacks of import duty and sales tax; and other sales tax exemptions (Ariff, Mahani, and Tan 1997: 20). The government also provides non-tax incentives such as export credit refinancing facilities and export credit insurance.

Institutions

The most important institutional means of achieving selective intervention in the economy has been the New Economic Policy (NEP), introduced following the inter-ethnic riots of 1969 to guide all socioeconomic planning in the country. One of the key objectives of the NEP was economic growth, which was to be achieved by accelerating industrialization, with the manufacturing sector as the engine of growth. The government actively courted FDI as part of this drive toward industrialization. A second main goal of the NEP was the redistribution of the ownership of wealth to ensure an equitable distribution among Malaysia's various ethnic groups. This too led to substantial interventions in economic activities. For example, the government imposed quotas of 30 percent in employment and equity ownership for the *bumiputera* (comprising the Malays, Ibans and other early inhabitants of Peninsular Malaysia, Sabah, and Sarawak) to increase their participation in the economy. These are enforced to this day to fulfill the redistribution objective.

The enforcement mechanism for the NEP was a licensing system set up under the Industrial Coordination Act of 1975. It empowered the Minister of Trade and Industry to impose any condition (including compliance with

*Table 6.6   Malaysia: List of Major Investment Incentives for the
Manufacturing Sector*

Incentive	Concession
Pioneer status	Five-year exemption from income tax for high-technology companies and companies in an approved industrial linkages scheme, thereafter a 30% corporate tax rate (15% for Sabah, Sarawak, Labuan, and designated parts of the Eastern Corridor of Peninsular Malaysia).[a]
Investment tax allowance	An allowance of 60% (80% for Sabah, Sarawak, Labuan, and designated parts of the Eastern Corridor of Peninsular Malaysia) on qualifying capital expenditure incurred during the first five years of operation. The allowance can be offset against 70% (85% for Sabah, Sarawak, Labuan, and designated parts of the Eastern Corridor of Peninsular Malaysia, and 100% for high-technology companies) of statutory income in the year of assessment, with any unutilized allowance carried forward to following years.
	For companies specializing in R&D activities, an allowance of 100% for R&D, contract R&D, and technical/vocational training companies (50% for in-house R&D companies) of qualifying capital expenditure incurred during the first ten years of operation. The allowance can be offset against 70% of statutory income in the year of assessment, with any unutilized allowance carried forward to following years.
Reinvestment allowance	An allowance of 60% on capital expenditure incurred by companies. The allowance can be offset against 70% (100% for Sabah, Sarawak, Labuan, and designated parts of the Eastern Corridor of Peninsular Malaysia) of statutory income in the year of assessment for companies that carry out reinvestment that will significantly improve their productivity levels. The allowance is given for a period of five years beginning from the first year of reinvestment. On expiry of the allowance, companies producing promoted products or engaging in promoted activities are eligible for an accelerated allowance on capital expenditure that enables capital write-off within three years.
Industrial adjustment incentives	Given to manufacturing industries for industry-wide reorganization, reconstruction, or amalgamation leading to improvements in industrial self-sufficiency, industrial technology, productivity, and the use of manpower and resources.

a   The Eastern Corridor of Peninsular Malaysia comprises the states of Kelantan, Trengganu, and Pahang, and the district of Mersing in Johor.

Table 6.6 (continued)

Incentive	Concession
Incentives to strengthen the industrial linkages scheme	For large companies: tax deductions for expenditure on employee training and product development. For suppliers: pioneer status or investment tax allowance for five years, with 100% exemption on statutory income.
Export incentives	Double deduction for expenditure on export-related activities (overseas advertising, freight charges, export credit insurance premiums); tax exemption on any increase in the value of exports in the services sector; industrial building allowance; export credit refinancing scheme.
Incentives to promote Malaysian brand names	Double deduction for expenditure on local advertising and professional fees paid to promote products carrying Malaysian brand names.
Training incentives	Single deduction for training expenses incurred before the commencement of the business. Double deduction for training expenses incurred at an approved training institution, for companies that do not contribute to the Human Resource Development Fund.[b]
Infrastructure allowance	100% allowance for expenditure on qualifying capital infrastructure incurred by companies in the manufacturing/commercial sectors in East Malaysia and the Eastern Corridor. The allowance can be offset against 85% of statutory income in the year of assessment, with any un-utilized allowance carried forward to following years.
R&D incentives	R&D company: Eligible for pioneer status with full income tax exemption at the statutory level for five years, or for an investment tax allowance of 100% of qualifying capital expenditure incurred within ten years. The allowance can be offset against 70% of statutory income in the year of assessment.
	Contract R&D company: Eligible to apply for an investment tax allowance of 100% of qualifying capital expenditure incurred within ten years. The allowance can be offset against 70% of statutory income in the year of assessment.
	In-house research: Eligible to apply for investment tax allowance of 50% on qualifying capital expenditure incurred within ten years.

b   The Human Resource Development Fund was launched in 1993 to encourage direct private sector participation in skills development. It operates on a levy/grant basis.

Source: Ministry of Finance (2003), *Economic Report 2002/2003*, Kuala Lumpur.

NEP targets) on the issuance and renewal of licenses. Initially, manufacturing companies with capital of more than RM250,000 and at least 25 full-time employees were required to apply for a manufacturing license from MIDA, which had been set up in 1967 under the auspices of the Ministry of International Trade and Industry (MITI) as an investment approval and promotion agency. (The limits have subsequently been revised to RM2.5 million and 75 full-time employees). Non-manufacturing activities had to seek investment approval from the Foreign Investment Committee, which was established in 1974 to ensure the fulfillment of NEP goals.

Nevertheless, the government took a pragmatic approach to the implementation of NEP targets in the manufacturing sector, as Rasiah (1993: 129) documents for the case of fully foreign-owned firms operating in free trade zones (FTZs) during the 1970s. This flexible implementation of targets in the manufacturing sector contrasted sharply with their stringent application in the domestic banking sector, such that the foreign share of banking had declined to less than half by the mid-1970s (Edwards 1995: 690). The government's pragmatic approach was again illustrated in its willingness to remove all equity constraints and export conditions in the manufacturing sector in response to the fall in inflows of FDI during the 1997–98 crisis.

The licensing system is also used to ensure that approved projects meet the current development needs of the country. Since November 1995, MIDA has used a minimum capital investment per employee ratio of RM55,000 as one of the criteria for foreign investment approval, in line with the loss of comparative advantage experienced in labor-intensive industries and the desire to encourage industrial projects with a higher level of value added (MIDA 2003: 3).

In response to inefficiencies, including the involvement of up to 29 government ministries and departments or agencies in the licensing process (Tham 1995: 9), MIDA has established a one-stop agency called the Center on Investment. Officials of the major ministries involved in foreign investment policy-making are represented at the center, thereby minimizing inter-ministerial delays as well as shortening the approval process. Manufacturing licenses can now be approved in six weeks, as opposed to two years previously. There is also a fast-track approval process whereby an interim letter of approval can be issued in seven days. This applies to straightforward cases that do not require the involvement of other agencies, and to products other than the seven on the government's 'sensitive' list.[2]

MIDA and MITI officials regularly promote Malaysia as a destination for investment during their numerous trade and investment missions abroad. Although diffficult to quantify, it is believed that these missions have also contributed to the relative success of Malaysia in attracting inflows of FDI.

Malaysia's labor laws have been designed to reduce the likelihood of poor labor relations becoming an issue for investors. The Trade Unions Act of 1959 grants the registrar of trade unions considerable discretionary power to reduce the power of the unions (Mohd. Nazari 1995: 49). The Industrial Relations Act of 1967 also contains a number of provisions that prevent unions in pioneer industries from negotiating collective agreements. It limits the areas subject to collective bargaining by unions and curtails the right of workers to strike by designating various issues 'non-strikeable.'

The first wave of export-oriented foreign firms to Malaysia was attracted by the establishment of the country's first FTZ in 1972. According to Rasiah (1995a: 177), the FTZs provided a well-policed, coordinated, and administered environment for MNEs in which they could be ensured of security, quick customs turnaround, and an efficient operating environment. Licensed manufacturing warehouses, offering the same set of incentives as FTZs, were introduced in locations where an FTZ would not have been feasible. Malaysia currently has 14 FTZs, numerous licensed manufacturing warehouses, as well as a number of specialized industrial estates and technology parks (Tham 1998: 109).

As mentioned earlier, in 1996 the government launched a new type of zone equipped with state-of-the-art infrastructure: a 15 x 50 kilometer strip near Kuala Lumpur called the Multimedia Super Corridor (MSC). The government hopes that the MSC will help Malaysia achieve competitiveness in high-tech industries, to lead the country into the next phase of development based on high technology and services. In a bid to entice leading global IT, multimedia, and software companies to make major investments in R&D in the new zone, the MSC offers both investment incentives and waivers from NEP requirements on equity ownership and hiring. Companies in the MSC are allowed to make duty-free imports of multimedia equipment as well as benefiting from competitive telecommunications tariffs (OECD 1999: 123).

To promote the development of linkages, in 1989 the state government of Penang helped found the MNE-run Penang Skills Development Center. Other states then set up similar industry-run training centers based on this model, such as the Kedah Industrial Skills and Management Development Center in 1993 and the Selangor Skills Development Center in 1994. In 1995, MITI established the Small and Medium Industries Corporation (SMIDEC) as a one-stop center providing advisory services, guidance, and assistance to SMEs, to enhance their competitiveness and assist them to develop linkages with MNEs.

Performance Requirements

In exchange for a relaxation of the NEP's equity requirements, the Malaysian government required firms operating in the FTZs to export at least 80 percent of their output. Two important changes were made to this regime as part of a liberalization of FDI implemented in 1986 (Felker 2001: 136). First, the liberalized foreign equity guidelines were extended to indirect exporters, that is, to firms producing parts or components for downstream assemblers of manufactured products. Second, exports were defined to include all sales from Malaysia's principal customs area to the FTZs and licensed manufacturing warehouses. These changes provided a strong incentive for large foreign manufacturers to encourage their home country suppliers to relocate to Malaysia, as the latter would no longer need to seek a local investment partner for production sites located outside the FTZs.

Following the financial and economic crisis of 1997–98, the government relaxed its rules on foreign equity to allow 100 percent foreign ownership in manufacturing without export conditions. Foreign manufacturers were even permitted to sell to the domestic market: all existing companies that had previously received incentives based on their level of exports could now apply to MITI for approval to sell up to 50 percent of their output on the domestic market (OECD 1999: 124). This temporary relaxation of export conditions was also extended to new companies approved before 31 July 1998. Once a certain level of equity participation had been approved, a company could be sure that it would not be required to restructure its equity at any time, provided that it continued to comply with the original conditions of approval and retained the original features of the project for which it had been approved. The post-crisis liberalization of FDI was extended to 31 December 2003, with the exception of the seven products on the sensitive list. However, as of 17 June 2003, the government had fully liberalized equity holdings in all manufacturing industries, so that there are currently no negative lists and the manufacturing sector is completely open to foreign investment (Rafidah 2003: 5).

Malaysia's concern to increase local content in the manufacturing sector was noted in the First Industrial Master Plan (1986–95). Thus, for the electronics sector, the plan noted the need to 'intensify vertical integration for higher local content, for which detailed localization programs should be annually reviewed and publicized by MIDA' (MIDA/UNIDO 1986: 3, as quoted in Felker 2001: 178). Nevertheless, initial attempts to increase local content did not take the form of mandatory local content rules. Instead, the government utilized indirect means to foster the development of local supply linkages, setting up a subcontract exchange scheme in 1986 (Felker 2001: 155). The scheme aimed to match supply and demand for components and parts by building a database of large assemblers and their requirements for inputs together with a registry of locally owned SME suppliers.

The government launched a formal local content policy for the electronics industry in 1990 because it was dissatisfied with the pace of technology deepening. But significantly, this policy did not distinguish between locally and foreign-owned suppliers and did not include any monitoring or enforcement provisions. In 1993, MITI launched a new vendor development program that was intended to offer a comprehensive strategy for linkage development, specifically for the electronics and automotive sectors (Felker 2001: 158). For the first time, 100 percent foreign-owned electronics assemblers were included in the plans to coordinate and monitor MNEs' subcontracting performance. Multinationals that signed formal agreements with MITI as anchor companies could choose among designated vendors supplying a broad spectrum of components. They would also receive incentives in return for providing guaranteed purchasing contracts and technical support to local suppliers.

In line with the renewed emphasis on linkage development in the Second Industrial Master Plan (1996–2005), in 1996 SMIDEC launched an industrial linkages program focusing on technology transfer and industrial deepening in leading manufacturing sectors. It had three main components: fiscal incentives; business matching; and programs to strengthen industrial linkages through technology development, skills upgrading, export market development, and the provision of industrial sites for SMEs (UNCTAD 2001: 207).

In 1999, the government went a step further with the launch of a global supplier program. It aimed to strengthen the competitiveness of Malaysian SMEs to the point where they could supply not only to the foreign affiliates of MNEs operating in Malaysia, but to MNEs located anywhere in the world. One critical component of the program was that it required a significant commitment from large corporations, who would have to 'adopt' local SMEs and assist them to upgrade their leadership skills and technology. In this way, it was envisaged that SMEs would become integrated into the supplier development programs of the MNEs, and their global manufacturing operations.

The latest government initiative to propel SMEs toward global supply was a RM5 million grant allocated in the 2002 budget to promote the adoption of RosettaNet standards for the electronic sharing of business information (Ernst 2002: 53). Approximately 10 percent of the grant has been used to set up the local operations of RosettaNet, with the Penang State Center responsible for providing the backbone infrastructure. In addition to incentives to persuade suppliers to use the new system, the adoption of a common standard to manage the supply chain is in itself a strong incentive for lower-tier SME suppliers to participate in RosettaNet.

International Obligations

At the bilateral level, Malaysia had concluded 45 agreements on the avoidance of double taxation as of 2002. As of 2001, it had also concluded 69 investment guarantee agreements. Such agreements essentially aim to protect foreign investors from the expropriation and nationalization of assets. In the event of a dispute, they offer recourse through the International Centre for Settlement of Investment Disputes. Malaysia, as a member of both the Asia Pacific Economic Cooperation (APEC) forum and ASEAN, has obligations under APEC's non-binding investment principles as well as to the ASEAN Investment Area. These are in addition to its commitments as a signatory to the WTO Agreement on Trade Related Investment Measures (TRIMs), discussed in greater detail below. Malaysia's current negotiations with six countries on bilateral free trade areas may have a greater impact on the investment climate, as these will focus specifically on trade and investment liberalization.

An Evaluation of Malaysia's FDI Policies

The large inflows of FDI experienced before the 1997 financial crisis cannot be attributed solely to Malaysia's proactive policy measures; the country has also benefited from fortuitous timing in the liberalization of its trade and FDI policies. The opening of FTZs in the 1970s coincided with the internationalization of the production process in the electrical and electronics industry. At the time, Malaysia's policy environment as well as its production environment were well suited to the requirements of MNEs in search of low-cost production sites. Similarly, the liberalization of FDI policies in 1986 coincided with demand for lower-cost production sites from East Asian MNEs whose domestic cost advantage had deteriorated. Thus, in the 1970s as well as in the late 1980s and early 1990s, Malaysia was fortunate in being able to offer a policy and production environment that matched the needs of MNEs looking to relocate production abroad.

The financial and economic crisis of 1997–98 did not cause any reversal in Malaysia's FDI policies. Rather, the sharp drop in the economic growth rate in 1998 compelled the government to further liberalize its FDI policies. However, the capital controls imposed in September 1998 created heated debate about the effect of such controls on capital flows, both port-folio and long-term, about the independence of monetary policy, and about the sustainability, efficacy, and necessity of controls as well as their impact on Malaysia's short and long-term economic growth.

In view of the importance of foreign investment to the economy, the government took measures to ensure that FDI was not affected by the selective capital controls. Thus, no controls were placed on current account transactions; on the repatriation of profits, dividends, interest, fees, com-missions, and rental income from portfolio investment and other forms of ringgit assets; or on FDI inflows and outflows.

Although critics claim that the controls adversely affected FDI by caus-ing a loss of confidence in the consistency and credibility of Malaysian policy-making, there is no substantive evidence so far to suggest that the drop in inflows in 1998 was significantly correlated to the capital controls. Some other countries in the region, such as Indonesia, the Philippines, and Singapore, also experienced lower FDI flows, while the relatively higher flows to Korea and Thailand can be attributed largely to the acquisitions, restructurings, and recapitalizations undertaken in these countries under IMF agreements. The relative importance of Japanese direct investment in Malaysia implies that the poor performance of Japanese companies in 1997–98 would have had a marked influence on FDI flows into Malaysia in 1998. Moreover, the data shown in Table 6.1 indicate that inflows recov-ered in 1999, although they have yet to recapture their pre-crisis peak of 8.7 percent of GDP in 1992.

In terms of the long-run impact, all that is left of the capital controls since 1 May 2001 is the pegging of the ringgit to the US dollar and some limits on outflows of domestic capital by individuals. Regardless of how one evaluates the effectiveness of the peg, a key issue will be its sustainabil-ity and its impact on the cost competitiveness of the economy, which then affects the relative attractiveness of Malaysia as a host economy. But the recent weakening of the US dollar has in fact boosted the export competi-tiveness of Malaysia as a result of the peg, reinforcing the government's preference to maintain it. While there have been numerous calls to de-peg, the government believes that this is unnecessary in view of Malaysia's rel-atively large current account surplus and robust reserves since 1997.

The cost of incentives to the country in terms of forgone revenue amounted to RM1.57 billion in 1988; this was 10 percent of manufactur-ing value added, 5.8 percent of manufactured exports, and 1.7 per of GDP (Table 6.7). More recent estimates are not available, despite the wide array of incentives offered by the government. However, MITI does publish data

Table 6.7   Malaysia: Tax Revenue Forgone due to Fiscal Incentives, 1988

Incentive	Value		Revenue Forgone as % of		
	(RM million)	(% of total)	Manufac- turing Value Added	Manufac- tured Exports	GDP
Pioneer status	294.6	18.8	1.9	1.1	0.3
Investment tax allowance	438.8	27.9	2.8	1.6	0.5
Locational allowance to encourage regional development[a]	0.3	0.0	0.0	0.0	0.0
Abatement of adjusted income for export[a]	297.5	18.9	1.9	1.1	0.3
Double deduction for export promotion	11.3	0.7	0.1	0.0	0.0
Export abatement[a]	503.3	32.0	3.2	1.9	0.6
Export allowance[a]	25.5	1.6	0.2	0.1	0.0
Total	1,571.3	100.0	10.1	5.8	1.7

a   This type of incentive no longer exists.
Source: Doraisami and Rasiah (2001: 261).

on the double deduction for R&D expenditure, which it reports as the main form of R&D incentive utilized thus far (MITI 2002: 153). The cost of the double deduction amounted to RM52.4 million in 1998 (0.018 percent of GDP) and RM51 million in 2000 (0.015 percent of GDP) (MASTIC 2002a: 216). Although the cost of incentives infers a loss to the country in terms of forgone tax revenue, this has to be weighed against their potential positive impact on investment, output, employment, and the creation of linkages, as will be examined in the following section.

4   IMPACT OF FDI ON THE MALAYSIAN ECONOMY

Ownership of Share Capital

Given the importance of the redistributive objective in Malaysia, it is per- tinent to consider the impact of FDI policies on the ownership of share cap-

Table 6.8 *Malaysia: Ownership of Share Capital of Limited Companies by Ethnic Group, 1970–99 (%)*[a]

Ownership Group	1970	1982	1990	1995	1999
Bumiputera	2.4	15.6	19.3	20.6	19.1
Other Malaysian	34.2	49.7	46.8	43.4	40.3
Chinese	27.2	33.4	45.5	40.9	37.9
Indian	1.1	0.9	1.0	1.5	1.5
Other	5.9	1.6[b]	0.3	1.0	0.9
Foreign	63.4	34.7	25.4	27.7	32.7
Nominee companies	n.a	5.0	8.5	8.3	7.9

a   Estimated using the par value of share capital.

b   The shares of the subgroups do not sum to the total shown because locally controlled companies that record the total value of share capital without disaggregating ownership by ethnic group have been excluded from the 'other' group.

Source: 1970: OECD (1999); 1982: Fifth Malaysian Plan (1986: 109); 1990: Seventh Malaysian Plan (1996: 86); 1995 and 1999: Eighth Malaysian Plan (2001: 64).

ital. Table 6.8 shows that foreign ownership of share capital fell progressively from 63.4 percent in 1970 when the NEP was launched to 25.4 percent in 1990, while that of the *bumiputera* increased from 2.4 percent to 19.3 percent. With the liberalization of FDI policy since 1985, the share of foreign ownership has again increased, to 27.7 percent in 1995 and 32.7 percent in 1999. The share accruing to the *bumiputera* increased to 20.6 percent in 1995 but had fallen slightly to 19.1 percent in 1999.

Table 6.9 provides a detailed picture of ownership patterns by sector for limited companies in 1999. The foreign share of share capital in the manufacturing sector increased from 39.5 percent in 1990 to 56.3 percent in 1999. The financial sector also witnessed an increase in the foreign share of share capital from 17 percent to 26 percent over the same period, with a converse trend seen in the case of agriculture. As Table 6.9 shows, the *bumiputera* share of the manufacturing and utilities subsectors was the smallest relative to other subsectors in 1999.

With the overall equity ownership share of the *bumiputera* still below the 30 percent target, it is envisaged that Malaysia's redistributive policies will remain in place until this goal has been achieved. It is extremely unlikely that the government will forgo control over equity shares in its

*Table 6.9   Malaysia: Ownership of Share Capital of Limited Companies
by Ethnic Group and Sector, 1999 (%)*[a]

Ownership Group	Agriculture	Mining	Manufac-turing	Utilities	Construc-tion
Bumiputera	28.5	19.0	12.5	12.2	26.5
Individuals	16.9	12.1	6.7	10.7	11.2
Institutions[b]	8.8	0.1	3.7	0.1	7.5
Trust agencies[c]	2.8	6.8	2.1	1.4	7.8
Non-*bumiputera*	39.3	58.4	27.3	31.1	50.2
Chinese	37.3	55.8	26.7	30.8	48.5
Indian	1.2	1.5	0.3	0.2	1.5
Other	0.8	1.1	0.3	0.1	0.2
Foreign	23.9	18.0	56.3	32.5	17.9
Nominee companies	8.3	4.6	3.9	24.2	5.4
Total	100.0	100.0	100.0	100.0	100.0

a   Estimated using the par value of share capital.

b   Refers to shares held by unit trusts and institutions such as the Pilgrims' Fund Board (Lembaga Tabung Haji).

c   Refers to shares held by agencies such as the National Investment Corporation

FDI policies in the near future. Domestic equity requirements will therefore continue to constitute an investment barrier in all but a few selected subsectors.

Output, Employment, and Wages

Table 6.10 shows the contribution of foreign establishments to gross value of output, value added, and employment in the manufacturing sector. The liberalization of FDI policy and subsequent increase in inflows has seen the number of foreign establishments increase from 488 (8.4 percent of total establishments) in 1986 to 1,696 (8.3 percent of total establishments) in 2000.

Despite their relatively small number and fairly stable share of total establishments, the contribution of foreign establishments to gross value of output and value added has been substantial: the foreign share of output

Table 6.9 (continued)

Ownership Group	Wholesale & Retail Trade	Transport	Finance	Other	Total
Bumiputera	15.2	24.2	20.5	20.5	19.1
Individuals	8.6	22.7	17.9	16.9	14.3
Institutions[b]	4.2	0.0	1.9	0.3	3.1
Trust agencies[c]	2.4	1.5	0.7	3.3	1.7
Non-*bumiputera*	43.8	47.4	43.2	46.3	40.3
Chinese	42.0	45.2	39.7	41.4	37.9
Indian	1.5	1.8	2.0	4.5	1.5
Other	0.3	0.4	1.5	0.4	0.9
Foreign	36.4	20.2	26.0	26.6	32.7
Nominee companies	4.6	8.2	10.3	6.6	7.9
Total	100.0	100.0	100.0	100.0	100.0

(Permodalan Nasional Berhad) and the State Economic Development Corporation.

Source: Government of Malaysia (2001: 94), *Third Outline Perspective Plan: 2001–2010.*

increased from 36.7 percent in 1986 to 50.3 percent in 2000, while the foreign share of value added rose from 33.4 percent to 44.2 percent. Over the same period, the number of workers employed in foreign establishments increased from 30.3 percent to 38.1 percent of total employees. It can be seen that foreign establishments in Malaysia are on average relatively larger than their domestic counterparts, whether this is measured in terms of value added per establishment or number of workers per establishment.

However, the data shown in Table 6.10 underestimate the contribution of FDI to manufacturing output and employment, for the following reasons. First, the data are constrained by the definitions used by the Department of Statistics. Non-Malaysian and jointly owned establishments are defined by the department to be those in which 50 percent or more of the equity is held by non-Malaysian residents. A lowering of this cut-off point would increase the number of foreign establishments, and thus their contribution to the economy as measured by the statistics. Second, the data do

Table 6.10   Malaysia: Output, Value Added, and Employment in the Manufacturing Sector, 1986–2000[a]

Year	Establishments (no.)	Gross Value of Output (RM million)	Value Added (RM million)	Workers (no.)
Non-Malaysian and jointly owned establishments				
1986	488 (8.4)	15,560.5 (36.7)	4,062.0 (33.4)	145,237 (30.3)
1990	1,013 (15.0)	43,660.0 (45.6)	10,307.5 (42.0)	358,649 (42.5)
1994	1,260 (15.1)	96,196.9 (48.9)	21,824.5 (44.1)	529,168 (43.2)
1996	1,474 (7.3)	126,959.2 (46.4)	31,216.4 (43.6)	555,495 (38.3)
1997	1,866 (8.1)	140,855.5 (47.4)	35,487.6 (44.8)	558,441 (39.6)
2000	1,696 (8.3)	221,514.7 (50.3)	46,887.3 (44.2)	600,698 (38.1)
Malaysian establishments				
1986	5,326 (91.6)	26,866.2 (63.3)	8,092.4 (66.6)	333,683 (69.7)
1990	5,718 (85.0)	52,153.8 (54.4)	14,222.1 (58.0)	486,084 (57.5)
1994	7,068 (84.9)	100,715.5 (51.1)	27,707.5 (55.9)	696,228 (56.8)
1996	18,730 (92.7)	146,479.9 (53.6)	40,322.0 (56.4)	893,339 (61.7)
1997	21,163 (91.9)	156,274.8 (52.6)	43,685.4 (55.2)	853,006 (60.4)
2000	18,759 (91.7)	218,490.0 (49.7)	59,189.8 (55.8)	974,099 (61.9)

a   Data are available only to 2000. Figures in parentheses indicate the percentage of the total.

Source: Industrial Survey 1986, 1990; Annual Survey of Manufacturing Industries 1994, 1997; Census of Manufacturing Industries 2001.

not capture the indirect impact of MNEs operating in the manufacturing sector, in that the linkages multinationals establish with the domestic economy contribute to the output and employment of their domestic subcontractors and suppliers. Third, the data do not reflect the contribution of foreign investment to the improvement in overall productivity in the manufacturing sector between 1986 and 1991 (Tham 1997: 337).

The buoyant growth of the manufacturing sector, owing much to inflows of FDI and their spillover effects, has transformed the Malaysian economy, ending the country's reliance on primary products and consolidating its position as a producer of manufactured goods. This can be seen in the rising share of manufacturing in GDP, employment, and total exports since Malaysia achieved independence in 1957. The sector's share of GDP increased significantly from 13.9 percent in 1970 to a peak of 35.7 percent in 1997. Its contribution to total employment rose from 8.7 percent in 1970 to a high of 27.1 percent in 1997, while its share of exports increased from 11.9 percent in 1970 to 86.4 percent in 2001.

The rapid growth of the manufacturing sector drove unemployment down from 6.9 percent in 1985 to 2.8 percent in 1995 (Lee 1998: 182), creating labor shortages toward the end of the period. Consequently, the real monthly wage rate rose by an average of 3.7 percent per annum over 1991–93, pushing up labor costs and decreasing Malaysia's locational advantage for labor-intensive manufacturing. In an effort to overcome labor shortages, both domestic and foreign firms in the manufacturing sector resorted to importing unskilled and semi-skilled foreign workers, legally and sometimes illegally, from neighboring countries.

More importantly, the increase in wages was not matched by a commensurate increase in productivity during this period of rapid growth. Tham and Liew (2002: 8) found the annual rate of growth in real productivity to be smaller than the annual rate of growth in real wages and salaries for the manufacturing sector as a whole, before the emergence of the crisis in 1997. The result was a decline in the real cost of labor measured in terms of value added per ringgit, which reduced the competitiveness of labor utilized in the manufacturing sector.

The crisis reversed this trend: the growth rate of real productivity exceeded the growth rate of real wages and salaries in 1997 and 1999 due to the contraction in the manufacturing sector and fall in demand for labor during that period. As a result, the shortage in the labor market eased considerably. With the economy recovering in the third quarter of 1999, employment in the manufacturing sector also picked up, to comprise 27.6 percent of total employment in 2000.

Table 6.11   Malaysia: Value of Exports of Limited Companies by Ownership and Sector, 1990 and 1995 (RM million)[a]

Company Type	Rubber	Other Agriculture	Tin Mining	Other Mining	Manu-facturing	Construc-tion
1990						
All limited companies	159.6	983.6	5.3	10,740.5	44,208.3	77.2
	(100.0)	(100.0)	(100.0)	(100.0)	(100.0)	(100.0)
Locally controlled	116.2	835.7	5.3	8,879.4	16,022.8	73.5
	(72.8)	(85.0)	(100.0)	(82.7)	(36.2)	(95.2)
Foreign controlled	n.a.	36.2	n.a.	402.3	27,493.4	3.7
	n.a.	(3.7)	n.a.	(3.8)	(62.2)	(4.8)
Malaysian branches	43.4	111.7	n.a.	1,458.8	692.0	n.a.
	(27.2)	(11.4)	n.a.	(13.6)	(1.6)	n.a.
1995						
All limited companies	37.7	1,070.5	0.0	6,939.0	123,597.0	98.0
	(100.0)	(100.0)	(100.0)	(100.0)	(100.0)	(100.0)
Locally controlled	36.2	617.8	_c	6,215.6	33,437.6	55.2
	(95.8)	(57.7)	_c	(89.6)	(27.1)	(56.4)
Foreign controlled	_b	452.0	_c	581.4	89,941.2	19.3
	_b	(42.2)	_c	(8.4)	(72.8)	(19.7)
Malaysian branches	1.6	0.6	_c	142.1	218.1	23.4
	(4.2)	(0.1)	_c	(2.1)	(0.2)	(23.9)

n.a.: not available.

a   Figures are based on the transaction value of exports. It includes adjustments for timing, coverage, and valuation, and so may differ from the customs value. Figures in parentheses indicate the percentage of the total.

Exports, Imports, and the Balance of Payments

Based on the Financial Survey of Limited Companies in Malaysia conducted annually by the Department of Statistics, the share of foreign establishments (comprising foreign-controlled companies and the Malaysian branches of limited companies) in total manufacturing exports increased from 64 percent in 1990 to 73 percent in 1995, while that of locally controlled companies declined from 36 percent to 27 percent over the same period (Table 6.11). Overall, the contribution of foreign establishments to exports is significantly higher for manufacturing than for other sectors.

Table 6.11 (continued)

Company Type	Wholesale Trade	Retail Trade	Banks & Financial Institutions	Other Industries	All Industries
1990					
All limited companies	6,241.1	446.9	165.1	40.0	63,064.3
	(100.0)	(100.0)	(100.0)	(100.0)	(100.0)
Locally controlled	4,914.4	426.0	165.1	22.9	31,461.2
	(78.7)	(95.3)	(100.0)	(61.9)	(49.9)
Foreign controlled	927.2	20.9	0.0	13.7	28,897.5
	(14.9)	(4.7)	(0.0)	(37.2)	(45.8)
Malaysian branches	399.4	n.a.	n.a.	0.3	2,705.6
	(6.4)	n.a.	n.a.	(0.9)	(4.3)
1995					
All limited companies	11,064.6	73.1	306.3	177.8	143,364.0
	(100.0)	(100.0)	(100.0)	(100.0)	(100.0)
Locally controlled	8,966.4	29.9	230.6	133.4	49,722.6
	(81.0)	(40.9)	(75.3)	(75.0)	(34.7)
Foreign controlled	1,905.5	43.3	63.8	44.4	93,051.0
	(17.2)	(59.2)	(20.8)	(25.0)	(64.9)
Malaysian branches	192.8	n.a.	11.9	0.0	590.5
	(1.7)	n.a.	(3.9)	(0.0)	(0.4)

b   Consolidated under 'other agriculture.'

c   Consolidated under 'other mining.'

Source: Department of Statistics (1990, 1995), *Report of the Financial Survey of Limited Companies.*

The share of foreign firms in total exports was 50 percent in 1990, increasing to 65 percent in 1995. However, as with the manufacturing statistics discussed earlier, if the equity threshold for a foreign-controlled company were lowered, then the contribution of foreign firms to manufacturing exports and total exports would be greater.

Because of their participation in regional production networks, foreign establishments have been responsible for substantial levels of imports: 60 percent of all manufacturing sector imports in 1990, rising to 72 percent in 1995. Over the same period, the contribution of locally controlled companies to manufacturing sector imports declined from 40 percent to 28 percent, in tandem with the decline in their share of exports. Although the share of foreign establishments in manufacturing sector imports is high, their share of mining sector imports is higher still, at 76 percent in 1995. The contribution of foreign establishments to total imports of all industries amounted to 51 percent in 1990, increasing to 64 percent in 1995.

In the manufacturing sector, the value of exports net of imports for foreign establishments increased three-fold from RM11 million in 1990 to RM33.4 million in 1995. The increase for locally controlled companies was smaller at RM4.5 million in 1990 and RM11.7 million in 1995. Similarly, for all industries, the value of exports net of imports for foreign establishments increased almost three-fold from RM10.0 million in 1990 to RM27.4 in 1995 whereas that of locally controlled companies increased from RM10.5 million to only RM12.2 million.

Unfortunately the Department of Statistics terminated its financial surveys in 1995. However, the Census of Manufacturing Industries conducted in 2001 included, for the first time, data on the exports and imports of manufacturing sector establishments (Table 6.12). In 2000 foreign establishments held a 69.5 percent share of manufacturing exports and a 69.1 percent share of manufacturing imports; thus the shares of Malaysian establishments were clearly much smaller at 30.5 percent and 30.9 percent respectively. The value of exports net of imports for foreign establishments amounted to RM69 million in 2000, and RM29.7 million for Malaysian establishments.

Technology, Technology Transfer, and Diffusion

Although R&D represents only one dimension of technology deepening, it is nevertheless a commonly used indicator to measure technology development in a country. Historically in Malaysia, it has been public research institutes such as the Rubber Research Institute that have contributed most to the country's R&D efforts; private sector efforts have by contrast lagged.

Nevertheless, the participation of the private sector has increased over time. According to the Malaysian Science and Technology Center, government research institutes and institutes of higher learning respectively accounted for 46.0 percent and 9.2 percent of total R&D expenditure in 1992 compared with a private sector share of 44.8 percent (MASTIC 2002b: 50). By 2000, the contribution of the private sector had grown to 57.9 percent while that of the government research institutes had fallen to 25.0 percent; institutes of higher learning accounted for the remaining 17.1 percent. The increasing importance of R&D over time is reflected in an

Table 6.12 Malaysia: Exports and Imports of Manufacturing Establishments, 2000 (RM million)[a]

Ownership	Exports	Imports
Total	226,059.8	127,340.9
	(100.0)	(100.0)
Malaysian establishments	69,038.3	39,312.5
	(30.5)	(30.9)
Foreign establishments	157,021.5	88,028.4
	(69.5)	(69.1)

a   Figures in parentheses indicate the percentage of the total.
Source: Unpublished data from the Census of Manufacturing Industries 2001.

expanded share of GDP: R&D spending as a percentage of GDP rose from 0.37 percent in 1992 to 0.5 percent in 2000 (MASTIC 2002b: 10).

Table 6.13 shows private sector R&D expenditure by industry and ownership for the year 2000. Although a smaller number of foreign-owned and controlled companies were reported to have made R&D expenditures (29 percent of all establishments), the total amount spent by these companies (RM635.9 million, or 64 percent of the total) far exceeded that reported for Malaysian companies (RM355.8 million, or 36 percent of the total). The share of foreign companies in total R&D spending amounted to 0.19 percent of GDP in 2000. The electrical and electronics subsector (comprising office, accounting, and computing machinery, electrical machinery and apparatus n.e.c., and radio, television, and communication equipment and apparatus) received almost 40 percent (RM253.7 million) of the total amount of R&D reported for foreign companies in that year. According to the Malaysian Science and Technology Center, Japanese companies spent most on R&D (RM175.8 million), followed by American companies (RM35.5 million) and Singaporean firms (RM15.8 million) (MASTIC 2002a: 38).

Turning to technology transfer, it is important to note at the outset that there has been no systematic assessment of the effectiveness of policy instruments in fostering local input linkages and technology transfer in Malaysia (UNCTAD 2001: 188). The lack of formal, systematic, *ex post* evaluation programs is rather incongruous given the government's concern

Table 6.13   Malaysia: Private Sector R&D Expenditure by Industry and Ownership, 2000 (RM million)[a]

Industry	Foreign		Malaysian		Total
	Owned	Controlled	Owned	Controlled	
Food & beverages	2.6	259.4	3.8	1.6	267.3
Textiles	0.3	–	4.1	0.1	4.5
Wearing apparel, dressing & dyeing of fur	–	–	0.9	0.3	1.1
Wood, wood & cork products except furniture, articles of straw, & plaited materials	0.4	0.7	0.1	0.7	2.0
Paper & paper products		0.1			0.1
Publishing, printing, & reproduction of recorded media	–	–	0.5	–	0.4
Coke, refined petroleum products, & nuclear fuel	–	–	–	0.3	0.3
Chemicals & chemical products	0.6	1.9	6.5	5.0	13.9
Rubber & plastic products	6.9	1.6	2.9	2.3	40.1
Non-metallic & mineral products	–	–	8.0	1.2	9.2
Basic metals	–	–	0.1	0.4	0.5
Fabricated metal products except machinery & equipment	0.2	0.2	1.5	0.2	2.1
Machinery & equipment	106.4	–	0.7	–	107.1
Office, accounting, & computing machinery	6.9	0.3	2.8	–	10.0
Electrical machinery & apparatus n.e.c	223.4	–	7.3	3.5	234.2
Radio, television, & communication equipment & apparatus	23.1	–	8.0	0.3	31.4
Medical & precision optical instruments, watches & clocks	0.9	–	0.8	–	1.7
Motor vehicles, trailers, & semi-trailers	–	–	0.6	257.6	258.2
Other transport equipment	–	–	5.3	–	5.3
Furniture, manufacturing n.e.c.	–	–	2.0	0.3	2.3
Total	371.7	264.2	55.8	273.6	991.7
(% of total)	(37.0)	(27.0)	(8.0)	(28.0)	(100.0)

a   A dash indicates a value of zero or close to zero.
Source: MASTIC (2002b: 135).

over these issues as reflected in its numerous policy initiatives to enhance technology deepening in the country.

Nonetheless, given its importance to the economy, the electrical and electronics subsector has received considerable attention from the research community. In particular, the issue of technology transfer as evidenced by the development of backward linkages in this sector has been assessed in several studies based on firm-level interviews, especially before the financial crisis. Other avenues of technology transfer, such as training and the building of human capital as well as the development of linkages between universities and firms, have received less attention.

Several key features of technology transfer emerge from these studies. First, the extent of backward linkages has changed over time. Studies conducted in the late 1970s and early 1980s find few backward linkages between MNEs and the domestic economy, but subsequent surveys conducted mostly in the first half of the 1990s find evidence that such linkages had begun to evolve.

Second, the technology transferred to the domestic economy, whether in the form of human capital formation or subcontracting ties, appears to have emerged outside the domain of formal technology transfer agreements (Rasiah and Anuwar 1998: 68; Hobday 1999: 91).

Third, external forces are identified as a major factor in motivating the development of backward linkages. MNEs have responded to growing competitive pressures in the global electronics sector to reduce the cost of production in Malaysia by investing in automation and flexible production systems that require proximate sourcing and a higher level of outsourcing. As observed by Narayanan (1997: 25), Rasiah (1995a: 193), Mohd. Nazari (1995: 215), and Hobday (1999: 89), the need to automate in order to improve efficiency and precision as well as the parallel need to modify and adapt machinery provided the impetus to forge these backward linkages.

Fourth, in the area of policy effectiveness, there is some evidence that local content requirements did force firms seeking incentives to expand their domestic purchases, thereby increasing the level of domestic sourcing of electronic inputs and stimulating the development of the local machine tool industry (Rasiah 1995b: 190). Similarly, in his study of 43 Japanese consumer electronics firms operating in Malaysia in 1995, Capannelli (1999: 220) found that policies to increase local content had had a positive and significant effect on the local procurement ratio.

However, it has to be remembered that the number of firms involved in programs to increase local sourcing is tiny. In 1996, of the estimated 20,200 manufacturing establishments operating in Malaysia, 18,948 (93.8 percent) were SMEs (SMIDEC 2002: 31). Of these only 256 (1.4 percent) were involved in a vendor development program. Furniture making and electronics were the major subsectors involved, each with about 25 percent of the total number of participating firms. Similarly, only 128 SMEs (0.7 percent of the total) were participating in the industrial linkages program, with electronics as the major subsector. Nine MNEs were reported to have adopted ten SMEs under the aegis of the global supplier program (SMIDEC 2002: 23). In short, the number of SMEs involved in a vendor development program, industrial linkages program, or global supplier program is extremely small, and the impact of such programs has therefore been very limited.

Programs to increase local sourcing have been complemented by business-matching and other programs to improve the technology capacity of SMEs (Rasiah 1999: 238). As described by Narayanan (1997: 29), in the early 1970s and 1980s Penang's chief minister took a personal interest in promoting the electronics industry. At his instigation, the state economic development corporation, Penang Development Corporation, collaborated with business associations and MNEs to ensure the rapid development of local linkages in the state. For instance, the corporation surveyed likely supplier firms, published sourcing guides, helped suppliers locate in the FTZs, and assisted them to obtain investment incentives from MIDA (Felker and Jomo 2000: 30).

In contrast, the state leadership in Selangor, where the dynamic Klang Valley is located, was preoccupied with other concerns such as the implementation of the NEP. Narayanan (1997: 29) postulated this difference in institutional support between the two states to be one of the reasons for the greater degree of linkage development found in Penang than in the Klang Valley. This suggests that the incentives offered by performance requirement programs are insufficient in themselves to induce technology transfer; extensive proactive government support is also needed in terms of business-matching and complementary programs to enhance the capabilities of local firms before they can supply to MNEs.

The pooling of the NEP target of promoting *bumiputera* entrepreneurship with the economic target of increasing the value and technological content of the MNEs' subcontracting networks has been observed to be a major obstacle to the effectiveness of the vendor development program (Felker 2001: 160). The government contends that the program is open to all SMEs regardless of ethnic ownership, but the list of potential vendors supplied by MITI nevertheless appears to have an ethnic bias. Capannelli (1999: 223) has further noted that some of the firms on the list of potential suppliers lack competitiveness in areas such as pricing and quality, even with respect to other Malaysian suppliers. In addition, the lack of proper monitoring of the program means that some buyers have sought to fulfill government requirements by providing only a minimal volume of business to local suppliers.

Although the government's policy measures may have contributed to the development of backward linkages, it is important to note that an increase in 'made in Malaysia' inputs is not equivalent to an increase in inputs 'made by Malaysians.' As noted by Capannelli (1999: 221), while the share of parts and components procured from firms located in Malaysia was close to 35 percent in 1995, the proportion procured from Malaysian-owned firms was below 7 percent. Moreover, the parts supplied by Malaysian firms were at the lower end of the technology scale. Even then, some of these input makers were joint ventures with firms from third countries such as Singapore and Taipei,China.

Therefore, much of the technology deepening that appears to be taking place in Malaysia is in fact intra-MNE, or a transfer of technology from MNE parent companies to their subsidiaries in Malaysia (Norlela and Bell 1999: 179). This certainly differs from the situation in Korea and Taipei,China, where the predominant mode of development in the electronics industry has been locally owned firms. The lower participation rate of locally owned firms in Malaysia indicates the weaker capacity of these firms as well as a lack of systemic coordination and network cohesion, especially in the case of industry in the Klang Valley (Rasiah 2002: 121). Although Penang has fared better due to the stronger intermediary role of the state government and the Penang Development Corporation, nevertheless it too suffers from the critical nationwide shortage of technical personnel, engineers, and scientists.

Competition and Competition Policy

According to Lee (2003: 3), the regulation of competition in Malaysia has been virtually non-existent and the impact of government policies on competition has not been addressed. However, Nor Ghani et al. (2000: 18) found that even in the absence of any kind of competition policy, the ten-year trend from 1985 to 1994, using standard measures of market concentration such as the four-firm concentration ratio and the Herfindahl index, indicated that 40–45 percent of the Malaysian industrial sector had been evolving toward a more competitive environment. Since no test was conducted for the factors that had contributed to this increasingly competitive structure, it is not possible to assess the impact of FDI on the market structure of the manufacturing sector. Nevertheless, in the electronics subsector where FDI predominates, the authors did find a significant downward trend for both measures of market structure.

Currently Malaysia does not have a national competition policy or law. However, the government has made a formal commitment in its latest five-year development plan (2001–05) to implement a fair trade policy and law that will prevent anti-competitive behavior such as collusion, cartel price-fixing, market allocation, and the abuse of market power (Government of Malaysia 2001: 467).

Domestic Attitudes toward FDI

Although in principle investment incentives are available to all investors, it has been alleged that foreign investors have been able to access them more easily than domestic investors. This allegation has not, however, been verified. Anuwar and Tham (1993: 3) have noted that the lower tax contribution of foreign-controlled companies in 1970–90 could be due to their greater ability to appropriate the incentives provided by the government. But it may also imply transfer pricing, as the prevailing tax rate in Malaysia was relatively high at that time.

While comments on the apparent bias of the government toward foreign investors have occasionally been aired, in general this has not attracted any significant protest. Felker (2001: 137) attributes the passive response of the Malaysian business world to the process of investment policy reform to the possibility that

> overt collective efforts to influence policy have long been forestalled by ethnically defined differences in business interests toward state regulation, and the predominance of clientelist networks as the primary mode of access to state resources.

Thus, although the specialized infrastructure and incentives for high-technology offered by the government are unlikely to be appropriated by local firms due to their lower technological capability, there has been no call to reverse such policies.

Although the local business community appears to accept the government's emphasis on foreign investment, it has at times appealed for special incentives for domestic investment. In 1993 the government launched a domestic investment initiative in response to criticism that the country's investment policies gave priority to foreign over domestic investment. It nevertheless rejected the notion of implementing a tighter screening of foreign investment in order to favor local industry (Felker 2001: 153). Indeed, the renewed emphasis on domestic investment should not be construed in any way as a strategy to curtail FDI; the initiative merely called for a more selective approach toward FDI (Anuwar and Tham 1993: 10).

The fall in inflows of FDI since the financial crisis has been of great concern to the local business community. During its 2003 annual dialogue with MITI, the Federation of Malaysian Manufacturers urged the government to abolish the equity requirements for FDI altogether ('StarBiz News,' *Star*, 22 April 2003: 7). It called for the aggressive pursuit of FDI, citing its role as a source of technology and markets and as a major contributor to national output, exports, and employment. Thus, in contrast to its previously passive domestic support for FDI policies, the local business community has been spurred by the post-crisis drop in inflows to press for greater liberalization of foreign investment.

Income and Income Distribution

The rapid economic growth enjoyed by Malaysia between 1971 and 1990 resulted in a significant increase in per capita gross national product (GNP) from RM1,937 to RM4,268 (in 1978 constant prices) (Ishak 2002: 23). This was accompanied by a reduction in unemployment and a fall in the absolute poverty rate from 52.4 percent in 1970 to 16.5 percent in 1990. Moreover, income differentials in Peninsular Malaysia as indicated by the Gini coefficient declined from 0.493 in 1979 to 0.445 in 1990. The fall in inequality during this period has been attributed to the success of the numerous strategies and programs adopted to eradicate poverty and reduce the income gap between ethnic groups, regions, and income groups.

Of these strategies, the government's concerted effort to foster industrial growth stands out as explaining much of Malaysia's success in reducing absolute poverty and narrowing income differentials. It has been argued that the rapid growth of the industrial sector, through labor-intensive, export-oriented manufacturing, reduced unemployment. Productivity increases, particularly in the manufacturing sector, drove increases in wage rates, thereby reducing poverty. At the same time, income differentials narrowed as the incomes of those at the lower end of the scale rose. In so far as FDI has facilitated the growth of labor-intensive, export-oriented manufacturing, its role in increasing national income, reducing poverty, and narrowing the income gap can thus be considered positive.

Despite the crisis, Malaysia's history of rapid economic growth before the crisis and its swift recovery afterwards enabled it to continue to sustain growth in per capita income: real per capita GNP attained RM8,035 in 2001 and RM8,189 in 2002. Although the crisis did increase the incidence of poverty, with the proportion of people living in poverty rising from 6.1 percent in 1997 to 8.5 percent in 1998, only a year later the poverty rate had fallen back to 7.5 percent (Government of Malaysia 2001a: 57). However, the trend for the income gap to narrow appears to have halted, with the Gini ratio increasing from 0.45 in 1990 to 0.47 in 1997 (Ishak 2002: 34).

Ishak (2002: 25) contends that the increasing use of automation by both foreign and domestic firms may have exacerbated income differentials by generating greater demand for skilled than for semi-skilled and unskilled labor. This would imply that the Gini ratio for urban areas, where most manufacturing industries are located, should be increasing. But Ragayah (2002: 13) found that the urban Gini ratio actually fell from 0.501 in 1979 to 0.427 in 1997 and 0.416 in 1999, whereas the rural Gini ratio increased from 0.409 in 1990 to 0.414 in 1995 and 0.424 in 1997 before moderating to 0.418 in 1999. Hence, the resurgence in income disparity is probably due to a widening of income inequality in rural areas. There is no evidence to suggest that FDI has contributed to the increased income disparity observed between 1990 and 1997.

5   WTO STATUS AND TRIMS IMPLEMENTATION

Malaysia participated actively in the Uruguay Round negotiations and has been a member of the WTO since its inception in 1995. Malaysia's compliance with the TRIMs Agreement is incomplete, with the country continuing to implement local content requirements for motor vehicles produced by both new and existing firms. However, as of 1 January 2000, it had eliminated other local content requirements tied to investment incentives, and the local content policy on automobiles was phased out on 31 December 2003.

Malaysia's major international investment obligations are confined to its bilateral investment guarantee agreements and its commitments as a member of the ASEAN Investment Area (Table 6.14). The former are mainly intended to protect foreign investors from the possibility of expropriation and nationalization. In the case of the latter, Malaysia's interest lies more in facilitating and promoting FDI, as ASEAN and non-ASEAN investors in the manufacturing sector are already treated equally.

The Malaysian government's current position on the WTO's proposed multilateral rules for investment is not to commence negotiations until the various issues involved have first been clarified (MITI 2002: 50). Because they would require national and MFN treatment to be granted to all, such rules might impinge on the development of policies needed to achieve the country's socioeconomic and development objectives (MITI 2002: 50). Limits on the use of technology-licensing agreements, incentives and performance requirements, and the screening of investments across sectors might also constrain domestic policy-making. Moreover, the government is not convinced that there is any direct correlation between multilateral rules on investment and FDI flows.

Malaysia would therefore prefer that the WTO develop best practice

Table 6.14   Malaysia: Summary of the Main Elements of Investment Guarantee Agreements

Element	Details
Definition of investment	Broad asset-based definition covering tangible and intangible assets as well as FDI
Application to investment	Usually post-establishment
National and MFN treatment	MFN treatment accorded; national treatment rarely given
Expropriation and nationalization	Main focus is to protect investors from expropriation and nationalization; in the event that either of these occurs, compensation that is freely transferable must be provided
Transfer of funds	Free transfer without unreasonable delay in any freely traded currency
Dispute settlement	Provides for arbitration between states, or between investors and states, under the International Centre for Settlement of Investment Disputes
Treatment of investors	Must be fair and equitable

Source: Interview with official from the Malaysian Industrial Development Authority, 31 July 2003.

modules in the areas of investment, competition, and government procurement. These would provide benchmarks to assist WTO members to improve their own practices and rules, without having to subscribe to multilateral rules linked to a dispute mechanism.

The clarification of issues emphasized by the Malaysian government nevertheless includes having matters of importance to the country incorporated in any multilateral framework on investment (MITI 2002: 50). The government recognizes the importance of continuing to participate actively in the clarification process so as to ensure that Malaysia's concerns and interests are represented, and its socioeconomic and development needs accommodated, in any new investment framework (Sidek 2002: 6). The government is in favor of using new approaches to deal with new issues.

Thus, non-binding guidelines that carry no penalty clauses or dispute settlement procedures have been suggested as one possible approach to the development of a multilateral framework on investment (Rafidah 2001: 3).

The main factor that may encourage the government to reconsider its position is the increasing tendency for Malaysians to invest abroad. This trend is likely to continue based on the country's savings–investment gap. As the export of capital becomes increasingly important, local investors will demand greater legal certainty, increased transparency, adequate protection and compensation, and a liberal and non-discriminatory environment for their overseas investments (Low 2003: 3). Since these are also issues that would be addressed by a multilateral framework on investment, the government may eventually be persuaded that such a framework would be in the interests of Malaysians investing abroad.

6   CONCLUSION AND RECOMMENDATIONS

Summary

Malaysia has relied heavily on FDI throughout all the phases of its development, first in agriculture and later in manufacturing. Currently it is promoting FDI in selected service sectors such as information and communications technology. While external circumstances fortuitous to Malaysia helped to encourage outflows from source countries, the country's FDI policy regime was also important in encouraging a surge of capital inflows in the late 1980s and early 1990s.

Malaysia's FDI regime is relatively liberal. The government has invested heavily in basic infrastructure while nurturing macroeconomic stability. The legal framework has further enhanced the enabling environment for FDI. Progressive trade liberalization has added to the attraction of Malaysia as a host economy, as have the institutions created to enhance the investment environment.

The government has made liberal use of incentives to attract the 'appropriate' type of investment, where 'appropriateness' is increasingly taken to mean the contribution of the investment to technology development. Incentives have been tied to performance requirements since the early days when FTZs were used to attract export-oriented MNEs. The subsequent need to encourage technology deepening has led to the increasing use of incentives that are tied to the R&D efforts of MNEs. Since equity restrictions are a barrier to investment, these have been relaxed for selected industries targeted for development. The incentives offered to the firms in the MSC specializing in ICT are a case in point.

Current empirical evidence indicates that linkage development has improved since the early days of enclave production in the FTZs. However, the factors that have shaped this improvement cannot be attributed to the incentive structure per se. Rather, the evidence seems to indicate that a complex convergence of factors is behind the expansion in local sourcing. Among these, external factors such as the increasingly competitive international environment and dynamic changes in the production structure have been identified as a critical influence in changing the sourcing behavior of MNEs in Malaysia. The effectiveness of government policies to promote linkages is dependent on accompanying state intervention in terms of business-matching and supplementary training programs to enhance the capability of SMEs and their capacity to absorb new technologies. The number of SMEs involved in the numerous performance requirement programs linked to incentives is very small. Hence, most SMEs have not benefited from these programs. Another important lesson is that government policies must target the development of indigenous SMEs; otherwise the increase in local sourcing may end up being dominated by foreign component suppliers operating in the domestic market.

In compliance with the TRIMs Agreement, local content requirements were withdrawn for all sectors, including automobiles, by the end of 2003. The automobile sector illustrates some of the difficulties Malaysia has encountered with regard to the liberalization process under the WTO. The government's development agenda has led it to intervene selectively in the economy, and yet global rules press for a reduction of such interventions and a greater focus on functional intervention. Malaysia's experiment in infant industry protection for the automobile sector along with the provision of numerous subsidies has certainly promoted the development of a cluster of national suppliers—who may or may not be able to compete when this sector is liberalized under WTO rules. Even Proton, the national car, may not be able to withstand the impending liberalization under ASEAN Free Trade Area rules.

Given Malaysia's socioeconomic aspirations, it is understandable that the government is unwilling to embrace a global agreement on investment rules. Nevertheless, it is important that it examine whether this policy position is tenable in the long run given increasing outflows of capital and the country's positive saving–investment gap. The government needs to bear in mind that Malaysian investors abroad may stand to benefit from a multilateral framework on investment.

Recommendations to the Malaysian Government

First, the government should implement a monitoring mechanism to ensure that Malaysia captures the full benefits of its investment incentives.

This should take the form of an independent monitoring mechanism, informed by government and academic involvement, to review and assess the contribution of the MNEs that have received incentives.

Second, the government needs to review the incentive structure and how it is implemented. This review should include an estimation of the loss of revenue incurred by providing incentives, in order to make an effective cost–benefit analysis of their use and enable the government to ascertain which are useful and which are redundant. The importance of incentives relative to other locational advantages, as well as the problems encountered in implementing incentives, should also be studied. Alternative strategies such as a cut in the corporate tax rate may be less cumbersome to implement and would benefit domestic investors directly, thereby removing any real or perceived discrimination against them.

Third, the government should undertake a review of employment quotas on foreign workers. Since foreign 'knowledge workers'[3] are already allowed to work in Malaysia in order to facilitate the shift to a 'knowledge economy,' a relaxation of employment quotas in industry would provide temporary relief for the current skill shortages.

Fourth, the government should review the education system with a view to meeting the country's future industrial needs. While significant changes have been made to the education system, the most recent one being the introduction of the teaching of science and mathematics in English, the persistent shortage of skilled and professional workers requires better policy coordination between ministries, especially in the area of human resource planning. The proposed review would identify the main factors contributing to the current shortfall in skilled and professional manpower.

Fifth, data collection and dissemination procedures need to be improved. The Department of Statistics could be better resourced, to upgrade its capacity to collect data. The time lag between the collection and dissemination of data needs to be shortened so that researchers and policy-makers have access to the most up-to-date data available.

Finally, despite its current position on investment policy liberalization at the multilateral level, the government should prepare for change based on the trends in investment abroad. It appears that the government is more interested in negotiating trade and investment liberalization at the bilateral than at the multilateral level. However, as both theoretical and empirical evidence supports the clear superiority of multilateral liberalization, it is important that the government not neglect multilateral negotiations. Given its limited capacity to negotiate concurrently at the bilateral, regional, and multilateral levels, the government will have to determine its negotiating priorities.

Recommendations to the WTO

The WTO can facilitate capacity building by increasing awareness of WTO issues among both government officials and the public. While the WTO has conducted training programs for government officers, those who are not dealing directly with trade and investment issues remain generally uninformed about its role and its programs. SMEs in particular are ignorant of WTO rules, as the dissemination of information to these firms is poor. Since the government does not have the resources to educate the private sector about WTO issues, universities may be able to play a role in this respect. The WTO could contribute to this process by enhancing the capacity of the universities to educate the general public and the private sector.

APPENDIX 6.1   DEFINITION OF FDI IN MALAYSIA

Since 2001, Malaysia has adopted a definition of FDI that is in accordance with the standard given for the compilation of FDI data in the fifth edition of the IMF's *Balance of Payments Manual* (Central Bank of Malaysia 2000: 1). FDI, as defined in the manual, is an international investment made with the objective of obtaining a lasting interest, by an entity resident in one economy (direct investor) in an entity resident in another country (direct investment enterprise). These transactions include equity capital, retained earnings, and inter-company loans. This is also the definition used by the Malaysian Department of Statistics, which has reclassified the FDI data before 2001 to conform as closely as possible with the IMF definition. This level of coverage does not, however, allow a breakdown by country or by industry grouping.

MIDA, which reports data for the manufacturing sector, has adopted a different definition for FDI. Until 1999, it defined FDI as foreign equity plus loans, with the latter referring not only to loans by foreign investors to their foreign affiliates, but also to loans from other sources abroad, such as foreign financial institutions (Phang 1994: 189). Hence this definition omitted retained earnings but widened the definition of loans. MIDA's data capture all manufacturing projects with shareholder funds of at least RM2.5 million or a workforce of 75 or more employees. They also capture manufacturing projects with shareholder funds of less than RM2.5 million if the investor has applied for fiscal incentives; applications by existing companies to expand their production capacity for approved products, or diversify into the manufacture of additional products; and investments in hotels and agriculture if the investor has applied for fiscal incentives. MIDA data have the advantage of allowing a detailed breakdown by source country and subsector.

Since 1999, MIDA has included retained earnings in its definition of FDI; since 2000 it has defined FDI to be foreign equity, retained earnings, loans, and other sources of financing not yet determined at the time of an FDI application.

MIDA publishes two series of data, the first pertaining to manufacturing companies in production based on a survey of 2,500–3,500 manufacturing projects, and the second based on approved projects. Both pose some problems for the user: the data on companies in production have not been published since 1998, while the data on approved projects are overestimates, as some projects are approved but not realized.

Approved FDI for projects in the MSC are compiled separately by the Multimedia Development Corporation.

NOTES

1 The South Commission was set up in 1987 by Dr Mahatir Mohamad. Consisting of distinguished individuals from the South of different backgrounds and political persuasions, its purpose was to assess the South's achievements and failings in the development field and suggest directions for action.

2 These seven product areas are: paper and plastic packaging; film; plastic injection molded components; metal stamping and metal fabrication; wire harnesses; printing; and steel service centers.

3 In Malaysia, a 'knowledge worker' is defined as a worker with five or more years' professional experience in ICT or a field that makes heavy use of multimedia; a worker with a university degree in any discipline, or a graduate diploma from a technical college in multimedia or ICT, plus at least two years' professional experience in multimedia/ICT or a field that makes heavy use of multimedia; or a worker with a master's degree in any discipline.

7

Thailand

Somkiat Tangkitvanich, Deunden Nikomborirak,
and Busaba Krairiksh

1   INTRODUCTION

Thailand has been a preferred destination for foreign direct investment (FDI) in Asia for the past decade, ranking around fifth among Asian countries in terms of net FDI inflows.[1] During 1996–2000, FDI represented the most important type of private capital inflows for Thailand (Figure 7.1). It has proved to be a much more stable source of funding for the country than portfolio investment, bank loans, and other types of loans.

From a historical perspective, FDI was a key factor in Thailand achieving one of the world's fastest rates of economic growth until 1997. The country experienced an average growth rate of nearly 8 percent for three and a half decades until 1996. Despite a world recession in the mid-1980s, the Thai economy expanded at double-digit rates from 1988 to 1990, and by over 8 percent per year from 1991 to 1995. This growth was driven largely by increasing inward FDI flows.

FDI has been indispensable to the development of many sectors, particularly automobiles and electronics. As a developing country with a low technological capability, Thailand would not have been able to build up its industries to the extent that it did without FDI. In fact, like other 'Asian Miracle' countries, Thailand's success can be attributed to a combination of a favorable external environment and the country's ability to make use of FDI to transform itself from an agricultural to an industrial economy.

The shock of the economic crisis prompted the Thai government to re-evaluate its growth-oriented development policy. Structural flaws in both the industrial and the financial sector had contributed to the crisis. Compared with the People's Republic of China (PRC), labor was no longer

*Figure 7.1   Thailand: Net Private Capital Inflows, 1983–2002
          ($ billion)*

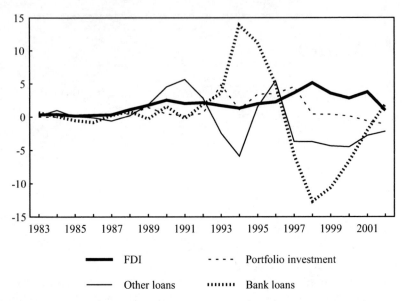

Source: Bank of Thailand, Bangkok.

cheap in Thailand. Limited public investment in training and education had rendered industry incapable of shifting from labor-intensive production toward activities with higher value-added. The absence of a coherent industrial policy meant that industries were constantly lobbying government for piecemeal policy changes to promote or maintain their competitiveness.

2   RECENT TRENDS AND DEVELOPMENTS IN FDI

Multinationals and Investment

Very little information is available about the number of establishments operated by multinational enterprises (MNEs) in Thailand or their levels of employment, sales, and exports. However, a survey conducted by the National Statistical Office in 1999 does provide some insight into the level of foreign ownership in the manufacturing sector (NSO 2000). The survey found that 19.2 percent of manufacturing firms in a wide range of subsectors had some level of foreign ownership. Table 7.1 shows the distribution

Table 7.1 *Thailand: Distribution of Firms with Foreign Ownership by Product Manufactured*

Product	Firms Surveyed (no.)	Foreign Firms (no.)	Foreign Firms (%)
1 Office & computing machinery	43	37	84.9
2 Electronic valves & tubes	219	144	65.8
3 Basic chemicals, except fertilizers	234	137	58.5
4 Medical & surgical equipment	52	29	55.8
5 Jewelry & related articles	184	100	54.5
6 Synthetic fiber	21	11	53.6
7 Electric motors, generators & transformers	332	146	43.9
8 Refined petroleum products	30	12	40.0
9 Optical instruments/photographic equipment	43	17	39.5
10 Pesticides & other agro-chemical products	443	161	36.4
11 Basic iron & steel	330	109	33.1
12 Engines & turbines, except aircraft	107	35	32.9
13 Knitted & crocheted fabric and articles	66	22	32.6
14 Motor vehicles	342	106	31.0
15 Treatment & coating of metals	183	56	30.4
16 Production, processing, & preserving of meat	78	22	28.2
17 Prepared animal feeds	121	33	27.3
18 Musical instruments	344	94	27.2
19 Bakery products	105	28	26.9
20 Starches & starch products	35	9	26.2
21 Sugar	83	21	25.7
22 Recycling of metal waste & scrap	12	3	25.0
23 Vegetable & animal oils & fats	64	15	22.7
24 Rubber tires & tubes	324	73	22.4
25 Processing & preserving of fruit/vegetables	184	41	22.0

Source: NSO (2000).

of firms with foreign ownership, classified by product manufactured, and ranked according to the ratio of firms with foreign ownership to total firms in the sector. Based on the same survey, Table 7.2 shows the distribution of firms with foreign ownership by nationality of investor. It can be seen that two economies, Japan and Taipei,China, accounted for more than half (about 55 percent) of firms with foreign ownership.

The investment policy regime has been continually revised to reflect the development of the overall economy in general and the trade regime in particular, from the era of import substitution to export promotion and post-crisis liberalization. Investment policy has become much more liberal during the past two decades. Table 7.3 summarizes major developments related to the FDI policy regime. The laws and policies implemented during the past two decades will be discussed in more detail in Section 3 below.

Thailand received relatively small amounts of FDI during the first half of the 1980s. Inflows began to pick up substantially during the second half of the decade, partly because of the 1985 Plaza Accord, which resulted in a sharp appreciation of the Japanese yen (Figure 7.1). This coincided with an increase in production costs in the Asian newly industrializing economies (NIEs)—Taipei,China; Hong Kong, China; and the Republic of Korea— making them less attractive locations for labor-intensive industries.

This was the period in which the Thai government managed to switch from an import substitution to an export-led growth strategy. The success of the export-oriented policy can be attributed to a number of factors, one being the country's fixed exchange rate regime whereby the Thai baht was pegged to the US dollar until the crisis in 1997. Businesses benefited from the currency stability and predictability this provided, coupled with occasional currency devaluations (in 1973, 1981, and 1984) to ensure that Thai exports remained competitive in the global market. Another key factor was low wages, which prompted major industrialized countries to relocate production of labor-intensive products to Thailand. This was made possible by the government's conservative minimum wage policy.

In 1987, the Investment Promotion Act was substantially revised to allow for increased tax privileges and the establishment of industrial and export-processing zones. As a politically stable country with few ethnic or religious conflicts, relatively cheap labor, and a strong work ethic, Thailand became an increasingly attractive destination for FDI, especially by Japanese manufacturers. The value of net FDI inflows increased twelve-fold between 1980 and 1996, from $189 million to $2.27 billion, while the inward FDI stock increased from $981 million to $28.2 billion (Table 7.4).

Following the economic crisis and the depreciation of the baht in 1997,

Table 7.2   Thailand: Major Foreign Investors in Manufacturing by Ownership

Economy/ Region	% of All Firms with Foreign Participation	Products Manufactured (ranked by number of firms in industry)	
Japan	37.9	1	Motor vehicles
		2	Electronic valves & tubes
		3	Basic iron & steel
		4	Pesticides & agro-chemical products
		5	Basic chemicals
Taipei,China	16.8	1	Plastic products
		2	Electric motors, generators, & transformers
		3	Non-structural ceramic ware
		4	Processing of fruit/vegetables
		5	Preparing/spinning of textile fiber
Europe	12.3	1	Jewelry & related articles
		2	Apparel, except fur apparel
		3	Electric motors, generators, & transformers
		4	General purpose machinery
		5	Pesticides & agro-chemical products
United States	7.5	1	Basic chemicals
		2	Electronic valves & tubes
		3	Dairy products
		4	Electric motors, generators, & transformers
		5	Processing of fish products
PRC	6.9	1	Apparel, except fur apparel
		2	Coating of metals
		3	Pulp, paper, & paperboard
		4	Rubber tires & tubes
		5	Motorcycles
Singapore	4.4	1	Musical instruments
		2	Pesticides & agro-chemical products
		3	Rubber tires & tubes
		4	Electronic valves & tubes
		5	Electric motors, generators, & transformers
Republic of Korea	2.5	1	Footwear
		2	Musical instruments
		3	Other general purpose machinery
		4	Office, accounting, & computing machinery
		5	Electric motors, generators, & transformers
Other	11.7		

Source: NSO (2000).

Table 7.3   Thailand: Major Developments in the FDI Policy Regime

Period	Development
State capitalism (1940s–1950s)	State monopolization of most imports and exports.
Import substitution (1958–71)	1st Economic Development Plan (1961–66) brings reduction in direct government involvement in the economy and greater promotion of private investment. Import substitution policy introduced. High levels of protection provided for capital-intensive industries such as automobiles. High tariffs imposed on finished consumer products. Industrial Promotion Act of 1960 establishes an organization that later becomes the Board of Investment, marking the beginning of tax concessions. Tariff structure revised several times to give greater protection to domestic industries. Balance of payments problems arise due to the import of parts and components, leading to discussion of the sustainability of the import substitution policy.
Export promotion (1972–92)	3rd Economic Development Plan (1972–76) brings shift to export promotion. Investment law revised in 1972 to provide exemptions from duty on raw materials and intermediate items for exporting industries. Alien Business Law of 1972 enacted, prohibiting foreigners from entering several business areas. 21 of 72 provinces designated investment zones. Investment Promotion Act enacted in 1977, introducing income tax holidays and 50% concessionary import duty on machinery. Four investment zones established in 1978. Tax incentives on raw materials and machinery reduced for Bangkok and Samut Prakarn, to promote deeper industrial decentralization. A series of baht devaluations takes place between 1983 and 1991.

Table 7.3 (continued)

Period	Development
	Investment Promotion Act revised in 1987, introducing tax privileges and refunds, industrial zones, and export-processing zones. 6th Economic Development Plan (1987–91) aims to improve income distribution and reduce income disparity.
Promotion of industrial decentralization (1993–96)	7th Economic Development Plan (1992–96) aims to reduce income disparity between urban and rural areas and promote sustainable development. Investment Promotion Act revised in 1993 to promote industrial decentralization, with generous incentives provided to encourage industries to locate outside Zone 1. Local content requirements eliminated for motorcycles in anticipation of the TRIMs Agreement of 1995.
Post-crisis liberalization (1997 – present)	Liberalization extended as part of the IMF-led reform package. Foreign Business Act of 1999 enacted, allowing full foreign participation in most manufacturing sectors. Condominium Act revised in 1998 to allow foreigners to wholly own buildings on two acres or less of land. Corporate Debt Restructuring Advisory Committee established to monitor and accelerate debt restructuring. ASEAN Investment Agreement adopted in 1998. Bankruptcy Act revised in 1999 to establish a central bankruptcy court. Local content requirements eliminated for vehicle assembly in 1999. Foreigners allowed to own 100% of shares in promoted manufacturing projects in 2000. Local content requirements eliminated in dairy products in 2003.

Source: Compiled by the authors.

Table 7.4   Thailand: Inward FDI Stock, 1980–2001 ($ million)

Year	1980	1985	1990	1995	2000	2001
FDI stock	981	1,999	8,209	17,452	24,468	28,227[a]

a   The value for 2001 is estimated by adding FDI inflows.
Source: Bank of Thailand, Bangkok.

net inflows of FDI increased sharply in both baht and dollar terms to reach a total of $3.6 billion in 1997 and $5.1 billion in 1998, before falling back to $3.6 billion in 1999 and $2.8 billion in 2000. They then increased once more to $3.7 billion in 2001. The growth of FDI in the post-crisis period can be attributed to the increase in loans provided to affiliates, and to the dramatic rise in the number of mergers and acquisitions (M&As). The baht depreciation reduced domestic production costs and asset values, making FDI more profitable during the economic downturn.

The more liberal FDI regime introduced as part of crisis management and corporate restructuring packages also opened up new opportunities for cross-border M&As, which increased sharply from $633 million in 1997 to $3.2 billion in 1998 (Table 7.5). As a result, net FDI inflows as a proportion of gross fixed capital formation increased from 3.0 percent in 1996 to 7.1 percent in 1997 and 20.5 percent in 1998 (Table 7.6). However, M&A activity subsided in 2002 along with the pace of debt restructuring, as the most attractive assets had already been sold.

The sources of FDI in Thailand have been fairly diversified; they include Japan, the United States, Europe, and the Asian NIEs. Japan has generally been the largest source of FDI since the late 1970s. In the late 1980s, Thailand was the major beneficiary of a massive relocation of industries from Japan brought on by a steep rise in the value of the yen. In 1988–90, for example, net FDI flows from Japan constituted about 40–50 percent of Thailand's total net flows. In recent years, however, the share has fallen due to weak economic conditions in Japan. The last few years has seen a sharp rise in FDI from Singapore, driven by that country's high levels of saving combined with an outward-looking strategy. Most of this investment has been concentrated in the finance, petroleum, and real estate sectors, arriving in the form of loans to affiliated companies. This contrasts

Table 7.5 *Thailand: Cross-border Mergers and Acquisitions by Value,*
1990–2001 ($ million)

Year	Amount
1990	70
1991	79
1992	498
1993	42
1994	89
1995	161
1996	234
1997	633
1998	3,209
1999	2,011
2000	2,569
2001	957

Source: UNCTAD, *World Investment Report 2002.*

Table 7.6 *Thailand: Ratio of Inward and Outward FDI to Gross Fixed*
Capital Formation, 1990–2000 (%)

Year	Inward FDI	Outward FDI
1990–95 (annual average)	4.4	0.6
1996	3.0	1.1
1997	7.1	0.9
1998	20.5	0.5
1999	13.9	1.3
2000	10.4	0.2

Source: UNCTAD, *World Investment Report 2002.*

Figure 7.2   Thailand: Net FDI Inflows by Sector (%)

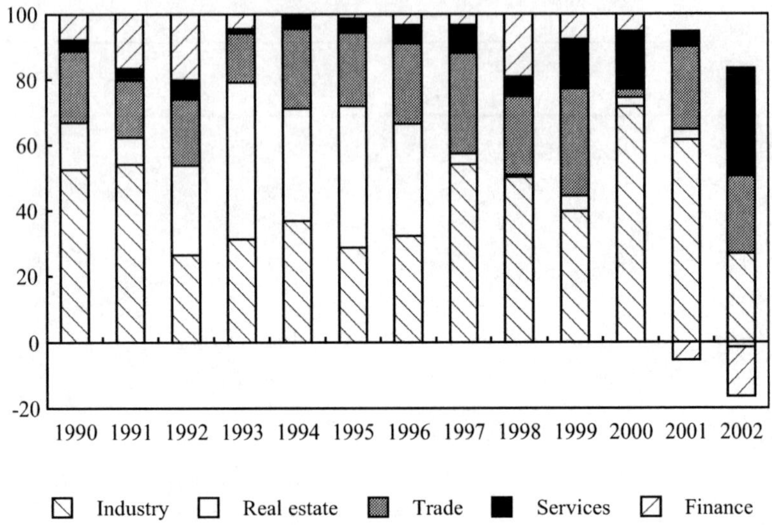

| ◨ Industry | ☐ Real estate | ▦ Trade | ■ Services | ▨ Finance |

Source: Bank of Thailand, Bangkok.

sharply with Japanese investment, which is concentrated in the manufacturing sector.

With the government actively encouraging manufactured exports through its investment policies, the manufacturing sector has consistently been the major recipient of FDI. It is followed by wholesale and retail trade (Figure 7.2). Within manufacturing, electrical appliances, machinery and transport equipment, and chemicals have received the largest amounts of FDI (Table 7.7). The automotive industry has been a major recipient since 1995 when production capacity was greatly expanded. Following the crisis, many Japanese companies injected capital into the industry in a bid to assist their subsidiaries and suppliers.

FDI in chemicals and petrochemicals increased sharply in 2000 when a number of local producers were restructured. The real estate sector attracted large flows in the early to mid-1990s, but this dried up when the property bubble burst in 1996–97. FDI in financial institutions rose significantly in 1998, when the government temporarily lifted limits on foreign ownership in this sector. However, these flows declined in 1999 and 2000, and net outflows were recorded in 2001 and 2002 (Figure 7.2).

There can be no doubt that the financial crisis was the key factor in the

Table 7.7 *Thailand: Net FDI Inflows to Manufacturing by Subsector,*
1995–2002 ($ million)

Sector	1995	1996	1997	1998	1999	2000	2001	2002
Food & sugar	39	45	226	74	93	94	108	–72
(%)	(6.9)	(6.3)	(12.4)	(3.3)	(7.3)	(5.2)	(5.0)	(–14.4)
Textiles	38	49	42	125	20	29	55	25
(%)	(6.7)	(6.9)	(2.3)	(5.7)	(1.6)	(1.6)	(2.6)	(5.0)
Metal & non-metallic products	92	113	216	342	263	93	355	90
(%)	(16.2)	(15.9)	(11.9)	(15.5)	(20.7)	(5.1)	(16.5)	(18.0)
Electrical machinery & appliances	234	241	604	264	425	298	662	–81
(%)	(41.3)	(34.0)	(33.2)	(12.0)	(33.5)	(16.4)	(30.7)	(–16.2)
Machinery & transport equipment	145	109	396	661	394	667	430	219
(%)	(25.6)	(15.4)	(21.8)	(29.9)	(31.1)	(36.8)	(20.0)	(43.7)
Chemicals & petro-chemicals	94	183	163	225	8	383	48	81
(%)	(16.6)	(25.8)	(9.0)	(10.2)	(0.6)	(21.1)	(2.2)	(16.2)
Petroleum products	–162	–250	10	329	8	30	277	32
(%)	(–28.6)	(–35.3)	(0.5)	(14.9)	(0.6)	(1.7)	(12.9)	(6.4)
Construction materials	25	3	–10	24	38	58	–3	21
(%)	(4.4)	(0.4)	(–0.5)	(1.1)	(3.0)	(3.2)	(–0.1)	(4.2)
Other	62	216	173	165	19	161	221	186
(%)	(10.9)	(30.5)	(9.5)	(7.5)	(1.5)	(8.9)	(10.3)	(37.1)
Total	567	709	1,820	2,209	1,268	1,813	2,153	501
(%)	(100.0)	(100.0)	(100.0)	(100.0)	(100.0)	(100.0)	(100.0)	(100.0)

Source: Bank of Thailand, Bangkok.

huge increase in M&As seen over the last few years, in particular in the automotive, electronics, and retail industries. The weakened baht placed a heavy burden on many local companies with foreign currency loans, at the same time as the country's battered commercial banks were unwilling to extend new loans to customers for fear of acquiring more bad debts. Faced with a severe liquidity crisis and a heavy debt burden, many local companies teetered on the brink of bankruptcy. Some relied on injections of new equity capital by a foreign partner, leading to a number of takeovers. Those that were not able to secure new loans or mobilize additional injections of equity had to submit to a debt restructuring process that often included a debt–equity swap.

Financial hardship has not been the only factor contributing to the increase in M&As in Thailand; the government's progressive liberalization of investment regulations has also had an impact on domestic industry. For example, the lifting of local content requirements in the automobile industry, which came into effect in January 2000, forced local parts suppliers into direct competition with foreign suppliers, because auto companies could now source their inputs globally. As a result, many local companies were bought out by foreign auto makers that were more experienced or had access to superior technology.

Thailand scores well on all the criteria determining a country's levels of FDI inflows, including exchange rate, economic growth rate, cost of labor, stability of political environment, and investment incentive regime. During the 1960s and 1970s, the country's high rate of domestic market growth, low wages, and range of investment incentives were among the important determinants of foreign investment in Thailand (Siamwalla, Vajragupta, and Vichyanond 1999). The stability of the currency until the 1997 financial crisis also reduced the foreign exchange rate risks associated with FDI.

An econometric study by Pupphavesa and Pussarangsri (1994) of net FDI inflows to Thailand in 1970–90 concluded that continuing high economic growth, the availability of physical infrastructure, and the appreciation of the Japanese yen against the US dollar were the major determinants. The average tariff rate was found to be unimportant before the Plaza Accord but important afterwards. Thus it appeared that protection through tariffs had become a barrier to FDI.

Every country has its share of nationalist sentiment, and Thailand is no exception. One concern that has been raised from time to time is that foreign investors are depriving Thailand of its national economic sovereignty. However, anti-MNE or anti-globalization sentiment is generally not strong, and appears to be concentrated in sectors such as finance, petrochemicals, and energy where a large number of domestic businesses fell into foreign hands as a result of the crisis. The Financial Restructuring Authority, the state agency placed in charge of 58 problem finance companies after the crisis, was subjected to harsh criticism when it closed all but two of these firms and auctioned off their assets—mainly to large, cash-rich foreign investors. Nationalist sentiment was fueled by the fact that local investors could not afford to participate in the mass auction of assets, which were sold to foreign buyers at deeply discounted prices. At the time, many Thai people believed that foreign investors had conspired to instigate the collapse of the baht in order to acquire Thai assets at fire-sale prices. But it is also worth observing that it was in the interest of some debt-ridden entrepreneurs to encourage this wave of nationalism, because they did not want their companies to fall into foreign hands. The owners of some bankrupt companies have stirred up anti-foreigner sentiment in order to undermine foreign creditors' plans to take control of their firms.

Compared with other countries in ASEAN, Thailand's MNEs appear to be relatively less active internationally. Of the top 50 non-financial MNEs from developing countries, ranked by foreign assets in 2000, six were from Singapore, four were from Malaysia, and one was from the Philippines—but none were from Thailand. This was partly an effect of the economic crisis. Before 1997, a number of Thai MNEs were actively investing abroad. The amount of net direct investment abroad was $422 million in 1994, rising as high as $835 million in 1996, equivalent to 31.8 and 41.7 percent of net FDI inflows respectively. Most of this outward FDI went to other ASEAN countries, where it was concentrated in manufacturing industries—especially electrical appliances—real estate, and telecommunications. After the crisis outflows dropped to less than $200 million per year, except in 1999 when Thai MNEs invested heavily in Hong Kong, China; the United States; and the PRC.

Future Prospects for FDI

In 1997–2000, a little less than one-third of Thailand's inward FDI came from Japan. In a survey of where Japanese manufacturers planned to direct their FDI over the next three years, the PRC emerged as the leading destination, with Thailand a distant second or third depending on the year (JBIC 2002). The PRC's accession to the World Trade Organization (WTO) is likely to lead to an increase in its inflows because investors will benefit from increased transparency in the domestic regulatory regime and better access to foreign markets. The real question is whether the increased flows to the PRC will mean that FDI is diverted away from Thailand. According to computable general equilibrium (CGE) modeling by Ianchovichina and

Walmsley (2002), only the Thai agricultural sector can expect to see an increase in FDI as a result of the PRC's accession to the WTO; flows to other sectors, such as manufacturing and services, are predicted to be adversely affected. These results were obtained by estimating the change in output level for each sector and the respective FDI/output ratios.

A survey by the Japan External Trade Organization in late 2001 somewhat soothed the concerns of Thailand and other ASEAN countries (JETRO 2001). It found that although one-fifth of Japanese MNEs planned to relocate production from Japan and other countries to the PRC after its accession to the WTO, 99 percent of those with investments in ASEAN countries would not relocate. Many Japanese companies remain concerned about the investment climate in the PRC, particularly about rules relating to establishment, the transparency of these rules, and the tax system.

Realizing that Thailand cannot compete directly with the PRC in terms of market size, production costs, or labor supply, the Thai government is positioning the country as an alternative investment destination for MNEs that would like to diversify the risks of investing in the PRC. In particular, it is highlighting the attractiveness of Thailand's transparent investment rules, tax system, and stability.

Thailand is currently engaged in bilateral and regional trade negotiations to establish free trade areas (FTAs) with a number of countries, including Japan, Australia, the United States, the PRC, India, and Bahrain. These 'new generation' FTA agreements are likely to include not only reductions in tariffs and non-tariff barriers, but also greater liberalization of services, trade facilitation measures, and improved investment rules. The new investment agreements of FTAs tend to be broader and deeper than traditional bilateral investment treaties, in particular because they aim to create a more transparent regulatory environment and provide non-discriminatory treatment not only for the manufacturing sector but also for a wide range of service industries, including finance and telecommunications.

Since Thailand has concluded only a few FTA agreements, all quite recently, it is too early to assess the effects of FTAs on FDI. However, it is possible to make some predictions about their impact. First, FTAs with developed countries in particular are likely to add credibility to the Thai government's policies and thus help to increase FDI inflows, especially from other parties to the agreement. Some have even argued that FTAs may work better than multilateral agreements in this respect (Schiff and Winters 2003). To begin with, FTA members have less scope for free riding and thus are more likely to retaliate in instances of violations. In addition, FTAs allow countries to make commitments on matters that are difficult to negotiate multilaterally, such as the harmonization of invest-ment codes.

Second, FTAs may stimulate FDI inflows from non-member countries. This is because, unlike firms located in a member country, firms located in a third country would not be able to enjoy the privileges of market access without relocating. It should be noted, however, that such 'tariff-jumping' or 'platform' FDI can reduce welfare in the host country, because tariffs would direct investment into sectors in which the host country does not have a comparative advantage. Therefore, the establishment of FTAs must be complemented by an overall reduction in external tariff walls.

The drawback of FTAs for small countries like Thailand is that they have less bargaining power in negotiating with developed countries and thus are likely to have to make more concessions. For example, both the United States and Japan are using bilateral FTAs concluded with Singapore as a blueprint for their agreements with other ASEAN countries. However, the bilateral agreements with Singapore are probably not the most suitable models for a bilateral agreement with Thailand because they contain no reference to agriculture. Agriculture is of the utmost importance to Thai-land and must be included in any FTA agreement. Another concern is the 'spaghetti bowl' effect that may arise from having too many FTAs and a multiplicity of trade and investment rules and regulations that becomes extremely complex and highly costly to manage.

3   THE POLICY REGIME FOR FDI AND RELATED TRADE ISSUES

The FDI Regime

The FDI regime in Thailand is shaped by two main laws, the Foreign Busi-ness Act of 1999 and the Investment Promotion Act of 1977, and their by-laws. The first prescribes the scope of foreign participation in local businesses while the latter stipulates investment incentives. The Industrial Estate Authority of Thailand Act 1979 also specifies incentives specifically for factories located in industrial estates. In addition to these general laws, some sectors—such as public utilities; petroleum, gas, and other natural resources; financial services; and certain business services—are covered by sector-specific legislation setting out the criteria for foreign participa-tion.

The Foreign Business Act

The Foreign Business Act of 1999 replaced National Executive Council Announcement 281 of 1972, more commonly known as the Alien Business

Law. The act determines the scope of foreign participation in domestic businesses. It defines an 'alien' as a natural person who is not of Thai nationality. The types of businesses covered by the act are juristic entities not registered in Thailand; juristic entities incorporated in Thailand with foreign shareholding accounting for one-half or more of the total number or value of shares; and limited partnerships or ordinary registered partnerships whose managing partner or manager is a foreigner.

Under the act, foreign corporations are free to operate in any industry that is not on any of the three 'prohibition lists' stipulated in the law. The first of these lists contains business activities that aliens are strictly prohibited from entering, including mass media, rice and animal husbandry, and other resource-based businesses. The second lists businesses concerned with national security or safety, art and culture, customs, traditional or folk handicrafts, and natural resources and the environment. Aliens are prohibited from operating in these areas without the permission of cabinet. The third list contains business activities that the government considers especially vulnerable to foreign competition. Aliens require the permission of the Director-General of the Business Development Department to operate in these areas.

The new law is less restrictive than its predecessor. For example, 21 of the 63 sectors in which foreign majority participation was restricted under the Alien Business Law—including drug manufacture, cement production, and animal feed processing—are no longer restricted under the Foreign Business Act. Certain sectors—construction, stockbroking and securities agencies, auction houses—that appeared on Lists 1 or 2 under the old law have been moved to the third list, where foreign majority participation may be permitted on a case-by-case basis. However, the act still imposes minimum capital requirements for foreign investors of B2 million for a business on List 1 and B3 million for a business on Lists 2 or 3.

The act also guarantees most favored nation (MFN) treatment for all except American investors, who are covered by the 1968 Treaty of Amity and Economic Relations between the Kingdom of Thailand and the United States of America. Under this bilateral arrangement, with the exception of six specified sectors, Americans have the same rights as Thai nationals with respect to the ownership and operation of businesses in Thailand.[2] The same rights are reserved for Thai nationals in the United States, but as the latter country generally does not impose any restrictions on foreign investors, in practice reciprocal treatment does not accord Thai nationals any special privileges.

The Investment Promotion Act

The Investment Promotion Act was originally enacted in 1977 but has subsequently been amended many times to reflect changes in government policy. It offers various incentives for foreign and domestic investment considered essential to the development of the Thai economy, while guaranteeing investors that they will be protected from potential adverse changes in government policies, rules, and regulations (such as price controls or export restrictions) as well as from competition from state enterprises and other government agencies, except those already in operation. The act established the Board of Investment (BOI) as the principal agency responsible for promoting investment through the granting of investment incentives and guarantees.

The BOI was given the authority to grant tax and non-tax investment incentives and privileges for projects that meet national economic development goals. These currently include exemption from or a reduction in import duties on imported machinery, materials, and components; exemption from corporate income tax for three to eight years, with permission to carry losses forward; and exemption from dividend tax during corporate income tax holidays. Foreign firms may also receive permission to bring in foreign technicians and experts to work on a promoted project: to own land in connection with a promoted project; and to operate a business indicated on Lists 2 or 3 of the Foreign Business Act.

The tax incentives currently provided by the BOI are summarized in Table 7.8. Broadly, they differ according to the zone in which the business is physically located and the sector or industry in which the firm operates. To encourage deconcentration of industrial development, the BOI divided the country into three zones based on proximity to Bangkok. Investment projects located in the zone farthest from Bangkok (Zone 3) are eligible to receive the highest tax incentives. In addition, only investments in certain pre-selected sectors are eligible for tax incentives. However, the sectoral dimension has been greatly diluted by the expansion of the list of promoted sectors.

The Industrial Estate Authority of Thailand Act

To promote the deconcentration of industry away from the Bangkok area, the Industrial Estate Authority of Thailand Act 1979 provides special incentives for investors locating in industrial estates situated in regional areas. These industrial estates comprise both general industrial zones and export-processing zones.

Some of the special privileges granted to businesses operating in

Table 7.8   Thailand: Summary of Tax Incentives Currently Offered by the Board of Investment

	Zone 1	Zone 2	Zone 3
Machinery	Standard duty of 5%, or 50% reduction of import duty, on machinery that is subject to an import duty of not less than 10%.	Same as for Zone 1.	Exemption from import duty on machinery for projects located in 40 designated provinces.
Raw materials	Exemption of import duty on raw materials used in the manufacture of export products for one year.	Same as for Zone 1.	Exemption from import duty on raw materials used in the manufacture of export products for five years, for projects located in 40 designated provinces.
Corporate tax	Tax holiday for three years for projects located in an industrial estate or promoted industrial zone, provided that they have invested capital of B10 million or more and obtain ISO9000 or similar international certification within two years of start-up; otherwise the tax holiday will be reduced by one year.	Same as for Zone 1 except that tax holidays are granted for five years.	Same as for Zone 1 except that tax holidays are granted for eight years. Projects located in 18 designated provinces are given the following additional privileges: a 50% reduction in corporate income tax for five years after the period of exemption; double deduction from income tax of transport, electricity, and water costs for ten years from the start of operations; and a 25% deduction from profit of the project's infra-structure/construction costs for ten years from the start of operations. Projects located within an industrial estate or promoted industrial zone are given the following additional privileges: a 50% reduction in cor-porate income tax for five years following the period of exemption; and double deduction from income tax of transport, electricity, and water costs for ten years from the date of first revenue derived from a promoted activity. Projects located outside an industrial estate or promoted industrial zone can deduct 25% of infrastructure and construction costs from profit for ten years from the start of operations.

Source: Board of Investment, Bangkok.

regional zones include the right to own land in an industrial estate, permission to obtain work permits for foreign technicians and experts, and the right to remit foreign currency abroad. Businesses operating in an export-processing zone are entitled to several additional tax incentives and privileges, including an exemption from special fees, import duty, value-added tax, and excise tax on machinery, equipment, and tools used in the manufacture of goods and in the construction of factories or buildings; a similar exemption for raw materials; an exemption from export duty, value-added tax, and excise tax on exported products; and an exemption from, or the refund of, taxes on goods destined for another export-processing zone.

The Trade Regime

Thailand was one of very few developing countries identified by Sachs and Warner (1995) as having 'always been open.' A country was judged by the authors to be open if it had none of the following characteristics: (i) a black market exchange rate that was more than 20 percent lower than the official rate, on average, during the 1970s or 1980s; (ii) a state monopoly on major exports; (iii) a socialist economic system; (iv) non-tariff barriers covering 40 percent or more of trade; and (v) average tariff rates of 40 percent or more. Thailand would be considered very open based on the first three criteria. On closer inspection, however, it is apparent that it has performed less well on the trade criterion. For example, its average tariff rate of 29 percent has been well above the average rate for developing countries of 22 percent. With regard to trade at least, the country is not as open as it seems.

Although Thailand officially abandoned its import substitution strategy in favor of an export-promoting strategy in 1972, the level of protection remained high for many years. In fact, the tariff rate was raised to increase government revenue shortly after the policy shift was announced, and non-tariff measures were also strengthened. Table 7.9 compares the use of non-tariff measures by a cross-section of Asian countries. The coverage of core non-tariff measures appears to be wider in Thailand than in Hong Kong, China and Singapore but narrower than in Indonesia, Korea, and Malaysia. Most such measures have targeted agricultural products, but, as discussed above, foreign investment has also been affected by the closure of businesses to foreign entry under the Alien Business Law.

The adverse effects of protection were moderated by 'protection offsets' such as the exemptions from corporate income tax and import duties and other investment promotion measures granted by the BOI.[3] Competition among government agencies also provided unintended remedies for the negative effects of protection (Rock 2001). It was not until the late

Table 7.9   Non-tariff Measures for All Products in Developing
             Economies, 1989–98 (%)[a]

Economy	Core Non-tariff Measures		Non-automatic Licensing		Prohibition	
	1989–94	1995–98	1989–94	1995–98	1989–94	1995–98
Hong Kong, China	2.1	2.1	2.0	2.0	0.0	0.0
Indonesia	53.6	31.3	53.0	31.0	5.0	0.0
Republic of Korea	50.0	25.0	32.0	0.0	0.0	0.0
Malaysia	56.3	19.6	55.0	20.0	4.0	14.0
Philippines	11.5	n.a.	7.0	n.a.	4.0	n.a.
Singapore	1.0	2.1	1.0	1.0	0.0	1.0
Thailand	36.5	17.5	36.0	11.0	0.0	6.0

n.a.: not available.

a   Non-tariff measures are calculated as frequency ratios as a percentage of all

1980s and early 1990s that a liberal trade regime was actually introduced. By 1993, non-tariff measures were applicable to 18 commodities only, partly to comply with the guidelines of the General Agreement on Tariffs and Trade (GATT). Thailand subsequently lifted its local content requirements in compliance with the TRIMs Agreement—the WTO Agreement on Trade-related Investment Measures.

Links between FDI and the Trade Regime

Thailand has continually revised its investment policy to reflect the development of the overall economy in general and the trade regime in particular. The process of industrialization since abandoning state capitalism in 1950 can be divided into four phases: import substitution, export promotion, industrial decentralization, and post-crisis liberalization (Table 7.3).

Import Substitution (1958–71)

In the late 1950s, the government imposed an escalating tariff structure, with the lowest rates placed on raw materials and the highest rates placed

Table 7.9 (continued)

Economy	Quotas		Tariff Quotas		Import Monitoring	
	1989–94	1995–98	1989–94	1995–98	1989–94	1995–98
Hong Kong, China	0.0	0.0	0.0	0.0	16.0	0.0
Indonesia	3.0	0.0	0.0	0.0	0.0	0.0
Republic of Korea	3.0	0.0	26.0	25.0	0.0	0.0
Malaysia	2.0	2.0	0.0	7.0	0.0	0.0
Philippines	1.0	n.a.	0.0	n.a.	0.0	n.a.
Singapore	0.0	0.0	0.0	0.0	0.0	0.0
Thailand	2.0	1.0	0.0	12.0	2.0	0.0

Harmonized System (HS) two-digit product categories. Core non-tariff measures include licensing, prohibitions, quotas, and administered pricing.
Source: Michalopoulos (1999).

on finished products. In 1971, at the end of the import substitution era, effective rates of protection in the Thai manufacturing sector ranged from –20.9 to 236.4 percent. This tariff structure was intended to foster the development of selected manufacturing industries. The government established a number of state enterprises during this period to promote industrialization and, in the early 1960s, also began to encourage private domestic investment. As MNEs were then regarded as 'exploitative,' FDI was strictly controlled.

The policy of import substitution proved incompatible with national economic goals. For instance, while the policy aimed to promote the utilization of domestic parts and raw materials, the tariff structure discriminated against many such activities. Also, while the national economic plan called for the development of household and small-scale industries, the BOI was targeting large-scale, capital-intensive industries (Poapongsakorn and Fuller 1997). By the early 1970s the import substitution policy had fallen out of favor. Industrial expansion had slowed markedly and the country's balance of payments was in deficit.

Export Promotion (1972–92)

The attitude to FDI changed dramatically with the switch to an export pro-motion strategy: it was now perceived as the means by which the country's balance of payments problems could be solved. However, although the BOI opted to provide an environment attractive to foreign investors, the trade regime remained unchanged: effective rates of protection widened to a range of –21.4 to 1,693.4 percent in 1982 (Mongkolsamai, Chunanun-tahum, and Tambunlerdchai 1985), and import-substituting activities con-tinued to be protected by very high tariff rates (Poapongsakorn and Fuller 1997). The export promotion strategy nevertheless proved effective, with exports consistently growing faster than GDP. The ratio of total trade to GDP rose steadily from less than 30 percent in 1970 to almost 50 percent in 1981 and nearly 70 percent by the beginning of the 1990s. The policy was successful in attracting foreign investment, particularly in labor-inten-sive activities.

Industrial Decentralization (1993–96)

As industrialization progressed, regional disparities became a major con-cern. The relative importance of the area around Bangkok increased dur-ing the 1980s, mainly due to its superior infrastructure. In order to reverse this trend of polarized industrial development, the government shifted to a policy of industrial decentralization. In 1993 the BOI radically redesigned the zoning system. For the first time, certain industries would no longer be promoted if they located in Zone 1, even if they were primarily exporters. For example, only textile producers locating in Zone 3 would be entitled to promotion, as would electronics firms locating in either Zone 2 or Zone 3. The government supported these initiatives by investing heavily in regional infrastructure. However, this strategy of industrial decentraliza-tion has yet to produce significant results.

Export promotion continued, and even flourished, during this period. A major change in the trade regime occurred in the early 1990s when the tar-iff schedule went through several revisions, partly to meet Thailand's obli-gations under the GATT. Tariff rates on most intermediate products and capital goods were reduced to 5–10 percent, and import bans on certain items such as automobiles were lifted.

Post-crisis Liberalization (1997 – present)

Following the economic crisis of 1997, the government had little choice but to rely on FDI to help it mobilize much needed foreign capital. The liberal-ization of foreign investment was also an important part of the IMF-led reform package. The post-crisis economic liberalization included plans to privatize state-owned enterprises in the infrastructure sector, and the deregulation of key service sectors such as banking and insurance. The government amended the Condominium Act in late 1998 to allow unrestricted foreign ownership of condominiums or apartment buildings built on two acres or less of land, and in 1999 it enacted the Foreign Business Act. Since 2000, the BOI has allowed foreigners to own 100 percent of shares in promoted manufacturing projects. The accession of the PRC to the WTO and its emergence as a major investment destination in Asia has also prompted the BOI to take a more aggressive stance toward attracting FDI.

Evaluation of Investment Policies

Foreign Business Act

Although the Foreign Business Act is considered to be more conducive to FDI than the previous Alien Business Law, several shortcomings remain. First, it is not clear how some of the classifications in the three lists of prohibited industries were arrived at. For example, forestry appears on List 3 as a business in which Thailand is not yet ready to compete, while wood fabrication for furniture appears on List 2 as a business related to natural resources and the environment. Such non-transparency leaves a wide margin for discretion on the part of the authorizing agencies.

Second, despite the fact that Article 9 of the Foreign Business Act requires the lists to be reviewed annually, recommending that a transparent and effective mechanism be established to carry out this task, in practice this is not being done to the specified standard because the criteria for evaluation have not been finalized.

Finally, although the Foreign Business Act appears to be more liberal in that it takes a 'negative list' approach to defining the sectors that are subject to investment restrictions, a 'positive list' approach still applies in practice in the services sector. This is because List 3 specifies many sectors that are subject to prohibitions, including 'other categories of service business except those prescribed in the ministerial regulations.' As a result, while the foreign investment regime in Thailand is relatively open for the manufacturing sector, it is very much closed for services. Laws specific to the sector remain important, such as the Telecommunications Act of 2001, which caps the foreign equity share of a facility-based operator at only 25 percent.

Locational Policy

FDI has always been considered a tool to promote regional development and industrial decentralization. Apart from investment incentives, however, a number of factors may affect the location of firms within the country. In some sectors, such as automobiles and electronics, firms tend to establish in clusters in order to take advantage of agglomeration economies. It is thus interesting to evaluate the extent to which the BOI's locational policies have contributed to industrial decentralization in Thailand.

Industrial decentralization has essentially been limited to Zone 2, despite the revision of the zoning policy in 1993. The share of GDP in Zone 1 grew continuously from 1982 to 1990, then declined steadily as a result of the congestion in and near Bangkok. The GDP and manufacturing shares of provinces that were either adjacent to Zone 1 or had access to the industrial estates along the eastern seaboard then rose dramatically, confirming that some progress had been made in industrial decentralization. This pattern indicates that, in response to the zoning policy, firms tried to locate as close to Zone 1 as possible, in order to maximize their access to good infrastructure while minimizing their taxation and transactions costs.

Very little decentralization has occurred in Zone 3. However, the GDP and manufacturing shares of some of the larger provinces—notably those situated in the north and northeast of the country—have increased, reflecting growth in the manufacturing production base of large provinces where an industrial estate is located and lower wage rates prevail. Industrial decentralization remains insignificant in the south, again with the exception of the largest provinces where most manufacturing industries are concentrated. In sum, the BOI's policies may be inducing decentralization, but only in a specific pattern and in conjunction with the availability of infrastructure.

A survey by the Foreign Investment Advisory Service confirms that the BOI's zoning policy has not made a significant contribution to industrial decentralization, particularly in Zone 3 (FIAS 1999). It found that 82.5 percent of the promoted firms in Zones 2 and 3 would have made the same choice of location even if they had been offered the same incentives as firms in Zone 1. Thus, while the level of investment in Zone 3 has no doubt increased, it is not conclusive that this was attributable to the investment incentives offered.

Investment Incentives

It is a complex exercise to assess the impact of tax incentives on investment. The marginal effective tax rate on company income, roughly defined as the proportional difference between the pre- and post-tax rates of return, provides a simple summary of the relative magnitude of taxes and tax incentives. For example, if the rate of return is 6 percent when taxes are applied and it rises to 10 percent after tax concessions, the marginal effective tax rate will be $(10-6)/10 = 40$ percent.

Table 7.10 *Marginal Effective Tax Rates in Selected Asian Countries (%)*

Tax Rate	Thailand	Singapore	Malaysia	Philippines
With interest deductibility	46	33	30	47
Adjusted for customs duty concessions	35	33	22	40
Adjusted for tax holiday	7	14	22	21
Adjusted for depreciation carried forward	7	−7	22	21

Source: FIAS (1999).

Table 7.10 compares the marginal effective tax rate for Thailand, Singapore, Malaysia, and the Philippines. After adjustment for interest deductibility, Thailand's rate is considerably higher than that of either Singapore or Malaysia and is on a par with that of the Philippines. However, after adjustment for tax holidays, Thailand's marginal effective tax rate drops to only 7 percent, which is higher only than the rate for Singapore. This implies that Thailand offers a much more generous tax holiday scheme than either Malaysia or the Philippines, resulting in potentially higher tax losses for the government. For example, tax losses due to investment incentives were estimated to be B18,370 million, or 0.39 percent of GDP, in 1996.

This could be justified if the incentives had proved effective in attracting additional investment, which generates large positive externalities for society. However, the Foreign Investment Advisory Service found that at least 70 percent of the promoted investments would have occurred even without tax incentives (FIAS 1999). It also estimated that these investment projects had created only 76,000 direct jobs between 1991 and 1996. Dividing the total tax revenue forgone by this number generates a net cost of B242,089 per job per annum. By 2001, the net cost of this job creation was expected to rise to B347,000, with a marginal cost of B1,171,000. This implies that the average tax revenue forgone per job created has been significantly higher than the opportunity cost of labor, as measured by the average rate of remuneration in the industrial sector of only B80,000.

Despite these adverse findings, the BOI continues to use tax-based incentives as its main instrument to encourage FDI. As in other countries, the investment authority is charged with promoting investment, but not with collecting revenue, and so is quick to hand out generous tax incentives. Moreover, the difficulty of measuring the revenue forgone through investment tax incentives allows bureaucrats to continue to pursue these seemingly costly promotional programs without being held accountable.

4   THE IMPACT OF FDI

Growth

Even though it is widely believed that FDI contributes to growth, the economist Jagdish Bhagwati among others has long argued that the growth-enhancing effect of FDI is not automatic but depends on various country-specific factors. In particular, Bhagwati claimed that the gains from FDI were significantly smaller, or even negative, under a strict import substitution regime compared with an export promotion regime. To test the Bhagwati hypothesis for Thailand, Archanun (2003b) examined the effect of the trade policy regime on the contribution of FDI to economic growth using time-series data for 1970–99. GDP was used as the dependent variable, and a number of variables—including total labor force, domestic capital formation, education expenditure, FDI, and the trade regime—were used as explanatory variables. The results confirmed Bhagwati's hypothesis that FDI had contributed positively to the growth of the Thai economy under an open trade regime.

The positive economic contribution of FDI is also validated in a study by Kinoshita (2001), who examined the contribution of FDI to GDP growth through three channels: fixed capital formation, imports, and exports. Results from a simulation model revealed that a 10 percent increase in FDI would increase fixed capital formation by 44.3 percent, imports by 2.0 percent, exports by 2.3 percent, and GDP by 1.6 percent at the peak period. The study thus confirmed that FDI has been one of the main drivers of economic growth in Thailand, in addition to other factors such as the appreciation of the Japanese yen and economic conditions in the United States and Japan. It also concluded that 'crowding out' impacts from FDI are unlikely.

Exports, Imports, and the Balance of Payments

It is widely believed that FDI promotes exports because large foreign companies that operate on a global scale enjoy significant economies of scale in marketing and possess a superior capability to access overseas markets. Foreign firms can also serve as a catalyst for domestic firms to increase their level of exports. According to BOI statistics, following the crisis the share of approved projects that were export-oriented (that is, that exported more than 80 percent of their total output) jumped from 30 percent of the total number of projects approved in 1997 to 65.5 percent in 1999, and remained relatively high through to 2001. These figures suggest that FDI has played a very important role in Thailand's export performance since the crisis.

Conversely, FDI may contribute to a deterioration in the trade account, since foreign firms generally display a higher propensity to import capital goods and raw materials than do local firms, as exemplified by FDI in the Thai electronics industry. Profit repatriation can also lead to a deterioration in the capital account. Since most MNEs do not have roots in the local economy, they are likely to repatriate profits at the earliest sign of an economic downturn. For an economy that is dominated by MNEs, a mass repatriation of profits is likely to exacerbate the difficulties experienced during a downturn. The net impact of FDI on the balance of payments is thus ambiguous. The net effects are found to be country-specific and sensitive to the type of investment, the industry mix, and the maturity structure of the investment.

Fry (1996, cited in UNCTAD 1997: 88) examined the effects of FDI in six Asian economies: Indonesia, Korea, Malaysia, the Philippines, Singapore, and Thailand. Through regression analysis, he found that balance of payments outcomes were explained by five factors, namely savings, FDI, exports, imports, and economic growth. The first four variables, including FDI, were found to contribute positively to the balance of payments, with a lagged response for exports. The results of a dynamic simulation showed that inflows of FDI were strongly associated with higher imports during the early stages of industrialization and thus tended to worsen the current account. However, in the long-run steady state, their contribution to economic growth generated net savings, thus leading to an improvement in the current account.

Labor Productivity

Ramstetter (2001) compared labor productivity in local and foreign-owned manufacturing plants in Thailand. His regression results showed the productivity difference to be insignificant. Even in the few isolated cases where a significant productivity gap was observed, there was little consistency in productivity differentials across years, industries, or nationality of ownership.

A study by Ito (2002) investigating productivity in foreign and local plants in the Thai automobile industry confirms Ramstetter's findings. She found, as expected, that labor productivity was higher in foreign plants.

However, this higher productivity was mainly attributable to the fact that foreign firms tended to employ capital more intensively than did Thai firms. There was no evidence to suggest that foreign plants had relatively higher total factor productivity. As we will see in the next section, however, the higher labor productivity of foreign firms has tended to translate into higher wages, irrespective of the causes of the productivity differential.

Wages

Matsuoka (2001) found evidence of a positive wage differential between foreign and local plants for both non-production and production workers, based on a survey of plants in 12 industries situated in and around Bangkok. In the first round, conducted in 1996, 2,407 plants were included in the survey. This was doubled to 5,122 in the second round, conducted in 1998. The 1996 round found that the average wage paid by foreign firms was 20 percent higher for non-production workers and 8 percent higher for production workers than the average wage paid by local firms. The wage differential was even larger in 1998, with foreign firms paying 28 percent and 12 percent more to non-production and production workers respectively.

The same study found that the foreign equity share and nationality of ownership of the foreign firm contributed to the wage differential. Surprisingly, the wage differential between a wholly owned foreign firm and a local firm was small and statistically insignificant. The gap between a joint venture and a local firm was, however, much more pronounced. This contradicts the finding of earlier studies (for example, Ramachandran 1993) that the larger a firm's foreign equity share, the higher its labor productivity and, hence, wages. This was explained by arguing that foreign firms were more willing to transfer technology to foreign subsidiaries the higher their ownership share.

Matsuoka found a larger wage gap for companies whose headquarters were in Japan, the European Union, or the United States. The gap was almost halved for firms from less developed countries such as the Asian NIEs. This can be explained by the fact that NIE companies tend to invest more in industries with low wages, such as textiles and electronic components. In contrast, firms from developed countries tend to invest in industries employing more sophisticated technology, and thus require more skilled and better paid workers.

In order to factor out the wage differential attributable to variables unrelated to a firm's nationality, Udomsaph (2003) conducted a similar regression analysis, but controlled for other possible explanatory variables. These included the level of education and skills of the worker, firm size, industry, and the location of the firm. The results confirmed Matsuoka's finding that foreign establishments offer a wage premium. However, in the case of the least skilled workers, the wage differential disappeared when other variables were controlled for. A wage differential was still present for highly skilled workers, but it was much smaller than that found in the previous study. Udomsaph attributed the wage differential for highly skilled labor to search costs for professional and skilled workers in the local labor market, as well as the firms' attempts to retain highly skilled employees by offering them higher wages.

Technology Transfer

Pupphavesa and Pussarungsri (1994) examined technology transfer between manufacturers and suppliers in Thailand through a survey of nine foreign-owned buyers and five suppliers. They found that all of the suppliers had acquired a basic level of three types of technology: product technology, quality control technology, and process technology. This included a knowledge of product specifications, standard manufacturing practices, and basic operation. However, only three of the five suppliers had acquired a medium level of all three types of technology, and only one claimed to have accessed a high level of technology, including product design, improvement of product/process performance, and process operation and adaptation skills.

Urata (1996) reached a similar conclusion. His survey found that Japanese firms operating in Thailand were more willing to transfer technology relating to manufacturing or assembly operations. Less than half of the firms had transferred technology related to tools development, and only 20–30 percent had transferred knowledge and skills related to technological improvements and development of the manufacturing process.

In contrast, a recent examination of inter-firm technology transfer in the Thai automobile industry by Techakanont (2002) found that Japanese firms *were* willing to transfer technology, not only to their own affiliates but also to local suppliers. The technology was transferred by information sharing and the provision of advice with regard to technological activities such as value analysis, value engineering, and quality control. However, the relative success of local parts suppliers in Thailand cannot be attributed entirely to the Japanese automobile manufacturers: Japanese parts suppliers have also played an important role as partners in joint ventures. The author concluded that the creation of strong technical linkages had been the most important factor in the successful development of a local supporting industry.

As mentioned earlier, technology transfer may occur through job mobility. Pupphavesa and Pussarungsri (1994) showed that the degree of job turnover was much lower in foreign firms than in Thai firms. They also found that workers in foreign firms tended to move to other foreign firms rather than to Thai firms. So did workers in Thai firms, partly because of the higher salaries and greater job security offered by foreign firms. The authors were thus skeptical about the possibility of mobility from foreign firms to Thai firms being a vital channel of technology diffusion: the direction of job mobility reflected a 'brain drain' rather than a diffusion of technology.

R&D and Innovation

Many studies have found that MNEs conduct little R&D outside their home bases (see, for example, Amsden, Tschang, and Goto 2001). A survey of 1,019 Thai firms conducted in 2001 by the Brooker Group (2001) confirms the above pattern for Thailand. It found that wholly locally owned firms had an R&D intensity ratio (defined as the ratio of R&D expenditure to annual sales) that was on average twice that of foreign companies. Interestingly, R&D intensity was considerably lower among joint ventures, implying that firms are less willing to invest in R&D when ownership is shared. The same study found a similar pattern for innovation. Again, wholly locally owned firms exhibited an innovation to sales ratio that was roughly three times that of the other groups (Table 7.11). One possible explanation is that local firms may have more limited avenues to acquire new technology than foreign firms, and thus have to resort to in-house R&D. Another hypothesis is that local and foreign firms may be producing different products that require different levels of technology. For example, the former may face a greater need to customize products for the local market than the latter.

It is also clear that very little R&D is conducted by the private sector in Thailand, regardless of firm nationality. The major reason lies in the lack of a well-developed human capital base. Thailand has been criticized for under-investing in post-primary education and training, with the result that Thai employees have a limited capacity to absorb and benefit from technology transfers and spillovers.

Competition and Concentration

How FDI affects concentration and the level of competition in the domestic market will depend largely on the degree of contestability.[4] If the market is open and conducive to competition from new entrants and imports, then the nationality of the players in the market matters little, as no firm will be able to carry out anti-competitive practices. The concern arises

Table 7.11   Thailand: R&D and Innovation Intensity by Ownership (%)

Ownership	R&D Expenditure/Sales	Innovation Expenditure/Sales
Wholly locally owned	2.15	3.25
More than 70% locally owned	0.17	0.66
50–70% locally owned	0.65	1.33
Less than 50% locally owned	0.23	0.61
Wholly foreign-owned	1.06	0.90

Source: Brooker Group (2001).

when the market is not contestable, in that new entry or competition from imported products is obstructed either by regulatory restrictions (such as licensing or import duties) or by market failure (whereby the industry displays significant economies of scale, giving an advantage to the larger players in the market). In this case, the type of FDI may have an impact on market concentration and competition, at least in the short run.

The experience in Thailand has been mixed. In banking, the post-crisis emergence of several foreign banks resulting from a series of takeovers of ailing domestic banks has contributed significantly to creating a more competitive environment. The pre-crisis banking industry was one in which a market leader (the largest bank) set interest rates for all other banks to follow. This guaranteed a healthy profit for the banks but contributed very little to improvements in service quality and service differentiation. The Association of Thai Commercial Banks provided a convenient forum for collusive practices. The entry of foreign banks such as ABN Amro, United Overseas Bank, and Standard Chartered Bank has broken the cartel, bringing about a remarkable improvement in service. Customers now enjoy longer banking hours, more diversified savings packages, more competitive lending rates, and an improved range of credit card services.

The story is different for industries with few players such as cement, however. Cement was one of the industries worst hit by the crisis: the local construction industry came to a halt with the collapse of the finance and real estate markets. A few firms were taken over by foreign companies such as Holcim of Switzerland and Cemex of Mexico. In 2001, the second largest player in the market, Siam City Cement (which is majority owned by Holcim), made a bid for TPI Polene Co. Ltd, which was subject to a debt restructuring process. Holcim reportedly announced that it expected to see a doubling of the price of cement in the domestic market once the takeover was completed. The merger does not appear viable since the merger provision in the Trade Competition Act of 1999 was not (and still is not) effective. This is because the act has yet to specify in detail its regulations relating to the approval of mergers. Almost every analysis has concluded that the merger will lead to collusion and, hence, an increase in the price of cement.

Retailing is another industry that has fallen into foreign hands as a result of the crisis. Most discount stores in Thailand are now owned by foreign multinationals such as Tesco of the United Kingdom, Carrefour and Casino of France, and Royal Ahold of the Netherlands. While these foreign retail companies compete vigorously among themselves and with Thai department stores, their extremely aggressive business culture has created tremendous friction with suppliers. Some of their business practices, such as mandatory enrollment of suppliers in price promotion schemes, preferential treatment for house brand products, and the collection of various service fees, borders on anti-competitive conduct. The Thai Trade Competition Commission has recently published a Retail Industry Code of Ethics in response to suppliers' complaints.

These three cases show that FDI may promote or restrict competition. It would be fair to say that all companies, whether foreign or local, will try to restrict competition if it is in their interest and legally feasible to do so. Therefore, in markets where concentration tends to be high due to economies of scale or scope, or due to the presence of a strong industry network, the best protection against the restrictive business practices of MNEs is to ensure that the market is contestable, that is, that new competitors and imported substitutes are able to enter the market freely. In addition, an effective competition regime needs to be established to guard against potentially abusive practices that cannot be solved by competitive pressures alone, and to ensure that the market structure is conducive to competition.

FDI in the Automobile and Electronics Industries

Automobiles and electronics are examples of two industries in Thailand in which MNEs have played a crucial role. Thailand currently ranks fourth in automobile production in Asia after Korea, the PRC, and Taipei,China, and first among ASEAN countries in terms of the number of establishments and employees in the industry. In the electronics industry, the country is a production base for many global manufacturers of hard disk drives.

The Automobile Industry

The automobile industry was one of the first industries to be promoted by the BOI because of its large upstream linkages—nearly 20,000 parts are required to make an assembled car. Japanese auto makers have been crucial to the development of the industry.

During the import substitution regime, imports of completely built-up vehicles were banned. By the end of the 1960s, Japanese assemblers had built a manufacturing base for automobile assembly. However, the import substitution policy created trade deficits because domestic car manufacturers were heavily reliant on imported parts and machinery. As a result, the government introduced a policy in the 1970s to rationalize the industry and increase economies of scale by restricting assemblers to the production of either passenger cars or commercial cars. Under the policy, existing producers of passenger cars would be allowed to produce no more than three models. The government also introduced local content requirements, which were gradually increased until they reached 50 percent by value in 1983. Such restrictions gave Japanese firms a competitive edge over American and European auto makers, since the cars sold by the latter rarely met the local content requirements.

The number of cars assembled in Thailand expanded quickly throughout the 1980s when the country was experiencing rapid economic growth. Investment in automotive parts also increased. In recognition of the high costs of protection, the government gradually reduced import duties, exposing assemblers to external competition and forcing them to improve their efficiency and quality. The TRIMs Agreement accelerated liberalization by providing for the abolition of local content requirements. High tariff rates remained as the only source of protection.

The formation of the ASEAN Free Trade Area in 1992 provided a further impetus for investment by global auto assemblers and parts suppliers. Most notably, the 'Big Three' US manufacturers, namely General Motors (GM), Ford, and DaimlerChrysler, announced their intention to set up assembly plants in Thailand, in recognition of the country's potential as an export hub for Southeast Asia. Within a few years production capacity had been greatly expanded. Planned capacity exceeded 1 million units in 1999.

Thailand has exported cars in increasing numbers since the 1997 financial crisis. Its transformation into an export base for automobiles owes much to Japanese assemblers, who decided to maintain levels of production in the country in spite of the economic difficulties caused by the crisis. Their main motivation appears to have been to retain scarce skilled labor in preparation for a future recovery in demand. In order to help financially distressed firms, the BOI removed the restriction on foreign shareholding in November 1997, allowing foreign investors to become majority shareholders. It also tried to reduce the production costs of Thai exporters by granting tariff exemptions for machinery imported by firms located in Zones 1 and 2.

The Hard Disk Drive Industry

The electronics industry is not as well developed as the automobile industry in terms of cluster formation. Hard disk drives (HDDs) are the only product made in Thailand by global players in the electronics industry. The BOI played a part in persuading major players to invest in Thailand, even though the incentives it offered could not compare with those provided by Malaysia and Singapore. It has been argued that whereas Thailand has taken a 'generalist' approach to industry promotion, offering broad incentives such as corporate tax exemptions and duty-free import of inputs, Singapore and Malaysia have taken a firm-specific approach, offering incentives to MNEs almost on a case-by-case basis (Poapongsakorn and Fuller 1998).

The emergence of an HDD manufacturing capability in Thailand can be traced to Seagate's decision in 1983 to shift its assembly operations from Singapore to Thailand. At the time the BOI offered only general tax incentives adopted as part of the government's export promotion policy, so it appears that investment incentives did not contribute to Seagate's decision to relocate. Neither did Thailand have the infrastructure to support an HDD industry at the time. However, it was able to offer cheaper labor and a stable economic and political environment, and these are believed to have been the main motives behind Seagate's decision to relocate. Other HDD manufacturers such as IBM and Fujitsu and their first-tier suppliers followed Seagate to Thailand in the 1990s, forming a large production cluster in the country. However, only modest agglomeration effects and technological spillovers have been evident, as most suppliers tend to serve only one producer. The problem with FDI in this industry is that technology transfer seems to be limited to production, and most activities still involve labor-intensive assembly. Deeper technological linkages are urgently needed if the Thai HDD industry is to compete with new players, especially the PRC.

5   THE WTO AND INTERNATIONAL OBLIGATIONS

The TRIMs Agreement

The TRIMs Agreement negotiated during the Uruguay Round of the GATT aims to discipline investment policies that are inconsistent with Article III (on national treatment) and Article XI (on quantitative restrictions) of the GATT; that is, it deals with the investment dimension of the GATT trade agreement. The agreement obliges all WTO member countries to phase out local content and export performance requirements imposed on foreign firms. Thailand previously imposed local content requirements on three industries—milk and dairy processing, car assembly, and motorcycle manufacturing—and had export performance requirements for investment projects applying for BOI investment incentives. In particular, projects in Zones 1 or 2 were required to export more than 80 percent of their output to qualify for corporate tax holidays, in addition to complying with other conditions.

The TRIMs Agreement was instrumental in achieving investment policy reform in Thailand. To comply with its terms, Thailand gradually abolished its TRIMs. New projects approved to receive investment incentives after April 1993 were no longer subject to local content requirements, except in the dairy product and vehicle assembly industries. The local content requirements for vehicle assembly were eliminated in 1999, with those for dairy products to be phased out by the end of 2003. Export performance requirements were lifted in August 2000.

It should be noted that the TRIMs Agreement is relatively limited in scope compared with the bilateral and regional agreements that have proliferated among member countries, in that it deals narrowly with trade-distorting investment measures.

Bilateral Investment Agreements

The purpose of bilateral investment treaties is to create a more favorable investment climate for signatory countries, in addition to granting special investment incentives. Thailand has concluded 34 bilateral investment treaties since 1954. Most of the treaties signed by the Thai government have the same format and similar substantive provisions, as summarized in Table 7.12. As already mentioned, the United States receives the most favorable treatment under the Treaty of Amity and Economic Relations between the Kingdom of Thailand and the United States of America. And, as noted above, Thailand is also currently engaged in negotiating a number of bilateral and regional trade agreements with several countries with a view to establishing FTAs.

The Regional Investment Framework

In addition to negotiating bilateral investment treaties with a number of countries, Thailand has pursued several initiatives to foster regional investment cooperation, the main ones being the non-binding investment princi-

Table 7.12   Thailand: Obligations under Bilateral Investment Treaties

Core Provisions	Details
Definition	Thailand has opted for a broad definition of investment to cover every kind of asset held by an investor/ company, including movable and immovable property and property rights.
Scope of the treaty	Investment privileges granted by bilateral investment treaties must be approved in writing, with the scope of the provisions depending on the agreement that Thailand has concluded with the signatory country.
National and MFN treatment	Thailand has granted both national and MFN treatment to signatory country investors at the post-entry level. Where some industries are exempted from national treatment at the pre-entry level, Thailand offers only MFN treatment. Members of the ASEAN Investment Area are also granted national treatment at the pre-entry level.
Expropriation and compensation	The Expropriation Act of Thailand of 1987 guarantees that the investments of signatory country investors will not be expropriated or nationalized except on a non-discriminatory basis for a public interest purpose. In such cases, compensation that is commensurate with the market value of the investment must be paid.
Transfer of funds and repatriation	Under Thailand's Exchange Control Act of 1942 and Article 8 of the IMF Agreement, Thailand allows the free transfer of funds and payments, including the trans-fer of capital and investment returns, the transfer of proceeds from the sale or liquidation of an investment, the repayment of loans, royalties, and fees, and the pay-ment of compensation, which must be made without delay at the rate of exchange applicable at the date of transfer.
Dispute settlement	Dispute settlement provisions have implicitly guaran-teed that the standards of treatment and protection offered to investors by Thai law will be implemented and enforced effectively. Thailand recognizes that dis-putes may occur between the private investors of states that are party to a treaty, between one state and the investors of another state, or between states themselves.

Source: Compiled by the authors.

ples of the Asia Pacific Economic Cooperation (APEC) forum, and the ASEAN Investment Area. APEC's investment principles, concluded in 1994, include transparency, non-discrimination, and a number of investment guarantees. The ASEAN Investment Area, concluded in 1998, provides an investment framework for ASEAN countries (Table 7.13). It requires members to grant national treatment to ASEAN investors by 2010, although exclusions are allowed. As with the ASEAN Free Trade Area, these exclusions include (1) a list of temporary exclusions that will gradually be phased out; (2) a list of sensitive items that will not be phased out but will be reviewed periodically by the ASEAN Investment Area Council; and (3) a list of general exceptions consisting of industries that, on grounds of national security, public morals, public health, or environmental protection, will not be open to foreign investment or granted national treatment. New members of ASEAN will be given a transition period in which to meet the terms of the agreement.

A Multilateral Framework on Investment

We believe that a positive list approach of the type adopted in the General Agreement on Trade in Services (GATS) offers a realistic way of approaching any eventual multilateral negotiations in the area of investment. In particular, it strikes a balance between the need for liberalization and the need for developing countries to have the flexibility to make commitments commensurate with their individual development needs. Legal experts also note that there is no rule of customary international law requiring a state to allow entry to foreign investment, and that the concept of an unconditional right of entry does not exist in practice.

The WTO should not aim to achieve a horizontal liberalization of investment. Individual member states should maintain their sovereignty over foreign investment policy; that is, they should be the ones to decide when, where, and how foreign investment should take place to be of greatest benefit to the domestic economy. The WTO's existing trade agenda already faces multiple challenges, with many issues at a standstill. It would be better to deepen rather than widen the present WTO agreements in order not to overstretch the limited resources of members—particularly developing country members.

Nevertheless, the task of constructing a positive list for WTO members is a crucial one. Each government needs to adopt transparent mechanisms and criteria to justify which business activities should be included in such a list, and to prevent domestic firms from benefiting from backdoor dealings with government authorities.

The Thai government would have no contention with the inclusion of

Table 7.13   Application of ASEAN Investment Area Provisions

Core Provisions	Application within the ASEAN Investment Area
Definition of investment	Covers all direct investment except portfolio investment.
Scope of framework	Uses a negative list approach, consisting of a temporary exclusion list and a sensitive list, with a transition period for new members.
National and MFN treatment	All ASEAN member countries are required to provide national and MFN treatment to all ASEAN investors, with the exception of investments on the temporary exclusion and sensitive lists.
Expropriation and compensation	As with the bilateral investment treaties, the provisions on expropriation and compensation for the ASEAN Investment Area fall under the Expropriation Act of Thailand of 1987. It guarantees that the investments of signatory country investors will not be expropriated or nationalized except on a non-discriminatory basis for a public interest purpose. In such cases, compensation that is commensurate with the market value of the investment must be paid.
Transfer of funds and repatriation	Thailand allows the free transfer of funds and payments, including the transfer of capital and investment returns, the transfer of proceeds from the sale or liquidation of an investment, the repayment of loans, royalties, and fees, and the payment of compensation, which must be made without delay at the rate of exchange applicable at the date of transfer.
Dispute settlement	The protocol for an ASEAN Dispute Settlement Mechanism adopted in 1996 provides ASEAN members with a regional dispute settlement mechanism.

Source: Compiled by the authors.

guarantees against expropriation without due compensation in a multi-lateral framework on investment, if the relevant terms were properly defined. Such a provision would be consistent with Thailand's Exchange Control Act of 1942 as well as its commitment to guarantee the free transfer of funds and payments under Article 8 of the IMF Agreement. Various bilateral investment treaties and the ASEAN Investment Area also contain provisions against expropriation.

General and other exceptions to GATT and GATS rules leave room for WTO members to regulate certain areas, in the public interest, in ways that would otherwise be inconsistent with their obligations to the WTO. These exceptions cover the areas of national security, public safety, health, environment, and culture, but must not involve arbitrary or unjustifiable discrimination or create disguised trade restrictions. The GATT and GATS also allow member countries to restrict imports to safeguard their external position and balance of payments, as long as the measures taken are temporary and subject to a clear time frame for removal. They should also be as undisruptive as possible and should not exceed what is necessary to address the problem. To ensure that the safeguard measure is not used to protect a specific industry, import controls must not be sector-specific. Procedural conditions for notification, consultation, and regular reporting are also required.

Similar exceptions and safeguards should apply to any proposed multilateral investment framework, with some modification to accommodate the specific characteristics of trade in goods, trade in services, and investment. Although such exceptions and safeguards are uncommon in bilateral investment treaties, and not available in the ASEAN Investment Area, this may be explained by the fact that the entry of foreign investment under bilateral and regional treaties is subject to national rather than multilateral laws and regulations.

An issue that needs to be resolved is whether the dispute settlement mechanism of any multilateral framework on investment would handle disputes between a state and an investor of another state in addition to disputes between states. The inclusion of a state-to-investor dispute settlement mechanism would place an excessive burden on the legal machinery of developing countries, and pose a politically unacceptable threat to national sovereignty. It would also be in conflict with the functioning of the WTO as an inter-governmental organization. Thus, a dispute settlement mechanism should handle only disputes between states.

It is not clear how a multilateral framework on investment that contained provisions that significantly constrained the ability of a host country to develop national policies would contribute to the development of member economies. Many studies of the effects of FDI on economic development have indicated that active government regulation is required to maximize the benefits of FDI, particularly when MNEs are not themselves subject to any multilateral rules.

According to this view, developing countries have little incentive to accept the proposed multilateral framework on investment. Some have suggested that investment, along with other Singapore issues, was introduced by the European Union simply to serve as a bargaining chip in a larger scheme known as 'grand bargaining,' that is, bargaining between the North and the South for liberalization in agriculture. In other words, by proposing an investment agenda that developing countries could not accept, the European Union hoped to have an excuse not to open up its agriculture market. Thus, developing countries were advised to just say 'no' to the proposed multilateral framework on investment in order to ensure that there would be no incentive to introduce new issues into the WTO when existing issues, in particular agriculture, had not yet been sufficiently dealt with.

We therefore suggest that developing countries take control of the design of any multilateral framework on investment, to ensure that it is 'development friendly.' Such a framework might include binding provisions disciplining MNE conduct, which is often beyond the reach of domestic laws and authorities; the free movement of labor tied to that of capital; and multilateral rules to promote better coordination of investment incentives and minimize the cost of 'incentive wars'—mainly among developing countries that are in dire need of foreign capital.

6   CONCLUSIONS AND RECOMMENDATIONS

Although Thailand has benefited significantly from FDI, it has yet to realize its full potential, especially in the area of technology. Moreover, current investment promotion practices are very costly. We therefore recommend that the Thai government reform existing investment incentive schemes to reduce these costs, and increase the level of technology transfer by promoting linkages between domestic firms and MNEs.

Tax holidays are not a cost-effective means of attracting FDI. Since the profits of firms, however large, are tax exempt, the most profitable investment projects are the greatest beneficiaries of the scheme. Projects like these are likely to be implemented even without the provision of incentives. Tax holidays are rarely important enough to significantly influence firms' investment decisions. It is often argued that tax holidays are needed to compensate firms for the high costs arising from poor infrastructure and a lack of qualified labor. If that were the case, it would be more cost effective to abolish tax holidays and use the tax revenue thus recovered to build better infrastructure and train workers. Another option would be to lower the corporate tax rate and cut tariffs across the board.

We have argued that local firms benefit from the transfer of basic production technology from MNEs. However, the transfer of more advanced technology, such as product design, is virtually absent. The acquisition of advanced technology is essential if Thai firms are to climb the comparative advantage ladder and compete with countries with lower labor costs such as the PRC and Viet Nam. The Thai government should therefore place more emphasis on technology transfer by giving incentives to MNEs at the post-entry level as provided in the National Science and Technology Development Act of 1991. To qualify for a subsidy, an MNE would have to introduce a technology that is more sophisticated than that which is currently available, and that is likely to foster technological upgrading in other firms and industries, including suppliers. Modest incentives for in-house training by MNEs for the staff of other companies could also be considered, as multinationals also have a part to play as training suppliers.

NOTES

1   Thailand's definition of FDI is modeled on that of the IMF: FDI is the lasting interest of a non-resident in a resident entity of another economy. A direct investment may take the form of equity capital, loans to affiliates, or reinvested earnings. Investment in equity is where the direct investor owns 10 percent or more of the ordinary shares or voting power of an incorporated enterprise. Loans to affiliates refers to lending between direct investors and their subsidiaries, branches, and associates. Reinvested earnings are investment earnings not distributed as dividends or remitted to direct investors. The Bank of Thailand currently excludes the third type of FDI when compiling data.

2   The six exceptions are communications, transport, fiduciary functions, banking involving a depository function (including non-bank financial institutions), exploitation of natural resources or land, and domestic trading in indigenous agricultural products.

3   Protection offsets are 'measures offsetting the cost-increasing effect of tariffs on the price of intermediary inputs entering into the production of exportables' (Cuyvers et al. 1997).

4   This section draws on Nikomborirak (2000).

8

Viet Nam

Tuan Bui

INTRODUCTION

Until the mid-1980s, Viet Nam followed the model of a centrally planned economy. Its commercial relationships were mainly with the Comecon block of communist countries and it had very little contact with the West. During the early 1980s the country experienced a severe economic crisis. However, with the introduction of a program of economic reform (*doi moi*) in 1986, Viet Nam achieved significant progress, especially in macro-economic stabilization and opening up the economy. Economic growth averaged 7.5 percent during the 1990s. The structure of the economy changed, with the share of industry and services increasing. Living standards improved and the number of poor households fell. Poverty incidence declined from over 70 percent at the end of the 1980s to 58 percent in 1993 and 37 percent in 1998.

Among the factors that led to this success, foreign direct investment (FDI) played a crucial role. The Law on Foreign Investment, promulgated in December 1987, liberalized the FDI policy regime. As a result, FDI inflows grew substantially throughout the 1990s, the level of exports rose, and economic growth expanded. The impact of FDI can be seen in many aspects of the economy, including capital formation, the transfer of technology and management skills, and market access.

Despite the important contribution of FDI to the economy, some key analytical and policy issues remain. The benefits generated by FDI have been uneven due to the country's distorted trade and commercial policy regime. There are high levels of protection in many sectors, pressure on foreign investors to form joint ventures with highly inefficient state-owned enterprises (SOEs), wasted fiscal incentives, and a lack of transparency and predictability in the legal environment. These problems have arisen principally from the government's hesitant approach to reform. The share of SOEs actually increased during the years of reform because the government has continued to believe that state ownership should play a leading role in the economy. The private sector is encouraged officially, but in practice it still suffers from discrimination.

This chapter attempts to analyze recent developments in FDI, changes to the institutional environment for FDI, the impact of foreign investment on the economy, and emerging issues related to FDI and trade-related investment measures (TRIMs). The chapter is organized as follows: Section 2 discusses the policy regime and trends in FDI inflows, Section 3 analyses the nature of the FDI regime and related trade issues, and Section 4 considers the impact of FDI on the economy. The last section provides conclusions and some policy recommendations.

2   RECENT TRENDS AND DEVELOPMENTS IN FDI

Data

Viet Nam has a weak FDI database, with different sources producing conflicting data. Official data provided by the Ministry of Planning and Investment differ from those used by some other organizations, mainly because the ministry's data include domestic equity in foreign-invested entities whereas, for example, IMF data do not. The treatment of FDI in the oil and gas industry also varies.

This chapter uses the data provided by the Ministry of Planning and Investment. These cover all sectors and refer to two kinds of FDI, 'investment capital' and 'realized capital.' Investment capital is defined as the capital required for implementing an investment project, and comprises legal capital and loan capital. Legal capital refers to the capital required to establish an enterprise, and is prescribed in the charter of the enterprise. Realized capital is defined as the actual disbursement of the investment capital. Typically this has only been about half of the licensed approvals in any given year. Other frequently used terms are 'registered capital' and 'approved capital.' These refer to capital committed in the investment license, and can therefore be understood as 'committed capital.'

Capital that is reinvested in FDI projects is incorporated in investment capital. Usually, at start-up, an enterprise implements only a part of its registered/approved capital. Another portion is made up of any earnings or profits that are reinvested in the enterprise. Unless the new investment exceeds its registered capital, the enterprise does not have to apply to the

Ministry of Planning and Investment to increase its approved capital. Note also that, in principle, the FDI data include investments by Vietnamese expatriates. However, much of this capital is regarded as domestic investment because businesses owned by expatriates are often registered under the names of relatives still living in Viet Nam.

Trends in FDI Inflows

The 1987 Law on Foreign Investment was a bold measure implemented as part of a reform package implemented in the late 1980s. It was designed to attract foreign capital in the wake of an economic crisis and a sudden reduction in aid from the former Soviet Union and other socialist countries. From 1988 through to March 2003, Viet Nam licensed 4,650 FDI projects with a value of about $50.6 billion.[1] Total realized FDI to the end of 2002 is estimated to be about $22.1 billion. FDI has contributed at least 18 percent of total investment in Viet Nam in recent years.[2] These are remarkable figures given the country's prior history of isolation. However, they are modest compared with flows to other countries in the region such as the the People's Republic of China (PRC). Viet Nam attracts only about 0.2 percent of total FDI flows to developing countries.

The history of FDI in Viet Nam can be divided into two periods. The first runs from 1988, when the Law on Foreign Investment started to take effect, to 1996, the year before the onset of the Asian crisis. The second is from 1997 to the present. In the first period, inflows peaked at $8.5 billion of registered capital in 1996. Average growth in approved capital inflows and realized capital was 48 percent and 72 percent respectively. Most of this FDI came from East Asia, which accounted for about 70 percent of the total in 1996. Underpinning this growth were both push and pull factors, including rapid East Asian economic growth and a desire on the part of foreign investors to obtain early entry into a high-growth, latecomer economy.

However, FDI policy in the first period lacked any clear strategic direction. Very little effort was made to fit FDI inflows into a more general, strategic economic development plan. Incentives were granted liberally according to very broad criteria, including project size, level of exports, degree of import substitution, level of technology, and capacity to generate employment.

Toward the end of this period, a clearer strategy emerged, focused on industrialization, modernization, and a reduction in spatial disparities. The Law on Foreign Investment was revised in 1996 to specify clearer guidelines for FDI in key industries such as metallurgy, basic chemicals, machinery, petrochemicals, fertilizers, and the manufacture of electronic components, automobiles, and motorcycle parts. The SOE sector continued to receive powerful support in senior policy circles.

The second period commenced with the downturn in FDI associated with the Asian economic crisis of 1997–98. Flows to Viet Nam fell sharply to $1.6 billion in 1999, about one-fifth of their 1996 level (Table 8.1). Realized FDI showed little change. The main reason for this decline was that almost all the major Asian investing countries were suffering from the financial crisis. Their levels of outward FDI fell, causing Viet Nam's inflows to decline. In addition to the external factors depressing FDI, the pace of domestic economic reform slowed; in a lower-growth environment, endemic problems such as lack of policy transparency, inconsistent regulations, and administrative bottlenecks became more serious. As a result of the downturn in FDI, there was actually a net outflow of capital in 1999 and 2000, owing to loan repayments. From 2000, however, FDI began to recover. Committed investment capital grew by 22 percent in 2000 and 20 percent in 2001 before falling by 16 percent in 2002. The average annual committed investment during this period was just over $2 billion. Realized capital grew weakly by about 3 percent per annum over these three years.

Investors from 74 countries and territories have invested in Viet Nam. Asian investors have dominated with 69.7 percent of the total, followed by Europe (25.7 percent), the Americas (3.1 percent), and Australia (1.3 percent). Singapore has been the largest investor, with around $7 billion in 311 projects. Other major investor countries include Taipei,China ($5.3 billion, 823 projects), Japan ($4.1 billion, 339 projects), the Republic of Korea ($3.5 billion, 403 projects), and Hong Kong, China ($2.8 billion, 234 projects). Investment from the PRC has been miniscule at only $30 million, similar to its investment in Lao PDR and about one-third that in Cambodia.

Industry and services have absorbed most of Viet Nam's FDI inflows (Table 8.2). Manufacturing has been the largest single subsector, with 65 percent of total FDI projects in 2002, followed by real estate and associated services (11 percent).

Initially, most FDI projects were located in urban areas and areas with better developed infrastructure. The spatial distribution of FDI in the post-crisis period has been relatively more balanced. As of the end of 2002, all 61 provinces and cities in Viet Nam had received some FDI. While the central areas attracted little of this owing to their poorly developed infrastructure, the cities and provinces in the southeast attracted more than half of FDI inflows (Table 8.3). The two largest cities, Hanoi and Ho Chi Minh City, have accounted for almost half (47 percent) of the total.

Table 8.1   *Viet Nam: Registered and Realized FDI, 1988–2002*
           ($ million) a

Year	Registered Capital	Realized Capital
1988	372	
1989	583	
1990	839	
1991	1,322	221
1992	2,165	398
1993	2,900	1,106
1994	3,766	1,515
1995	6,531	2,652
1996	8,497	2,371
1997	4,649	2,950
1998	3,897	1,900
1999	1,568	2,156
2000	2,012	2,150
2001	2,536	2,300
2002	1,557	2,345
Total	43,194	22,064

a   Registered capital does not include supplementary capital invested in projects
licensed in previous years, or investment in oil exploration.
Source: General Statistical Office (2003), *Statistical Yearbook*; Ministry of Planning and Investment.

The government has focused on developing industrial zones with good infrastructure as a means of attracting investment. Of the country's 76 industrial zones, 18 were built with FDI—one is 100 percent foreign-owned and the rest are joint ventures. The industrial zones have attracted 1,202 foreign projects with approved capital of $9.4 billion, and 1,035 domestic projects worth about $2.8 billion. FDI in the zones accounts for more than 23 percent of Viet Nam's total FDI, and 40 percent of FDI in the industry and construction sector.

According to the Law on Foreign Investment, FDI may take various forms, including joint ventures, 100 percent foreign-owned enterprises, and business cooperation contracts (BCCs). These are defined in Appendix 8.1. Foreign investors investing in infrastructure projects may sign build–

Table 8.2   Viet Nam: FDI by Sector, 2002[a]

Sector	Projects		Total Realized Capital	
	(no.)	(% of total)	($ million)	(% of total)
Industry & construction	2,576	68.9	14,617	67.6
Manufacturing	2,439	65.2	10,037	46.4
Construction	69	1.9	576	2.7
Mining	48	1.3	3,196	14.8
Electricity & gas production & supply	20	0.5	808	3.7
Services	790	21.1	5,594	25.9
Real estate, consultancy	394	10.5	1,770	8.2
Hotels & restaurants	108	2.9	1,820	8.4
Transportation, storage, information	112	3.0	987	4.6
Culture & sport	51	1.4	321	1.5
Finance & credit	39	1.0	517	2.4
Trade	40	1.1	125	0.6
Health	16	0.4	37	0.2
Education & training	30	0.8	16	0.1
Agriculture, forestry, & aquaculture	373	10.0	1,404	6.5
Agriculture & forestry	312	8.3	1,298	6.0
Aquaculture	61	1.6	106	0.5
Total	3,739	100.0	21,616	100.0

a   As of 31 December.
Source: Ministry of Planning and Investment.

operate–transfer (BOT), build–transfer–operate (BTO) and build–transfer (BT) contracts with the authorized state agency. The law stipulates that FDI in the fields of oil exploration and telecommunications must be in the form of a BCC. In some sectors, such as transportation, port construction, airport terminals, forestry plantations, tourism, culture, and the production of explosives, FDI must be in the form of a joint venture. In others, foreign investors are unrestricted as to the form of the enterprise.

Table 8.3   *Viet Nam: FDI by Province/City, 2001*[a]

Province/ City	No. of Projects	Total Investment ($ billion)	Legal Investment ($ billion)	Disburse- ment ($ billion)
Ho Chi Minh City	1,039	10,213	4,986	4,820
Hanoi	398	7,801	3,423	2,975
Dong Nai	327	5,036	1,954	2,174
Binh Duong	478	2,549	1,195	1,243
Ba Ria-Vung Tau	69	1,859	669	423
Quang Ngai	6	1,332	814	283
Hai Phong	101	1,284	586	988
Lam Dong	49	843	105	102
Hai Duong	32	512	219	132
Thanh Hoa	9	452	142	397
Ha Tay	27	413	168	198
Kien Giang	5	393	192	394
Khanh Hoa	25	335	127	229
Vinh Phuc	36	332	122	269
Long An	42	310	131	208
Quang Ninh	10	248	102	48
Nghe An	35	246	99	159
Tay Ninh	44	213	173	115
Da Nang	41	204	88	152
Bac Ninh	8	152	61	132
Thua Thien-Hue	12	134	70	111
Phu Tho	7	130	66	118
Can Tho	28	114	48	55
Phu Yen	13	107	34	32
Other	182	839	404	425
Offshore Oil	23	1,809	1,328	2,511
Total	3,046	37,861	17,308	18,694

a   As of 31 December.
Source: Ministry of Planning and Investment.

Table 8.4   Viet Nam: Types of FDI, 2001[a]

Investment Form	Number of Projects	Approved Capital ($ million)	Realized Capital ($ million)	Project Size ($ million)	Disburse-ment Ratio (%)	Approved Capital/ Total Capital (%)
	(A)	(B)	(C)	(D)	(C)/(B)	
BOT	6	1,228	40	204.7	3.3	3.2
BCC	139	4,052	3,274	29.2	80.8	10.7
Foreign	1,858	12,414	5,663	6.7	45.6	32.8
JV	1,043	20,167	9,716	19.3	48.2	53.3
Total	3,046	37,861	18,694	12.4	49.4	100.0

BOT: build–operate–transfer; BCC: business cooperation contract; foreign: 100 percent foreign-owned enterpise; JV: joint venture.

a   For effective projects, as of 31 December.

Source: Ministry of Planning and Investment.

The preferred form of FDI has gradually been shifting from joint ventures to 100 percent foreign-owned enterprises. Owing to the preferential treatment they receive with regard to land ownership and access to credit, in the late 1980s joint ventures accounted for more than 70 percent of licensed projects, whereas wholly foreign-owned enterprises accounted for just 5–10 percent. As of the end of 2001, however, 100 percent foreign-owned projects accounted for 61 percent of licensed projects and 32.8 percent of approved capital, while joint ventures accounted for 34.2 percent and 53 percent respectively (Table 8.4). Two factors explain these changes. First, regulations on the entry of 100 percent foreign-owned enterprises have been liberalized. And second, many foreign investors found joint venture arrangements unsatisfactory, especially their dealings with SOEs, which until recently constituted the only feasible option for a domestic partner.

Table 8.4 shows that the average size of joint venture projects is larger than that of 100 percent foreign-invested enterprises. BOTs have the largest average size but accounted for only a small share of total approved capital, while the disbursement ratio for BCCs was the highest.

An increasing proportion of FDI has gone into export-oriented indus-

Table 8.5   Viet Nam: Contribution of FDI to Non-oil Exports,
1991–2000

Year	Total Exports ($ million)	Total Manufac- turing Exports ($ million)	Exports by FDI Firms ($ million)	FDI Firms/ Total Exports (%)	FDI Firms/ Total Manu- facturing Exports (%)
1991	1,314	158	52	4.0	32.9
1992	2,724	1,145	112	4.1	9.8
1993	3,190	1,423	269	8.4	18.9
1994	3,589	1,322	352	9.8	26.6
1995	5,600	2,846	495	8.8	17.4
1996	5,502	2,657	920	16.7	34.6
1997	6,969	3,932	1,790	25.7	45.5
1998	7,693	4,526	1,982	25.8	43.8
1999	7,931	4,718	2,590	32.7	54.9
2000	9,832	5,850	3,320	33.8	56.8

Source: Doanh (2003).

tries. It is difficult to separate the share of total foreign capital in export-oriented industries, because many firms in such industries produce goods for both the export and domestic markets. Nevertheless, the concentration of foreign capital in export-oriented industries is reflected in the location in industrial and export-processing zones of 933 FDI projects with registered capital of $11.1 billion—or more than one-fifth of total investment—as of the end of 2001. This trend is also reflected in the rising share of foreign firms in total exports, from 4 percent in 1991–92 to 34 percent in 2000 (Table 8.5). In labor-intensive industries, foreign firms accounted for 55 percent of fiber exports, 30 percent of fabric exports, 49 percent of footwear exports, 18 percent of garment exports, and 25 percent of food and beverage exports. Clearly Viet Nam is attracting FDI to labor-intensive, export-oriented industries where the country has a comparative advantage.

However, a significant part of FDI has also gone into protected, 'strategic' industries. For example, the stock of FDI in one of the most highly protected industries, automobiles, was nearly 5 percent of the total in 2001.

Currently, foreign firms account for 100 percent of production in automobiles, oil and gas, washing machines, refrigerators, air conditioners, and office equipment, 60 percent in steel, 28 percent in cement, 33 percent in electrical and electronic appliances, and 76 percent in health care equipment. Due to the concentration of inflows in capital-intensive industries, only a minor share of direct employment has been generated by foreign firms—about 620,000 jobs or less than 2 percent of the total workforce.

A study by the Institute of World Economy of foreign firms in the manufacturing sector showed that they had very weak linkages with supplying and supporting industries (Le, Bui and Dao 2002). Supporting this result is the low share of local inputs used in the export-oriented garment and textiles industry, and the low level of local content in electronics, motorcycles, and automobiles. In view of the low share of domestic value added in export-oriented products (20 percent in textiles and garments, for example), Viet Nam should strive for more active foreign participation in the value chain of export production. However, local content regulations would almost certainly be counterproductive (STAR/CIEM 2003).

Policy Regimes for FDI and Related Trade Issues

FDI Policy

Regulations on FDI since the initial Law on Foreign Investment have been amended and revised several times, notably in 1990, 1992, 1996, 2000, and 2003. The revisions have addressed a broad range of issues, from the business environment to management issues in foreign-invested enterprises. The regulatory changes have included the following:

- removing some of the operational obstacles and difficulties facing foreign-invested enterprises;
- reducing risks for foreign-invested enterprises in land clearance, and shifting responsibility for employee compensation and land clearance from the foreign to the Vietnamese partner;
- allowing foreign-invested enterprises to mortgage their land use rights to borrow from banks;
- relaxing currency balancing regulations on foreign-invested enterprises;
- giving greater autonomy to foreign-invested enterprises, and reducing the range of issues that require a consensus from the management boards of joint ventures;
- giving investors greater freedom to change an investment form, reorganize enterprises, and transfer capital;
- improving government regulatory procedures for FDI;

- giving greater preference to foreign investors, increasing the scope for import tariff exemptions and reductions, and reducing the tax on profit remittances;
- allowing 100 percent foreign-owned enterprises and the foreign partner of a BCC to carry losses forward; and
- allowing foreign-invested enterprises to recruit workers freely.

In 2001 there was a significant shift in official government policy on FDI when the 9th Communist Party Congress recognized the 'foreign-invested economic sector' as an independent economic sector for the first time. Previously, the Communist Party had identified the main ownership groups as being the state, cooperative, private and household, and state capitalist sectors, and had policies corresponding to each. Foreign investment was considered part of the latter sector. The change confirmed the importance of the FDI sector for social and economic development, especially given the target for Viet Nam to become an industrialized country by 2020.

In spite of these reforms, the numerous remaining restrictions on FDI need to be emphasized. One relates to regulations on the stake and legal capital held by the foreign partner of a joint venture. The minimum share of the foreign partner is required to be not less than 30 percent of the total legal capital of the joint venture, although this may be lowered to 20 percent depending on the field of operation, technology, market, business efficiency, and socioeconomic benefit of the particular project.

In addition, the government places restrictions on entry into certain sectors, and on the forms of FDI. For example, only BCCs are allowed in oil exploration and telecommunications, and FDI must take the form of a joint venture or BCC in air transportation and airport construction, industrial explosives production, forestry, culture, and tourism. Some industries have requirements for the proportion of output to be exported. For others, such as dairy production and dairy processing, sugar and sugar cane, natural oil, and wood processing, FDI projects must include investment in associated processing activities. FDI is excluded in activities that may harm national security, the country's historical heritage, or the environment, or that produce toxic substances.

Local content requirements in the electronics and engineering industries also restrict FDI. For instance, a 1994 guideline of the Ministry of Planning and Investment stipulated that foreign motorcycle assemblers would have to achieve a local content ratio of 5–10 percent in the second year of operation, and 60 percent within five to six years. Additional regulations in 2000 and 2002 intensified these localization measures, specifying import tariffs according to local content ratios. A complicated method of calculating the local content ratio has added to the confusion for manufacturers.

Labor agreements are another area of difficulty for foreign-invested enterprises, in particular the requirement that if a temporary labor agreement is signed three times then it is considered to become permanent. In addition, the current regulation that provides preferential treatment for projects that export over 30 percent of production and use up to 30 percent local materials may run counter to the TRIMs Agreement.

These restrictions essentially aim to protect the SOE sector, and reflect an ambivalence toward FDI. The 9th Communist Party Congress in 2001 clearly stated that 'the State sector should have a leading role in the economy and is an important force and instrument to stabilize and orient the economy.' It is therefore not surprising to find that the share of the state sector in GDP remains very high and has hardly changed during the reform period (Table 8.6), that is, to find that the policy framework continues to favor the state sector. Moreover, joint ventures (mainly with SOE partners) continue to receive more favorable treatment than 100 percent foreign-invested enterprises. The fact that only joint ventures and BCCs are allowed to operate in a number of fields is another indication of preferential treatment for the state sector.

Viet Nam offers preferential taxes, tariffs, and land rent to lure FDI. Currently, the tax rate on profits is only 25 percent for foreign-invested enterprises compared with 32 percent for domestic enterprises, and in some circumstances can be reduced further to 10 percent. Depending on the sector and locality of the investment, foreign-invested enterprises and the foreign partner in a BCC may receive tax exemptions for a period of two years from the commencement of operations, and a 50 percent reduction in profit tax for the subsequent two years. Some firms receive tax exemptions for up to eight years. The government also offers other incentives such as exemptions from or reductions in land rent, and preferential treatment of losses, reinvestment, and remittances.[3]

The most recent change in the FDI regime occurred in April 2003, when foreign-invested enterprises were allowed to become shareholding companies. This means that 100 percent foreign-invested enterprises can now establish joint ventures. Those producing mechanical spare parts or operating in the electrical and electronics industry may receive zero tariffs on imported inputs for five years. They may also recruit workers directly, use their land rights and related assets as collateral for borrowing from financial institutions, and cooperate with foreign business entities to implement BCCs.

However, there is a gap between the content of official FDI policies and

Table 8.6   Viet Nam: Share of GDP by Ownership, 1995–2001 (%)

Ownership	1995	1996	1997	1998	1999	2000	2001[a]
State	40.2	39.9	40.5	40.0	39.7	38.5	38.6
Collective	10.1	10.0	8.9	8.9	8.8	8.6	8.2
Private	3.1	3.4	3.4	3.4	3.4	3.4	3.8
Household	36.0	35.3	34.3	33.8	32.9	32.3	32.1
Mixed	4.3	4.1	3.8	3.8	3.9	3.9	4.2
Foreign	6.3	7.4	9.1	10.0	12.2	13.3	13.1
Total	100.0	100.0	100.0	100.0	100.0	100.0	100.0

a   Estimate.
Source: General Statistical Office (2002), *Statistical Yearbook.*

their implementation in practice. Although the regulations are designed to improve the investment environment, a lack of policy transparency and problems with the legal system continue to hinder foreign investors. Administrative obstacles and red tape have not been significantly reduced. Many foreign investors complain about the limited opportunities for participation in the process of policy reform. Other common complaints concern lack of policy consistency, complicated legal procedures, and the double price system for the 'foreign' and 'domestic' sectors.

A good example of the difficulties faced by foreign investors resides in the local content requirements for the motorcycle industry. The quality of local materials remains poor. Manufacturers can use imported inputs, but this raises their costs of production because high import duties apply. This situation puts manufacturers in a difficult position: both using local inputs to meet local content regulations, and not using them in order to raise quality, lead to competitive disadvantages. As a result, widespread smuggling of cheap parts occurs, particularly from the PRC.

The Trade Regime

Viet Nam has undertaken a series of trade reforms, two of which have been particularly important. The first was the liberalization of trading rights in the 1990s. Before *doi moi* in 1986, all foreign trade activities were the monopoly of the state. Prices, commodities, export and import markets, and the exchange rate were all state regulated. In the early 1990s, in order to get an import/export license, a business enterprise needed to obtain a foreign trade contract and shipment license, and meet the requirements on minimum working capital and 'skills' in trade. In 1996, the requirement for a foreign trade contract and shipment license was eliminated, and the barrier to trade was further lowered by reducing the number of imported goods for which an import/export license was required. From January 1997, all enterprises with an import/export license were encouraged to export not only registered items, but also many other commodities they had not themselves produced. In July 1998, the government decreed that all enterprises would be permitted to trade in the goods registered in their business license without the need for an import/export license, except for four groups of 'special' goods.[4] Foreign-invested enterprises were also encouraged to export goods produced by other firms, providing an additional avenue for domestic manufacturers to export their products. Restrictions on trading rights were removed in August 2001, when all legal entities were allowed to export most goods without a license.

The second important trade reform was to reduce quantitative restrictions. This process accelerated throughout the 1990s, until the onset of the Asian economic crisis temporarily reversed this trend. The number of commodities and products subject to import quotas increased sharply in 1999, but subsequently fell to just three groups by mid-2003 (Table 8.7).

Although trade liberalization has progressed, a number of problems remain, particularly in the context of Viet Nam's aspiration to join the WTO. The first is the country's relatively high average tariff rate. Viet Nam's nominal tariff rates and tariff dispersion are somewhat above East Asian norms, though not markedly so (Table 8.8). As a member of the ASEAN Free Trade Area, Viet Nam must reduce tariff rates on all but a few items to meet its commitments under the Common Effective Preferential Tariff scheme. By 2002, about 5,558 tariff lines out of 6,324 were already on the 'inclusion list.' The scheme requires that the rate on these lines be reduced to under 5 percent by 2006.

The second trade policy challenge is Viet Nam's high effective rates of protection, biased in favor of several industries. Athukorala (2002) has shown that effective rates of protection in manufacturing and export-oriented industries are high compared with those in other countries in the region. He found that import-competing motor vehicles had the highest rate (559 percent), followed by sugar (366 percent) and wearing apparel (181 percent). This implies a bias in favor of import-competing industries. Moreover, as the first two industries are dominated by SOEs, the trade regime in effect subsidizes the SOE sector.

The third challenge is the many complex measures used to promote

Table 8.7   Viet Nam: Products Subject to Quantitative Restrictions,
1998–2003

1998	Petroleum, sugar, fertilizer, steel, cement/clinker, glass, motorcycles, cars, paper
1999	Petroleum, sugar, fertilizer, steel, cement/clinker, glass, motorcycles, cars, paper, electric fans, ceramic tiles, porcelain, caustic soda, bicycles, plastics, plastic packaging
2000	Petroleum, sugar, steel, cement/clinker, glass, motorcycles, cars, paper, vegetable oil
2001	Petroleum, sugar, steel, cement/clinker, motorcycles, cars, vegetable oil
2002	Petroleum, sugar, cement, motorcycles
2003[a]	Petroleum, sugar, motorcycles

a   As of 30 June.
Source: STAR/CIEM (2003); unpublished report by the Ministry of Trade.

Table 8.8   Comparison of Tariff Rates in East Asian Countries, 2000

	Tariff Measure	All Products	Primary Products	Manufac- turing
PRC	Mean	15	14	15
	Maximum	100		
Indonesia	Mean	8	7	16
	Maximum	170		
Malaysia	Mean	10	5	15
	Maximum	300		
Philippines	Mean	8	6	8
	Maximum	60		
Thailand	Mean	18	16	19
	Maximum	80		
Viet Nam[a]	Mean	16	19	14
	Maximum	120	120	50

a   Figures for Viet Nam are for 2002.
Source: Athukorala (2002).

exports, including duty drawback schemes and export subsidies. The first duty drawback scheme, which began in 1991, offered rebates on import duty for intermediate goods used in export production. It was supplemented in 1993 by a regulation allowing exporters to suspend duty payments on imported inputs for 90 days (275 days since 1998). The subsidies on exports take indirect forms. Exporters can avail themselves of preferential credit access from a number of funds established to support exporters. These include the Development Assistance Fund and the Credit Fund for Supporting Exports. As SOEs are often in a better position to access state financial institutions (using their reputation as collateral, for example), these funds have been of particular benefit to SOEs.

Export tax rates have been changed frequently. For example, the export duty on rice was reduced from 10 percent to 1 percent in 1991; revised twice in 1995, from 1 percent to 2 percent in September and from 2 percent to 3 percent in October; reduced to 2 percent in 1997; and reduced to zero in 1998. The objectives of the tax differ from product to product. The zero tax rate on rice is designed to encourage rice exports, while the high tax rate on metal scrap is meant to assist local steel producers. And, as already noted, some FDI projects receive tax exemptions.

The Law on Foreign Investment governs the trading activities of foreign-invested enterprises. They are granted the same export rights as domestic firms, but are subject to more restrictive measures with regard to imports. Foreign-invested enterprises in manufacturing industries are allowed to import inputs used in the production process, but no other goods. The recent amendments to the Law on Foreign Investment have not addressed this situation.

Foreign invested enterprises are not permitted to borrow from abroad except in special situations, and then only with approval from the State Bank of Viet Nam. In 2000, the foreign exchange balancing requirements for foreign-invested enterprises were relaxed. Foreign-invested enterprises are now able to obtain foreign currency from domestic banks to pay off the principal, interest, and fees on short-term loans from offshore banks, and to make repayments on longer-term loans from offshore banks, as long as the loans are registered with the State Bank.

Viet Nam's participation in regional and international initiatives has facilitated trade liberalization. In July 1995, Viet Nam became a member of ASEAN, and subsequently committed the country to implementing the Common Effective Preferential Tariff. The relationship between Viet Nam and the United States was also normalized in 1995, and a bilateral trade agreement between the two countries was signed in July 2000, coming into effect on 10 December 2001. The agreement specifies reciprocal commitments by both countries to reduce barriers to bilateral trade and investment. It covers many issues related to trade in goods and services, intellectual property rights, investment, and business facilitation, and requires Viet Nam to reduce its tariffs (mostly on agricultural products) and remove quantitative restrictions on imports. The commitments under the bilateral trade agreement are to be phased in over one to ten years, but most will be implemented within three to four years.

Many obligations in the agreement are internationally recognized rules and regulations already incorporated in the WTO. As the bilateral trade agreement includes broad obligations related not only to import tariffs and quotas, but also to transparency, dispute settlement, investment, intellectual property protection, market access for services, and business facilitation, implementing the agreement should facilitate Viet Nam's accession to the WTO. The implementation of the agreement also places further pressure on Viet Nam to bring its legal and governance system in line with international standards. Thus the signing of the bilateral agreement with the United States has strengthened the reform process in Viet Nam and moved it along the path to becoming a WTO member.

4   IMPACT OF FDI

Contribution to Investment and the State Budget

FDI has made an important contribution to total investment in Viet Nam. It accounted for 25 percent of total investment on average in 1991–95, and 21.6 percent in 1996–2002 (Figure 8.1). The contribution of FDI to GDP has also been significant. In the early 1990s the share was modest, at 2–4 percent of GDP, rising to over 13 percent in recent years. The FDI sector contributed about $1.5 billion to the state budget in 1996–2000, or 6–7 percent of total revenue. If oil and gas revenues are included, the FDI share rises to about 20 percent (Luan, Hai, and Quan 2003).

Contribution to Exports

With foreign investors increasingly attracted to export-oriented industries, FDI has played an important part in Viet Nam's exports (Ba, Chung, and Huong 2003). Exports of foreign firms, excluding oil and gas, increased rapidly to $4.5 billion in 2002, when they accounted for over 25 percent of total exports (Figure 8.2). Both the value of FDI exports and the contribution of FDI to total exports have increased strongly over time, including during the Asian financial crisis. The role of FDI is especially important in some key export industries, such as footwear, where it accounts for about 42 percent of exports, garments and textiles (25 percent), and electronics,

*Figure 8.1   Viet Nam: FDI by Value and Share of Total Investment,
1996–2002*

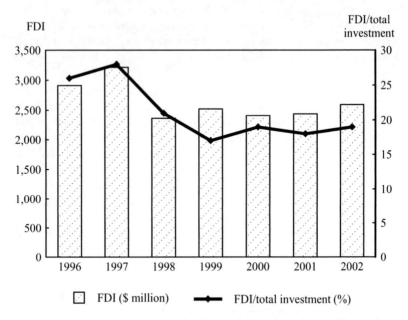

FDI data include supplementary capital invested in projects licensed in previous years and investment in oil exploration.
Source: Ministry of Planning and Investment.

computers, and supplies (84 percent). FDI has also played an important role in several service sectors, especially tourism and hotels.

Contribution to Economic Restructuring

Policies to encourage FDI in preferred regions and industrial zones have been consistent with Viet Nam's industrialization and modernization objectives. In the early years after the enactment of the Law on Foreign Investment, much FDI went into real estate. However, in 1996–2000, FDI gradually shifted toward production and export-oriented processing industries. Compared with the previous five-year period, the number of FDI projects in real estate fell by 52 percent during this period, while the number in infrastructure (such as telecommunications and technical services) rose by 40 percent. FDI has been particularly important in crude oil, automobiles, refrigerators, air conditioners, computers and office equipment, electronic tubes, and telecommunication switchboards (in all of which it

Figure 8.2   Viet Nam: Exports of FDI Sector by Value and Share of Total Exports, 1991–2002

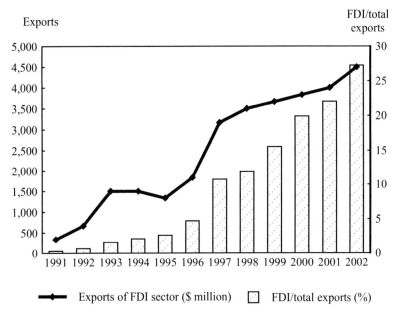

Source: Ministry of Planning and Investment; General Department of Statistics.

accounted for 100 percent of output), laminated steel (60 percent), cement (28 percent), electronics (33 percent), precision medical tools (76 percent), fiber (55 percent), cloth (30 percent), footwear (49 percent), garments (18 percent), and foodstuffs and beverages (25 percent).

Many new and modern technologies have been imported into Viet Nam through FDI projects, especially in telecommunications, oil and gas, chemicals, electronics, computers, automobiles, and motorcycles (Le, Bui and Dao 2002). The technology introduced by foreign firms has had spillover effects on other sectors: to survive in a more competitive market, SOEs and private enterprises have been forced to upgrade their technology, and have made efforts to adapt technologies to local conditions.

Contribution to Employment and Human Resource Development

FDI has contributed to employment in Viet Nam, albeit on a small scale. The FDI sector has created 620,000 direct jobs, as well as thousands of indirect jobs in supporting industries. The employment share of the FDI sector in 2000 was still small, at about 2 percent of the total. Most of the jobs created have been in industry and construction (Table 8.9). By sector, FDI accounts for about 6.4 percent of employment in industry and construction, 0.2 percent in agriculture, forestry, and aquaculture, and 0.4 percent in services.[5]

Based on data on FDI in four manufacturing industries in 2000, the Institute of World Economy found that the share of unskilled labor in the FDI sector was relatively high compared to SOEs, but similar to that in the domestic private sector (Le, Bui and Dao 2002). This result is somewhat unusual for a developing country. It can be explained by the fact that two labor-intensive industries (textiles and garments and food-processing industries) were among the four industries in the sample. Also, many 'skilled' graduates of training centers could not meet the standards of foreign investors and were therefore counted as 'unskilled.' The same study found that the average wage of workers in foreign firms was much higher than that in private and state firms. Thus, besides the benefits of knowledge and skills transfer, FDI has made an important contribution to raising the living standards of foreign sector employees.

5   WTO STATUS AND TRIMS IMPLEMENTATION

Viet Nam submitted an application to join the WTO in January 1995. The following year, it submitted a Memorandum on the Foreign Trade Regime and Economic Policy for examination by the WTO working group set up to oversee Viet Nam's entry. This was followed by studies to clarify domestic policies and institutions related to trade, goods, custom duties, investment services, and intellectual property rights. Other issues of interest to members include the trade regime, institutional structures, the privatization process, and the ability of the government to fulfill its WTO commitments.

Eight years after applying to join the WTO, Viet Nam has completed the stage of clarification of its trade and commercial policy regime, and has moved to the negotiating stage. The most important issue under negotiation is the opening up of the domestic market. Viet Nam is working to resolve the issues of most concern to WTO members, with the ambitious target of joining the WTO in 2005.

In the process, Viet Nam has had to review many of its regulations that do not currently comply with the requirements of the TRIMs Agreement. However, its existing bilateral and multilateral investment agreements with 45 countries, territories, and international organizations have given it some experience in fulfilling international obligations. The bilateral trade agreement with the United States is one of the most important examples.

Table 8.9   *Viet Nam: Direct Jobs Created by FDI, 2000–01 (no.)*

Sector	2000	2001	2002
Agriculture, forestry, & aquaculture	33,313	40,957	63,224
Industry & construction	304,418	362,068	512,189
Services	38,469	42,959	46,085

Source: Ministry of Planning and Investment.

In keeping with the standards for investment promotion and protection provided under the bilateral trade agreement framework, Viet Nam has made binding commitments to grant most favored nation (MFN) and national treatment to US investors for a specified period of time. Viet Nam does not maintain any exceptions to MFN treatment, but has excluded certain sectors from national treatment, while providing a timetable for the phasing out of most of these exceptions. Certain sectors are permanently exempt from national treatment obligations.

Viet Nam's commitments include reducing and eventually eliminating restrictions on US investment. For example, within five to seven years of the commencement of the agreement, Viet Nam will eliminate some measures that are inconsistent with the TRIMs Agreement. These include export requirements for certain products, the mandatory development of local raw materials for paper processing, vegetable oil, milk, cane sugar, and wood processing, and local content requirements for automobiles, motorcycles, and electrical and electronic products. Viet Nam will eliminate all other TRIMs no later than five years after the commencement of the agreement. In addition, within three to seven years, US investors will be allowed to set up joint ventures or 100 percent US-owned enterprises to conduct import and export activities with respect to all but a few specified goods.

As a member of ASEAN, the Asia Pacific Economic Cooperation (APEC) and Asia Europe Meeting (ASEM) forums, Viet Nam has dealt with the issue of international investment integration on both a bilateral and multilateral basis. In October 1998, ASEAN member countries signed a Framework Agreement on an ASEAN Investment Area, with the objective of enhancing the region's attractiveness to, and competitiveness for, foreign investment. One important aspect of the agreement is that the signatories have agreed to implement national treatment and open their industries to foreign investment from ASEAN investors, with the exception of sectors specified in the temporary exclusion list and the sensitive list.[6]

However, there are still some important issues that need to be addressed to meet the requirements of the TRIMs Agreement. First, although the original local content requirements have expired, they remain part of the investment license appraisal process and are a condition for the application of preferential rates of import duty on imported accessories and spare parts in automobiles, motorcycles, and electronics production and assembly. The application of local content requirements as a condition for granting investment licenses as well as preferential rates of import duty is inconsistent with the TRIMs Agreement. Under its bilateral trade agreement with the United States, Viet Nam has agreed to abolish this requirement within five years. It now has to continue in this direction and abolish it for investors from all WTO members.

Second, the requirement for the development and use of local materials and resources in the production of sugar, vegetable oil, milk, and wood processing also violates the TRIMs Agreement. Under its bilateral trade agreement with the United States, Viet Nam has agreed to eliminate this requirement. This too should be extended to all WTO members.

Viet Nam faces many other challenges in meeting the requirements of WTO accession. First, it must open its market to foreign goods, investment, and services. Creating a business environment in which domestic and foreign enterprises are treated equally will force many Vietnamese enterprises, especially those in highly protected sectors, into fierce competition with more able, foreign-owned competitors.

Second, Viet Nam faces the challenge of implementing its strategy of industrialization and modernization, part of which is based on import protection and export promotion, while being obliged to reduce or remove these restrictions within a defined period of time. Investment licensing procedures and the regulation of foreign-invested enterprises need to be liberalized further to reduce the extent of state intervention in foreign investment activities. Tax incentives, reductions in land rent, and other subsidies given to foreign-invested enterprises need to be phased out to the extent that these favor foreign over domestic enterprises.

And third, Viet Nam must find a way to create a comprehensive, transparent, and predictable legal system by 2005. The current laws and policies on FDI contain numerous defects, contradictions, overlaps, and inconsistencies, and are subject to constant change. Many legal documents are not sufficiently specific, leaving them open to a number of interpretations. In addition, the enforcement of laws has not been effective. The criteria for the issuance of investment licenses are not transparent, and in some cases are inconsistent. Procedures related to project implementation, such as land usage, construction, and customs, are still cumbersome.

In summary, the requirements of WTO accession in general, and of TRIMs Agreement implementation in particular, are having a major impact on commercial policy and the legal environment in Viet Nam. The difficulties and challenges associated with accession to the WTO and compliance with the TRIMs Agreement are massive.

6 CONCLUSIONS AND RECOMMENDATIONS

Viet Nam is a poor country in transition from being a centrally planned economy. With the enactment of the 1987 Law on Foreign Investment, the government recognized the importance of FDI for economic development. The country has attracted considerable FDI, even though in the early years the authorities lacked a strategic vision of how to use FDI as an engine for development. The policy framework has been revised several times, and now has a clearer rationale together with more effective implementation. A range of incentives has been employed to attract FDI, including financial measures, preferential treatment of losses, rent reductions, and import protection. The restrictions on FDI include requirements relating to minimum capital shares, sector regulations, the types of FDI permitted, export performance, and local content.

The FDI sector has made a very important contribution to the transfer of technology, management, and skills, to government revenue, to export market access, and to employment. Areas of concern include FDI in heavily protected, inefficient industries, the relatively poor linkages between foreign and domestic firms, and the limited development of human resources.

The WTO framework and accession process have had a positive impact on Viet Nam by creating pressure to accelerate economic reform. Viet Nam has gradually been removing investment restrictions that are not compatible with the TRIMs Agreement. Its membership of ASEAN, APEC, and ASEM, and its various bilateral and multilateral trade and investment agreements, especially with the United States, have assisted its progress. However, Viet Nam still faces the major challenge of achieving its socioeconomic development targets while adjusting its domestic policies to comply with WTO requirements. The 2005 WTO membership target is extremely ambitious and will require a great effort on the part of both government and business. We conclude this chapter by highlighting some key challenges.

For the government, the major imperative is to continue to implement economic reform, specifically by reducing the restrictions on foreign investment. These relate to market access in manufacturing, opening the services market, and gradually opening all other sectors except those related to national security, historical and cultural concerns, traditional customs, and the environment. It is important that the government enhance the clarity, transparency, consistency, and predictability of Viet Nam's laws and policies, to create the legal basis of a competitive environment for both domestic and foreign enterprises.

Specific reforms to improve the environment for FDI include:

- allowing flexible conversion among the various investment forms open to foreign firms;
- gradually eliminating restrictions on the capital contribution of foreign-invested enterprises, in particular, removing restrictions on the minimum capital ratio contributed by foreign investors in joint ventures (30 percent) and the minimum ratio of legal capital to the total investment capital of foreign-invested enterprises (30 percent); and
- building a unified legal foundation for tax, financial, and investment costs for both domestic and foreign-invested enterprises.

In the framework of the second stage of tax reform, the government has issued and/or amended the Value Added Tax Law, Special Consumption Law, and Enterprise Income Law. As a result of the implementation of these laws since 1999, some duties and fees inconsistent with the economic policy framework have been removed or amended. Moreover, the government now has a 'roadmap' to adjust fees and charges on some goods and services, including water and tourism, but excluding electricity and domestic civil aviation.

The Law on Corporate Income Tax and the Law on Foreign Investment should be amended with a view to removing the withholding tax on repatriated profits and applying a unified corporate income tax schedule for both domestic and foreign enterprises. It is also important to develop a uniform system of markets, consistent with trade and investment liberalization. In particular, policies that enhance the business environment for enterprises—especially those concerning land usage, foreign exchange management, labor recruitment, technology transfer, and the environment—should be improved. The government should actively promote the development of markets for capital, real estate, scientific and technological services, and labor. The financial system should be strengthened and the process of SOE reform accelerated.

Finally, a key objective will be to improve investment procedures and the government's regulation of FDI by simplifying licensing and investment procedures. The registration regime for investment licensing should be expanded, while narrowing the scope of so-called Group A projects that require prime ministerial approval. The rights of Provincial People's Committees and industry zones' management boards to issue licenses and manage foreign investment activities should be expanded, while ensuring nationally consistent FDI policies are pursued.

APPENDIX 8.1 TYPES OF FDI SPECIFIED BY THE LAW ON FOREIGN INVESTMENT

Foreign investment in Viet Nam can be carried out in any of the following forms.

i   A business cooperation contract (BCC) is an arrangement by which two or more parties (a foreign investor and a Vietnamese partner) enter into a business, in the form of profit sharing, product sharing, or some other form of cooperation. BCCs do not involve the creation of a legal entity and are more easily amended and more flexible than either joint ventures or 100 percent foreign-owned projects. Parties agree to implement a project and produce certain goods or provide certain services for the duration of the relationship as defined in the contract. BCCs generally place no limitation on management structure or the repatriation of profits.

ii A joint venture is an enterprise established in Viet Nam on the basis of a contract signed by one or more Vietnamese parties (including existing joint ventures) and one or more foreign parties, in order to invest and carry on a business in Viet Nam. A joint venture enterprise is established in the form of a limited liability company and is a legal entity in accordance with the law of Viet Nam. Each joint venture party is responsible to the other party and to the joint venture to the extent of its contribution to legal capital.

The legal capital of a joint venture must be not less than 30 per cent of invested capital. In respect of infrastructure construction projects in regions with difficult economic and social conditions, this ratio may be reduced to 20 percent with the prior approval of the body issuing the investment license. The capital contribution of the foreign party or parties is decided between the joint venture parties, but should be not less than 30 percent of the legal capital of the joint venture.

iii A 100 percent foreign-owned enterprise is one owned and established in Viet Nam by a foreign investor who manages the enterprise and takes full responsibility for its business results. Such an enterprise is a legal entity under Vietnamese law, has limited liability, and is distinct from the parent company. As with a joint venture, the prescribed capital of a 100 percent foreign-owned enterprise should be equivalent to at least 30 percent of the total investment capital, unless a specific exemption has been obtained from the Ministry of Planning and Investment. The enterprise is not allowed to reduce the level of its prescribed capital during the course of its operations.

iv Other forms of FDI include export-processing zones and build–operate–transfer (BOT), build–transfer–operate (BTO), and build–transfer (BT) arrangements.

NOTES

1 Most of the figures used in this chapter are from the Ministry of Planning and Investment, but some have been provided by the General Statistical Office. Note that the ministry's figures do not always coincide with those of the General Statistical Office; they often tend to be higher because they include projects that are registered but not yet realized.

2 Figures are from General Statistical Office (various years).

3 Losses incurred by joint ventures can be carried over to the next year and set against investment returns for up to five years. The remittance tax for joint ventures is rather low, 3–7 percent depending on the capital contribution of the investor. To encourage expatriates to invest, the government offers them a 20 percent reduction in income tax. Remittance tax is only 3 percent for expatriates, foreign investors in industrial zones, and foreign investors located in favored localities. Foreign-invested enterprises producing mechanical, electronic, and electrical spare parts can be exempted from tariffs for up to five years.

4 These were a group of commodities subject to quotas; a group of prohibited commodities; a group of commodities under government management; and a group under specialized management.

5 Author's calculation, using the number of employed people aged 15 years and over in 2000 as total employment.

6 The time frame for removing sectors from the temporary exclusion list is the same as for AFTA+3 (ASEAN plus the PRC, Japan, and Korea), that is, 2013 for Viet Nam, 2010 for original member countries, and 2015 for Lao PDR and Myanmar. The sensitive list includes measures and/or sectors not yet covered by market access and national treatment obligations.

References

ADB (Asian Development Bank) (2003), *Asian Development Outlook 2003*, ADB, Manila.

Agarwal, A. (2001), 'Liberalization, Multinational Enterprises and Export Performance: Evidence from Indian Manufacturing,' *ICRIER Working Paper No. 69*, Indian Council for Research on International Economic Relations, New Delhi.

Agosin, M.R., and R. Mayer (2000), 'Foreign Investment in Developing Countries: Does it Crowd in Domestic Investment?' *UNCTAD Discussion Paper No. 146*, United Nations, Geneva.

Ahluwalia, I.J, and I.M.D. Little (eds) (1998), *India's Economic Reforms and Development: Essays for Manmohan Singh*, Oxford University Press, Delhi.

Ahluwalia, S., Y.V. Reddy, and S.S. Tarapore (eds) (2003), *Macroeconomics and Monetary Policy: Issues for a Reforming Economy*, Oxford University Press, New Delhi.

Aitken, B., G.H. Hanson, and A.E. Harrison (1997), 'Spillovers, Foreign Investment and Export Behaviour,' *Journal of International Economics*, 43: 103–32.

AMCHAM Korea (American Chamber of Commerce in Korea) (1998), 'Meet Jeff Jones: The New AMCHAM President,' *The Journal*, 46(5): 18–19.

AMCHAM Korea (American Chamber of Commerce in Korea) (2002), 'Korea as the Next Business Hub of Asia,' *The Journal*, 60(8): 22–7.

Amsden, A. (1989), *Asia's Next Giant: South Korea and Late Industrialization*, Oxford University Press, New York.

Amsden, A. (2001), *The Rise of the Rest: Challenges to the West from the Late-Industrializing Economies*, Oxford University Press, New York.

Amsden, A., T. Tschang, and A. Goto (2001), 'Do Foreign Companies Conduct R&D in Developing Countries? A New Approach to Analyzing the Level of R&D, with an Analysis of Singapore,' *Working Paper Series No. 14*, ADB Institute, Tokyo.

Anuwar, A., and S.Y. Tham (1993), Domestic Investment and Foreign Direct Investment: Seeking the Right Balance, Paper presented at the Malaysian Institute of Economic Research (MIER) 1993 National Outlook Conference, Kuala Lumpur, 7–8 December.

Archanun, K. (2003a), Foreign Direct Investment and Technology Spillover: A Cross-industry Analysis of Thai Manufacturing, Unpublished paper, Australian National University, Canberra.

Archanun, K. (2003b), Foreign Trade Regimes and the FDI–Growth Nexus: A Case Study of Thailand, Unpublished paper, Australian National University, Canberra.

Ariff, M. (1989), 'TRIMs: A North–South Divide or a Non-issue?' *World Economy*, 12(3): 347–60.

Ariff, M. (1991), *The Malaysian Economy: Pacific Connections*, Oxford University Press, Singapore.

Ariff, M., Z.A. Mahani, and E.C. Tan (1997), *Trade and Investment Policies in Developing Countries: Malaysian Case Study*, Institute of Developing Economies, Tokyo.

Athreye, S., and S. Kapur (1999), 'Foreign-controlled Manufacturing Firms in India: Long-term Trends,' *Economic and Political Weekly*, 34: M-149–51.

Athreye, S., and S. Kapur (2001), 'Private Foreign Investment in India: Pain or Panacea?,' *World Economy*, 24(3): 399–424.

Athukorala, P.-C. (2001), *Crisis and Recovery in Malaysia: The Role of Capital Controls*, Edward Elgar, Cheltenham.

Athukorala, P.-C. (2002), Trade Policy Reform, Export Strategies and the Incentive Structure in Vietnam (draft), Hanoi, World Bank, March.

Athukorala, P.-C. (2003), 'FDI in Crisis and Recovery: Lessons from the 1997–98 Asian Crisis,' *Australian Economic History Review*, 43(2): 197–213.

Athukorala, P.-C., and C. Manning (1999), *Structural Change and International Migration in East Asia: Adjusting to Labour Scarcity*, Oxford University Press, Melbourne.

Athukorala, P.-C., and H. Hill (2002) 'Host Country Impact of FDI in East Asia,' in B. Bora (ed.), *Foreign Direct Investment: Research Issues*, Routledge, London: 168–94.

Ba, L.X., T.K. Chung, and T.T. Huong (2003), Attracting FDI from the Angle of Impact on Trade Activities in Viet Nam in the Past, Paper presented at the workshop, New Economic Context, Foreign Investment Inflows, and Development of Trade and Markets in Asia and in Vietnam, Hanoi, 13–14 February.

Balasubramanyam, V.N. (1991), 'Putting TRIMs to Good Use,' *World Development*, 19(9): 1,215–24.

Battat, J., I. Frank, and X. Shen (1996), *Suppliers to Multinationals: Linkage Programmes to Strengthen Local Capabilities in Developing Countries*, Foreign Investment Advisory Service, Washington DC.

Berezin, P., A. Salehizadeh, and E. Santana (2002), 'The Challenge of Diversification in the Caribbean,' *IMF Working Paper, WP/02/196*, Washington DC.

Blomstrom, M., and A. Kokko (1998), 'Multinational Corporations and Spillovers,' *Journal of Economic Surveys*, 12: 247–77.

Bora, B. (2001), *Trade Related Investment Measures and the WTO: 1995–2001*, United Nations Conference on Trade and Development, United Nations, Geneva.

Bosworth, B.P., and S.M. Collins (1999), 'Capital Flows to Developing Economies: Implications for Saving and Investment,' *Brookings Papers on Economic Activity*, 1: 143–69.

Brecher, R., and C. Diaz-Alejandro (1977), 'Tariffs, Foreign Capital and Immizerising Growth,' *Journal of International Economics*, 7(3): 317–22.

Brooker Group (2001), *Technology Innovation of Industrial Enterprises in Thailand 2001*, Brooker Group, Bangkok.

Brooks, D.H., E.X. Fan, and L.R. Sumulong (2003a), 'Foreign Direct Investment: Trends, TRIMs, and WTO Negotiations,' *Asian Development Review*, 20(1): 1–33.

Brooks, D.H., E.X. Fan, and L.R. Sumulong (2003b), 'Foreign Direct Investment in Developing Asia: Trends, Effects and Likely Issues for the Forthcoming WTO Negotiations,' *ADB/ERD Working Paper No. 38*, Asian Development Bank, Manila.

Buckley, P. (2003), 'The Challenges of the New Economy for Multinational Firms: Lessons from Southeast Asia,' in F. Bartels and N. Freeman (eds), *The Future of Foreign Investment in Southeast Asia*, Routledge-Curzon Press, London: 15–31.

Capannelli, G. (1999), 'Technology Transfer from Japanese Consumer Electronic Firms via Buyer–Supplier Relations,' in K.S. Jomo, G. Felker, and R. Rasiah (eds), *Industrial Technology Development in Malaysia: Industry and Firm Studies*, Routledge, London: Chapter 8.

CEAF (Centre for Economic Analysis and Forecasts) (2003), *An Analytical Report on Investment of Chinese Enterprises: 2003* [in Chinese], CEAF, Peking University, Beijing.

Central Bank of Malaysia (2000), *Third Quarter Bulletin 2000*, Central Bank, Kuala Lumpur.

Central Bank of Malaysia (2001), *Central Bank Annual Report 2000*, Central Bank, Kuala Lumpur.

Chen, C., L. Chang, and Y. Zhang (1995), 'The Role of Foreign Direct Investment in China's Post-1978 Economic Development,' *World Development*, 23(4): 691–703.

Chi, P.S.K., and C. Kao (1994), 'Foreign Investment in China: A New Data Set,' *China Economic Review*, 5(2): 149–55.

Cline, W.R. (1987), 'Discussion (of Chapter 3),' in D.R. Lessard and J. Willanson (eds), *Capital Flight and Third World Debt*, Institute for International Economics, Washington DC.

Cooper, R.N. (2002), 'Growth and Inequality: The Role of Foreign Trade and Investment,' in World Bank (ed.), *Annual World Bank Conference on Development Economics 2001/2002*, World Bank, Washington DC.

Correa, C.M., and N. Kumar (2003), *Protecting Foreign Investment: Implications of a WTO Regime and Policy Options*, Zed Press in association with Research and Information System for the Non-Aligned and Other Developing Countries (RIS), London and New York.

Crafts, N. (2000), 'Globalization and Growth in the Twentieth Century,' *IMF Working Paper, WP/00/44*, Washington DC.

Cuddington, J.T. (1986), 'Capital Flight: Estimates, Issues, and Explanations,' *Princeton Studies in International Finance*, 58: 1–40.

Cuyvers, L., P. de Lombaerde, B. Dewulf, and D. Bulcke (1997), 'Export Strategies and Policies in Thailand until 1995,' *CAS Discussion Paper No 10*, Centre for International Management and Development, Antwerp.

Dahlman, C.J., and T. Andersson (2000), *Korea and the Knowledge-based Economy: Making the Transition*, World Bank/OECD, Washington DC and Paris.

Dai, D. (2003), 'How to Assess the Exaggeration Issue of China's FDI Statistics,' <http://www.tdctrade.com/econforum/boc/boc030101.htm2003>, accessed May 2003.

Doanh, L.D. (2003), Foreign Direct Investment and Trade Development in Vietnam, Paper presented at the workshop, New Economic Context, Foreign Investment Inflows, and Development of Trade and Markets in Asia and in Vietnam, Hanoi, 13–14 February.

Doraisami, A., and R. Rasiah (2001), 'Fiscal Incentives for Promotion of Manufactured Exports in Malaysia,' in K.S. Jomo (ed.), *Southeast Asia's Industrialization: Industrial Policy, Capabilities and Sustainability*, Palgrave, Hampshire: Chapter 9.

Dunning, J.H. (1998), 'Globalization and the New Geography of Foreign Direct Investment,' *Oxford Development Studies*, 26(1): 47–70.

Economic Research Centre, State Committee of Economics and Trade (2002), *Cadre's Training Reading Book for China's WTO Accession* [in Chinese], revised edition, Press for the Central Party School of the Communist Party, Beijing.

Edwards, C. (1995), 'The Role of Foreign Direct Investment,' in *Malaysian Development Experience: Changes and Challenges*, National Institute of Public Administration Malaysia (INTAN), Kuala Lumpur: Chapter 26.

Eng, I., and Y. Lin (1996), 'Seeking Comparative Advantage in an Emergent Open Economy: Foreign Direct Investment in Chinese Industry,' *Environment and Planning*, A28: 1,113–38.

Ernst, D. (2002), 'Global Production Networks in East Asia's Electronics Industry and Upgrading Perspectives in Malaysia,' *East–West Center Working Papers, Economics Series, No. 44*, East–West Center, Hawaii, March.

Fan, E.X. (2003), 'Technological Spillovers from Foreign Direct Investment: A Survey,' *Asian Development Review*, 20(1): 34–56.

Felker, G. (2001), 'The Politics of Industrial Investment Policy Reform in Malaysia and Thailand,' in K.S. Jomo (ed.), *Southeast Asia's Industrialization: Industrial Policy, Capabilities and Sustainability*, Palgrave, Hampshire: Chapter 6.

Felker, G., and K.S. Jomo (2000), 'New Approaches to Investment Policy in the ASEAN-4,' <http://www.adbi.org/para2000/papers/Jomo.pdf>, accessed 18 April 2003.

FIAS (Foreign Investment Advisory Service) (1999), *A Review of Investment Incentives: Thailand*, FIAS, International Finance Corporation and World Bank, Washington DC.

Fikkert, B. (1994), An Open or Closed Technology Policy? The Effects of Technology Licensing, Foreign Direct Investment, and Technology Spillovers on R&D in Indian Industrial Sector Firms, PhD dissertation, Yale University, New Haven CT.

Freeman, J.N. (1994), 'Vietnam and China: Foreign Direct Investment Parallels,' *Communist Economics and Economic Transformation*, 6(1): 75–97.

Freeman, N. (2003), 'The Prospects for Foreign Direct Investment in the Transitional Economies of Southeast Asia,' in F. Bartels and N. Freeman (eds), *The Future of Foreign Investment in Southeast Asia*, Routledge-Curzon Press, London: 170–87.

French, H. (1998), 'Capital Flows and Environment,' *Foreign Policy in Focus*, 3(22): 1–4.

Fry, M.J. (1992), 'Foreign Direct Investment in a Macroeconomic Framework: Finance, Efficiency, Incentives and Distortions,' *PRE Working Paper*, World Bank, Washington DC.

Fry, M.J. (1996), 'How Foreign Direct Investment in Pacific Asia Improves the Current Account,' *Asian Economics*, 7(3): 459–86.

Fukasaku, K., D. Wall, and M. Wu (1994), *China's Long March to an Open Economy*, OECD, Paris.

Ganesan, A.V. (1998), 'Strategic Options Available to Developing Countries with Regard to a Multilateral Agreement on Investment,' *UNCTAD Discussion Paper No. 134*, United Nations Conference on Trade and Development, Geneva.

Garnaut, R., and L. Song (eds) (2003), *China: New Engine of World Growth*, Asia Pacific Press, Canberra.

General Statistical Office (various years), *Statistical Yearbook*, Statistical Publication, Hanoi.

Gomez, E.T., and K.S. Jomo (1997), *Malaysia's Political Economy: Politics, Patronage and Profits*, Cambridge University Press, Cambridge.

Gordon, J. (2002), 'Foreign Direct Investment and Export', Presentation to the Indian Institute of Foreign Trade, 20 September, available at <http://www.imf.org/external/country/>.

Government of Malaysia (2001), *The Eighth Malaysia Plan: 2001–2005*, Malaysian National Printers Corporation, Kuala Lumpur.

Greenfield, G. (2001), 'The WTO Agreement on Trade-related Investment Measures (TRIMs),' *CCPA Briefing Paper Series: Trade and Investment*, 2(1): 1–8.

Hallward-Dreimeier, M. (2003), 'Do Bilateral Investment Treaties Affect Foreign Direct Investment? Only a Bit … and They Could Bite,' *Working Paper No. 3121*, World Bank, Washington DC.

Han, J. (1999), 'An Empirical Analysis of China's Capital Flight: 1989–1998' [in Chinese], *Journal of Hebei Economic and Trade University*, 12, Shijiazhuang.

Hardin, A., and L. Holmes (2002), 'Measuring and Modelling Barriers to FDI,' in B. Bora (ed.), *Foreign Direct Investment: Research Issues*, Routledge, London: 253–72.

He, M. (2002), *Key Points of China's Commitment and Adjustment of Policies and Laws in WTO Accession* [in Chinese], China Material Press, Beijing.

Hiemenz, U. (1989), 'Foreign Direct Investment and Capital Formation in China since 1979: Implications for Economic Development,' in D. Cassel and G. Heiduk (eds), *China's Contemporary Economic Reforms as a Development Strategy*, Nomos Verlagsgesellschaft, Baden-Baden: 85–108.

Hill, H. (1988), *Foreign Investment and Industrialization in Indonesia*, Oxford University Press, Singapore.

Hill, H. (2002), 'Spatial Disparities in Developing East Asia: A Survey,' *Asian-Pacific Economic Literature*, 16(1): 10–35.

Hobday, M. (1999), 'Innovation in Electronics in Malaysia,' in K.S. Jomo, G. Felker, and R. Rasiah (eds), *Industrial Technology Development in Malaysia: Industry and Firm Studies*, Routledge, London: Chapter 4.

Huang, F. (1995), 'China's Utilization of Foreign Capital and the Related Policies,' *Journal of Asian Economics*, 6(2): 217–32.

Huang, Y. (2001), 'Internal and External Reforms: Experiences and Lessons from China,' *Cato Journal*, 21(1): 43–64.

Huang, Y., and T. Khanna (2003), 'Can India Overtake China?' *Foreign Policy Magazine*, July–August 2003, available at <http://www.foreignpolicy.com/story/>.

Hwang, S.-I., and I. Shin (2000), 'The Liberalization of Banking Sector in Korea: Impact on the Korean Economy,' *KIEP Working Paper 00-13*, Korea Institute for International Economic Policy, Seoul.

Hwang, S.-I., I. Kim, and I. Shin (2001), 'The Liberalization of the Banking Sector and the Effect of Foreign Entry in Korea' [in Korean], *KIEP Policy Analysis 01-03*, Korea Institute for International Economic Policy, Seoul.

Ianchovichina, E., and T. Walmsley (2002), Regional Impact of China's Accession, World Bank, Washington DC, mimeo.

IFC (International Finance Corporation) (2000), *China's Emerging Private Enterprises: Prospects for the New Century*, IFC, Washington DC.

IMF (International Monetary Fund) (2003), *World Economic Outlook Database*, September.

Ishak, S. (2002), *The Earth for all Humanity: Managing Economic Inequality in the Era of Globalization*, Universiti Kebangsaan Malaysia Publishers, Bangi.

Ito, K. (2002), 'Are Foreign Multinationals More Efficient? Plant Productivity in the Thai Automobile Industry,' *ICSEAD Working Paper Series Volume 2002-19*, International Centre for the Study of East Asian Development (ICSEAD), Kyushu, July.

JBIC (Japan Bank for International Cooperation) (2002), 'JBIC FY2001 Survey: The Outlook of Japanese Foreign Direct Investment,' *Journal of the Research Institute for Development and Finance*, 9(January): 4–38.

JBICI (Japan Bank for International Cooperation Institute) (2002), 'Foreign Direct Investment and Development: Where Do We Stand?,' *JBICI Research Paper No. 15*, JBICI, Tokyo.

JETRO (Japan External Trade Organization) (2001), *17th Survey on Japanese Manufacturing Affiliates in Europe/Turkey*, JETRO, Tokyo.

Jiang X. (2002), *The Foreign-invested Sector in China: Its Contribution to Economic Growth, Structural Upgrading, and Competitive Power* [in Chinese], People's University Press, Beijing.

Jomo, K.S. (1994), 'The Proton Saga: Malaysian Car, Mitsubishi Gain,' in K.S. Jomo (ed.), *Japan and Malaysian Development: In the Shadow of the Rising Sun*, Routledge, London: Chapter 11.

Jomo, K.S. (2002), 'Introduction,' in K.S. Jomo (ed.), *Ugly Malaysians? South–South Investments Abused*, Institute for Black Research, Durban: Chapter 1.

Jomo K.S., and G. Felker (eds) (1999), *Technology, Competitiveness, and the State: Malaysia's Industrial Technology Policies*, Routledge, London.

Jomo K.S., G. Felker, and R. Rasiah (eds) (1999), *Industrial Technology Development in Malaysia: Industry and Firm Studies*, Routledge, London.

Joshi, V. (2003), 'India and the Impossible Trinity,' *World Economy*, forthcoming.

Joshi, V., and I. Little (1997), *India's Economic Reforms 1991–2001*, Oxford University Press, Oxford.

Kamath, S.J. (1990), 'Foreign Direct Investment in a Centrally Planned Developing Economy: The Chinese Case,' *Economic Development and Cultural Change*, 39(1): 107–30.

Kamath, S.J. (1994), 'Property Rights and the Evolution of Foreign Direct Investment in a Centrally Planned Developing Economy: Reply,' *Economic Development and Cultural Change*, 42(2): 419–25.

KIET (Korea Institute for Industrial Economics and Trade) (2001), *Five Economic Effects of FDI*, [in Korean], KIET, Seoul.

Kim, J.-D. (1997), 'Impact of Foreign Direct Investment Liberalization: The Case of Korea,' *KIEP Working Paper 97-01*, Korea Institute for International Economic Policy, Seoul.

Kim, J.-D. (1999), 'Inward Foreign Direct Investment Regime and Some Evidences of Spillover Effects in Korea,' *KIEP Working Paper 99-09*, Korea Institute for International Economic Policy, Seoul.

Kim, J.-D. (2003), 'Inward Foreign Direct Investment into Korea: Recent Performance and Future Agenda,' *KIEP Discussion Paper No. 03-01*, Korea Institute for International Economic Policy, Seoul.

Kim, J.-D., and S.-I. Hwang (2000), 'The Role of Foreign Direct Investment in Korea's Economic Development: Productivity Effects and Implications for the Currency Crisis,' in A.O. Krueger and T. Ito (eds), *The Role of Foreign Direct*

Investment in East Asian Economic Development, NBER East Asia Seminar on Economics, Vol. 9, University of Chicago Press, Chicago and London: 267–94.

Kim, J.-I., and J.-D. Kim (2003), 'Liberalization of Trade in Services and Productivity Growth in Korea,' in T. Ito and A.O. Krueger (eds), *Trade in Services in the Asia-Pacific Region*, NBER East Asia Seminar on Economics, Vol. 11, University of Chicago Press, Chicago and London: 179–202.

Kim, L. (1997), *Imitation to Innovation: The Dynamics of Korea's Technological Learning*, Harvard Business School Press, Boston MA.

Kim, L. (2000), 'Korea's National Innovation System in Transition,' in L. Kim and R.R. Nelson (eds), *Technology, Learning, and Innovation: Experiences of Newly Industrializing Countries*, Cambridge University Press, Cambridge: 335–60.

Kinoshita, S. (2001), 'East Asia Economic Growth and a Quantitative Model of Trade and FDI: The Case Study of Thailand,' *ICSEAD Working Paper Series Volume 2001-27*, International Centre for the Study of East Asian Development (ICSEAD), Kyushu.

Kojima. K. (1996), *Trade, Investment and Pacific Economic Integration*, Bushindo, Tokyo.

Krueger, A.O. (ed.) (2002), *Economic Policy Reforms and the Indian Economy*, Oxford University Press, New Delhi.

Kueh, Y.Y. (1992), 'Foreign Investment and Economic Change in China,' *China Quarterly*, 129–132(5): 637–90.

Kumar, N. (1990a), *Multinational Enterprises in India: Industrial Distribution, Characteristics and Performance*, Routledge, London and New York.

Kumar, N. (1990b), 'Mobility Barriers and Profitability of Multinational and Local Enterprises in Indian Manufacturing,' *Journal of Industrial Economics*, 38: 449–61.

Kumar, N. (1991), 'Mode of Rivalry and Comparative Behaviour of Multinational and Local Enterprises: The Case of Indian Manufacturing,' *Journal of Development Economics*, 35: 381–92.

Kumar, N. (1998a), 'Liberalization and Changing Patterns of Foreign Direct Investments: Has India's Relative Attractiveness as a Host of FDI Improved?' *Economic and Political Weekly*, 33(22): 1,321–9.

Kumar, N. (1998b), 'Emerging Outward Foreign Direct Investments from Asian Developing Countries: Prospects and Implications,' in N. Kumar (ed.), *Globalization, Foreign Direct Investment and Technology Transfers: Impacts on and Prospects for Developing Countries*, Routledge, London and New York: 177–94.

Kumar, N. (1998c), 'Multinational Enterprises, Regional Economic Integration, and Export-Platform Production in the Host Countries: An Empirical Analysis for the US and Japanese Corporations,' *Weltwirtschaftliches Archiv*, 134(3): 450–83.

Kumar, N. (2000a), 'Explaining the Geography and Depth of International Production: The Case of US and Japanese Multinational Enterprises,' *Weltwirtschaftliches Archiv*, 136(3): 442–76.

Kumar, N. (2000b), 'Mergers and Acquisitions by MNEs: Patterns and Implications,' *Economic and Political Weekly*, 35(32): 2,851–8.

Kumar, N. (2001a), 'Indian Software Industry Development: International and National Perspective,' *Economic and Political Weekly*, 36(45): 4,278–90.

Kumar, N. (2001b), 'Determinants of Location of Overseas R&D Activity of Multinational Enterprises: The Case of US and Japanese Corporations,' *Research Policy*, 30: 159–74.

Kumar, N. (2002), *Globalization and the Quality of Foreign Direct Investment*, Oxford University Press, Delhi.

Kumar, N. (2003a), Performance Requirements as Tools of Development Policy: Lessons from Experiences of Developed and Developing Countries, Paper presented at the International Conference on Trade, Investment and Development organized by the Government of India and UNCTAD, New Delhi, 18–20 May 2003. Revised version available as *RIS Discussion Paper No. 52*, available at <www.ris.org.in>.

Kumar, N. (2003b), Liberalization, Foreign Direct Investment and Economic Development: The Case of India, Paper presented at the Conference on Foreign Direct Investment and Economic Development in East Asia, World Bank Institute, Fukuoka, June.

Kumar, N. (2003c), 'Investment on WTO Agenda: A Developing Country Perspective and the Way Forward for the Cancun Ministerial Conference,' *Economic and Political Weekly*, 38(30): 3,177–88.

Kumar, N., and A. Agarwal (2000), 'Liberalization, Outward Orientation and Inhouse R&D Activity of Multinational and Local Firms: A Quantitative Exploration for Indian Manufacturing,' *RIS Discussion Paper No. 07/2002*, Research and Information System for the Non-Aligned and Other Developing Countries (RIS), New Delhi.

Kumar, N., and J.P. Pradhan (2002), 'Foreign Direct Investment, Externalities and Economic Growth in Developing Countries: Some Empirical Explorations and Implications for WTO Negotiations on Investment,' *RIS Discussion Paper No. 27/2002*, Research and Information System for the Non-Aligned and Other Developing Countries (RIS), New Delhi.

Kumar, N., and J.P. Pradhan (2003), 'Export Competitiveness in Knowledge-based Industries: A Firm-level Analysis of Indian Manufacturing,' *RIS Discussion Paper No. 43/2003*, Research and Information System for the Non-Aligned and Other Developing Countries (RIS), New Delhi.

Kumar, N., and N.S. Siddharthan (1994), 'Technology, Firm Size and Export Behaviour in Developing Countries: The Case of Indian Enterprises,' *Journal of Development Studies*, 31(2): 289–309.

Kumar, N., and N. Singh (2002), *The Use and Effectiveness of Performance Requirements: The Case of India*, Research and Information System for the Non-Aligned and Other Developing Countries (RIS), New Delhi.

Lall, S., and S. Urata (eds) (2003), *Competitiveness, FDI and Technological Activity in East Asia*, Edward Elgar, Cheltenham.

Lan, P., and S. Yong (1996), 'Foreign Direct Investment and Technology Transfer: A Case-study of Foreign Direct Investment in North-east China,' *Transnational Corporations*, 5(2): 57–83.

Lardy, N.R. (1996), *The Role of Foreign Trade and Investment in China's Economic Transformation*, Oxford University Press, Oxford and New York.

Le, B.L., T. Bui, and D.V. Hung (2002), FDI and Development of Manufacturing Industries in Vietnam, Project Report, Project funded by Canadian International Development Assistance (CIDA) and International Development Research Center (IDRC), Hanoi: Institute of World Economy.

Lee, B. (2002), *Productivity Spillovers to Domestic Firms from Foreign Direct Investment: Evidence from Korean Manufacturing* [in Korean], Korea Economic Research Institute, Seoul.

Lee, C. (2003), Implementing Competition Policy in Malaysia, Paper presented at a workshop on Malaysia: Selected Economic Issues and the Challenges Ahead, Institute of Southeast Asian Studies, Singapore, 27 March.

Lee, K.H. (1998), 'Labour Market Issues: Skills, Training and Labour Productivity,' in S.L. Ying and S. Nagaraj (eds), *The Seventh Malaysia Plan: Productivity for Sustainable Development*, University of Malaya Press, Kuala Lumpur: Chapter 12.

Lee, S.-B. (2000), 'Korea's Overseas Direct Investment: Evaluation of Performances and Future Challenges,' *KIEP Working Paper 00-12*, Korea Institute for International Economic Policy, Seoul.

Lee, S.-B. (2001), 'Tax Benefit Analysis of Incentives for Foreign Direct Investment in Korea,' *International Tax Review*, 29(12): 396–401.

Lee, S.-B., and M. Yun (2002), Assessment of Foreign Direct Investment Liberalization in Korea, Paper presented at the Korea Institute for International Economic Policy International Seminar, Seoul, 7 March.

Lim, E.-G. (2001), 'Determinants of, and the Relation between, Foreign Direct Investment and Growth: A Summary of the Recent Literature,' *IMF Working Paper WP/01/175*, Washington DC.

Lipsey, R. (2001), 'Foreign Direct Investment in Three Financial Crises,' *NBER Working Paper No. 8084*, Cambridge MA.

Little, I.M.D., D. Mazumdar, and J. Page (1987), *Small Manufacturing Enterprises: A Comparative Study of India and Other Economies*, Oxford University Press, New York.

Low, P.S.K. (2003), Investment, Trade and Competition Policies: Interface with National Policy Objectives, Paper presented at the UNDP Asia Trade Initiative, University of Malaya, and Malaysian Institute of Economic Research (MIER) Conference on Investment, Energy and Environmental Services at Cancun: Promoting Human Development in WTO Negotiations, Kuala Lumpur, 7–8 August.

Luan, P.V., H.V. Hai, and L. Quan (2003), Some Present Issues on FDI in Vietnam, Paper presented at the workshop, New Economic Context, Foreign Investment Inflows, and Development of Trade and Markets in Asia and in Vietnam, Hanoi, 13–14 February.

Machado, K. (1994), 'Proton and Malaysia's Motor Vehicle Industry,' in K.S. Jomo (ed.), *Japan and Malaysian Development: In the Shadow of the Rising Sun*, Routledge, London: Chapter 12.

MASTIC (Malaysian Science and Technology Center) (2002a), *Malaysia Science and Technology Indicators Report 2000*, MASTIC, Kuala Lumpur.

MASTIC (Malaysian Science and Technology Center) (2002b), *National Survey of Research and Development 2000*, MASTIC, Kuala Lumpur.

Mathews, J.A. (1995), *High-technology Industrialization in East Asia: The Case of the Semiconductor Industry in Taiwan and Korea*, Economic Analysis No. 4, Chung-Hua Institution for Economic Research, Taipei.

Matsuoka, A. (2001), Wage Differentials among Local Plants and Foreign Multinationals by Foreign Ownership Share and Nationality in Thai Manufacturing, Unpublished paper, International Center for the Study of East Asian Development, Kitakyushu.

McCulloch, R. (1991), 'Investment Policies in the GATT,' *NBER Working Paper Series No. 3672*, National Bureau of Economic Research, Cambridge, Massachusetts.

McKendrick, D.G., R.F. Doner, and S. Haggard (2000), *From Silicon Valley to Singapore: Location and Competitive Advantage in the Hard Disk Drive Industry*, Stanford University Press, Stanford CA.

Mehta, R. (2003), *Indian Industrial Tariffs: Towards WTO Development Round Negotiations*, Research and Information System for the Non-Aligned and Other Developing Countries (RIS), New Delhi.

Menon, J. (2000), 'How Open is Malaysia? An Analysis of Trade, Capital and Labor Flows,' *World Economy*, 23(2): 235–56.

Michalopoulos, C. (1999), 'Trade Policy and Market Access Issues for Developing Countries,' *World Bank PRWP No. 2214*, Washington DC.

MIDA (Malaysian Industrial Development Authority) (2003), *Report on the Performance of the Manufacturing Sector 2002*, MIDA, Kuala Lumpur.

MIDA/UNIDO (Malaysian Industrial Development Authority and United Nations Industrial Development Organization) (1986), *Medium and Long-term Industrial Master Plan (1986–95): Executive Summary*, UNIDO, Kuala Lumpur.

Ministry of Commerce, Industry, and Energy, Korea (1999), *Patterns of FDI in 1998 and Policy Measures Needed* [in Korean], Seoul.

MITI (Ministry of International Trade and Industry, Malaysia) (2001), *Malaysia: International Trade and Industry Report 2000*, MITI, Kuala Lumpur.

MITI (Ministry of International Trade and Industry, Malaysia) (2002), *Malaysia: International Trade and Industry Report 2001*, MITI, Kuala Lumpur.

Mohd. Nazari, I. (1995), *Transnational Corporations and Economic Development: A Study of the Malaysian Electronics Industry*, University of Malaya Press, Kuala Lumpur.

Mongkolsamai, D., S. Chunanuntahum, and S. Tambunlerdchai (1985), 'Fiscal Policy and Investment Incentives: Effectiveness and Effect on Government Revenue' [in Thai], *Thammasat Journal of Economics*, 3: 39–80.

Moran, T.H. (1998), *Foreign Direct Investment and Development*, Institute for International Economics, Washington DC.

Moran, T.H. (2001), *Parental Supervision: The New Paradigm for Foreign Direct Investment and Development*, Institute for International Economics, Washington DC.

Moran, T.H. (2002a), *Strategy and Tactics for the Doha Round: Capturing the Benefits of Foreign Direct Investment.* Asian Development Bank, Manila.

Moran, T.H. (2002b), *Beyond Sweatshops: Foreign Direct Investment and Globalization in Developing Countries*, Brookings Institution Press, Washington DC.

Morgan Guaranty Trust Company (1986), 'LDC Capital Flight,' *World Financial Markets*, Morgan Guaranty Trust Company, New York, March.

Morisset, J., and N. Pirnia (2002), 'The Impact of Tax Policy and Incentives on FDI,' in B. Bora (ed.), *Foreign Direct Investment: Research Issues*, Routledge, London: 273–291.

Mundell, R. (1957), 'International Trade and Factor Mobility,' *American Economic Review*, 47: 321–35.

Narayanan, S. (1997), 'Technology Absorption and Diffusion among Local Supporting Firms in the Electronics Sector: Explaining the Divergence between Penang and the Klang Valley, Malaysia,' *Institute of Malaysian and International Studies (IKMAS) Working Papers, No. 9*, IKMAS, Bangi, June.

Nayyar, D. (1978), 'Transnational Corporations and Manufactured Exports from Poor Countries,' *Economic Journal*, 88: 59–84.

NBS (National Bureau of Statistics, China) (various years), *China Statistical Yearbook*, China Statistics Press, Beijing.

Nikomborirak, D. (2000), *Cross-border Mergers and Acquisitions in Thailand*, Thailand Development Research Institute, Bangkok.

Nor Ghani, M.N., Z. Osman, A.Z. Abdullah, and C.Y. Jun (2000), 'Trends in the Malaysian Industrial Market Structure,' *Jurnal Ekonomi Malaysia*, 34: 3–20.

Norlela, A., and M. Bell (1999), 'Firms, Politics and Political Economy: Patterns of Subsidiary–Parent Linkages and Technological Capacity-building in Electronics TNC Subsidiaries in Malaysia,' in K.S. Jomo, G. Felker, and R. Rasiah (eds), *Industrial Technology Development in Malaysia: Industry and Firm Studies*, Routledge, London: Chapter 7.

NSO (National Statistical Office of Thailand) (2000), 'Report of the 2000 Manufacturing Industry Survey: Whole Kingdom,' available at <www.nso.go.th>, accessed 15 July 2003.

NWMI (Nationwide Web for Mini-auto Information) (2002), *Selections of Auto Information, 2002*, NWMI, Beijing.

O'Donovan, D. (2000), 'Economy-wide Effects of Direct Foreign Investment: The Case of Ireland,' Paper presented to the Inter-American Development Bank, 18 September.

OECD (Organisation for Economic Co-operation and Development) (1996), *Trade and Competition: Frictions after the Uruguay Round*, OECD, Paris.

OECD (Organisation for Economic Co-operation and Development) (1999), *OECD Proceedings: Foreign Direct Investment and Recovery in Southeast Asia*, OECD, Paris.

OECD (Organisation for Economic Co-operation and Development) (2003), *OECD Investment Policy Reviews: China's Progress and Reform Challenges*, OECD, Paris.

Osman-Rani, H. (1992), 'Industrial Decentralisation, Foreign Direct Investment and Regional Competition,' in M. Ariff, and H. Yokoyama (eds), *Foreign Direct Investment in Malaysia*, Institute of Developing Economies, Tokyo: Chapter 6.

Padayachee, V., and I. Valodia (2002), 'Developing South–South Links? Malaysian Investment in Post-Apartheid South Africa,' in K.S. Jomo (ed.), *Ugly Malaysians? South–South Investments Abused*, Institute for Black Research, Durban: Chapter 4.

Pan, W., and D. Parker (1997), 'A Study of Management Attitude: Chinese State-owned Enterprises, Collective and Joint Ventures,' *Asia Pacific Business Review*, 3(3): 38–63.

Panagariya, A. (2002), 'Developing Countries at Doha: A Political Economy Analysis,' *World Economy,* 25(9): 1,205–33.

Pfeffermann, G. (2002), Business Environment and Surveys, Paradoxes: China vs. India, Presentation made at the 2002 PSD Forum Session on Investment Climate Assessment Methodology: The Investment Climate in India and China: Which Is Better? available at <http://rru.worldbank.org/psdforum/forum2002/documents/Pfeffermann.ppt>.

Phang, H.E. (1994), 'Foreign Direct Investment in Malaysia,' in T. Azizah (ed.), *Foreign Direct Investment in the SEACEN Countries*, South East Asian Central Banks (SEACEN) Center, Kuala Lumpur: Chapter 4.

Poapongsakorn, N., and B. Fuller (1997), 'Industrial Location Policy in Thailand, Industrial Decentralization or Industrial Sprawl?' in S. Masuyama, D. Vandenbrink, and C.S. Yue (eds), *Industrial Policies in East Asia*, Nomura Research Institute and Institute of Southeast Asian Studies, Singapore.

Poapongsakorn, N., and B. Fuller (1998), The Role of Foreign Direct Investment and Production Networks in the Development of the Thai Auto and Electronics Industries, Paper presented at the JETRO–IDE Joint Symposium, Can Asia Recover Its Vitality? Globalization and the Roles of Japanese and US Corporations, Tokyo.

Pomfret, R. (1991), *Investing in China: Ten Years of the Open Door Policy*, State University Press, Ames IA.

Pomfret, R. (1994), 'Foreign Direct Investment in a Centrally Planned Developing Economy: Lessons from China. Comment on Kamath,' *Economic Development and Cultural Change*, 42(2): 413–18.

Pupphavesa, W., and B. Pussarungsri (1994), *Foreign Direct Investment and Industrial Restructuring in Thailand*, Thailand Development Research Institute, Bangkok.

Rafidah, A. (Minister for International Trade and Industry) (2001), Statement on Malaysia made at Doha, Qatar, in November 2001, <www.myGlobal.gov.my>, accessed 6 February 2003.

Rafidah, A. (Minister for International Trade and Industry) (2003), Speech delivered at the Annual Luncheon of the Malaysian International Chamber of Commerce and Industry, 17 June.

Ragayah, M.Z. (1999), 'Malaysian Reverse Investment: Trends and Strategies,' *Asia-Pacific Journal of Management*, 16: 469–96.

Ragayah, M.Z. (2002), The U-Turn in Malaysian Income Inequalities: Some Possible Explanations? Paper presented at the Fourth International Regional Science Association (IRSA) International Conference, Bali, 20–21 June.

Ramachandran, V. (1993), 'Technology Transfer, Firm Ownership, and Investment in Human Capital,' *Review of Economics and Statistics*, 75(4): 664–70.

Ramstetter, E. (1999), 'Comparisons of Foreign Multinationals and Local Firms in Asian Manufacturing over Time,' *Asian Economic Journal*, 13(2): 163–203.

Ramstetter, E. (2001), 'Labor Productivity in Local Plants and Foreign Multinationals by Nationality in Thai Manufacturing, 1996 and 1998,' *Working Paper Series 2001-31*, International Centre for the Study of East Asian Development (ICSEAD), Kyushu, November.

Rasiah, R. (1993), 'Free Trade Zones and Industrial Development in Malaysia,' in K.S. Jomo (ed.), *Industrialising Malaysia: Policy, Performance and Prospects*, Routledge, London: Chapter 4.

Rasiah, R. (1995a), 'Malaysia,' in B.S. Atipol (ed.), *Transnational Corporations and Backward Linkages in Asian Electronics Industries*, Monograph No. 5, ST/ESCAP/1528, United Nations, New York: Chapter 5.

Rasiah, R. (1995b), *Foreign Capital and Industrialization in Malaysia*, St. Martin's Press, London: Chapter 9.

Rasiah, R. (1999), 'Government–Business Coordination and the Development of Eng Hardware,' in K.S. Jomo, G. Felker, and R. Rasiah (eds), *Industrial Technology Development in Malaysia: Industry and Firm Studies*, Routledge, London.

Rasiah, R. (2001), Government–Business Coordination and Small Business Performance in the Machine Tools Sector in Malaysia, Unpublished paper., United Nations University, Maastricht.

Rasiah, R. (2002), 'Systemic Coordination and the Development of Human Capital: Knowledge Flows in Malaysia's TNC-driven Electronics Cluster,' *Transnational Corporations*, 11(3): 89–129.

Rasiah, R., and A. Anuwar (1998), 'Governing Industrial Technology Transfer in Malaysia,' in Y. Ishak and I. Abd. Ghafar (eds), *Malaysian Industrialization: Governance and Technical Change*, UKM Publishers, Bangi: Chapter 2.

Razin, A., E. Sadka, and T. Coury (2002), 'Trade Openness and Investment Instability,' *NBER Working Paper No. 8827*, National Bureau of Economic Research, Cambridge, Massachusetts.

Rock, M. (2001), 'Thailand's Old Bureaucratic Polity and Its New Semi-democracy,' in R. Doner and R. Ansil (eds), *Rents, Rent-seeking and Economic*

Development: Theory and Evidence in Asia, Cambridge University Press, Cambridge.

Rokiah, A. (1996), *Industrialisation in Malaysia: Import Substitution and Infant Industry Performance*, Routledge, London.

Sachs. J., and A. Warner (1995), 'Economic Reform and the Process of Global Integration,' *Brookings Papers on Economic Activity*, 1(1): 1–118.

Schiff, M., and L.A. Winters (2003), 'Stimulating Investment,' in M. Schiff and L.A. Winters (eds), *Regional Integration and Development*, Oxford University Press, New York: 101–22.

Shan, J., G.G. Tian, and F. Sun (1997), The FDI-led Growth Hypothesis: Further Econometric Evidence from China, Unpublished paper, Australian National University, Canberra.

Sharma, K. (2000), 'Export Growth in India: Has FDI Played a Role?' *Center Discussion Paper No. 816*, Economic Growth Center, Yale University, New Haven CT.

Siamwalla, A., Y. Vajragupta, and P. Vichyanond (1999), *Foreign Capital Flows to Thailand: Determinants and Impact*, Thailand Development Research Institute, Bangkok.

Sidek, H. (2002), Doha Development Agenda: Critical Issues and Challenges, Paper presented at the 'Seminar on Future Environment: WTO Post Doha and AFTA,' Institute of Public Administration (INTAN), Kuala Lumpur, 26 February.

Smarzynska, B.K. (2002), 'Composition of Foreign Direct Investment and Protection of Intellectual Property Rights: Evidence from Transition Economies,' *World Bank Policy Research Working Paper No. 2786*, Washington DC.

SMIDEC (Small and Medium Industries Corporation) (2002), *SMIDP: SMI Development Plan (2001–2005)*, National Printing Corporation, Kuala Lumpur.

Smith, H. (2000), *Industry Policy in Taiwan and Korea in the 1980s: Winning with the Market*, Edward Elgar, Cheltenham.

Sohn, C.-H., J. Yang, and H.-S. Yim (1998), 'Korea's Trade and Industrial Policies: 1948–1998,' *KIEP Working Paper 98-05*, Korea Institute for International Economic Policy, Seoul.

Song, W. (1999), 'A Study of the Issue of China's Capital Flight: 1987–1997' [in Chinese], *National Economic Research Institute Working Paper No. 99-001*, National Economic Research Institute, Beijing.

Srivastava, S. (2003), 'What Is the True Level of FDI Flows to India?' *Economic and Political Weekly*, 38(7): 608–10.

STAR/CIEM (Support for Trade Acceleration and Central Institute of Economic Management) (2003), *An Assessment of the Economic Impact of the United States–Viet Nam Bilateral Trade Agreement*, Annual Economic Report for 2002, STAR and CIEM, Hanoi.

Stiglitz, J.E. (2001), 'From Miracle to Crisis to Recovery: Lessons from Four Decades of East Asian Experience,' in J.E. Stiglitz and S. Yusuf (eds), *Rethinking the East Asian Miracle*, Oxford University Press, New York, for the World Bank.

Techakanont, K. (2002), A Study on Interfirm Technology Transfer in the Thai Automobile Industry, PhD dissertation, International Development and Cooperation (IDEC), Hiroshima.

Teng, B. (2003), 'The Three Phases of Historical Development of China's Motor Vehicle Industry: A 50 Years Review' [in Chinese], China Auto Industry Association Website, <www.caam.org.cn>, accessed July 2003.

Tham, S.Y. (1995), An Assessment of Investment Protection in Malaysia, Country report submitted to the UN Economic and Social Commission for Asia and the Pacific (ESCAP), Bangkok.

Tham, S.Y. (1997), 'Determinants of Productivity Growth in the Malaysian Manufacturing Sector,' *ASEAN Economic Bulletin*, 13(3): 333–43.

Tham, S.Y. (1998), 'Foreign Direct Investment Policies and Related Institution-building in Malaysia,' in *Foreign Direct Investment in Selected Asian Countries: Policies, Related Institution-building and Regional Cooperation*, ESCAP Development Papers No. 19, ST/ESCAP/1809, United Nations, New York: Chapter 5.

Tham, S.Y., and C.S. Liew (2002), Foreign Labour in Malaysian Manufacturing: Enhancing Malaysian Competitiveness, Paper presented at the International Conference on Globalisation, Culture and Inequalities: In Honour of the Work of the Late Prof. Dr. Ishak Shari (1948–2001), Bangi, 19–21 August.

Toh, K.W. (2002), The Political Economy of Industrialization in Penang, Paper presented to a conference on Malaysian industrialization, Australian National University, Canberra.

Udomsaph, C. (2003), *Premiums to Employment in Establishments with Foreign Direct Investment: Evidence from Thai Manufacturing*, University of California, Berkeley CA.

UNCTAD (United Nations Conference on Trade and Development) (1997), *World Investment Report*, United Nations, New York.

UNCTAD (United Nations Conference on Trade and Development) (2001), *World Investment Report 2001: Promoting Linkages*, United Nations, New York.

UNCTAD (United Nations Conference on Trade and Development) (2002), *World Investment Report*, UNCTAD, Geneva.

UNCTAD (United Nations Conference on Trade and Development) (2003a), Foreign Direct Investment Database, accessed 15 September.

UNCTAD (United Nations Conference on Trade and Development) (2003b), *Use and Effectiveness of Performance Requirements: Select Case Studies*, United Nations, New York (forthcoming).

UNIDO (United Nations Industrial Development Organization) (2002), *Industrial Development Report 2002/2003: Competing through Innovation and Learning*, UNIDO, Vienna.

Urata, S. (1996), 'Foreign Direct Investment and Technology Transfer in Asia,' in K. Yuthasak and S. Prasobsuk (eds) (2001), *Foreign Direct Investment and Technology Transfer in Thailand*, Thailand Board of Investment and National Economic and Social Development Board, Bangkok.

Urata, S. (2001), 'Emergence of an FDI–Trade Nexus, and Economic Growth in East Asia,' in J.E. Stiglitz and S. Yusuf (eds), *Rethinking the East Asian Miracle*, Oxford University Press, New York, for the World Bank.

USTR (United States Trade Representative) (2001), *Foreign Trade Barriers: Republic of Korea*, USTR, Washington DC.

Wang, X. (2000), 'Sustainability of China's Economic Growth and Institutional Changes' [in Chinese], in X. Wang and F. Gang (eds), *Sustainability of China's Economic Growth*, Economic Science Press, Beijing, 3–68.

Wells, L.T. (1983), *Third World Multinationals*, MIT Press, Cambridge MA.

Wells, L.T. Jr., and A.G. Wint (1991), 'The Public–Private Choice: The Case of Marketing a Country to Investors,' *World Development*, 19(7): 749–61.

Wong P.K. (2003), 'From Using to Creating Technology: The Evolution of Singapore's National Innovation System and the Changing Role of Public Policy,' in S. Lall and S. Urata (eds), *Competitiveness, FDI and Technological Activity in East Asia*, Edward Elgar, Cheltenham: 191–238.

World Bank (1985), *World Development Report*, World Bank, Washington DC.

World Bank (2002), *World Development Report*, World Bank, Washington DC.

WTO (World Trade Organization) (2001a), *Doha Ministerial Declaration*, WTO, Geneva.

WTO (World Trade Organization) (2001b), 'Accession of the People's Republic of China, Decision of 10 November 2001,' cited by the Ministry of Commerce of the People's Republic of China, available at <http://www.moftec.gov.cn>, accessed February 2003.

Yang H., and J. Chen (2000), 'China's Capital Flight: Estimation and International Comparison' [in Chinese], *World Economy*, 1: 21–9.

Yun, M. (2000), 'Foreign Direct Investment: A Catalyst for Change?,' *The Korean Economy in an Era of Global Competition*, Joint US–Korea Academic Studies, Vol. 10, Korea Economic Institute of America, Washington DC: 139–74.

Yusuf, S., and S.J. Evenett (2003), *Innovative East Asia: The Future of Growth*, Oxford University Press, New York, for the World Bank.

Zhou, C. (2001), 'Security Times of Panorama Web,' [in Chinese], <http://finance.sina.com.cn>, accessed July 2003.

Zuo, D. (2000), 'China's Strategic Options in Foreign Trade' [in Chinese], *Strategy and Administration*, 4, Beijing: 40–45.

Author Index

Subject Index

Argentina, 18, 27n
Asia Europe Meeting (ASEM), 301
Asia Pacific Economic Cooperation
  (APEC), 212, 275, 301, 303
Asian Development Bank (ADB), xv,
  xvi, xviii
Asian financial crisis, 2, 3, 11, 31, 38,
  49, 154, 158, 161, 176, 190, 201,
  210, 228, 239, 248, 284, 294
Association of South East Asian
  Nations (ASEAN), 52, 123, 164,
  204, 212, 230, 245, 253, 270, 274,
  275, 276, 277, 294, 296, 301, 303
  Dispute Settlement Mechanism,
  276
  Free Trade Area, 52, 75n, 271, 275
Australia, 284

banks/banking, 66
  see also [name of country], banking
Brazil, 18, 21, 124

Cambodia, 284
Canada, 16, 187n
capital
  inflows, 34–5
  modalities of flows, 34–5, 47–8
  see also [name of country], capital
  inflows; FDI

China
  see People's Republic of China
Colombia, 18
commercial environments, 30, 53–5,
  70, 72
  see also [name of country], commercial environment
Common Effective Preferential Tariff
  Scheme, 294, 296
competition, 61, 67–8, 96–100,
  268–70
corruption, 32n, 33, 41–2, 52, 54, 64,
  67, 70, 73, 82, 90

decentralization, 42, 43, 60, 73, 77n,
  80
Deng Xiaoping, 80–1
Developing Asia
  FDI recipients, 4, 5
diaspora, 36, 37, 51, 53
domestic/foreign firm linkages, 13, 63,
  64–5, 77n, 100–3, 148, 209, 225
Dutch disease, 7

economic indicators, 31, 32–3
economic reform, 41–3
education, 33, 36, 37, 53, 54, 55
  see also [name of country], education